THE BUFFALO WAR

THE
BUFFALO WAR

The History of the Red River Indian Uprising of 1874

JAMES L. HALEY

University of Oklahoma Press : Norman

Library of Congress Cataloging-in-Publication Data

Haley, James L.
  The Buffalo war.

  Reprint. Originally published: Garden City, N.Y.: Doubleday,
1976.
  Bibliography: p.
  Includes index.
  1. Red River War, 1874-1875. I. Title.
[E83.875.H34   1985]   973.8'2   85-40484
ISBN 0-8061-1957-8 (pbk.)

To My Grandparents
Foster and Hazel Lewis

PREFACE

On a summer dawn a century ago, in present Hutchinson County, Texas, five hundred Comanche, Kiowa, Cheyenne, and Arapaho Indian warriors swooped down on a sleepy-looking settlement of sod-and-picket hovels hunched near a sluggishly flowing little creek. The Indians knew the buildings were occupied by the most hated of white men, professional buffalo hunters, men who killed hundreds of bison every day, animals that the Indians needed to survive, stripping off the hides and leaving the precious meat to rot. In a period of three years the hunters had virtually denuded the Indians' reservations of buffalo, shooting hundreds of thousands of animals on land where, by signed and ratified treaty, they had no shadow of a right to set foot.

Futilely the Indians had begged for justice from the white government, but ran head-on into an administration grimly determined to break the proud South Plains tribes to the plow and the schoolroom. With the buffalo fast disappearing, the Indians concentrated at the agencies to learn the white road, only to find that "Washington" could not or would not feed them, quite literally leaving them to starve to death. The government would not protect them from white horse thieves who decimated their pony herds, nor from the profiteering whiskey peddlers and gun runners who kept them in a constant state of excitement. For the hungry Indians, swindled, defrauded, and betrayed at every turn, only one course of action remained open. Now, led by their greatest war chiefs and protected by the medicine of a tribal prophet, they had embarked on a war to destroy those who had, in effect, destroyed them already.

The Red River War of 1874–75 is an anomaly in all of American history. At its conclusion General Philip Sheridan, who engineered it, called it "the most successful of any Indian campaign in the country since its settlement by whites." Recently a prominent historian called it "forgotten." The importance of the Red River War in the history of our nation is undisputed. It saw the final subjugation of three of America's most famous and powerful Indian tribes accomplished by the most massive use of troops ever thrown against Indians to that time. It saw the extermination of the bison from the South Plains, and it safeguarded the opening of the territory from central Kansas to central Texas to white settlement. And it even awakened the consciences of a few to the barbarity of the government's treatment of her primitive wards. Yet the curious fate of its written history has so disposed itself as to delay for one hundred years the appearance of a volume devoted to its recounting and analysis.

Many factors have conspired to make this a difficult book to write. Among secondary sources, some phases of the war are so well known as to have been elevated to the level almost of tradition, while the rest of it has all but disappeared entirely. On the one hand, therefore, while so much was written about the Battle of Adobe Walls that it was a problem to separate the valid from the folklorish, on the other hand so little study had been done on the causative factors of the war that almost all research had to be done in original letters and documents. This imbalance was aggravated by the complexity of the Red River War itself. It contained not one conflict but several, each one bearing in some degree upon the others: the hostile Indians against the whites, the Peace Indians against the War Indians, the Army against the Indian Bureau, ambitious army officers fighting each other for commands and promotions, and the Indian agents fighting the insensitivity of their own bureaucracy were all important segments of the whole story.

Of the many hundreds of pieces that have appeared in the past century that deal in part with the Red River War or some phase of it, each of them either overshoots or undershoots. A general history of the American Indian wars will give it a few pages or at most a chapter, while scholarly papers on some portion of a cause or complication so far exceed the boundaries of the war as to contain little perspective on it within themselves. Research, where present, was often solid, but seldom went far enough beyond the specific topic at hand to give more than a two-dimensional view of it, and usually did not place the narrow subject in terms of the 1874 uprising. Hence, the task was mine to relate for the first time this intricate and amazing mosaic in all its lights and perspectives, describing the events and explaining the causes, all the while sorting out and discarding the widely varying prejudices of at least three generations of literary commentary.

I earnestly hope that I have in some degree advanced our understanding of the forgotten Buffalo War.

James L. Haley

Arlington, Texas

ACKNOWLEDGMENTS

The assimilation and writing of successful history is not the result of the work of one individual. It requires the efforts of numbers of people, the author serving as final editor, compilator and interpreter of the contributions of others. I take great personal satisfaction in paying the greatest debts herewith.

The Buffalo War, moreso than other books known to me, had a precariously delicate infancy, and any early failure of support or enthusiasm on the part of several people would have resulted in the abandonment of the project. Most prominent in this category were my mother and late father, whose faith that I could handle the project was always greater than my own. Other critical nurturing came from historian, teacher, and friend Mrs. Dale Summers. For his skill and patience in managing a first-book author, thanks are due my editor, James J. Menick.

Of all who provided technical assistance, I am particularly grateful to the following: at the Amon Carter Museum of Western Art, Ms. Marjorie Morey, archivist; at the Panhandle-Plains Historical Museum in Canyon, Texas, Mr. Rolla Shaller, curator of exhibits, and Ms. Claire Kuehn, archivist-librarian; at the Kansas State Historical Society, Mr. Eugene Decker, archivist; at the Texas State Library in Austin, Ms. Carol Carefoot; at the Oklahoma Historical Society, Ms. Manon B. Atkins and Ms. Martha Blaine; at the Montana Historical Society, Ms. Harriet C. Meloy; at the National Archives Federal Records Center in Fort Worth, Director C. George Younkin; at the Smithsonian Institution, Ms. Paula Richardson and Ms. Stephanie Krumrein; at the Jenkins Garrett Collection of the University of Texas at Arlington, Ms. Margaret F. Morris and Ms. Mary Van Zandt, and in the Interlibrary Loan facility, Ms. Mary Alice Price.

Additional aid was generously forthcoming from Dr. Elliott West, assistant professor of history at the University of Texas at Arlington; Ms. Karen D. Petersen of St. Paul, Minnesota; Gillett Griswold, Curator of the Fort Sill Museum; Charles G. Anderson of Snyder, Texas; and George F. Schesventer, Superintendent of the Castillo de San Marcos National Monument, St. Augustine, Florida. Also, special thanks are due Mr. Paul Heffron at the Library of Congress for locating the Scott manuscript on the sign language.

For reading copy and making valuable suggestions, assisting in preparation of the manuscript, for accompanying me on research trips, and above all for bearing three years of my tirades over setbacks and blunders with unfailing patience and good humor, I owe an unredeemable debt to Jim Huggins of Irving, Texas.

CONTENTS

	PREFACE	vii
	ACKNOWLEDGMENTS	xi
	LIST OF ILLUSTRATIONS	xv
I.	The Buffalo Indians	1
II.	The Indians' Commissary	21
III.	The Gathering Storm	37
IV.	The Buffalo War	59
V.	The Battle of Adobe Walls	67
VI.	Lone Wolf's Revenge: The Lost Valley Fight	79
VII.	The United States Goes to War	95
VIII.	Internment: The Anadarko Fight	107
IX.	The Great Dry Time: The Miles Expedition and the Battle of Red River	125
X.	Medicine Water: The Lone Tree Massacre and the German Kidnapings	139
XI.	The Anadarko Renegades: The Battle for Lyman's Wagon Train and the Battle of Buffalo Wallow	147
XII.	The Mackenzie Column: The Battle of Palo Duro Canyon	169
XIII.	The Wrinkled-hand Chase	185
XIV.	The Collapse of Indian Resistance	197
XV.	Prison	211
	NOTES	223
	BIBLIOGRAPHY	261
	INDEX	279

LIST OF ILLUSTRATIONS

(following page 122)

1. Quahadi Comanche camp, 1872; man sitting at left is He Bear, or Bull Bear (Parra-o-coom)
2. Columbus Delano, Secretary of the Interior
3. Tabananica (Sound of the Sun), a chief of the Yapparika Comanches
4. Billy Dixon
5. Bat Masterson
6. Josiah Wright Mooar
7. John Wesley Mooar
8. Dead buffalo on the Plains, early 1870s
9. Skinning a buffalo on the Texas Plains, 1874
10. General John Pope. Commanding the Military Department of the Missouri
11. General Philip H. Sheridan, Commanding the Military Division of the Missouri
12. Rath Hide Yard, Dodge City, c. 1874; Charlie Rath (inset)
13. Háhki oomah (Little Robe), a chief of the Southern Cheyennes
14. Buffalo hunters' camp, Texas Panhandle, 1874
15. John D. Miles, Cheyenne-Arapaho Indian agent
16. James M. Haworth, Kiowa-Comanche Indian agent
17. Big Bow, a chief of the Kiowas
18. Enoch Hoag, superintendent of the Indian Territory agencies
19. Little Robe
20. Ado etta (Big Tree), a Kiowa war chief
21. Set-tain-te (Satanta, or White Bear), a leading chief of the Kiowas
22. Téné-angopte (Striking Eagle), a chief of the Kiowas
23. Gui-päh-go (Lone Wolf), principal chief of the Kiowas
24. Nap-a-wat, a Kiowa medicine man
25. Quanah Parker, a war chief of the Nokoni Comanches
26. Isa Rosa (White Wolf), a chief of the Yapparika Comanches
27. Kobay-o-burra (Wild Horse); after 1874 first chief of the Quahadi Comanches
28. Isa-tai (Wolf Shit), a medicine man of the Quahadi Comanches

(following page 146)

29. Red Moon, a Cheyenne war leader
30. John B. Jones, major of the Frontier Battalion of the Texas Rangers
31. Tsen-tonkee (Hunting Horse), a Kiowa warrior
32. Colonel Nelson A. Miles, 5th Infantry
33. Minninewah (Whirlwind), a chief of the Cheyennes
34. Tape-day-ah, a Kiowa warrior
35. Captain Wyllys Lyman, 5th Infantry
36. William F. Schmalsle, scout
37. Lieutenant Frank D. Baldwin, 5th Infantry
38. Tsen-tain-te (White Horse), a Kiowa war chief
39. Mow-way (Push Aside), first chief of the Kotsoteka Comanches
40. Minimic (Eagle Head), a Southern Cheyenne war chief
41. Man-yi-ten (Woman's Heart), a Kiowa war chief
42. Kiowa warriors; left to right, Chief Poor Buffalo, Kaw-tom-te, Short Greasy Hair, Silver Horn, and Feather Head
43. Do-hauson the Younger, a Kiowa warrior, in war shirt
44. Tau-ankia (Sitting in the Saddle), Lone Wolf's son
45. Eonah-pah (Trailing the Enemy), a Kiowa warrior
46. Upper Palo Duro Canyon
47. Colonel Ranald S. Mackenzie, 4th Cavalry
48. Catherine German, captive of Medicine Water
49. Sophia German, captive of Medicine Water
50. Adelaide and Julia German, captives of Gray Beard
51. Medicine Water, a Cheyenne war chief, leader of the German family massacre and kidnaping
52. Mochi (Buffalo Calf Woman), wife of Medicine Water
53. Stone Calf, a Cheyenne chief, and his wife
54. Indian prisoners arrive at Fort Marion
55. Hach-i-vi (Little Chief), a Cheyenne warrior, on the way to prison, May 10, 1875
56. Lined up in prison: left to right, Chief Heap of Birds (Cheyenne), Hummingbird, Mountain Bear, unknown, Zotom, Chief White Horse (all Kiowas)
57. Black Horse, second chief of the Quahadi Comanches, poses in Fort Marion
58. Lieutenant Austin Henely, 6th Cavalry

THE BUFFALO WAR

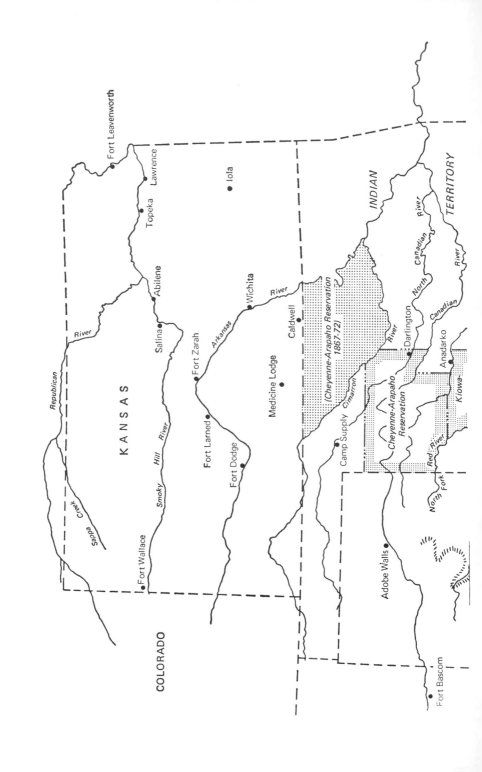

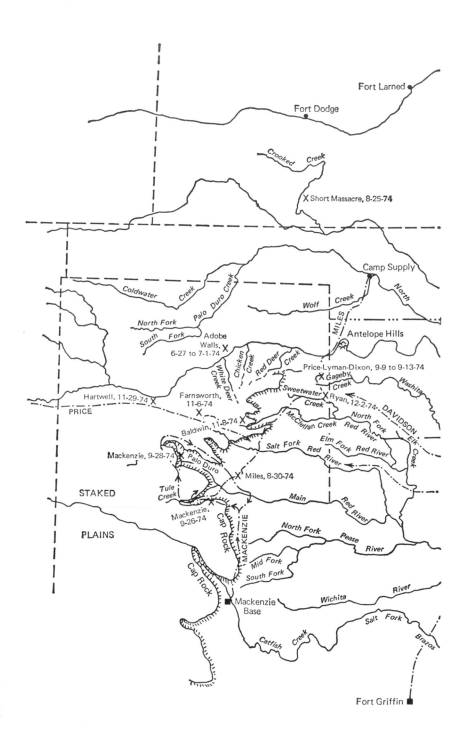

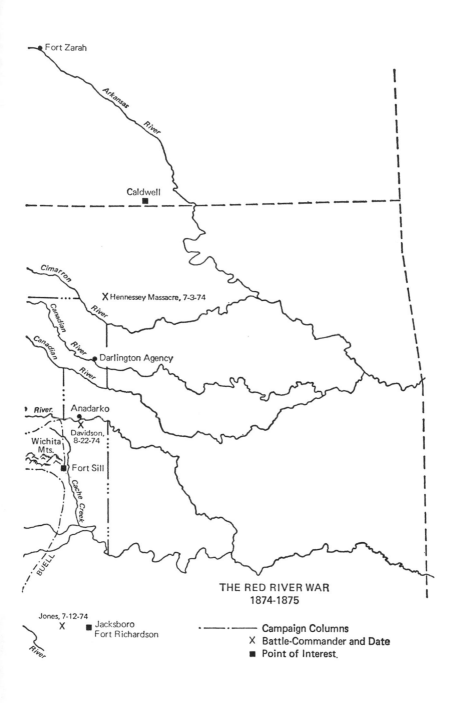

●Fort Zarah

Arkansas

River

Caldwell■

Cimarron

X Hennessey Massacre, 7-3-74

Canadian

River

Canadian

River

River

●Darlington Agency

❭ *River.*

Anadarko●

X
Davidson,
8-22-74

Wichita
Mts.

■ Fort Sill

Cache Creek

BUELL

THE RED RIVER WAR
1874-1875

Jones, 7-12-74
X   ■Jacksboro
Fort Richardson

River

———·—— Campaign Columns
X   Battle-Commander and Date
■   Point of Interest.

I. The Buffalo Indians

The situation of the South Plains Indians in 1874 was the product of a crazyquilt history that few people, the Indians least of all, understood, even though that history had left them impoverished and materially wretched, dominated by another race of men to whom they had been exposed for only a few decades, and gnawed by a horrible intuition that their entire social structure was doomed, and the days of their tribes, numbered.

To begin, none of the tribes had originated on the South Plains. All were emigrés of fairly recent coming: the Comanches, Kiowas, and Katakas from the North Plains, the Cheyennes and Arapahoes from the western Great Lakes, via the North Plains. The Comanches were the first to arrive, becoming fairly well entrenched by early in the eighteenth century. When the Kiowas followed later, years of war ensued over control of the hunting grounds before the two called a peace and confederated about 1795. The Cheyennes and Arapahoes came later (after 1830), offshoots of their main tribes who had migrated south for trading benefits to be had along the Arkansas River. Though they maintained close ties with those of their people left behind, they soon gained recognition as independent tribes, the Southern Cheyennes and Southern Arapahoes, and after eight years of bloody contention the allied Comanches and Kiowas accepted them into the South Plains confederation in 1840.

All were "buffalo Indians," the epitome of what has become in the modern mind's eye the stereotype of the American Indian: proud, fiercely romantic, superstitious, impressionable as a child, easily transformed by treachery real or imagined from lofty contemplator to walleyed savage. Closer to the root of their present dilemma was their lack of sophistication: They were too simple to realize that, in a few generations' dependence on the wandering herds of buffalo, they had become not so much the practitioners of their culture as its prisoners. After their acquisition of Spanish horses and later firearms, the once sedentary Plains Indians became nomads, living off the fringe of the mighty herds of buffalo until they became utterly dependent on the rugged animals for virtually their entire existence—for food, clothing, shelter, utensils, even for a medium of barter. But, just as in nature any race that sacrifices its adaptability for the conveniences of overspecialization is in the greatest danger of extinction, just so were the buffalo Indians overspecialized, and in the post-Civil War era these Indians, sensing outsiders hemming them in tighter with every passing season, faced the bleak necessity of having to suddenly recapture their adaptability and switch to a new and in-comprehensible—and therefore frightening—mode of living, else die. Yet the nomadic life suited them so well—their romanticism, their closeness to nature, their wanderlust—that they were not prepared to abandon the chase of the buffalo unless these white outsiders could prove demonstrably that a better way of life lay in store for them if they did.

The buffalo Indians needed also to apply an adaptability to another facet of their culture that was incompatible with the in-creasing presence of large numbers of white men, namely, the im-portance and esteem that their society placed on the martial arts. The experience of their history, like that of all primitive peoples, was that one occupied a hunting ground precisely as long as one could hold it by force of arms. Indeed, the very migration of the "South Plains" tribes to the South Plains had occurred because a powerfully expanding Sioux Nation had physically driven them from their old territories, and when they arrived on the South Plains and found them already occupied by Apache Indians, the latter had then to be vanquished and driven into the deserts of the Southwest. War had always been survival, and in addition had become a cultural proving ground for their men, whose social standing depended almost entirely on their prowess in the field. But now the white outsiders, who hopelessly outnumbered them, and against whom the Indians increasingly felt a need to defend themselves by war, were telling them that war was, in and of itself, bad. It was a premise many of the chiefs were willing to accept, but the decision that the Plains Indians had to make to end their ways as pillaging raiders would certainly have been easier had it not been shoved at them by whites whose primary interest was the Indians' land and the advancement of their own civilization.

Through their history the outsiders had been of three kinds: Mexicans, Texans, and Americans. By 1874 the Indians regarded the latter with a complex balance of emotions, largely no doubt because the Americans quarreled so much among themselves about what to do with them and treated them in so many different ways at the same time; the two former were regarded much more simply, particularly by the Kiowas and Comanches, as objects of unspeakable vilification and hatred, fit to be but the Indians' victims of war.

Certainly the roots of these two tribes' dealings with the Mexicans and, soon after their independence, the Texans, were as strong as they were hateful and bloodsmeared. The principal source of the trouble was probably the Indians whom the Kiowas and Comanches had first driven from the grassy plains, the Apaches. That tribe, sandwiched between expanding Comanche-Kiowa power on the north and expanding Spanish power on the south, played the two giants off against each other, and succeeded in fostering a deeply vindictive hate between them, which reached full flower by 1757, when Comanches razed the Spaniards' San Saba Mission and slaughtered every living being they could find. The situation was aggravated by the way in which the exhausting succession of Spanish royal governors, and after 1822 the provincial governors of the Mexican Republic, treated the Kiowas and Comanches. There were dozens of the executives, seldom holding office for more than a few months (sometimes four in one year), each pursuing largely independent policies toward the Plains Indians. Hence, Mexican diplomacy toward them veered unpredictably from mustache-twirling sweet talk to Inquisitorial butchery, the former employed more than once to arrange for the latter. To the Indians the Mexican manner was detestable; the Indians themselves observed rigid rules of war, and once an expression of friendship or hospitality was made it might not be dishonored. As Thomas Battey observed, even when an avowed enemy came to one's tipi and asked for food and a night's lodging, they were given, and safe passage accorded. Hence, the Mexicans' sometime practice of luring the Indians into settlements with promises of food and talk, then sealing them off and murdering them, was eminently hateful.

Traders in the northern part of New Spain, later New Mexico, complicated matters still further. Generic ancestors of the latter-day Comancheros, they had little in common with other Mexicans far to the south, and they actually encouraged the Plains Indians to make raids deep into Old Mexico (better there than in their own settlements), and then turned a shady profit by trading for stolen goods with the returning Kiowa and Comanche warriors. By the opening of the 1800s the killing of Mexicans, stealing their stock, and slave-trading their women and children were practices firmly assimilated into the Indians' overall cultural scheme.

The hatred that the Comanches and Kiowas had for the Texans was of a more recent origin. One of their first contacts with the Texans, or more accurately, American colonists in Mexico north of the Rio Grande, was in the spring of 1822, when Stephen F. Austin and two companions were waylaid and threatened by a band of about fifty Comanches on the Nueces River. When the Indians discovered their captives were not Spanish but Americans, Austin and the others were released unharmed. During the Texas war for independence neither side apparently tried hard to employ the Plains Indians against the other, at least not until after the Mexicans' disaster at San Jacinto, when the Mexicans reportedly offered to divide Texas with the Kiowas and Comanches in exchange for their hostility toward the rebels. The Indians, made wise to Mexican doubletalk by the endless parade of primping royal governors, refused to make any arrangement.

On the part of the young republic, her second President was Sam Houston, himself an adopted Cherokee chief, who gave at least the outward appearance of having a compassionate understanding of Indians' thinking, and who undeniably strove to make fair territorial arrangements with the Texas Indians. Other members of his government rode roughshod over such sentimentality, however, and almost from her first year, Texas marked her Indians for extermination. Houston's successor, Mirabeau Lamar, called for—and prosecuted—"an exterminating war upon their warriors; which will admit of no compromise and have no termination except in their total extinction or total expulsion."

After one year of Lamar the Comanches sued for peace, and the commander of the garrison at San Antonio agreed to receive a delegation, provided they surrender all their white captives and stolen goods, and bring in future Indian raiders for trial. The Indians agreed to this, and the commander readied two companies of regulars to deal with any emergency. On March 19, 1840, more than sixty Comanches, men, women, and children, entered San Antonio for the *parlez,* led by twelve chiefs. The Comanches had only one white captive with them, and when the dozen chiefs entered the "Council House" they were arrested and told they would not be released until all the captive Texans were returned safely. One of the chiefs tried to escape, and after the smoke of the ensuing Council House "fight" had cleared, thirty-five Comanches lay dead in their blood, including every one of the chiefs. Twenty-nine, nearly all women and children, were taken prisoner; one got away.

Thereafter the Comanches and allied Kiowas never made the slightest pretense of appeasing the hated "Tehannas"; they were locked in a war to the death that spanned the next thirty-five years, and their furious depredations on the Texas frontier were given further impetus by the same New Mexican traders who encouraged the raids into Old Mexico. The Comancheros and their ofttimes respectable backers offered a market for all the Texans' property and stock—especially cattle, which helped deflate the price of beef in New Mexico settlements—that the warriors could obtain by raid and pillage, thus making war on Texas a matter of profit as well as revenge. Before long raids into Texas, like the raids into Old Mexico, were a way of life as integral as hunting the buffalo, providing in addition to the profit an acceptable outlet for their cultural heritage of war, without arousing the anger of the powerful people who loomed to the east, north, and northwest: the Americans.

As with the Texans, the Kiowas' and Comanches' first contact with the Americans was cordial enough. It was in 1834 that General Henry Leavenworth located the camp of Kiowa principal chief Do-hauson (Little Mountain), and returned to the tribe a young girl who had been taken captive by the Osages. It was the

Kiowas' first close look at the white man's warrior society and, deeply impressed at the trouble they had taken to return the girl, then pledged their friendship. The next year the Comanches made their first treaty with the whites, an agreement of friendship not involving any cession of the Indians' land, the same terms as the Kiowas' first treaty, made in 1837.

Nine years after independence and five years after the Indians' bitter lesson at the Council House, the Republic of Texas applied for admission to the Union, and soon all-out war flared between the United States and Mexico over the maverick state. Once again soldiers entered the realm of the Comanches and Kiowas, and like the times before, they brought gifts, though now for a more mercenary reason. The main route to the theater of war was over the Santa Fe Trail, by the late 1840s a steady source for the Indians of sugar, coffee, and other white commodities for which the Indians had acquired a liking. The government wanted to make certain the pacification of the South Plains confederation, lately swelled to four by the addition of the Southern Cheyennes and Arapahoes. Some forty-one chiefs, therefore, were taken up to see the Great Father, President Polk, in Washington, and were awarded a large amount of goods to assure their neutrality. It was the very first time the Indians had received a government appropriation; to get it they gave up nothing and continued to raid in Old Mexico, now as the *de facto* allies of their friend, Washington. It was all good business as far as the Indians were concerned.

After the war against Mexico was won, however, the white man's political maneuverings became too much for the savages to understand, and the seeds of discontent began to take an alarming hold. First, Texas was admitted to the Union, and her frontier patrolled, not by Texans, but by soldiers from Washington. To the Comanches and Kiowas it was sheerest nonsense to think that their mortal enemies, the "Tehannas," who slaughtered them at council meetings, had inexplicably and in the twinkling of an eye become a part of Washington, which embraced the red man and gave him presents. Similarly, under the terms of the Treaty of Guadalupe-Hidalgo ending the Mexican War, the United States agreed to keep its Indians from raiding in Old Mexico, a provision which, obviously, nobody negotiated with the most powerful force in the area, the Plains Indians themselves. The United States had, in effect, pulled a stunt worthy of Baroque Europe: conquered an enemy and then, content to seize nearly half her territory, made a separate peace and turned upon her ally. When Washington began to dot the open country with forts, the Indians were shocked, bewildered, and maddened to discover that the soldiers came, not to bring presents as always before, but to tell the Indian how to live, where he might hunt, not to raid ever again on anybody—white, Texan, or Mexican—and then to make war when the Indian did not obey the soldiers' orders.

When General Leavenworth had located Do-hauson's Kiowas in 1834, there was among them a war leader in the prime of life named Set-ankia (Satank or Sitting Bear). A third of a century later it was a shriveled and silver-haired old Set-ankia whose tongue stung the conscience of the Medicine Lodge Council with his accounting of the treachery: "The white man grows jealous of his red brother. The white man once came to trade; now he comes as a soldier. He once put his trust in our friendship and wanted no shield but our fidelity. But now he builds forts and plants big guns on their walls. He once gave us arms and bade us hunt the game. We loved him then for his confidence. . . . He now covers his face with the cloud of Jealousy and anger and tells us to be gone, as an offended master speaks to his dog."

The other half of the South Plains coalition, the Cheyennes and Arapahoes, had been so long linked together that they were almost always referred to in common, like the Sauk-and-Fox. At one time they were northwoods Algonquian farmers, neighbors of the Canadian Ojibway, but the Sioux and their allies had driven them to the North Plains by 1680, where they continued to farm for more than a century. Only when further pressure from the marauding Sioux forced them to abandon their log houses and cornfields did they become buffalo Indians, living day to day in skin tipis. They adapted well, though, and soon their agricultural life was a dim memory; by the opening of the nineteenth century they were making long-distance horse-stealing raids to Mexico and making war on the Kiowas of the Upper Missouri Valley for the latter's hunting territory, and successfully drove them southward to the domain of the Comanches.

After the move south in 1832, the Southern Cheyennes and Arapahoes, numbering perhaps thirty-five hundred in all, had less to do with war on Texas and Mexico, but their relations with the American Government and pioneers had been stormier, and more tainted with massacre and victimization. By no stretch of the imagination were the problems that they faced in 1874 new on the scene. The following report on their condition, for instance, was written in 1859: "A smothered passion for revenge agitates these Indians, perpetually fomented by the failure of food, the encircling encroachments of the white population, and the exasperating sense of decay and impending extinction with which they are surrounded. . . . These numerous and warlike Indians, pressed upon all around by Texans, by the settlers of the [Pike's Peak] region, by the advancing people of Kansas, and from the Platte, are already compressed into a small circle of territory, destitute of food. . . . A desperate war of starvation and extinction is therefore imminent and inevitable, unless prompt measures shall prevent it."

In 1861 the federal government concluded the Fort Wise Treaty, by which the Cheyennes and Arapahoes were given a farcically small reservation in the southeast corner of Colorado, but the frontier population took a dim view of any federal Indian policy not spoken with powder and shot. When the United States Army's presence on the frontier diminished during the Civil War, ranchers and businessmen, backed by expansionist journalists and politicians, declared open season on the Indians of their region. What resulted was a spectacle in November of 1864 that left most of the nation speechless with horror: John Chivington's massacre of Black Kettle's village on Sand Creek. The Indians were encamped under the specific protection of their agent, and suspected nothing. Chivington and his army of ranchers and "volunteers" wrought a butchery on the Southern Cheyennes and Arapahoes that staggered imagination. As the Medicine Lodge Commission reflected three years later: "The particulars of this massacre are too well known to be repeated here. . . . It is enough to say, that it scarcely has its parallel in the records of Indian barbarity. Fleeing women holding up their hands and praying for mercy were brutally shot down; infants were killed and scalped in derision, men were tortured and mutilated in a manner that would put to shame the savage ingenuity of interior Africa."

The Cheyenne-Arapaho and Comanche-Kiowa affiliations made their first joint treaty with the whites in October 1865, at the mouth of the Little Arkansas River. In it the government gave them a huge but unfortunately bogus reservation covering parts of Kansas and Colorado and nearly all the Texas panhandle. Senate amendments clipped off the Colorado and Kansas lands, and in Texas the federal government owned not one acre of land to give anybody, thus rendering the Indians officially homeless in their own homeland. During the negotiations for the Little Arkansas Treaty, it is said that old Do-hauson, the Kiowa chief who had greeted General Leavenworth thirty years before, revealed shortly before he died a disillusioned insight into the jingoistic, expansion-minded American Government. "There are three chiefs," he said, "the White Chief, the Spanish Chief, and me. The Spanish Chief and myself are men. We do bad towards each other, sometimes steal horses and take scalps, but do not get mad and act the fool. The White Chief is a child and gets mad quick when my young men, to keep their women and children from starving, take from a white man . . . a cup of sugar or coffee. The White Chief is angry and threatens to send soldiers. He is a coward. Tell him what I have said."

The ink was hardly dry before Washington failed to live up to its provisions as, among other things, the commander of the Military Department of the Missouri, the vain and arrogant General Winfield Scott Hancock, outlawed distribution of any firearms to the Indians. If they wanted to hunt buffalo they could do it with bows and arrows, as they had in the days before they had guns. The Comanche-Kiowa and Cheyenne-Arapaho agents gasped at the danger involved in such a statement, and the Indian chiefs made rankled threats. In mid-March General Sherman told Hancock that the situation "cannot be tolerated for a moment. If not a state of war, it is the next thing to it. . . ." Hancock, a brave soldier but hopelessly ignorant of Indian affairs, took the field in early April with fourteen hundred troopers from Colonel George A. Custer's 7th Cavalry, to teach the Indians a lesson. It was Colonel Custer's first Indian expedition and, as Hancock told the men, "We go prepared for war, and will make it if a proper occasion presents. . . . No insolence will be tolerated." He would hold a series of meetings with the chiefs, delivering the message that, if they wanted a war, he would fight them; if they wanted peace, they must reconcile themselves to having no more guns, and they must not go near the white man's roads any more.

The first of these meetings took place thirty-five miles up the Pawnee Fork from Fort Larned, at a large village of Southern Cheyennes and visiting Sioux. Irritated that only two big chiefs, Tall Bull and White Horse, both prominent leaders of the Cheyennes' "Dog Soldier" warrior society, came out to meet him, Hancock told them he would march his fourteen hundred men to their camp to meet the rest of the chiefs. It was just over two years since the Sand Creek massacre, and the Indians fled for their lives in fear, abandoning their tipis and belongings. Hancock interpreted this as an act of war and paused only long enough for the agents to tell him he was making an awful mistake before he burned the 250 lodges to the ground. President Andrew Johnson found Hancock's manner an acute embarrassment and removed him before he could do any more damage, and in October of 1867 another Peace Commission came to the South Plains Indians to try to quell "Hancock's War."

Thousands of the Indians of all the tribes gathered at Medicine Lodge Creek, Kansas, seventy miles south of Fort Larned (and about one hundred miles from the ashes on Pawnee Fork) to receive them, and during the week of October 21–28 concluded comprehensive treaties. The commissioners, who had just come from a similar peace mission on the North Plains, conducted themselves faultlessly while among the Indians. After reviewing the history of the southern frontier, they absolved the tribes from blame for the failure of the Little Arkansas Treaty, placing the culpability rather on the federal government, complaining eloquently in their report to Congress, "If the lands of the white man are taken, civilization justifies him in resisting the invader. Civilization does more than this; it brands him as a coward and a slave if he submits to the wrong. Here civilization made its contract and guaranteed the rights of the weaker party. It did not stand by the guarantee. The treaty was broken, but not by the savage. If the savage resists, civilization, with the Ten Commandments in one hand and a sword in the other, demands his immediate extermination. . . ."

Of all the treaties' provisions, two were of particular importance. First, the Indians agreed to live only on reservations, and the government set aside for them two areas within the Indian Territory, spacious by today's standards but woefully insufficient to meet the needs of the nomadic tribes. The one in the Southwest was for the Comanches, Kiowas, and Katakas, the one in the North for the Cheyennes and Arapahoes. Second, regarding the use of the areas by white men, the words of the treaties offer the clearest explanation: "[The reservations are] hereby set apart for the absolute and undisturbed use and occupation of the Indians herein named . . . and the United States now solemnly pledges that no persons except those herein authorized . . . shall ever be permitted to pass over, settle upon, or reside in the territory described. . . ."

To partially compensate for the restrictions placed on the Indians, another clause was added, that the Indian tribes "yet reserve the right to hunt on any lands south of the Arkansas River so long as the buffalo may range thereon," thus allowing the Indians to continue hunting their precious buffalo in all of Kansas south of the Arkansas. Many of the chiefs vigorously opposed the imposition of any more restrictions on their life style but, influenced partly by the huge piles of gifts their people would receive for signing, and partly by the belief that the new treaty was ironclad (an erroneous assumption, since last-minute verbal persuasions were never written down), they accepted them.

The following summer, however, the issuance of arms and ammunition was again delayed, as the Cheyenne agent and his superintendent found themselves at odds over whether they should be distributed. A small amount of arms were finally approved at the agent's insistence, but not before a small party of Cheyennes, sensing another betrayal, set off on a string of depredations. Although the large majority of Indians had nothing to do with the raids, the army's reaction was swift and unequivocal: All the South Plains tribes were now to suffer war without quarter, a war that, in Sherman's words, "If it results in the utter annihilation of these Indians, it is but the result of what they have been warned again and again. . . . I will say nothing and do nothing to restrain our troops from doing what they deem proper on the spot, and will allow no mere vague general charges of cruelty and inhumanity to tie their hands . . . these Indians, the enemies of our race and of our civilization, shall not again be able to begin and carry out their barbarous warfare on any kind of pretext they may choose to allege . . . these Indians will seek some sort of peace, to be broken next year at their option; but we will not accept their peace, or cease our efforts till all the past acts are both punished and avenged."

In addition, this war would have a new aspect: It would be carried, in winter, into the Indian camps, placing the Indians at a tremendous disadvantage. Since known as the "Winter Campaign," the most famous engagement occurred on November 27, the "Battle" of the Washita. Eight hundred troopers of the 7th Cavalry, led by Colonel Custer, who was freshly reactivated after having been once convicted and removed for dereliction, swooped down upon a village of about fifty Cheyenne tipis. Unfortunately, it was the camp of the peace chiefs Little Robe, Little Rock, and the survivor of Sand Creek, Black Kettle, who had all come in close to Fort Cobb to escape the war. Although Black Kettle and Little Robe had ridden to the fort to announce their presence and peaceful intentions, there was evidence that some of their young men had been raiding, and in a saber-swinging dawn attack through the village about one hundred Cheyennes, including Little Rock and Black Kettle, were cut down.

At once a furious and disgusted Agent Wynkoop resigned charge of the Cheyennes, and Custer was vehemently attacked as another Parson Chivington, but the war went on until the South Plains Indians were humiliated to the satisfaction of most of the army generals and frontier settlers.

In 1869 the federal government took a whole new approach to the problem of Indian management when President Ulysses S. Grant inaugurated his famous "peace policy" of replacing military agents with religious officers, charged to talk the Indians in, civilize, and ultimately Christianize them. The change settled a debate that had been raging for years over who should control the Indian Bureau. Originally the ministering agency was the War Department. At the creation of the Department of the Interior in 1849 it assumed control, and the army had been fighting ever since to get it back. Sentiment in Congress had swung like a pendulum, as whenever the flagrant graft and corruption within the Indian Office led them to the verge of letting the army hold sway, news would reach Washington of another grisly massacre like Sand Creek or the Washita, and the transfer bills would be killed.

When religious leaders approached President-elect Grant and volunteered the good names and reputations of the churches to care for the American Indians, the former General of the Army confused and incensed his Indian-fighting subordinates—particularly Sherman and Sheridan—by blessing them to try. A Board of Indian Commissioners was established to advise the Secretary of the Interior on Indian affairs, and the tribes of the South Plains were given over to the care of the Society of Friends, or Quakers. The headquarters of the superintendency was located in Lawrence, Kansas, under the direction of Friend Enoch Hoag, a middle-aged civil libertarian who went west with no reservation but that the Indians, if only treated with sympathy and dignity, could in time be enlightened to the virtues of Christian civilization. Often denounced by a military establishment never really willing to give him a chance at being a "pious visionary," he was never given full credit for grappling with the tremendous problems that faced him. The agency for the Cheyennes and Arapahoes was set up first at Camp Supply, a military outpost in the northwest part of the Indian Territory, but was soon moved a hundred miles down the North Canadian by the agent, Friend Brinton Darlington, to lessen what was considered to be the deleterious effect of the military presence on the Indians. When the elderly Darlington died in 1872 the agency was named after him, and the agent for the Kickapoo Indians, bearded, energetic John D. Miles, was transferred to assume his duties. The Kiowa and Comanche agency was established at the newly created Fort Sill, in the southwestern Indian Territory, at the eastern edge of the ruggedly beautiful Wichita Mountains. When the first agent, Lawrie Tatum, resigned in 1873, he was replaced by James M. Haworth, 43, of Olathe, Kansas, a man whose close intellectual affiliation with Superintendent Hoag led to his equally ugly castigation by the army. As a result Haworth gained undeserved the reputation of a weak-willed, temporizing apologist. Actually, many Quakers had opposed his appointment as Indian Agent because he had raised a company of volunteers to fight in the Civil War. Attaining the rank of major, he at one time was aide-de-camp to General James

A. Garfield, but his health gave out after a few months and he returned home to recuperate. He was still basically a pacifist but a strong, capable, and determined administrator. A round-faced, russet-bearded farmer, it took the Kiowas only a short time to select a name for him: Simpo-goodl (Red Beard).

It had been several years since George Bent had characterized the Southern Cheyennes as "these numerous and warlike Indians," but when the Quaker agents assumed their posts the designation was still applicable in some degree to all the South Plains Indians. First among equals in the doomed Stone Age coalition were the Comanches. Numbering probably less than twenty-five hundred individuals, their language had become the *lingua franca* of intertribal commerce. They were by far the best horsemen, and they were the craftiest raiders; in fact the symbol in the intertribal sign language for "Comanche" was a wriggling motion of the hand, signifying snake. By the end of the Americans' Civil War the dozen or more principal bands of the Comanche tribe had been almost totally absorbed into the five largest: the Penateka, Kotsoteka, Yapparika, Nokoni, and Quahadi.

The Penatekas, or "honey eaters," were at one time the southernmost of the bands, having occupied the Texas Hill Country as early as the late 1700s. Once as warlike as the other bands, prolonged contact with the white men altered their disposition, until by the 1870s they were the most easily pacified, often displaying a testy independence from the other bands in maintaining good relations with the whites. The two leading chiefs of the Penatekas, Isa-havey (Milky Way) and Asa-toyah-teh (Striding Through the Dusk), were probably Agent Haworth's closest allies when he came to Fort Sill.

The other bands were less tractable. Although Haworth had among the Yapparikas ("root eaters") important allies in the minor chiefs Quirts Quip (Elk Chewing) and Ho-weah (Clearing in the Woods), a much larger following was commanded by two tough old war chiefs, Tabananica (Sound of the Sun) and his brother-in-law Isa-Rosa (White Wolf). Though the latter two did consent to draw rations from Haworth, the agent considered them the two most dangerous of all the Comanche chiefs who stayed more or less near the agency. Unswerving in his contempt for reservation life, Tabananica had disrupted the 1872 Alvord Council when, in response to the government's milk-and-honey description of settling down and raising crops, he rose and snarled vehemently, "I have kept out on the plains because the whites were bad. Now you come here to do good, you say, and the first thing you want to do is pen us up in a narrow territory. Ugh! I would rather stay out on the plains and eat dung than come in on such conditions!" When he ran out of verbal invective he still hissed and spit for scorn. The Quaker schoolteacher to the Kiowas, Thomas Battey, once stayed overnight in Isa-Rosa's tipi, but condemned both chiefs as being the only ones who stayed near the agency who refused to forbid their young men from raiding in Texas.

The Kotsotekas ("buffalo eaters") were evidently one of the smaller bands, as they boasted only one influential chief, though he was indeed a dominant personality: Mow-way (Push Aside). His acclaim for bravery was truly widespread; in the scalplock over his craggy face was strung a gigantic claw, a trophy taken from a grizzly bear that the chief killed with a knife as the animal was mauling one of his braves. His band was one of the widest ranging of all, having traveled far enough west at one time to have allied with the Mescalero Apaches. He always represented himself to the Americans as friendly, having boasted on receiving a government medallion that he had never made war on Washington; during the "Winter Campaign" of 1868 the military agent listed him as a valuable friend of the government. His good will, however, did not extend to Texans and Mexicans, and he was jailed for raiding in Santa Fe, New Mexico, in 1869. He also was outspoken in his displeasure with Indians who settled on the reservations as long as there were buffalo to hunt, as he told the Alvord Council in 1872 that, to bring him in to the reservation, "I was promised lots of things, but I don't see them. . . . When the Indians in here are better treated than we are outside, it will be time enough to come in."

The Nokoni ("wanderer") Comanches were evidently split into two factions. The group favoring peace and adoption of white ways followed the lead of a senior chief, Horseback. At one time his band had numbered some two hundred people, and he had enjoyed wide influence, even among the Quahadi chiefs, who respected his bravery and skill as a fighter. Frail now, and elderly, riddled with tuberculosis, Horseback had moved in near the agency as early as 1868 because, he said, he was too sick to either fight or run away if he were attacked; he became one of Agent Haworth's most trusted informants. A sizable group of more independent and conservative Nokonis gravitated about another chief, Pe-arua-akup-akup (Big Red Meat) reputedly the bravest fighter in the Comanche tribe, while at the same time some of the more determined young raiders probably followed a rising young war chief, Qua-nah (Fragrance) Parker, the son of the chief who had given the band its name, when Quanah left the Nokonis to live with the Quahadis.

Traditionally conservative isolationists, the Quahadi ("antelope eater") Comanches of the Texas panhandle had never been party to a treaty with the white men, seldom went near the agency, did not draw rations, and indeed they mingled only infrequently with the other bands of Comanches. Their haunts were the high "Staked Plains" (El Llano Estacado), a well-defined plateau of lush prairies abounding in buffalo, pronghorn, and other game. By far the most warlike and dreaded of the Comanche bands, their first chief, until his death in 1874, was Parra-o-coom (He Bear or Bull Bear), who reputedly drew his greatest pleasure from hand-to-hand fighting; the leaders under him, Second Chief Kobay-o-burra (Wild Horse), who succeeded as first chief in 1874, and Kobay-o-toho (Black Horse), who became second chief, were no less ferocious in demeanor.

Where the Comanche chiefs wielded little exercisable authority and the widely ranging bands tended toward political anarchy, the Kiowas, numbering about 1,300, concerned themselves perhaps overmuch with formal politics, and the death of old Do-hauson in 1865 left that tribe saddled with divisive political struggles. Do-hauson had named to succeed him as principal chief a distinguished though aging war chief, Gui-päh-go (Lone Wolf), perhaps a result of his growing disillusionment with the Americans whom he had once trusted. Although a member of the Tsetanma warrior society and the on-de aristocratic caste, Lone Wolf had never been able to command Do-hauson's universal following, a predicament due largely to the ambitions of other chiefs possessing greater personal magnetism.

Two influential chiefs in particular detracted from Lone Wolf's following, both of them senior members of the highest of the six warrior societies, the Kaitsenko. The first was Set-ankia (or Satank, Sitting Bear), often referred to in veneration as "Highest of the Tribe," who was at least seventy years old, and the second was Set-tain-te (or Satanta, White Bear), somewhat over sixty. Unquestionably the most famous and celebrated of all the South Plains chiefs, Satanta always professed friendship toward the white Americans, although he was a ferocious raider and had always resisted with vehemence all attempts to transform the Kiowas into pastoralists or anything but buffalo Indians. Of large stature for an Indian—he stood about five feet ten—Satanta was an influential speaker possessing tremendous personal charisma, although his popular appellation, "Orator of the Plains," was evidently given him in jest of his strutting, boasting behavior at the Medicine Lodge Council of 1867. In 1871 Satank and Satanta were arrested, along with the lesser young war chief Ado etta (Big Tree), for their part in the famous Warren Wagontrain massacre. Satank committed suicide before he could be tried, but Satanta and Big Tree were conveyed to Texas, convicted by a pistol-toting cowboy jury in Jacksboro, and sentenced to hang. When Texas governor E. J. Davis bowed to pressure from eastern reformers and commuted the sentences to life imprisonment, and then released them in 1873 as part of a political "deal" with the Kiowas, the United States Army and the settlers on the frontier fumed, but Satanta had become rather more tractable. Still, he remained a powerful voice for conservatism, often taking Lone Wolf's part in council meetings.

Until his death in 1865 Do-hauson had pursued a policy of peace and conciliation toward the white men, notwithstanding the Americans' self-contradictions and growing deviousness. After 1869 this legacy was taken up by a handsome young chief of great intellectual ability, wisdom, and power of persuasion: Téné-an-gopte (Eagle That Strikes with Talons, or more simply, Striking Eagle). Like Lone Wolf a member of the Tsetanma warrior society, Striking Eagle's tremendous ability early overcame the social prejudice attached to his being a nonfull-blood—his grandfather was a Crow Indian—and he avowedly sought to intergrate his people into the white civilization in a manner that would not confuse and frighten them. This stance brought him into bitter

and often ugly confrontation with the more conservative chiefs—
Lone Wolf most particularly—but Striking Eagle always held his
own. When a rumor campaign started against him in 1870, whis-
pering that he befriended the whites because he had become a
coward, Striking Eagle led a raid, not against isolated settlers, but
against a force of more than fifty troopers of the 6th Cavalry,
killing three bluecoats and wounding twelve. During this fight
Striking Eagle proved that he not only had bravery equal to the
more conservative war chiefs (he had personally speared one of
the soldiers), but also superior tactical and maneuvering ability.
After that he let no one doubt that he pursued the white road out
of conviction, not weakness. Soon after Agent Haworth's arrival,
he and Striking Eagle became close, indeed intimate, friends.
When the Quaker administration sent out an educator, Thomas C.
Battey, to open a school among the Kiowas in 1873, it was done at
Striking Eagle's instigation, and it was primarily his influence that
guaranteed Battey's safety among them.

By 1874 the majority of the Kiowas accepted Striking Eagle's
lead, but numerous lesser war chiefs, who had gained prominence
by fighting and depended on it to maintain their social status (and
whose intellects were for the most part insufficient to merit their
having influence in anything but war), adhered to the more conservative Lone Wolf faction. The oldest of them was probably
Medicine Lodge Treaty signer Man-yi-ten (Woman's Heart), but
the bulk of their strength lay in war chiefs of Striking Eagle's own
generation, most prominently Zepko-etta (Big Bow), about forty
years old. A handsome, barrel-chested playboy, Big Bow had
stolen his first wife when he was only eighteen, the same year he
had been first recognized a war chief. His reputation was almost
matched by that of another war chief, Tsen-tain-te (White
Horse). Younger than his close companion Big Bow by several
years, White Horse had earned a reputation for being exceptionally "tough and reckless," a demeanor masked by his soft eyes
and nearly effeminate face. Soldiers in Texas had killed his
younger brother two years before, to which White Horse responded by leading the bloody Lee massacre. In April 1872, Big
Bow and White Horse together led the Howard's Well wagon train
massacre, where White Horse had personally slain three of the
seventeen Mexican drivers.

Still prominent, though of lesser influence, were such war chiefs as Poor (meaning Skinny) Buffalo, Big Tree, and Gui-ka'ti (Wolf Lying Down). The division between the conservative and liberal factions was distinctly marked, and virtually all of the Kiowas' forty-odd headmen had aligned themselves with one group or the other. Even the two medicine men who have come down as the most influential in that tribe belonged to opposing factions: Maman-ti (Swan, or Walks-in-the-Sky), was also a prominent war chief; the more respected Nap-a-wat (No Moccasins) tended to back Striking Eagle.

Like the Comanches, the Cheyennes and Arapahoes were essentially apolitical, or were at least only rarely as vocally political as the Kiowas, and after the Sheridan "winter campaign" of 1868 they presented little obstacle to peace. Among the Arapahoes the principal proponent of keeping good relations with the whites was Chief Powder Face, at one time an awesome warrior who commanded universal respect, but who now used all his dominating influence to keep at bay the less willing members of the Arapahoes' Tomahawk warrior society. Like the twice-widowed Striking Eagle, Powder Face kept only one wife—to whom incidentally he was famously devoted—and like Striking Eagle, Powder Face became as trusted a friend to Agent John D. Miles as the Kiowa was to Haworth.

Among the Cheyennes the man who bore the greatest responsibility for keeping peace was Chief Little Robe, the survivor of the massacre on the Washita that took the lives of the two other peace chiefs, Little Rock and Black Kettle. When in 1869 members of the Cheyennes' militant "Dog Soldier" warrior society challenged his liberal rule and threatened to recommence raiding, Little Robe succeeded in driving some of them north to the old homeland and effectively cowed the rest, likely aided in the coup by the influence of three other elder peace chiefs, Stone Calf, White Shield, and Old Whirlwind.

Yet, if the rising influence of the liberal, prowhite chiefs in 1870 presented a favorable omen for the future, that influence was only barely able to stand the pressures that dogged the tribes over the next four years. Except for the beneficence of the government issue, which was not enough to subsist them, all the tribes were still basically hunters and gatherers, peculiarly susceptible to adverse changes in their environment. Seen in that light, the systematic decimation by white hunters of the buffalo herds on which the Indians did subsist, which began in that year, fell upon the South Plains Indians as the most gross and disastrous affliction imaginable.

II. The Indians' Commissary

The actual train of events leading up to the Red River uprising
begins three years after the treaty council at Medicine Lodge, in
the fall of 1870, when a young New Englander named Josiah
Wright Mooar came west and founded the business of hunting
buffalo for hides. Barely nineteen years old, blond, blue-eyed, just
under six feet tall, he arrived in Fort Hays, Kansas, filled with
visions of "the grandeur and dangers of the Wild West." The
realities of the world caught up with him there, however, and he
was obliged to support himself on the dangerous and romantic job
of supplying the local army post with wood, for which he was paid
two dollars per cord. At Fort Hays he made friends with one
James White, whose not too dissimilar task was to keep the post
commissary stocked with meat. White was a buffalo hunter, and
like all the others he took only the choice cuts, leaving the rest of
the carcass, including the hides, lying on the prairie. White, and
the many other buffalo hunters on the Great Plains, had made
some noticeable inroads in the tremendous herds of buffalo, but
still the animals numbered so many millions that they literally
blanketed vast stretches of country.

Mooar and White often talked of the waste of skins, wondering
if perhaps they could not be useful as leather. A market had been
growing back east, for furry buffalo robes to use as sleigh
blankets, for instance, and Indians had certainly tanned buffalo
leather for centuries, but their idea gained no impetus until an
English firm contracted a Leavenworth, Kansas, robe and meat
trader, for five hundred hides. They too were interested in experi-
menting on the skins for tanning, and a subcontract fell to a

hunter named Charlie Rath, who in turn contacted his friends, among them Wright Mooar. The youngster from Vermont fulfilled his part of the quota and found himself with a surplus of fifty-seven hides; wondering if there might not be an American market for them, rather than letting England take the whole business, he sent the skins to his elder brother, John Wesley Mooar, in New York, to try to sell to an American tannery.

The hides were something of a novelty in New York—not too many had been seen there—and they were to be put on display until they were purchased. Two tanners from Pennsylvania saw the hides being pulled down Broadway in an open wagon, and later in the day called on the elder Mooar. They offered him $3.50 apiece for the hides, which Mooar accepted readily, and a few weeks later they contacted him again. They said they had experimented on the skins, were satisfied that they were useful, and inquired whether the Mooars would be interested in a contract for 2,000 skins at $3.50 apiece, a total of $7,000. John Mooar instantly departed New York for the Great Plains, and the Mooar brothers began hunting buffalo together more purposefully than anyone ever had before them.

Though the Mooars had always stayed a couple of jumps ahead of the pack, the promise of easy, fast money to be had by preying upon the huge herds of buffalo attracted opportunists like the rotting buffalo carcasses attracted flies; the business fairly exploded. Dodge City, in southwestern Kansas, became the center of the trade, and perhaps the best records of the carnage were preserved by the commander of the local military post (Fort Dodge), Major Richard Irving Dodge: In 1873 alone, the three rail lines serving Dodge City carried away over 750,000 hides, "exclusive of robes"; the figure for the three years 1872–74 totals an incredible 4,373,730 buffalo killed. That figure, said Dodge, was for the rail exports alone; other sources added at least 1 million more to the total.

Though the Indians to the south abhorred the wanton slaughter, they made no concerted move to stop it, as the depredations were confined to lands north of the Arkansas River. Country to the south of the Arkansas was considered Indian hunting ground, with the Arkansas River as the boundary—the famous "dead line"—between the two, a boundary that the hide hunters respected, at least in the early years of the Medicine Lodge Treaty. Their aversion was due principally to two factors: the abundance of buffalo still left in the north of Kansas, and the ferocity of the Indians south of the Arkansas and in the Indian Territory.

English adventurer and Americanophile William Blackmore, writing in 1877, recalled, "In the autumn of 1868 [one year after the signing of the Medicine Lodge Treaty], whilst crossing the plains on the Kansas Pacific Railroad—for a distance of upwards of 120 miles, between Ellsworth and Sheridan [far to the north of the Arkansas River] we passed through an almost unbroken herd of buffalo. The plains were blackened with them, and more than once the train had to stop to allow unusually large herds to pass. A few years afterwards, when travelling over the same line of railroad, it was a rare sight to see a few herds of from ten to twenty buffalo."

In 1873 a plague of grasshoppers destroyed the settlers' crops in the Republican River Valley, again far to the north of the Arkansas. Although Mooar and the others had been in business only three years, when the army sent "several companies" of troops to shoot buffalo to keep the farmers from starving, the troops found to their great consternation that there were virtually none left. The Mooars and the swarms of buffalo hunters who followed them were doing their business with unbelievable efficiency. As far as the Arkansas River hunting boundary was concerned, William Blackmore went with an army scouting party on a trip along the Arkansas east of Fort Dodge in 1872. They found, he wrote later, ". . . a continuous line of putrescent carcasses, so that the air was rendered pestilential and offensive to the last degree. The hunters had formed a line of camps along the banks of the river, and had shot down the buffalo, night and morning, as they came down to drink." One of the Dodge City buffalo hunters was William "Billy" Dixon, of West Virginia, no older than Wright Mooar; Dixon was rapidly gaining a reputation as one of the finest marksmen and most successful of them all. "During the fall and winter of 1872 and 1873," Dixon wrote later, "there were more hunters in the country than ever before. . . . I feel safe in saying that 75,000 buffaloes were killed within sixty or seventy-five miles of Dodge. . . . We had to make hay while the sun shone. . . ."

But none of the hunters dared cross the river, and the "dead line" held, because for the first five years of the treaty (to 1872), to cross the Arkansas with buffalo guns and a wagon was to risk a horrible death at the hands of the Indians. A few desperate or greedy men did chance it, but then only in winter, when the Indians seldom left their camps, and with light, strong wagons and fast horses. And even then, a number of them were picked off and scalped; it was obvious that the tribes of the South Plains had been driven back as far as they intended to go.

Only after the northern Kansas buffalo herds were gone did the hunters venture in force into the Indian hunting ground south of the Arkansas; they went down as far as, but rarely crossed, the boundary between the state of Kansas and the Indian Territory. In only one season they mowed down the southern Kansas buffalo like a scythe. On a scout from Dodge City to the Indian Territory, Blackmore recorded, "In 1872 . . . we were never out of sight of buffalo. In the following autumn, while travelling over the same district, whilst the whole country was whitened with bleached and bleaching bones, we did not meet with buffalo until we were well into Indian country, and then only in scattered bands."

The suddenness of it all was appalling. As much as it strains today's imagination, the white men slaughtered their buffalo in the hundreds of thousands, utterly obliterating in one season's kill the southern Kansas herds on which the Cheyennes and Arapahoes had, in large measure, subsisted. The Indians were powerless before the onslaught of an entire army of buffalo "runners," as the hidemen called themselves, and had retreated to the sanctity of their reserve, where, the government promised them, white men would not—could not—follow. But follow they did, and with more alacrity than when they crossed the Arkansas. During the year that the southern Kansas buffalo were exterminated, Cheyenne and Arapaho war parties still managed to drive off those of the whites' hunting outfits that crossed the border into the "exclusive" domain of the Indians, but by the next year (1873), raids on the Indians' game became more and more frequent, and the Indians, fighting now within their own territory, became less and less capable of fending off the tide of poachers.

One can wonder here what the United States Army was doing all this time, since under the terms of Medicine Lodge they were supposed to be patrolling the Kansas-Indian Territory boundary to see that nobody crossed. The troops were indeed watching over the border, but from an early date they had worked out a happy arrangement with the hunters to look the other way whenever the latter made a foray into the forbidden country. The prevalent view of the army men was best summed up by General Philip Sheridan, when in 1875 he lectured a session of the Texas legislature to defeat a conservation bill that would have preserved the buffalo from extinction. The buffalo hunters "have done more in the last two years," he said, "to settle the vexed Indian question than the entire regular army has done in the past thirty years. They are destroying the Indians' commissary. . . . Send them powder and lead, if you will; but, for the sake of lasting peace, let them kill, skin, and sell until the buffaloes are exterminated. Then your prairies can be covered with speckled cattle and the festive cowboy, who follows the hunter as a second forerunner of an advanced civilization."

As Phil Sheridan was the commander of the Military Division in which the slaughter was taking place, it seemed unlikely that·the buffalo runners would meet any opposition from the army; indeed, the soldiers enjoyed a buffalo hunt as much as anybody, and they did not even take the hides; they were just after the sport. As early as the campaigns of the 1860s the men under Colonel George A. Custer, operating as part of Sheridan's famous "winter campaign," when not hunting for Indians, divided into small squads to see which could kill the most buffalo in one day. Tallies were kept by cutting out the animals' tongues, later fed to camp dogs, and the general rule was that the losing party had to fix dinner for the others. At the Medicine Lodge Council in 1867, the Kiowa chief Satanta had become violently angry when he saw the government's soldiers amusing themselves by shooting down buffalo.

With the army standing idly by, the "dead line," once accepted to be the Arkansas River and then moved south to the border of the Indian Territory, was moved south yet again in 1873, on a *de facto* basis, all the way to the next large river south of the Arkansas, the Cimarron. That meant that the Indians had lost all control over what had been the reservation given them at Medicine Lodge, of which the Cimarron was the *southern* boundary.

The Indians were left to look for game in lands to the south and west.

For the buffalo runners, the 1873 killing season on the Cimarron was in turn so successful that the Great Southern Herd would never again migrate that far north. The voracious hide hunters had done their bloody business so well that in the space of a single year the bison, because of their reduced numbers, would stop short their migration at the Canadian River, which at the Texas panhandle meridian is some one hundred miles *south* of the Cimarron. To gain any sense of the proportion of the slaughter one must trace the carnage on a map: from the Arkansas to the territorial border to the Cimarron to the Canadian, the prairies denuded of their thundering black herds and left silent and white with millions of skeletons bleaching in the sun—all in the space of the three years 1872–74. The Indian tribes reeled before the juggernaut, struggling in vain to find a foothold.

Their plight notwithstanding, however, the hunters determinedly began to lay plans for the 1874 hunt on the Canadian. That, however, meant a one hundred miles' deeper penetration into the Indian Territory, which was a bit much for even the bravest of them to risk. Since none of them wished to isolate himself smack in the middle of hostile Indian country, two of the plainsmen, Wright Mooar, by now a leader of the hunters and still very much in the vanguard of their movements, and John Webb, rode south into the panhandle of Texas, where very little hunting had ever been done except by the Comanche and Kiowa Indians, to investigate the rapidly proliferating rumors that the prairies there were still grazed by huge and untouched herds of buffalo. Mooar and Webb did indeed find them, and on their return they confirmed the stories, relating the scene of "an almost solid mass" of hundreds of thousands of bison. Commented Mooar, "All day long they opened up before us and came together behind us."

At this time, in the fall of 1873, the Kansas hunters began to worry that the army might for once try to hinder their crossing Indian land, and sent emissaries in the persons of Wright Mooar and another hunter, Steele Frazier, to Major Richard I. Dodge, the commander of Fort Dodge, whose job it was to patrol the border. The hunters were about to risk their lives by operating the farthest yet from any settlement, and any interference from the army would put an end to their schemes altogether, so they could not settle for a noncommittal answer. Anxious to make a good impression on the major, Mooar and Frazier bathed (reputedly an extreme measure for a buffalo hunter), and wore brand-new suits of clothes to the interview. Mooar's specific question to Dodge was: "Major, if we cross into Texas, what will be the government's attitude toward us?" Even to cross Indian land was declared illegal by the Medicine Lodge Treaty, but it was the only way to get from Kansas to Texas, and besides it could be argued, technically, that a crossing would not be illegal if it were made over the so-called "No Man's Land," to the west of the actual Cheyenne-Arapaho Reservation. On the other hand, they would have no license to hunt there, and Texans might feel differently about shooting their buffalo, not because they were against killing buffalo, but because they might feel that the presence of buffalo in the panhandle helped keep the Kiowas and Comanches out of central Texas settlements.

Mooar and Frazier soon found their caution unnecessary, however. Major Dodge, himself a "sportsman" and hunter, received them warmly, and finally confided, "Boys, if I were a buffalo hunter, I would hunt where the buffaloes are." And thus was formalized the unwritten alliance between the hidemen and the United States Army. Major Dodge would give the hunters a free rein anywhere they wished to shoot.

The buffalo runners therefore agreed to carry out the next season's hunt high on the "Staked Plains" (El Llano Estacado) of the Texas panhandle, the vast, grassy plateau that rises abruptly from the flat lowlands. This would put them west of the Indian Territory and outside the Indians' hunting reserves, the northern part of which of course they had already depleted. Hunting in Texas, the Indians should have no quarrel with them, except for the brief but necessary trespass, if indeed it were a trespass. The hunters knew, however, that the Indians would not see it that way. As far as the Indians were concerned, all the buffalo south of the Arkansas River were theirs, and the whites had stolen from them. The heat for revenge was high; the presence of white hunters among the last herds of buffalo on the South Plains would likely touch off a savage Indian war, and the hunters knew it.

Most of the hidemen spent the winter of 1873–74 holed up in

Dodge City, but some of the hardier outfits wasted no time and headed for the Texas ranges that very fall. With very little delay, the Mooars reloaded their own wagons and headed back to Texas, the dangers posed by the Indians notwithstanding. Also going south with his own outfit was Billy Dixon, now at twenty-three one of the ablest and most respected marksmen on the plains. The actual process of hunting the buffalo on the range that autumn was best explained by Wright Mooar himself. "Each outfit would take a wagon, a keg of water, a roll of bedding, and a little grub and, with a four-mule team, would drive out on the divide between the North Palo Duro and the Canadian. There we would intercept the herds that were crossing, east to west, from the headwaters of Wolf Creek to the Blue and the Coldwater. We stayed there on the divide until we loaded out the wagon with hides and meat. We could haul 10,000 pounds when the ground was frozen. We would load, come back to camp, unload, and go back out again. We could keep track of the Wheelers' outfit [another team of hunters], and his of ours, by the sound of the guns. If either of us got into trouble, the sound of the buffalo guns would be interrupted with the reports of lighter guns."

Back in camp the skins were pegged out to dry in the sun, and any extra meat they had brought back, particularly tongues, for which there was still a paying market, were hung up to dry. At night the autumn cold of the Staked Plains was never a problem as, in Wright Mooar's words, "The camp bed of a frontiersman was a thing of art. A tarp was spread upon the grass, the blankets spread upon it and the tarp was drawn back over the top and carefully folded in at the sides. The sleeper then crawled in at the head of his bed and drew the tarp entirely over his head, thus encasing him, shutting out the cold and prowling animals and snakes." When Wright Mooar's brother John had first tried this type of bed a couple of years before, the New Yorker had "crept in with his trousers on, but soon found the bed so snug and warm, in spite of the November chill, that he had to shed them. Two inches of snow fell during the night, and when the tarp was thrown back the next morning we looked out on a white world."

In the mornings, breakfasts were hurriedly consumed, and the day's work began all over. There were several techniques of shooting the buffalo, but the most effective, and therefore most favored, was the "stand." When a herd was found, the hunter would pick out an exposed place some hundreds of yards away, from where he could fire in relative comfort and not alarm the animals. Setting up the forked rest sticks on which he set the heavy barrel of his buffalo gun, he first picked out and shot the leader of the herd. With no leader to start a stampede, the animals milled about until the hunter shot as many as his skinners could handle. That done, the skinners would go out (the hunter usually had three or four in his employ) to rip off the hides. A good hunter could kill fifty animals in a stand before the herd bolted or wandered out of range. Billy Dixon, one of the best, "once took 120 hides without moving his rest sticks." Other top scores for stands were, Wright Mooar, 96; Charlie Rath, 107; and Frank Collinson, 121. Hunters making a stand would not kill all the buffalo they could, but only as many as their skinners could do in a day. Frank H. Mayer, one of the last surviving buffalo runners, recalled not long before his death, "Killing more than we could use would waste buff, which wasn't important; it would also waste ammunition, which was."

The favorite gun of all the buffalo hunters was the Sharp's "Big Fifty" buffalo rifle, a .50-caliber octagonal-barreled cannon which, with its 2,000 foot-pounds of muzzle energy, could put a heavy ball probably farther and more accurately than any rifle before or since. One model weighed 16 pounds, but Mooar and most of the others preferred the lighter kinds. "I killed 6,500 buffaloes with my fourteen-pound gun," recalled Mooar, "and 14,000 with the eleven-pounder." Mooar and the other professionals always insisted on making their own bullets, melting their own lead, and overloading the three-inch bottlenecked cartridges with up to 110 grains of powder. There should only have been 90 grains, but the massive, eight-sided barrels had no trouble handling the extra charge. A weapon of this type could kill the strongest buffalo at 600 yards; some of them were equipped with 10x and 20x telescopes, and a well-placed ball could drop an animal at three quarters of a mile. Each man followed his own eccentricities in loading his gun, and tastes varied to the degree that one could recognize any hunter on the plains merely by the peculiar "boom" of his Sharp's Fifty. One other rather grim article that each hunter carried with him at all times was his "bite," a Big Fifty cartridge emptied of its powder and filled with cyanide, a guaranteed quick death infinitely preferable to the tortures devised by the Indians, and insurance as well against mutilation. The warriors would only scalp or "count coup" on a victim they had actually killed; hunters who "bit the bite" were never butchered, and their remains were found intact.

Each outfit, of course, carried all the necessary supplies with them. A party of four, the functional unit of a buffalo hunting team, subsisted mostly off what they shot, but there were other necessities. One historian noted that "A sack of flour, five pounds of coffee, ten pounds of sugar, a little salt, a side of bacon, and a few pounds of beans, was a month's supply store." They also had to carry hardware, and they carried their own ammunition; one party listed "sixteen hundred pounds of lead, and four hundred pounds of powder," and accessories like paper caps and shells.

This dependence on a supply base was a source of worry to the hunters. Shooting in the Texas panhandle was dangerous enough without having to risk their scalps to shuttle back and forth through hostile country to pick up supplies in Dodge City, and moreover they had the problem of how to dispose of the skins they took. Here again, they did not want the responsibility of freighting them through Indian Territory, but neither did they want to sit in their camps with several hundreds or even thousands of skins and so present an even greater temptation to the Indians than they already were. In the opening days of the spring of 1874, Billy Dixon set off on his own scout of the Texas high plains. When he returned to Dodge City at the end of March with the report that, although he had seen few buffalo, the range had been heavily grazed, and that he was sure a large herd would push through during the summer, those hunters who had waited out the winter in Dodge decided the time had come for them to move south in force. If they all went south together the Indians would be much less likely to attack them than they would small groups.

To accommodate the hidemen and ease the supply problem, one of the Kansas robe and meat traders, A. C. "Charlie" Myers, agreed to pack up his entire fifty-thousand-dollar business and move south with the hunters, to open a supply store and market center for their hides right there in the Texas panhandle. (This was hardly philanthropy on Myers' part. To keep his business going he needed buffalo, and there were none left in Kansas. He too had to follow the herds.) Renting space on the nearly empty wagons of the hunters heading south, as he had only two teams of his own, his caravan when it left Dodge consisted of some fifty men in thirty wagons. There was quite a celebration as the wagons rumbled down Front Street, with the men who decided not to go cheering from the sidewalks.

One man saw them but was not cheering: Amos Chapman, a half-bred Indian scout and interpreter at Camp Supply, a military outpost in the western Indian Territory. The husband of a Cheyenne woman, he often attended the councils of her people, and knew the mood that had been growing among them. He knew that the peace chiefs, Powder Face of the Arapahoes and Little Robe, Stone Calf, and White Shield of the Cheyennes, were having great difficulty in controlling their young men and that the patience of the older chiefs themselves was growing thinner by the day as the buffalo became scarcer, government rations dwindled or disappeared entirely, and white horse thieves from Kansas and Texas ran off with Indian ponies, which the government, in spite of the earnest pleas of the Indian agents, never even tried to get back. The war chiefs of the wilder Comanches and Kiowas were commanding larger and larger audiences among his wife's Cheyennes, and when Amos Chapman learned the wagon train's destination, he muttered darkly, "They's a lot of them Kiowas and Comanches down that way." But the white hunters merely derided him for trying to save the buffalo for the savages, and retorted that they could "shoot their way through all the Indian Nations of the Southwest" if they had to.

At the head of the caravan was Billy Dixon, now twenty-four, just returned from his scout. Also in the wagon train was another young hunter, Dixon's only close friend on the trip, and one with whom he had many things in common. He was only twenty years old, the youngest member of the expedition, but he was a year and a half veteran of buffalo hunting and showed great promise of being a fine shot. His name was William Barclay Masterson; to friends like Billy he was just "Bat." The two young men kept much to themselves, looking on the older hunters as a bunch of misfits, outlaws, and fugitives, which was, for the most part, a strikingly accurate assessment.

They were a colorful group, to put it charitably. Most of them clung to the edge of the frontier because they were for one reason or another simply unable to fit anywhere into normal society. Some had been loners so long they had forgotten—or at least had no reason to remember—their Christian names, and went merely by their nicknames: Shoot-'em-up Mike, Light-fingered Jack, Shotgun Collins, Prairie Dog Dave (who once got a thousand dollars for the white buffalo he shot), and young Dirty-face Jones, who boasted he had once made a stand of 106 buffalo "before breakfast." Some of them were downright notorious, like "Dutch Henry" Born, one of the most talented horse thieves in the history of the plains. He had started his career as a nondescript buffalo hunter, when one day Indians overran his camp and wounded him in the leg with an arrow. He hobbled several miles to an army post for a doctor, only to have the commanding officer, who thought little of buffalo hunters, order him off the post. Dutch Henry Born was still nominally a buffalo hunter, but since that day no head of government stock—or Indian pony, for that matter—was secure from his aberrant genius.

One of the more interesting, if rather less dangerous, characters was a young greenhorn from Illinois named Fairchild. A lawyer by profession, his knowledge of life in the wilds was limited to what he gleaned from the prevalent "dime novels" of the day. Anxious to get in on the adventures he had read about, he rode into Dodge City in the spring of 1874 slicked up in a "shiny broadcloth suit, plug hat, flowered vest," and a tie that one blinded onlooker could only compare to a Rocky Mountain sunset. To hear him talk, his greatest goal was to kill a red Indian and save the scalp for a souvenir. Young Fairchild did not, needless to say, make a terribly smashing impression on the "Shoot-'em-up Mikes" on the trip.

The wagon train headed south on a trail that was, by this time, beginning to be fairly well defined, and the first day's journey took them as far as Crooked Creek. There, after dinner, some of the men unpacked fiddles and harmonicas, as others pegged down a dried buffalo skin as a dancing platform. They performed jigs, and even, for comedy's sake, danced with each other. (Indeed, the thought of Dirty-face Jones dancing with Shotgun Collins is after a hundred years still enough to distract a historian from serious deliberations.)

The second day out they crossed the Cimarron, but only after much labor, as the wagon train had to pick its way through the broad bottoms, feeling as they went for the treacherous pockets of quicksand for which that river is justly famous. They camped on the south bank, just at the threshold of Indian country, and there the hidemen decided on a "policy" of Indian relations: If the savages left them alone, they would initiate no hostility. (They did not, obviously, consider "destroying the Indians' commissary" an act of hostility.) They would, however, keep a constant lookout for a surprise attack.

The next day's pull took them as far as the Beaver, a primary feeder stream of the North Canadian. Continuing on their way south, they passed the camps of the hunters already there, all of whom were greatly pleased to see present such a large force of armed white men. Now the expedition began to scout seriously for a location to set up their new town. They passed Palo Duro Creek and went on to swift, high-banked Moore's Creek. There was little grass there, however, so they followed it south, finally camping, about a week after they left Dodge, on the north bank of the Canadian River, the general destination, in what is present-day Hutchinson County, Texas. Their 150-mile trek had brought them to the ruins of an old, abandoned trading post, built in the 1840s by the entrepreneurs William Bent and Ceran St. Vrain, for purposes of trade with the Comanches and Kiowas, who had proven uninterested in such an arrangement. Here, ten years before, in 1864, some troops and Indian "auxiliaries" under Colonel "Kit" Carson had fought and defeated a band of hostile Kiowas; the crumbling walls now stood four and five feet high.

When the wagon train reached the main fork of the Canadian some of the men, with the strains of the journey behind them, decided to play a trick on the loud-mouthed greenhorn from Illinois, Fairchild. Since they had left Dodge the young lawyer had strutted about wearing a "bang-up brown duck suit," a sombrero wide enough to shade a buffalo, and outsized spurs clamped onto boots with heels so high he had difficulty walking straight (and this to impress a bunch of tobacco-chewing, whiskey-swizzling roughnecks who had been on the plains for years!). For days Fairchild, armed with a Sharp's Big Fifty, a revolver, and a huge butcher knife, had been loudly demanding a chance to kill and scalp an Indian, to "tell the folks about." The night they camped on the Canadian the veteran hunters decided to give Fairchild an opportunity to get his Indian.

In the brushy timber down by the river were roosting hundreds of wild turkeys, so to begin Fairchild's lesson, Charlie Myers and Bat Masterson (who was by all accounts one of the most resourceful practical jokers on the plains) suggested to Fairchild that they go out and shoot some. As they rode out of camp, two other men who were in on the scheme sneaked stealthily over to the timber and, by arrangement, built a campfire, "Indian style," and hunched in the bushes, waiting. Presently they heard the three men, Myers, Fairchild, and Masterson, ride around a bend in the river and pull up short when they caught sight of the fire.

"Indians!" wheezed Masterson, panicky.

"Nonsense!" huffed Myers disgustedly. "Pull yourself together, Masterson."

But Bat continued to snivel and whimper until Myers finally told Fairchild that they should ride on alone and send the "damned coward" back to camp. Besides, said Myers, if there were any trouble, this would be Fairchild's big chance to get his Indian. Fairchild suggested they not do anything hasty.

Suddenly the men in the brush screamed like red men and fired volleys of bullets into the treetops, and poor Fairchild never waited around to see if Myers and Masterson got out alive. Spurring his horse, he rode like a madman back to camp, where he half fell off the animal babbling bug-eyed to the other men that the woods were crawling with Indians, Myers and Masterson were dead, etc., etc.

One of the hunters exclaimed that Fairchild had been wounded, as another ripped off his shirt and somebody poured hot coffee over his back. Even Fairchild thought he was shot. After the "wound" was dressed, though, a gun was thrust into the poor tenderfoot's hands and he was hustled, protesting, off to the river to stand sentry over the camp. There they left him. When he finally wandered back into camp he found all the men helpless with laughter.

Fairchild was furious, but after he recovered he became a "fine fellow and good hunter."

When they were finally ready to begin scouting for a favorable location to set up shop, the hunters headed north along the Canadian, but stopped after they had gone about a mile and half, where they came upon a spot perfect for establishing a new settlement. Grass for the stock was abundant—sagebrush, pokeweed, bluestem, and beargrass—with water provided by a creek and fresh spring. Along the creek grew a gallery forest of willow, cottonwood, chinaberry, and hackberry, providing timber for the construction of buildings.

Four of them were eventually erected, all of them facing the east, all of them "soddies," built by standing logs on end in trenches and filling in the chinks with sod; roofs also were of sod, laid on wooden frames, good and thick as insulation against the coming summer's heat. Myers built his store on the north end of the line, hiring as many men as he could to cut timber; it formed the northeast corner of a large corral. At the south end of the corral one Tom O'Keefe built his blacksmith shop, about fifteen feet square, and next to it a hunter named James Hanrahan provided himself with a second source of income by opening a saloon, stocked with whiskey he had brought from Dodge. Not long after, Charlie Rath, the same who had shot buffalo for the English tannery years before, followed Myers in moving his business south to the new settlement. Like Myers, Rath was aware of the Indian danger, but did not concern himself unduly. "Sometimes the Indians threatened," he said later, "[but] they done that every year." His store, with its restaurant operated by William Olds and his wife, was the southernmost of the four buildings. Mrs. Olds was the only woman in town; it is said that many of the hunters wanted to bring along some of Dodge City's more "talented" saloon girls, but Myers forbade it.

Myers' and Rath's moving to Texas with their businesses was important because it gave some semblance of organization to the hunting tnere. Up to that time the hunting parties had ranged south one at a time, each one getting there as best it could, the sooner before its competitors the better, and when the wagons were full, the hunters freighted them back to Dodge themselves. There had been only one unifying factor: avarice. Myers' establishment of his supply post gave the hunters a much closer market for their hides, as well as a centralized base from where they could operate and obtain goods.

The new settlement was called Adobe Walls, after the nearby ruins of the old trading post. Its own walls were not of adobe; indeed, no really permanent buildings were required, as everybody planned to leave again, as soon as they killed all the buffalo. All four of its business establishments were receiving customers by the first of May, and immediately Adobe Walls became the center of the whole panhandle hide trade. All the outfits—Dixon's, the Mooars', and many others—operated from there—an estimated two hundred professional buffalo hunters. Summer came late, however, which delayed the migration of the great southern herd through that part of the country, giving the hunters only scattered bands of buff to shoot, and while the hunters lay mostly idle, Jim Hanrahan's saloon did a booming business. Summer did arrive, though, and with a sultry vengeance, and when the herds began to move through, the buffalo runners moved out en masse and cut them down by the thousands.

III. The Gathering Storm

If the government had lived up to its treaty obligations to protect the Indians from invasion by white buffalo hunters, there would have been little need for the war that ensued. But such was not the policy of the government, and it is difficult to imagine the privation that the eradication of the buffalo caused among the Indians. The primary staple of the tribes' diet was dried buffalo meat, gathered when the hunting was good, then stored by the ton in sacks of dried buffalo skin, the packages weighing perhaps a hundred pounds each. But the big shaggy animals were much more than the primary year-'round source of food. From the hides the Indians fashioned their clothing and the tipis they lived in, their war shields, cradles for their infants, even rude boats of hides stretched over willow saplings. They wove rope from the hair and stretched the tendons into bowstrings and thread. They fashioned the large bones into tools, rendered glue from the hoofs, even removed and dried the bladders to use as canteens. Brains were pounded into a pulp used as a tanning paste, as were extracts from fat and other organs. The horns were crafted into eating utensils; even the tails were dried to serve as war clubs and knife scabbards, and all these were just the utilitarian functions. The buffalo was the heart of Indian culture and Indian religion as well, and the South Plains Indians believed very simply that, when all the buffalo were gone, their world would come to its end.

Though the destruction of Indian buffalo was blatantly illegal, the agents lacked the police power to bring the poachers to justice. Only once, apparently, in early February 1874, was Cheyenne-Arapaho agent John D. Miles actually able to cause the arrest of some eleven buffalo hunters who were trespassing on Indian land, but even then he muffed his chance to act forcefully. Shortly after their arrest Miles let them go and even returned their outfits to them, the hunters having evidently done some fast talking. "They are all very poor," wrote Miles, "and they say that the cries of their children *for bread* is what induced them to engage in the chase. . . . I have no disposition to disbelieve. . . ." He added, rather naïvely, that he believed the hunters had learned their lesson and the incident would deter other hidemen from entering the reservation.

As far as higher authority was concerned, Interior Secretary Columbus Delano expressed the government's view of affairs in his annual reports of 1872 and 1873: "In our intercourse with the Indians it must always be borne in mind that we are the most powerful party. . . . We are assuming, and I think with propriety, that our civilization ought to take the place of their barbarous habits. We therefore claim the right to control the soil they occupy, and we assume it is our duty to coerce them, if necessary, into the adoption and practice of our habits and customs. . . . I would not seriously regret the total disappearance of the buffalo from our western prairies, in its effect upon the Indians, regarding it rather as a means of hastening their sense of dependence upon the products of the soil."

What makes that statement incomprehensible is the fact that the majority of the Indians were in fact willing to give the white man's road a chance. The Arapahoes, for instance, had been docile since the Medicine Lodge Treaty. Among the Cheyennes, there had not been an all-out war for six years—since 1868—and in 1869 that tribe's most influential spokesman for peace, Chief Little Robe, had actually banished from his camps the militant Dog Soldier Society. Its members drifted northward for a while, and when they returned the peace chiefs, Little Robe, White Shield, Stone Calf, and Old Whirlwind, were successful in controlling them. The Kiowas and Comanches had been officially tractable for an even longer period. When the Medicine Lodge Council convened in October of 1867, its commissioners agreed that "The testimony satisfies us that since October 1865 the Kiowas, Comanches, and Apaches have substantially complied with their treaty stipulation entered into at that time at the mouth of the Little Arkansas."

The only violation of which the commissioners found them guilty was the slaying in mid-August of 1866 of Texan James Box and the capture of his family. The Indians, of course, held that they were making war on the Tehannas, not Washington, and had not violated the treaty. The government's remonstrations to the contrary particularly confused the Indians, because during the Civil War Washington itself made war on Texas for four years. But the commission, of which Generals Sherman and Augur were both members, concluded, "We are aware that various other charges were made against the Kiowas and Comanches, but the evidence will pretty clearly demonstrate that these charges were almost wholly without foundation."

Though the wilder war chiefs continued to sporadically seek coups in Texas, most of the Kiowas and Comanches admitted that war against the whites was a hopeless proposition, especially after 1872, the year a few of the chiefs went to Washington and saw the power of the whites for themselves. Among the Kiowas tempers flared when those chiefs who stayed home refused to believe the tales of huge cities and gigantic stone tipis so large that all the Kiowa tribe could sit in a single one. When Thomas Battey, the Quaker schoolteacher to the Kiowas, produced stereo slides of the sights in the east, the war chiefs were struck dumb with amazement. "What you think now?" huffed Chief Sun Boy, who had made the trip back east. "You think all lie now? You think all chiefs who been to Washington fools now?" The warriors put their fingers over their open mouths. "Look! see what a mighty powerful people they are! We fools! We don't know anything! We just like wolves running wild on the plains!"

By 1874 most of the South Plains Indians were ready to come in to the agencies and learn the white man's ways, but their own primitiveness worked against them. The Kiowas, for instance, would not permit a census of their people because of a deathly tribal superstition against being counted. One of the Yapparika Comanche chiefs, Quirts Quip (Elk Chewing), once tried to learn how to farm, but as he prepared to move into his house a violent squall line of thunderstorms blew over. Refusing to defy such an omen, he had nothing more to do with farming.

But tribal superstitions were minor indeed compared to their greatest handicap. Without their buffalo the Indians were entirely dependent on government rations for their survival, but when they abandoned the hunt to come in to the agencies and learn the white road, they sat there and quite literally starved. Had the government only provided the Indians with some alternative source of food and supply, their transition to the white man's ways, though painful and clumsy, might well have been bloodless. But to obtain food for them the federal authorities relied on private contractors, a discredited system that never worked well, even in the best of times. In the case of the South Plains tribes it all but broke down completely, and during the blizzard-stricken winter of 1873–74 the Indians were forced to slaughter large numbers of their ponies just to stay alive. To make things worse, the cold weather was extremely protracted, lasting well into April, extending their hardship late into the spring. Unfed at the agencies when they stayed there, and accused of raiding when they left to hunt buffalo, the Indians were trapped between the proverbial rock and hard place. Probably no single factor was as influential in putting them on the warpath in the spring of 1874 than that one primary deprivation: They were hungry. Even Nelson A. Miles, who during the war prosecuted his campaign against the Cheyennes with all the fervor of an ambitious colonel after his star, reflected twenty years later, "One of the strongest causes of unrest among [the Indians] . . . was the fact that the promises made to induce them to go on to reservations were not always carried out by the government authorities. They had been removed from . . . the ranges of the buffalo, but under distinct treaty stipulation that they were to be provided with shelter, clothing, and sustenance. . . . They were sometimes for weeks without their rations. Their annual allowance of food was usually exhausted in six or seven months. . . ."

In late March 1874, Cyrus Beede, the chief clerk of the Central Superintendency and Enoch Hoag's right-hand man, toured the agencies and reported "very discouragingly" on the supply situations, especially at Fort Sill. He wrote that even Satanta and Lone Wolf, conceded to be the Kiowas' two biggest "problem" chiefs where pacification was concerned, were peaceable, but suffering from need of rations. "I believe the Indians are peaceably disposed, but the want of something to eat at the very commencement of the [spring] raiding season seems to me most suicidal."

In other words, if there were a general war, it would be starvation that would drive the Indians back out onto the plains, a view reinforced by Agent Haworth's report a few weeks earlier that his Indians were concentrating near the agency with peaceful intentions.

On April 8 Haworth too warned the Commissioner of Indian Affairs, Edward P. Smith, in Washington, "Our sustenance is getting very low & unless more is purchased soon we will be left with nothing to give them and they caused to seek it in other channels, which would be very unfortunate at this season of the year." When a large number of the Comanches deserted the agency in June, Haworth wrote dejectedly to Beede, "The shortness of our rations has had a bad effect upon all. I think it a great mistake in the government to allow the Commissaries, at the Agencies of the Wild Indians, to get out of supplies . . . to tell [the Indians] in the face of an empty Commissary, if you go away I won't feed you, would only have made them laugh."

Corroborating evidence that the want of food was driving a portion of the Kiowas and Comanches to war is not lacking. On February 17, 1874, famed army scout Ben Clarke, working out of Camp Supply, reported to his commanding officer that Big Bow, the Kiowa war chief, had been visiting a prominent Cheyenne warrior, Red Moon, at the same time as himself. "Big Bow said the Agent had sent for him to go down to Ft. Sill, [but] he did not want anything more to do with that Agency, [as] they never gave him or his band anything when they went there. . . . When he moved it would be in the direction of the Buffalo, west or southwest, which he expected to subsist upon."

Other letters scattered through the Indian Bureau letter files follow up on the lack of food and the alienation of the influential Big Bow from the peace party. On April 20 Haworth wrote to Hoag, "This week's issue will exhaust our supply of flour, which now amounts to only half rations. My teams are gone on the hunt for sugar, and coffee. I hope to have them back by issue day, with enough to give my people a little." They did not return in time, however, and Haworth's report of May 6 said almost wistfully, "Issue day is almost here, only one night off, and the sugar and coffee not here. I applied to the Post Commissary, but could not get any. . . ." Such was the situation when Big Bow came in for rations on May 7. Obviously discouraged, the chief said, "We come in from our camps on issue day, to get our rations, only we find little here. We carry that home, divide around among the people. It is soon gone, and our women and children begin to cry with hunger, and that makes our hearts feel bad. A white man's heart would soon get bad to see his wife and children crying for something to eat, when he had nothing to give them."

A couple of weeks later Haworth indicated that the lack of food was also responsible for the disaffection of the Comanches, stating that it was becoming increasingly difficult for those peaceably inclined to maintain any influence, when keeping the "good path" was rewarded with hunger and privation: "If I had supplies on hand," he wrote, "to help those who wanted to do right, it would be a great help to them. . . . Our scarcity of supplies is one of our greatest——in fact, is *the* greatest drawback, in governing these people. Give me plenty of supplies, and I will exert a controlling influence over them."

Throughout the spring, moreover, Agent Haworth had been laboring under the weight of a personal tragedy. On December 31, 1873, his only son, James Entricon, died at home in Kansas of spinal meningitis. The two had been unusually close, and Haworth had dashed home to be with him, but arrived too late. The death of his beloved "Entie" had afflicted him deeply and compounded his frustrated suffering on behalf of his Indians.

Haworth's personal safety, too, had been in jeopardy several times at the hands of the more hostile element, but his friends in the Kiowa and Comanche camps always kept him from harm. The Kiowa war chief White Horse, in particular, hatched at least two plots to assassinate him, one foiled by friendly Kiowas, and the other exposed at the last instant by the Kataka chief, Pacer.

At Darlington, meanwhile, Agent Miles was experiencing every bit as difficult a time obtaining food for his Cheyennes and Arapahoes. On March 21, 1874, an opportunity presented itself for Miles to pacify a large portion of the Cheyennes, as 140 lodges came into the agency, led by Minimic, White Shield, and Old Whirlwind. With them, very significantly, was White Horse, head chief of the historically implacable Dog Soldiers. It was, wrote Miles, the very first time any of the Dog Soldiers had come in for rations; they said the buffalo were scarce, and Miles believed they would stay in as long as he could feed them. But, he wrote ominously to Hoag in begging for more supplies, "We will soon be out of rations, and thou can then judge of our situation." Ten days later the warning took on an increased urgency: "We now have at this Agency over 500 lodges of Cheyennes and Arapahoes. . . ." Only Gray Beard and his 60 lodges were still out, and they were expected any day. "Our coffee, sugar, & bacon is exhausted," Miles continued, "and the beef contractor is *considering whether* he can furnish any more beef. . . . We cannot afford to let these people leave the Agency just at this time. They could not find buffalo nearer than 150 miles, and that in the direction of western Texas, just the place that we do not want them to go. . . ." He went on to say that he was expecting some fifty barrels of sugar, thirty bags of coffee, and a little bacon from Wichita, Kansas, but "what is this for so many people, for three months. What can be done?"

Miles was, in addition, expecting a visit from a party of 30 Northern Arapahoes under Chief Plenty Wolf. "They must be treated well," he wrote, or they could persuade his own Indians to forsake the agency and return to the plains, a danger heightened by Plenty Wolf's report on the disappearance of the buffalo. His band's trek southward had taken some three months, during which time "They saw but two buffalo en route."

No additional rations arrived, however. By April 4, Gray Beard had come in accompanied by another of the less friendly chiefs, Heap of Birds, which meant that virtually every Southern Cheyenne and Arapaho belonging to Miles' agency was present, accounted for, and hungry: On May 12 he wrote desperately to Hoag "It is *very important* NOW that these people be *fed!*"

His ration supply dwindled away steadily, though, until by the second week in May Miles had, however reluctantly, been forced to release those who wished to leave, to go west to find what buffalo they could. Thus, to Miles' intense frustration and dismay, the Cheyennes were forced to compete with the white buffalo hunters from Kansas for the last large segment of the great southern herd of buffalo, whose migration was at that time carrying it across the Staked Plains of the Texas panhandle. Although the Arapahoes and many of the Cheyennes told Miles that they would stay near the agency "No matter what," the conflict, and its ultimate outcome, were now inevitable.

Seen in this light, the outrage with which the South Plains Indians greeted the news that the Kansas buffalo hunters were decimating the last of the herds is all the more understandable. Yet, as heavy as its role was in alienating the South Plains Indians from the peace road, their extreme hunger was by no means the only irritation that contributed to their disaffection. Probably the second greatest cause, and one of the least studied, was the havoc wrought among the Indian pony herds by white horse thieves from Kansas and Texas. The Treaty of Medicine Lodge specifically provided: "If bad men among the whites . . . shall commit any wrong upon the person or property of the Indians, the United States will, upon proof made to the agent and forwarded to the Commissioner of Indian Affairs at Washington City, proceed at once to cause the offender to be arrested and punished according to the laws of the United States, and also re-imburse the injured person for the loss sustained." Where enforcement was concerned, "United States" meant the United States Army, yet it was in the face of a studied lack of co-operation that Agents Miles and Haworth labored to exhaustion to stamp out the theft of Indian stock. In 1873, Little Robe and several other Southern Cheyenne and Arapaho chiefs journeyed to Washington to beg for protection from the outlaws, and President Grant promised his aid, but few effective steps were ever taken at the Washington level to shield the Indians from the horse thieves.

In an attempt to get law-enforcement officers into the Indian Territory, Commissioner Smith did receive confirmation from Interior Secretary Delano that Indian Agents and the superintendent did in fact have authority to direct federal marshals to patrol Indian country to apprehend such outlaws. Two deputy marshals, E. C. Lefebvre and John H. Talley, were in fact based at Camp Supply, about one hundred miles upstream on the North Canadian from the Darlington Agency, at least as early as the first week of January 1874. A cover letter from the Attorney General of the United States, George H. Williams, to Interior Secretary Delano confirmed that Lefebvre and Talley were especially employed "to patrol that portion of Kansas bordering on the Indian Reservation, for the purpose of breaking up illicit traffic. . . ."

However, Lefebvre and Talley were federal deputy marshals of the state of Kansas, exceptionally authorized by the Indian Department to operate in the Cheyenne-Arapaho Reservation and surrounding country. When Commissioner Smith tried to get more manpower by having deputy marshals appointed specifically for the Indian Territory, the Attorney General claimed he had no authority. Williams excused himself from the subject on the grounds that: (1) deputy marshals could only be appointed within existing jurisdictions of federal marshals, of which the Indian Territory was not one; (2) the military had the responsibility of protecting the Indians; and (3) that the superintendent himself had the power to "enlist" individuals to help break up the illegal trade and depredations. Williams admitted, though, that such individuals would have no power to arrest offenders!

The net result of this studious investigation was precisely nothing. Lefebvre and Talley were only two men, given the impossible task of patrolling literally thousands of square miles of wild country; the raids on Indian stock by white outlaws continued unabated. The depredations' effect on the Indians is shown graphically in the well-known theft on about March 11, 1874, of forty-three ponies from the herd of Little Robe, one of the most consistently peaceful Cheyenne chiefs. It is widely accepted that this incident was of primary importance in putting many of the Cheyennes on the warpath, and as Agent Miles observed, "The Chiefs are very much provoked and discouraged . . . and express the fear that, should nothing be done . . . and another raid be made upon them, that it will be impossible for them to restrain their young men from making a like raid on the frontier of Kansas."

That was an understatement; the Cheyennes were furious, and an examination of agency correspondence shows that white inaction in the matter was actually more crass than has ever been written, in that the Indians knew the precise identity of the thieves— they were led by William "Hurricane Bill" Martin, a well-known ringleader of horse thieves, gun runners, and bootleggers as characterized by none less than George Bent, the half-bred Cheyenne interpreter at the Darlington Agency. Bent too, incidentally, lost his horse herd to the rustlers early in the spring.

The agent of course did what he could. In response to Miles'

stern, "This matter must have attention," Superintendent Hoag
sent a transcript of the marshals' report to Kansas' Governor T.
A. Osborn, who promised that the guilty men would be punished
—if they should happen to be found. Observed Hoag with a sting
rare in his reserved Quaker upbringing, "I do not apprehend the
State Authority will take any active steps in the case, so far as the
northern border of the Territory is concerned." Indeed, as this
Governor Osborn was the same who, less than two months later,
demanded of General John Pope that the latter supply troops to
protect the Kansas buffalo hunters at Adobe Walls, it seems
superfluous to add that, indeed, nothing was done.

Agent Miles, realizing fully the extreme danger of the situation,
took matters into his own hands and dispatched his two deputy
marshals to overhaul and apprehend the thieves by themselves.
Although Talley and Lefebvre succeeded in catching up with the
Martin gang, the marshals found themselves outgunned six to two,
and made no arrests. Miles was livid: "How are we to rid this
country of outlaws if our police force is inadequate . . . ?"
Regarding Attorney General Williams' pious assertion that protection of Indians was the responsibility of the military, Lefebvre and
Talley did try once to obtain the aid of troops in quashing the activities of outlaws, from General Brooke, commanding Camp Supply, which was the only outpost of troops in the Indian Territory
north of Fort Sill. Brooke refused them without explanation.

Had the military acted swiftly and decisively to recover Little
Robe's ponies, it is possible that few of the Cheyennes would have
had anything to do with the general outbreak. But as it happened,
Little Robe's son, Sitting Medicine, led a band of young warriors
to Kansas to get them back. Failing to find the horses, the young
men ran off some cattle belonging to a white rancher; a fight
ensued with a cavalry unit, and Sitting Medicine was wounded
twice seriously. False rumors spread to some Cheyenne camps
that the chief's son had been killed, and war parties set out southward at once for revenge, killing at least one white, a member of a
survey team. And in addition, "Hurricane Bill" Martin, in the absence of any retaliatory force, literally settled in near the
Cheyenne-Arapaho Agency, and regularly and without fear of
punishment stole stock from Little Robe, Whirlwind, Powder
Face, and even the agent himself.

In addition to their actual raids on Indian pony herds, the white thieves also had a bad effect on the overall situation in that, when they had occasion to murder another white, they often scalped their victim so that the crime would be laid to Indians. Almost unerringly, they succeeded. That they managed to stir up the already inflamed tempers of the frontier population against the Indians is shown by a report dated June 19, 1874, from Major C. E. Compton, then commanding Fort Dodge, Kansas, to the effect that the countryside was even then seized with a panic from just such a murder, which the major confided he believed to be the work of white men: "That Indians committed this crime I do not believe but am strongly impressed with the belief that horse thieves—who of late have become such a pest to this neighborhood—are responsible for the deed, the scalping having been done with a view of shielding themselves."

White horse thieves were also a chronic problem at the Kiowa-Comanche Agency. Even during the height of the war, before any major hostile groups had surrendered, Texans continued to steal horses from the peaceable Kiowas and Comanches who stayed under registration at Fort Sill. At one point Haworth was moved to write, "Since the Indians have camped near the Agency over one hundred head of their stock has been stolen and taken into Texas——and none recovered. . . . I have made an arrangement with the sheriff of Clay County, into which [the thieves] often go, to apprehend and bring them back here, for which I am to pay him a fair compensation, not exceeding ten dollars a head for returned horses." Whether payment of such bounty with Bureau funds was fully legitimate is not clear, but it does show to what lengths Haworth was willing to go to keep white outlaws from robbing from his Indians, and provoking more of them into raiding than were already hostile.

Still other horse thieves ran off Kiowa ponies, not to Texas, but to Chickasaw country, to the east. Haworth's men captured one of them there, but could not arrest him and bring him back because they had no authority to take anyone outside their own jurisdiction. The agent painstakingly spelled out his position to the authorities responsible for the Chickasaw lands, but complained to Hoag, "I might as well make no effort at all, as to wait to hear from [them]."

The problem of white outlaws impersonating Indians to commit crimes also existed at the Kiowa-Comanche Agency. Eight "Indians" were taken by soldiers scouting out of Fort Griffin, Texas, on suspicion that they had murdered a teamster near Fort Sill. Four were killed during the arrest, and the rest in an alleged escape attempt. "Instead of real Indians, they proved to be counterfeit—— white men in Indian disguise," seethed Haworth. "I am fully convinced that many of the offences charged to Indians are committed by white men in disguise." Similarly, Thomas Battey wrote that "On one occasion the sheriff of one of the northwestern counties of Texas informed me, that twice in his official capacity he had called out a portion of the militia to put down Indian depredators in his county, and in the ensuing skirmish one or two had been killed. The individuals killed on both these occasions proved to be white men, so thoroughly disguised with false hair, masks, and Indian equipage, as to be readily mistaken for Indians."

Battey, who at the time lived among the Kiowas, went even further, accusing that some of the white outlaws gave accounts of their own crimes to newspapers, describing them as Indian raids, which the expansionist newspapers were more than happy to publish: "It is a well-known fact," he wrote, "that there is a gang of desperadoes . . . who make a regular business of horse-stealing and other desperate deeds . . . passing readily for Indians when it suits their convenience to do so. . . . They [then furnish] telegrams and newspaper paragraphs—anonymous, of course, but giving the authority of Major or Captain Someone, who has lately arrived from such a place and reports so and so,—giving the details of their own deeds. Sometimes the Indians thus reported on the warpath have been sick in their own lodges, on their own reservations, or running buffalo hundreds of miles from the scene of the reported depredation.

"This has lately been the case with Satanta and Big Tree, whose doings in Texas since their release have furnished hundreds of paragraphs for newspapers, while to my certain knowledge the latter was at home, sick in his lodge, and the former enjoying—after two years confinement in prison—the pleasures of the buffalo chase, on territory assigned for the purpose."

Still other pressures were forcing the Indians toward war. Many of the whites who stole their horses were also guilty of smuggling them liquor, for which the warriors had acquired an inordinate fondness. The bootleggers would trade the Indians a few gallons of rotgut whiskey for a small fortune in buffalo robes, which were practically the Indians' only source of income. The Indians had existed for centuries without distilled spirits, and when it was finally introduced to them they proved as tragically susceptible to alcoholism as they were to smallpox or cholera or any other of the white man's diseases against which they had built no immunity. The Kiowas and Comanches acquired their "foolish water" mainly from the New Mexican Comancheros; the Cheyennes and Arapahoes, closer to the American frontier, suffered much more from its use, getting theirs also from the unscrupulous Kansas "businessmen." Among the Cheyennes the addiction became so widespread that at one time the Cheyenne women refused to work until their men promised to abstain. "If fifty-two kegs of whiskey in one day will make that article plenty," wrote Miles disgustedly, "then whiskey is plenty." Not fully understanding their peculiar susceptibility to the "foolish water," the Cheyenne warriors felt only a vague, sick resentment at their increasingly decrepit emotional state, and managed to perceive the white man as the source of their decline.

Government surveys of Indian lands also contributed to the tribes' unrest, and occasionally a surveyor would be found murdered in the field. Some Cheyennes massacred an entire survey party in 1873 in the northwest Indian Territory, but it was the Kiowas who most especially feared the demarcation of the land with the same superstitious dread they felt of head-counting. Even Striking Eagle said uneasily in late 1873, "This country . . . was given by Washington to his red children. It was a country of peace. I now see white men in it making lines, setting up stones and sticks with marks on them. We do not know what it means, but are afraid it is not for our good."

Gun running also contributed to the war momentum. The Plains Indians had been raiders too long and too successfully, and the Comancheros had made it too profitable, for them not to continue to spend large amounts of their material wealth on guns and ammunition. In this illegal trade, as in the liquor operation, the Comancheros and Kansas traders turned tremendous profits from their dealings with the Indians. Charlie Rath, in particular, had been sneaking guns to the Kiowas for at least seven years. Recent study has even unearthed evidence that the government licensed traders at the Darlington Agency, who turned in one meticulous report after another to Agent Miles accounting for every gun and box of ammunition sold to the Cheyennes and Arapahoes, but who actually ran guns, powder, and lead to the Kiowas and Comanches in quantities as large as those tribes could pay for. Haworth knew that something was amiss on April 20, when one of the post traders at Fort Sill complained that the Kiowas and Comanches did not sell them even one fourth the usual amount of up to ten thousand buffalo robes a year, because the traders would not exchange firearms for them. Haworth checked into the matter and was shocked to learn from a clerk of the Darlington traders that "under instructions from his employers he sold Ammunition including Powder Lead Caps and Cartridges in unlimited quantities to whatever Indians called for them—among whom were the Cotchatethkas [Kotsoteka Comanches]. . . . I cannot get any direct or positive information as to the sale of arms but am certain somebody has been doing it very extensively as a great many of my Indians are armed with the latest improved pistols and guns with large amounts of fixed ammunition to suit them."

The Indians had been hoarding arms for a long period, however, and it was only a matter of time before some incident occurred that would touch off a major war. In December 1873 a large raiding party of Comanches and Kiowas, understandably sick of their debilitating existence off the agency dole, sortied for Mexico. They had returned as far as the Double Mountain Fork of the Brazos River when they were intercepted and attacked by a sizable force of 4th Cavalry. Eleven of the Indians were killed and, in the rout, abandoned, but three of the casualties were especially incendiary: One was the uncle of a rising young medicine man named Isa-tai of the Quahadi Comanches. The other two were Tau-ankia (Sitting in the Saddle), the favorite son of Lone Wolf, principal chief of the Kiowas, and Tau-ankia's cousin Guitain (Heart of a Young Wolf), the son of Lone Wolf's brother, also a chief, Red Otter.

When Lone Wolf heard of the disaster he went absolutely wild with grief. He hacked off his hair, maimed his body fearfully, slaughtered his horses, burned his possessions, and vowed to get even. Red Otter and Lone Wolf's wife visited Haworth, explaining that Lone Wolf would calm down once the shock had passed, but when the old chief went to Texas in the spring to bury his son's decomposed body, and was himself attacked by soldiers and forced to abandon it once more, he was beyond the reach of reason. He would have war.

A few weeks after the losses to the 4th Cavalry, a second raiding party headed for Texas, but was attacked by Lieutenant Colonel George P. Buell, leading a large force of 10th Cavalry and 11th Infantry. In addition to another eleven warriors killed the renegades lost several dozen ponies captured. Again, about two weeks after this, a third raiding party was mauled and another ten Indians killed. These two defeats, plus that inflicted by the 4th Cavalry, resulting in at least 32 Indian dead, were major disasters for the small tribes—certainly of a proportion that they had never before let pass unavenged.

Chief Lone Wolf, like all the South Plains Indians, had only the dimmest notion of the historical forces working upon his people, but it was inevitable that by the spring of 1874 not just his camp, but nearly all the camps, were smoldering hotbeds of resentment. To their limited understanding, the Medicine Lodge Treaty of 1867 had guaranteed their reservations to them, for their free, unhampered, and "exclusive" use, but the white buffalo poachers had destroyed practically every buffalo herd in the northern part of the territory. It was Indian land and Indian buffalo, and the whites had stolen from them. The government had promised to subsist them and had lied. Except for their agents, who they discovered had no real power, Washington did nothing. It was evident enough to them that the white government had no intention of carrying out its part of the Medicine Lodge bargain, and this after defaulting on the Treaty of the Little Arkansas of 1865. The Indians may not even have known it, but had they tried, they would not have been able to negotiate a new treaty; in 1871 the Congress passed a law saying that no Indian tribe was any longer an "independent nation, tribe, or power with whom the United States may contract by treaty." They were officially wards of the government, like orphans, and had about as much legal leverage as the buffalo that were being slaughtered.

The Indian Bureau seemed helpless to aid them, and by the spring of 1874 the situation was ready to explode. In the tipis there was talk of war and killing, of driving the white man from the land, but as yet there had been little action. The Indians had surrounded and picked off isolated parties of buffalo poachers for years, but there had never been any general offensive. First, many of the Indians were slow to abandon Agents Miles and Haworth's hopeful promises of better times in the future, but probably more importantly, the Indians had had no leader to unite behind. The anger was there—pure anger—and the desire, long suppressed, to give vent to it, but movements of rebellion have always needed some catalytic embodiment, and there had been none. The Arapahoes had given up, the Cheyennes had no personality strong enough to hold together an intertribal alliance, the Kiowas were engaged in consumptive political quarrels, and the roving Comanches seldom stayed in one place long enough for any of the others really to know what they were up to. During the spring of 1874, however, the needed leader finally emerged in the person of Isa-tai (Wolf Shit), the adolescent but volatile medicine man of the wild Quahadi band of the Comanches.

He was a young warrior, deep in grief for his uncle, lately killed in the skirmish in Texas. As yet he was untried in battle, but throughout the year 1873 one thing had become certain to the Comanches: His medicine was strong. He said he had brought the dead back to life and that he was immune to the bullets of the white man. Those in themselves were not particularly impressive, since other great shamans had claimed those feats, but here Isa-tai surpassed the others. He claimed, and was supported by witnesses, that he could swallow and vomit forth at will wagonloads of cartridges. He had "ascended above the clouds, where he had communed with the Great Spirit." This also witnesses swore to. Many believed in him. A few may have doubted his self-proclaimed messianic role in driving away the white men, preferring to see him as just another young buck trying to get up a revenge raid for a slain relative, as indeed it was proper for him to do, but no one could doubt that, early in 1873, before the uncle was killed, when a brilliant comet had appeared, it was Isa-tai who predicted it would disappear in five days' time. The comet vanished on schedule. Later on, it was Isa-tai who had predicted the blizzards of the

1873–74 winter, and that had firmly established his reputation. The medicine of Isa-tai was strong indeed, and the young man was doing his best to incite a war against the whites and to avenge his uncle.

By May his influence had grown to the degree that he did an unprecedented thing: He sent out runners, summoning all the bands of the Comanches to attend a Sun Dance. It was a bold step, for the Comanches had never even been assembled all in one place before, let alone made tribal medicine. The Sun Dance was a ritual foreign to their culture, although among the other South Plains tribes it was an annual occurrence. In Isa-tai's mind the move was probably to accomplish two things: first, to capitalize on his newfound notoriety by assembling an audience to whom to preach his antiwhite doctrine, and second, to recruit the war party.

In the latter endeavor he would have help, as one of his earliest and strongest converts was the prominent war leader Qua-nah (Fragrance), better known with his white surname as Quanah Parker. The half-bred son of Nokoni Comanche chieftain Pe-ta and a white captive, Mrs. Cynthia Ann Parker, Quanah had lived among the Quahadis for many years, renowned as a fighter and leader.

First news of the young firebrand Isa-tai reached Agent Haworth on the night of May 5, when Old Horseback sought him out, warning him that he thought the Quahadis meant to go to war, even take Fort Sill. Of Isa-tai, Haworth wrote tongue in cheek to Hoag, "They have a new Medicine Man, who can accomplish wonders. Horse Back says he can furnish them an inexhaustible supply of cartridges, suited for any gun, from his stomach. Certainly a very valuable man to have around in time of war. He can also raise the dead, having recently done so." In a much more serious vein, Haworth also sent a peace feeler to the Quahadi camp, but their answer was not encouraging, telling him, in effect, that if he kept out of the way he would not be hurt. If he interfered, he and everyone else the Quahadis could find at the agency would be put to death. Strangely, though, on the thirteenth all the Comanche bands came in for issue, and of the meeting Haworth observed that they "never behaved any better, or showed less signs of bad intentions." But the Sun Dance was not called off, and the friendly Penatekas, Asa-toyah-teh and Isa-havey, kept

Fort Sill's military commander informed that Isa-tai's war message was drawing a large following.

Thus, at Isa-tai's call, the first Comanche Sun Dance was held in May 1874, on the banks of the North Fork Red River, near the boundary of the reservation, and all the bands did come, including the Penatekas, who made it clear, however, that they wanted no part of anyone's war. The Comanches had observed the Kiowa and Cheyenne Sun Dances for decades, and knew its forms and ceremonies, but, being a highly adaptable people and in a hurry, they stripped it of many of its formalities, like the Tai-me "grandfather gods" of the Kiowas. What the Comanches wanted was the spirit of the thing, a solemn appeal, "an invocation to the Great Power" to save their people from their desperation. The emphasis of the symbolism was placed, understandably enough, on the buffalo.

Four days were taken to gather materials for the circular medicine lodge before construction could begin. In its center was a large, forked ridgepole, surrounded by a circle of twelve more poles, the tops of which were connected by streamers to the fork of the center one. The spaces between the wall poles were filled in with brush, except for the space between the two easternmost, which was left open for an entrance. A newly killed buffalo, stuffed with willow twigs, was then hoisted to the top of the structure to watch over the proceedings.

While the medicine lodge was abuilding, mud-smeared clowns dressed in willow leaves entertained the other members of the tribe, galloping through the encampment and thumping the unwary with soft clubs of mudballs on willow switches. After the ceremonies began, the lodge was filled with the most earnest prayers and dances, all hoping for the return of the buffalo, as Isa-tai verbally lashed the braves into a fever for action. He said he had personally talked to the Great Spirit, who told him He would aid the Comanches if only they would fight to regain their lands.

At the Sun Dance some course of action would have to be decided upon. The old war chief of the Quahadis, Bull Bear (or He Bear, Parra-o-coom), lay dying of pneumonia, and his place of authority was assumed, reportedly, not by Second Chief Wild Horse, but by the dynamic young Quanah. And, since Quanah was the most vocal supporter of Isa-tai's medicine, little urging was needed for the bulk of the men to reach their decision: war. But where would they strike?

The first plan was to attack the Tonkawa Indians of Texas, long hated by the Comanches for their cannibalism, and later for their friendliness toward the whites, with whom the Tonkawas had allied in their continuing struggle with the Comanches. Quanah was himself waging a personal vendetta against the Tonkawas, who had recently killed a close companion of his. Many years later he remembered, "I had a friend killed by the Tonkaway at Double Mountain Fork Brazos in Texas. That made me feel bad —We grew up together, went to war together. We very sorry [for] that man. Tonkaway kill him, make my heart hot. I want to make it even.

"That time I was pretty big man, pretty young man and knew how to fight pretty good. I work one month; I go to Naconie Comanche camp, in head of Cache Creek. Call in everybody. I tell them my friend kill him Texas. I fill pipe—I tell that man, 'You want smoke?' He take pipe, smoke it.

"I give pipe to other man, he say 'I not want smoke,' if he smoke he goes to war—[but] he not refuse—God kill him he afraid.

"I go see Kiowas on Elk Creek and Quahadis, then I go Cheyenne—lots of them smoke pipe. . . . Lots Comanches there Otter Belt, He Bear, Tabananica; Old Man Isa Rosa (White Wolf) there—big village. Camps different places.

"They say, 'When you go to war, Quanah?'

"I say, 'Maybe tomorrow, maybe next day. Have dance to-night. . . .'

"I hear somebody call, 'Quanah, old men want to see you over here!' I see Old Man Otter Belt and White Wolf [Isa Rosa], lots old men.

"They say, 'You pretty good fighter Quanah but you not know everything. We think you take pipe first against white buffalo killers. You kill white buffalo hunters, make your heart good— after that you come back, take all the young men, go to war, Texas!' "

It is very interesting that it was the "old men," not the hot-blooded young war leaders, who directed that the war be fought, not against the Tonkawas or just anybody they happened across, but against the "white buffalo killers," who were, in the final analysis, their deadliest enemy. At the Comanche Sun Dance, Quanah no doubt remembered that experience before the old Yapparika chiefs, when he set forth the second, much bolder plan: They would attack and destroy the new settlement of buffalo hunters in the Texas panhandle, Adobe Walls.

The very day after deciding to go to war, the Comanches sent out messengers to the other tribes, all of whom were camped nearby, inviting them to join in the crusade and to attend a great medicine and war council. One emissary went to the close-by encampment of the Cheyennes at the site of their annual Sun Dance, at the head of the Washita River, where Crazy Mule had been making medicine. Others traveled to the Kiowas, Arapahoes, and Katakas. The great council convened on the North Fork Red River, at the mouth of Elk Creek, in what is now Kiowa County, Oklahoma, but the question of war had divided the other tribes.

The Katakas ignored it almost entirely, although reportedly a few were present. Chief Powder Face of the Arapahoes had too firmly committed himself to the white road to countenance any thought of war, but he was defied by one of his lesser chiefs, Yellow Horse, who rode into the encampment at the head of twenty-two renegades. Among the Cheyennes, three of the four important peace chiefs, Little Robe, Old Whirlwind, and White Shield, moved their camps in near the agency at the first hint of trouble, but among them they controlled only forty-one lodges. The Cheyennes had had enough of the peace road, and this time it was the Dog Soldiers who held sway; not forgetting that it was Little Robe who had faced them down and banished them in 1869, members of the warrior society shot the chief's horses as he moved in to the agency. The fourth peace chief, Stone Calf, journeyed to the war council, although undoubtedly because he hoped to exert a moderating influence. But sometime during the council he was summarily deposed in disgrace, and went with a few supporters to hunt in Mexico.

The war question cleft the Kiowas more deeply than ever, with Striking Eagle and his faction for peace, and Lone Wolf and his faction for war. Only a few Kiowas, the fiercest of the war chiefs, attended the council, for two basic reasons. The Kiowas had not yet had their annual Sun Dance, which was of such religious importance to them that few—only scoffers like Big Bow—would risk missing it by going off on a campaign. Second, a large number of friendly and neutral Kiowas had gone in to the agency in the first week in June for what they resolved would be one last time. If there were still no food for them, as Thomas Battey wrote, "they should conclude that the talk of its coming was all lie, and they should, after all, be obliged to go to the plains for subsistence . . . and throw Washington away." To Haworth's great relief a reasonably large shipment of foodstuffs arrived barely in time to buy their allegiance for a few weeks more, and the formal question of war was put off until the Kiowas could discuss it fully at the Sun Dance, the first week in July.

Precisely what happened at the war council has never been learned with great certainty. Most definite information about it came from the Penatekas and the friendly Yapparika chiefs, Quirts Quip and Ho-weah, who bolted the ceremony and returned to the agency, although they did so at no small risk to themselves, as the hostile faction threatened to shoot their horses and strand them afoot if they did not commit to the war movement. Haworth did learn that the Quahadi medicine man Isa-tai had staged a mystical display of his magic that utterly convinced the hostilely inclined that they would receive divine protection in their war effort. One of the Kiowa scoffers reportedly debunked the medicine show, whereupon Isa-tai sought to increase his reputation by making another of his uncanny predictions, this one for a summer-long drought. "I tell you," he said, "there will be a great dry time this summer." Haworth also learned from Quirts Quip that Mexican Comancheros were present at the encampment and that the liberal consumption of whiskey served mostly to harden the stand of the war faction, though they tended to make up their minds in drunken confusion. The leaders, said Quirts Quip, "have a great many hearts. . . . Make up their minds at night for one thing and get up in the morning entirely changed." In addition, Ho-weah told Haworth that the Cheyennes had ridden into the council brandishing not less than eighty mint-new breech-loading rifles.

During the ceremonies, which were held at the very fringe of the reservation, some of the war party slipped back to near Fort Sill and stole about fifty head of stock from the agency corral. Grim and sobered, Haworth reported the incident, adding, "I am at a loss to account for their actions, though [they were] much disappointed at the shortness of their rations." Still, he hoped, as he had written before, that "this cloud will, like many others since I came here, pass away, without a storm."

This time, however, he was wrong.

IV.   The Buffalo War

As the remaining peace chiefs saw the uneasy peace with the federal authorities begin to crumble, the chiefs tried harder than ever to make the agents realize the danger that the government was running by not holding the buffalo hunters in check. At Darlington the leader of the Cheyenne peace faction, Chief Little Robe, tried to explain the inequity under which his people had been living: "Your people make big talk," he said, "and sometimes make war, if an Indian kills a white man's ox to keep his wife and children from starving; what do you think my people ought to say when they see their [buffalo] killed by your race when you are not hungry?"

In mid-March Miles wrote that his Cheyennes "all seem in excellent humor and good spirits, except on the encroachment of buffalo hunters——and intimate trouble unless the whites are kept out."

On June 3 the faithful Striking Eagle of the Kiowas tried similarly to explain the importance of the buffalo to Agent Haworth: "The buffalo is our money. It is our only resource with which to buy what we need and do not receive from the government. The robes we can prepare and trade. We love them just as the white man loves his money. Just as it makes a white man feel to have his money carried away, so it makes us feel to see others killing and stealing our buffaloes, which are our cattle given to us by the Great Father above to provide us meat to eat and means to get things to wear."

Back at Adobe Walls, meanwhile, the business of "killing and stealing" the buffalo continued, unabated and smoothly, until, quite suddenly about the last of May, things began to go wrong. As Billy Dixon was trying to ford the swollen Canadian River on his way back to the walls with a load of hides, he learned that Indians had attacked the camp of hunter Joseph H. Plummer on Chicken Creek, only twenty-five miles downstream from his present position. The bodies of Plummer's two partners, Dave Dudley and Tommy Wallace, were found scalped and horribly mutilated. One was pinned to the ground by a wooden stake driven through his torso; they had been castrated and their ears were cut off, and their heads propped up so they could watch themselves die. The attack had taken place a few days since, and if the Indians were headed upriver they could easily be in any of the country surrounding Dixon, so he made for the safety of Adobe Walls, preferring to chance the swollen river to meeting the war party. In crossing the flooded Canadian his wagon overturned and had to be cut loose; it floated away, carrying with it the load of hides and Dixon's prized Big Fifty buffalo gun. On reaching the north bank one of the two mules lay down and died of exhaustion.

Straggling back to the Walls, Dixon bought the best rifle left for sale, a round-barreled Sharp's .44, and at once set about returning to rescue his crew of skinners, whom he had left in his camp. Before he departed, however, grim word came that the Indians had struck again, this time at a small camp on a feeder stream of the Salt Fork Red River. Two more hunters—John "Antelope Jack" Holmes, an Englishman, and a German called "Blue Billy" —had lost their lives. Dixon found his skinners unharmed, but most of the hunters in the area, Dixon among them, smelled trouble in the wind and rode for Adobe Walls, where on about June 18 a mysterious person arrived, under an escort of government troops.

It was Amos Chapman, the army scout and interpreter who had seen the hunters' caravan pull out of Dodge City. Word had come into Chapman's base, Camp Supply, that an attack on Adobe Walls was imminent. Precisely who gave this alarm is not clear, but most evidence points to the Penateka Comanches who managed to slip out of the war council and told all to Colonel Davidson, in command at Fort Sill, who forwarded it to Camp Supply. The warning reached the post traders, who decided to forward it to Charlie Rath, the partner of their friend R. M. Wright. They also applied for—and received—an escort of a half dozen army regulars to accompany Chapman.

When he arrived at Adobe Walls, the messenger immediately conferred with the proprietors of the three stores: Rath, Charlie Myers, and Jim Hanrahan, and told them they could expect a massive Indian attack on the morning after the next full moon: Saturday, June 27. The three merchants decided at once to keep the secret to themselves; if word got around, the hunters might clear out, leaving the valuable stock of supplies defenseless. To keep the secret a cover then had to be set up for Chapman; later, in Hanrahan's saloon, a soldier answered the hunters' queries by rather stupidly telling them they were looking for horse thieves. Although that may indeed have been all the soldiers were told of the purpose of their mission, many of the hunters had done a substantial amount of horse pinching in their time (already mentioned is Dutch Henry Born), and they decided Chapman must be a spy, either for the government, since he was escorted by troopers, or for the Indians, since his wife was a Cheyenne woman; they had an equally low opinion of both. Either way, they said, a lynching would not be out of order.

Seeing this, Hanrahan suggested to Amos Chapman that Chapman should pass the night with John Wesley Mooar in the latter's wagon, parked behind the Rath store, where the other hunters would not think to look. After dark, Chapman bought a drink and loudly told Hanrahan that he was going briefly to the Myers store (in the opposite direction), but would return to spend the night.

"All right," Hanrahan agreed. "Come back."

Outside, Chapman made for Mooar's wagon, as Hanrahan covered his getaway by yelling to the other men to belly up to the bar for a round of drinks, "on the house." Chapman advised Mooar of the pending attack, and Mooar let him bed down in the wagon with him on hearing of the danger the scout was in. The other hunters, meanwhile, had a few more drinks and went out looking for the halfbreed later, but failed to find him.

With the new day Mooar left for the range to fetch back his brother Wright, taking with him Philip Sisk and two others, making a total of four wagon teams. The Mooar camp was on the Salt Fork Red River, far to the south and east of Adobe Walls, and the men made forced drives, hoping to reach Wright and his men before the Indians found them. Discovering Wright and the others unharmed, John told him of the brewing trouble, adding that the main body of buffalo had gone as far north as Adobe Walls anyway, so the hunting there, nearer shelter, would be just as good as the present location. At once the men struck camp, loaded the wagons with the hides they had taken, and headed north at the best speed they could make.

On the second day out, however, thunderstorms began to boom overhead, and the trail turned to soupy muck in the rain. They stopped to rest and eat about noon near the headwaters of Red Deer Creek, freeing the stock to graze between two large pools of water. There were a great many buffalo in the area but the Mooars and the others, fearing the danger of an Indian attack, decided not to take the time. It was a good thing, too, as suddenly they noticed a big war party trailing them at a distance of about a mile. Strangely, the Indians were riding two abreast, cavalry style, and as they began to charge, the hideman heard a bugle signal the attack.

In an instant the men in the Mooar camp ran to gather and hitch the stock. Sisk and Lem Wilson were unarmed; they had not cleaned their guns since the last time they had shot buffalo, leaving Wright Mooar the only man in the group with a long-range rifle.

"Is your gun ready, Mooar?" screamed Lem Wilson as he scrambled to get the animals.

Mooar called back, "Yes, and I have forty rounds of ammunition."

"Well for God's sake hold 'em back and Sisk and I will get the stock."

Without delay Mooar knelt and fired a shot in front of the charging columns. Doubtless startled by the range of the Big Fifty, the Indians at the fore of the columns abruptly pulled up short, causing the rest of the formation to collapse behind them. Taking advantage of this, Mooar fired again, aiming a little closer to the Indians. Confused, the warriors milled about and then retreated a few yards. Again Mooar's Big Fifty boomed, felling an Indian's pony.

At this point the bugler sounded a rally; the Indians regrouped and began another assault, but again Mooar jumbled the formation with good placements from his Sharp's. All this time the other men worked feverishly to hitch the stock, and when the heavy wagons were finally ready to rumble northward the weather worsened, and rain came down in sheets. The Indians pursued at a distance, but just after the Mooar outfit crossed Red Deer Creek, about a mile from where they had camped, a flash flood roared providentially down the wash. "It flooded the crossing twenty feet deep," remembered Mooar, "completely cutting off the Indians from immediate pursuit."

The outfit made straight for Adobe Walls, and got to the south bank of the Canadian before evening of the third day. This stream too was in flood, so as the rest of the men camped the night on the south bank, Mooar and Sisk swam the torrent to reach Adobe Walls and obtain the use of Charlie Myers' teams of oxen. The Mooars' stock was insufficient to haul the cumbersome wagons across the wide Canadian, and additional pull was needed. The Indians who previously attacked the group had never given up on trailing them, and when Mooar and Sisk, the best shots in the camp, were gone, the warriors charged into the camp, upsetting cookery, scattering the hunters' belongings, and wreaking general havoc. The remaining hunters dove for cover, however, and were not injured, and the Indians too reportedly rode away without loss.

Mooar and Sisk came back the next morning, with John Webb, an experienced wagonmaster, and two large, empty, high-framed wagons (of the type used to haul big loads of hay), each pulled by two dozen yokes of oxen. They ploughed into the river and crossed it safely, swimming the deeper channel, and on reaching the south bank the Mooars' hides and equipment were reloaded into Myers' larger, sturdier wagons. Then the empty Mooar wagons were tied onto the rear, and the long oxteams hauled them back across, steered by mounted men. After that the Mooar stock was herded across, and the day by then was almost spent.

Webb returned to the Walls that night, but the exhausted Mooar group decided to camp there on the north bank. But again the Indian war party caught them off their guard with a surprise attack, staged just as the hunters were cooking their evening meal. All the hidemen escaped injury again, but this time believed they managed to wound a number of the hostiles as the latter charged about the camp.

The next day, after stopping briefly at the Walls, the Mooar brothers learned that Rath and Myers were preparing to send a shipment of hides north to Dodge, so they, with their own pile of skins to deliver, decided to go along. Rath and Myers themselves, however, told the Mooars that they were going to stay on and look after their interests, which the Mooars did not believe. Sure enough, the next day Rath and Myers both cleared out for Dodge, leaving their stores in the care of clerks. As a lone humane gesture John Mooar offered to take Mrs. Olds with them, using the pretext that she seek dental care for a tooth that had been bothering her. She refused, and the wagon train pulled out. Thus, of the original "in" group who received Chapman's warning, only one, Jim Hanrahan, remained in Adobe Walls. He had sunk his life savings into his hunting and drinking businesses, and had no choice but to stay and fight for them.

On the evening of June 26, the night before the impending attack, two brothers named Ike and Shorty Shadler arrived at the Walls, delivering a wagonload of goods. On their way south they passed the Mooars, who warned one of them, "Ike, you better hurry back or the Indians will get your scalp." Exact details were withheld, presumably lest word should spread to the other hunters. The Shadlers apparently took the warning seriously, unloading and reloading their wagon the same night they got there. They parked it on the north side of the corral near Myers' store and bedded down inside it, ready for an early start on Saturday morning. Also on the evening of the twenty-sixth, Jim Hanrahan the hide trader formed a partnership with Billy Dixon the hunter. Whereas Rath had about ten thousand buffalo hides stockpiled in his corral, Hanrahan had no really first-rate marksman to keep his skinners busy (he had come south with seven), and Dixon had too few skinners to keep his rifle booming. The affinity seemed obvious, and Dixon, satisfied with the new arrangment, by which he got 50 per cent of the income, loaded up his wagons to get started early the next morning. He bedded down under his wagon after leading the horses to pasture by the creek.

Hanrahan, too, was pleased with the new partnership, but was worried about the coming dawn, because he knew the settlement was in no shape to receive an attack. Still no lookouts were posted, and the walls of the buildings were so flimsy that holes could be bashed in the chinks with rifle butts. There might not be an attack; but then again there just might, and so Hanrahan agonized over his options. He could do nothing; if there were no battle, then no harm done. If there were, they would all be killed, himself included. He could have awakened everybody and warned them, but then whether or not a fight took place the other hunters would undoubtedly have hanged him for keeping Rath's and Myers' little secret and saying nothing sooner. It was with this burden on his mind that he, possibly with the help of Billy Dixon, set about a plan to save the settlement.

Throughout these days the main Indian war party had been riding steadily west, being joined on the way by smaller groups, until their numbers grew to several hundreds. Their exact number remains unknown; traditional history places it at seven hundred; Chief Whirlwind of the Cheyennes set the total at twelve hundred. But whatever the actual number was, it was the largest war party ever to assemble on the South Plains. Every night they reminded themselves of their purpose by smoking the sacred pipe, making medicine, and listening to the harangues of Isa-tai, who had been chosen war leader. Quanah remembered these hate sessions this way: "Isa-tai make big talk that time. He says, 'God tell me we going to kill lots white men—I stop bullets in gun—bullets not pierce shirts. We kill them all, just like old woman. God told me the truth.' . . . Before that pretty good medicine Isa-tai."

On the night of June 25–26, scouts were sent out to look over the situation; in 1897 Quanah gave an account in broken English for then Captain Hugh Scott of the next two days' activities. Scott recorded Quanah as saying that two nights before the battle:

"Pretty soon we move Fort Elliott—got no fort there that time. Pick out seven men go look for white men's houses on Canadian —Old Man White Wolf go with them. Gone all night. Next day a watcher on a little hill call out, 'Here they come!' We all see scouts circle four times right and we know they find houses. Women, children, everybody make long line in front of the village, Old Man Black Beard in the middle—Then seven scouts come single file in front of Old Man Black Beard.

"He say, 'Tell the truth, what did you see?'

"First scout say, 'I tell you true, see four log houses, I see horses moving about.' All scouts say same thing.

"Black Beard say, 'All right pretty soon we kill some white men.' "

On hearing the scouts' report the men mounted at once and made their final approach to the area of Adobe Walls. Once again, Quanah: "Everbody saddle up, take war bonnets and shields. We started sun there [about eleven in the morning], stopped sun there [around four in the afternoon]." The war party paused briefly on the south bank of the Canadian, and the warriors readied themselves for battle, as Isa-tai prepared the magic war paint, which he said would turn away the white man's bullets. Quanah:

"Put saddles & blankets in trees, hobble extra horses, make medicine, paint faces, put on war bonnets, then move in fours across Canadian sundown. Keep along river pretty near Red Hill near a little creek, where houses were. Everybody walk—[enemy] hear trot a long way off.

"At dark, somebody want to go to sleep. He Bear say, 'Dismount, hold lariats in your hand, I call, you mount again.'

"Some sleep, some smoke tobacco & talk. Finally He Bear and Tabananica call them, all mount again, travel until a little light— Pretty soon we make a line."

The formation went forward slowly and quietly, but some of the younger braves, anxious for the action, began to pull forward of the line: "All chiefs try to hold back young men, say, 'You go too fast. No good to go too fast.'

"Pretty soon they call out, 'All right go ahead!' We charge on horses pretty fast, dust thrown up high. Prairie dog holes—I see men and horses roll over & over."

V. The Battle of Adobe Walls

The night of June 26–27 passed away quietly at Adobe Walls, at least until the wee hours of the morning. At that time, Jim Hanrahan silently slipped out his pistol, pointed it into the air, and pressed the trigger. The two men sleeping inside his saloon jumped awake, to hear Hanrahan scream, "Clear out! The ridgepole is breaking!" Those inside, fearful of being smothered beneath the heavy sod roof that they believed was about to crash in upon them, dashed out into the night air; the commotion awakened other men. Some of them climbed onto the roof to lighten the load, while others started rummaging through the woodpile to find a log to replace the "damaged" ridgepole. They just happened to find one perfectly cut, which had been planted there by Hanrahan. Most of the men never learned of the trick, and died believing they had been saved from the Indians by the providential cracking of that ridgepole. The "repairs" took over two hours, during which time not one man noticed they were replacing a virtually undamaged, 2½-foot-thick ridgepole with an 8-inch-thick substitute. By the time the work was finished, about half the men in the settlement were awake, but then Hanrahan saw with horror that several of them were crawling back into their bedrolls. Having to think fast, he quickly did the only thing a bartender could have done: he loudly offered a round of drinks to everybody, "on the house," in appreciation for their help. The crustier men accepted; another reprieve for Hanrahan. Bat Masterson, still a bit tender to relish rotgut whiskey at five o'clock in the morning, made himself a cup of coffee. Hanrahan suggested to his new partner Dixon that since it was almost dawn, Dixon might do well to get his things together to head out, rather than go back to bed. Dixon found this sensible, if indeed he was not in on Hanrahan's plan, and sent a young assistant, Billy Ogg, to fetch Dixon's stock back from the creek.

Dixon himself began clearing the ground around his wagon, gathering up his Sharp's .44, which had lain next to him all night. As he bent over to pick up his bedroll, out of the top of his eye he caught the faintest glimmer of movement at the edge of the trees by the creek. Bat Masterson, standing behind him, saw him freeze. "What the hell is that?"

"I don't know," said Dixon, "but I don't like it."

Masterson hoped fervently it wasn't Indians. "Buffalo, sure enough," he said as the beats of thousands of hoofs became slowly more audible.

Straining his eyes, Dixon dimly made out the figures of mounted men, spreading out into a line. "No, I think it's Indians. A big war party." The thunder of the charging horses grew louder, then they could hear the terrible, ululant war whoops. It *was* Indians— hundreds and hundreds of Indians—covered with Isa-tai's bright ochre war paint, feathers and scalps fluttering from their bridles. Dixon thought for an instant they might be after the stock, and started to run to recover his favorite saddle horse, but the attackers, whipping their mounts mercilessly with short Mexican quirts, raced past the whites' horses and mules, straight at the buildings. Pausing only to fire one shot, Dixon turned and fled after Masterson into Hanrahan's saloon, and as he reached it the bullets were already kicking up dirt at his feet.

Somebody had closed the door! Dixon beat at it frantically until it was opened, and Billy Ogg, who had unbelievably survived the quarter-mile sprint from the creek, dashed through the door after Dixon and fell on the floor in exhaustion.

As the doors slammed shut the horde of Indians closed in around the buildings in the classic maneuver of Plains warfare, circling the buildings, a little closer each time, clinging to the far sides of their ponies at full gallop, using the animals' bodies as shields, firing from beneath the horses' throats by slinging one arm through a loop braided in the horses' manes and holding tight with the legs to their bodies. Although an attack was always planned by the war leader, once the fight started each brave was free to carry out his part however he thought best. Hence, some of the braves dismounted and took cover behind the wagons and corral fence, shooting into the sod houses. Others pulled out of the circle and reared their horses, with vulgar gesticulations taunting the whites to come out of the buildings and fight like men. Some of the younger warriors, seeking to prove their bravery and perhaps win places in the warrior societies, broke ranks and charged the houses, guns blazing.

Yet in spite of the spectacle, Indian warfare was not the romantic thing we are so often guilty of imagining. The Plains Indians' culture was after all advanced only a little from the New Stone Age. They were not revolted as whites were by the sight of gore; they could dissect a quivering carcass and devour the raw entrails. They saw nothing wrong as whites did with the cutting of trophies from an enemy's dead body. To be caught up in an attack by Indians was not romantic; it was a cold, mean, bloody, cruel, and terrifying experience. But above all it was a revolting, ugly thing.

The latter fact was quickly borne out by the fate of the two Shadler brothers, Ike and Shorty, who had worked late into the night to make sure they could leave before any trouble started. They had not awakened at Hanrahan's first pistol shot, nor during the ensuing noise. Now cut off from shelter, their doom was sealed. Some sixty-five years after the battle two Indian survivors, Yellow Fish and Tim-bo (the son of He Bear), both Comanches, recalled their end. Some Indians had been milling about the Shadler wagon for some time, but none of them guessed it might be occupied until one of their number, another Comanche named Mihesuah, lifted up the canvas cover with his bow to see if there was anything worth looting, and was met by a muzzle blast from one of the Shadlers' guns. Mihesuah was seriously wounded, but the Shadlers had given themselves away, and their wagon was quickly swamped and the brothers riddled with bullets and arrows. The warriors so collected the day's first two scalps, and throughout the day some of them paraded, just beyond accurate gun range, brandishing the bloody hair at the whites inside, teasing them, trying to lure them outside where they could be shot more easily. The Shadlers had been viciously defended by their big black Labrador, which had slept at their feet, and after the Indians killed it they recognized its bravery by cutting a fur "scalp" from its side.

The other twenty-seven whites were holed up in the three large buildings, isolated and with no contact among them except for shouting. The Rath store, far at the south end, was defended by the weakest party, six men and Mrs. Olds. Nine men had taken refuge in the saloon, including Hanrahan, Dixon, and Bat Masterson. The strongest garrison, eleven men, fought from the north end, by the corral. The hunters were awake when the Indians came, but other than that they were caught totally unawares; many of them fought in their underwear, ammunition belts slung over their longjohns. In each stronghold they hurriedly barricaded the doors with crates and grain sacks, and none too soon.

On one of the very first charges Quanah, in the lead and flanked by two other warriors, raced straight for one of the doors, whirled his pony around at the last second, and backed into the door, trying to break it down. Fortunately for the hunters the only trained carpenter at the Walls, a Swede named Andy Johnson, had spent his spare time early that summer fitting all the doors with reinforcing crossplanks, and the door held firm. Frustrated, Quanah dismounted and beat at it, unsuccessfully, with his rifle butt. The assaults continued all morning, and those in the Walls were astounded to discover that the Indians' movements—charge, circle, fall back, regroup, and charge again—were controlled by bugle calls. The men inside wondered aloud who the bugler could be; undoubtedly it was the same who had been with the war party that repeatedly attacked the Mooar outfit on their return from the Salt Fork Red River. Some thought he might be a deserter from the all-black 10th Cavalry, stationed at Fort Sill. Others held it may have been a particular Kiowa captive; in the 1860s some of that tribe had abducted a half-bred Mexican boy near the Rio Grande and, having raised the youngster, they could have won him over to their ways, which was not uncommon on the frontier.

Isa-tai, with the older chiefs, watched the proceedings from one of the surrounding buttes, but did not participate in the fight, as was his privilege as war leader. He was stark naked, except for a cap of sage stems; both he and his pony were coated solid with the magic yellow war paint. Early in the fight things went well; they had taken two scalps, had several wagons to loot, and had suffered few casualties. They had not killed the whites in their bedrolls, but other than that Isa-tai's success seemed complete.

Before long, however, the white hunters recovered from their surprise and began to return the fire. Shooting through the few windows and knocking chinks in the walls for additional shooting holes, the concussive buffalo guns began to boom regularly, interrupting the staccato of the smaller arms. But the Indians presented unbelievably difficult targets, circling the buildings and hanging from the protected sides of their ponies; their agility on horseback was incredible. Long famed as the most skilled with horses of all the Plains Indians, many of these same Comanches had seven years earlier staged a much more good-natured exhibition of their talent for some American dignitaries and a news reporter at the Medicine Lodge Treaty Council. The whites had come away dumfounded: "Riding at full gallop, the Comanches swung down the flanks of their ponies, shooting arrows into a brush target as they swept past. Shouting and waving [fourteen-foot] lances, they rode back and forth, full speed, hanging from their ponies' necks, rumps, and flanks, changing positions as easily as they might walk across the prairie. The well-trained hunting ponies turned and wheeled without any obvious command. . . ."

But despite the warriors' bewildering horsemanship, the supreme accuracy of the Sharp's buffalo guns began to take their toll. In the Myers store one of the veteran buffalo runners who was currently employed as Fred Leonard's cook, "Old Man" Keeler, who had often traded with the Cheyennes, recognized one of the first casualties as the son of Chief Stone Calf, and remarked, "Now them Cheyennes will fight like crazy, if Stone Calf has any say." Of course, the chances that Stone Calf himself was actually present are extremely meager, but his presence as a hostile in the battle could scarcely have given the other braves any greater fighting spirit.

During an early charge one of Quanah's companions was shot and killed almost at the door of one of the buildings. Indian warriors always expended every effort to recover their dead, and Quanah rode with the greatest courage straight into the muzzles of the buffalo guns, leaned down and plucked up his friend's body, then with almost superhuman strength carried it to safety, clinging to his horse with an arm and a foot.

Early in the fray an event occurred that most writers treat only as a colorful bit of bravado, but that may in retrospect be considerably more important. As related by Charlie Rath's partner Robert M. Wright, a certain magnificently clothed and mounted young man broke away from a group of warriors and rode straight for the side of one of the stores that had the greatest number of shooting ports. He had not been hit as he reached it, and once there he leaped from his pony, put the barrel of a revolver through a porthole, and emptied the chamber. The building was filled with smoke, but no one inside was hurt, and as the young man tried to get away he was felled by fire from the store. He struggled to his feet, but when he was shot again and fell, the young brave pulled out another pistol and shot himself through the head. Judging from the quality of his clothing, from the fact that Stone Calf's son was among the confirmed and probably unrecovered dead, and from the fact that suicidal bravery was an established avenue of restoring honor to oneself or family, it seems not unlikely that this was none other than the son of the old Cheyenne peace chief, at that time exiled in disgrace.

At about the same time another young brave, a Cheyenne named Horse Road, set out to prove his bravery. Already wounded at least once, he circled the buildings, jeering, then closed in and beat at a door with his gun butt. Andy Johnson's plank door held fast, and the young warrior was blasted point blank from within. Other Cheyennes known to have fallen throughout the day included Spotted Feathers, Coyote, Stone Teeth, and Walks-on-the-Ground.

The Indians' maneuvers were still controlled by the mysterious bugler, which was of no little aid to the defenders, since many of the army veterans recognized the signals and had their guns ready and waiting at each charge. The bugler himself braved the fire long enough to ransack the Shadler wagon, but as he ran northward, a can of coffee under one arm and a can of sugar under the other, skinner Harry Armitage set his Big Fifty and fired, and the bugler fell forward, a broad hole in his back. Years later Quanah settled the mystery of his identity: "One Comanche killed was a yellow nigger painted like Comanche. He had left nigger soldiers' company. . . ."

During a break between charges someone in the Myers store

shouted over to the saloon that one of their men had been hit. He was Billy Tyler, a young and inexperienced tenderfoot freighter who had arrived only the night before. On hearing the news, Bat Masterson climbed out the saloon window and dashed to the Myers store to be with the youngster, one of his closest friends back in Dodge. Tyler and Myers' partner Fred Leonard had run out the back door into the corral to try to save some of the stock. They failed, and as they were driven back inside, Tyler paused for one last shot, but was himself shot through the lungs; he knew he was dying, and as Masterson held him he begged for a drink of water. There was none left inside, where, in Old Man Keeler's words, it was "hot as a Dutch oven with the biscuits burning," and the well was in the middle of the corral, well covered by hostile fire. Masterson, either out of valor or blind grief, grabbed a bucket and ran for the back door. Seeing him, Old Man Keeler courageously took the bucket away from him, saying he knew many of the Cheyennes, and they wouldn't be so quick to shoot him as they would a stranger. Keeler's dog ran between his legs as he ran out the door, nearly sprawling him in the dust, as from the opposite fence he was met by a horrendous volley fire. It looked "as if the whole west side of the stockade was on fire," remembered Keeler's boss Fred Leonard. "They were all shooting at Keeler." But the Indians, incredibly, missed. Keeler drew the water and dashed back inside, miraculously unscathed, but his dog lay dead with, reportedly, twenty bullets in him. Back inside the store, Masterson recalled years later, "I took some water, washed Billie Tyler, bathed his face, and gave him a drink. Then his head fell over to one side and he was dead."

By late morning a crisis arose in the saloon; the men there were fast running out of ammunition, so Hanrahan and Dixon, crawling through a window, sprinted across the clearing to the Rath store, where cases of it were stocked. They got there safely, the Indians' long-range shooting being ineffective. Hanrahan returned to the saloon with a sackful of cartridges, but Dixon stayed there in the Rath store, at the wish of the people there, who pointed out that they were the weakest garrison, and "There was Mrs. Olds to protect." Mrs. Olds, a woman not yet thirty, had been loading and shooting as ably as the men, as the hunters proudly testified.

Dixon agreed to stay, and when a short while later the fighting diminished suddenly and markedly, the young hunter decided to take a look toward a large gravel hill that reared about fifty feet above the floodplain a few hundred yards to the west. There were no windows on the west side of the Rath store, but over the back door in the Olds' restaurant there was a crude transom. Bulky grain sacks had been thrown against the door as a barricade, and Dixon, a borrowed Big Fifty in one hand, delicately picked his way to the top of the pile to peek out. At first he saw little to note, but when he spied a movement in some tall grass he squirmed to plant one knee for balance, aimed the heavy weapon, and pressed the trigger. An experienced hunter like Dixon should have known better than to shoot from such a spraddled position; the buffalo rifle's tremendous recoil blew him backward off his perch like a child. The others in the store, fearful that he had been shot, rushed to his aid as he landed amid the crash of upset cookery and tinware.

Uninjured, Dixon again climbed back up to the transom. Once more he saw the grass move and, bracing himself more securely, shot at it again. He missed by several feet, but a third ball was true to its mark, and thereafter the clump of grass was still.

The fighting about noon had fallen off so noticeably that some hunters may have thought the Indians were growing discouraged, but there was a much more serious reason for the disengagement: Quanah Parker had been shot—from behind. During one of the early assaults, when he was about four hundred yards from the buildings, Quanah was spilled on the sun-baked ground when his horse was shot from under him, forcing him to seek cover behind a putrefying buffalo carcass. While he was there he was struck a terrific blow between the neck and the shoulder. The skin was only creased and he bled little, but the force left his arm paralyzed and useless for hours. Quanah had dragged himself to a thicket of plum trees, where he had lain all morning, until he was seen and snatched away by another warrior.

Actually he had been struck by a spent or ricocheted bullet, but the Indians did not understand the ballistics of bullets glancing off one object into another, and hurriedly called a council to determine who had shot the young chief. When every man denied being anywhere near Quanah, the only conclusion left them was that the white men had a fearsome new weapon that could make its bullets circle behind a man and shoot him in the back.

Isa-tai was silent at this. As the day wore on, the feeling grew that his medicine was worthless. The Indians had not caught the hunters sleeping, as he had promised they would, they had taken only two scalps, and moreover they had by this time lost dozens of their braves killed or wounded, including Tsa-yat-see, a brother of Yapparika chief Isa Rosa. Other Comanche dead later enumerated were Co-bay (Wild Mustang), Esa-que (Wolf Tongue), Tasa-vete (Sore Footed), and a Mexican-Indian named Sai-yan (Rag-Full-of-Holes).

This meeting was held on one of the buttes that surrounded Adobe Walls, but the Indians could not see the actual buildings because they were hidden behind the crest of the butte. As the council progressed it was interrupted by a sharp "splat," and when the warriors turned they saw Isa-tai's pony, solidly doused in the magic war paint, stagger and fall, its forehead split by a ball from a Big Fifty. That did it. In a rage a Cheyenne named Hippy, backed by a band of angry braves, advanced on Isa-tai to beat him with his quirt. Quanah himself remembered the scene: "All Cheyennes pretty mad Isa-tai, tell him, 'Whats matter your medicine? You got polecat medicine!'" Isa-tai was saved by the older chiefs, however, who told Hippy and the others that the medicine man's disgrace would shame him for life. That was enough, they said. Isa-tai retorted later that someone had killed a skunk, a powerful animal of Indian superstition, and that had broken his power.

Isa-tai's pony was of course hit by a stray bullet, but for all the Indians understood the whites had guns so powerful they could hit a target without even having to see it. And Isa-tai, contemplating his dead pony, was forced to concede, "The whites have a very strong medicine. Shoot today, maybe so kill you tomorrow."

After that the Indian force made no more frontal assaults on Adobe Walls, but maintained a sporadic lookout and siege. They had killed every last stock animal at the settlement, so they knew the whites were not going anywhere.

At about four o'clock the hunters began to venture cautiously from the buildings. Hanrahan rigged a black flag as a distress sig-

nal, as other men buried Billy Tyler and the Shadlers in one grave
by the corral. The dead stock, and what dead Indians were not
buried in pits, were dragged on buffalo hides a satisfactory distance from the buildings and left to the vultures. While this was in
progress some Indians appeared at a nearby hilltop; shots were
exchanged, and the Indians vanished.

Several hours later one George Bellfield rode into Adobe Walls
in his wagon, followed some time later by two buffalo hunters, Jim
and Bob Cator, just come in from their camp about twenty-five
miles away. None had seen any sign of Indians and were shaken
to discover that the dastardly savages would dare attack such a
stronghold. In fact they had thought the black flag was somebody's idea of a joke, until they got close enough to see the dead
stock. In 1892 Jim Cator described the scene: "Right on the West
of Mr. Rath's buildings were the hides, and below, two indians lay
there dead. Right at the next building, which was the saloon, I do
not think more than twenty-five or thirty yards [away] five indians
lay dead. A little farther west of them there was another indian
lying shot. He was dead. On the east side of A. C. Myers' building
one indian lay dead. Some of them that had been lying close to the
buildings had been drawn away. On the north side of Myers'
building another indian was dead. There were dead horses lying
all about. Some of the horses close up had been dragged away
from the house and a hole dug in the ground for them and partly
covered up."

One of the whites' horses killed was Mrs. Olds' pet mustang
colt. Given her by one of the hunters, he had become a community favorite; she had cared for him lovingly, even sewn him a
blanket of burlap bags to protect him from the voracious mosqui-
toes.

With live horses (Bellfield's and the Cators') once more within
the settlement, the people lost no time in summoning aid. Motivated by a consideration of two hundred fifty dollars, hunter
Henry Lease volunteered to run the gantlet to try to reach Dodge;
he left well after dark, armed to the teeth. Riding like the wind for
Dodge City, he arrived there safely only to find that no one there
had authority to dispatch a column of cavalry to rescue the hunters at the Walls. Word of the situation was sent to Governor Osborn, who interceded for them via telegraph with the senior mili-

tary officer of the region, Department Commander General John Pope.

They were barking up the wrong tree. No one had ever accused John Pope of being soft on Indians, but he was one of the few army men who had a conscience where Indians were concerned, and he laid the fault for the entire uprising exactly where it belonged: squarely on the Dodge City buffalo hunters. Still steaming mad at their illegal depredations in the Indian Territory and entry into Texas, Pope showed no sympathy whatever for the hunters, growling that they had "justly earned all that may befall them," and if he sent any troops at all to Adobe Walls, it would be to "break up the grogshops and trading establishments rather than protect them."

Little aid from the army was actually needed, however. The buffalo hunters had a reputation for looking out after their own, and soon a relief force under hunter Tom Nixon rode south.

The day after the battle, an event took place back at the Walls that ranks as one of the more remarkable of the time. Billy Dixon and some others had been keeping a lookout for hostiles, and when a party of about twenty warriors topped a small butte maybe a mile east of the post, some of the other men urged Dixon to demonstrate his famous marksmanship by trying a shot. Among the Indians was reportedly Quanah, with some other chiefs and braves, and as they sat their ponies to look over the buildings, they saw a puff of smoke jet from one of the hunters' gun barrels. An instant later a brave named To-hah-kah crumpled to the ground, and some seconds later the boom of Dixon's Big Fifty rolled across the valley. Indian informants evidently contradict each other on whether the warrior was killed or merely stunned by the spent bullet, but the Indians wheeled and fled, guardedly returning only to fetch the wounded (or killed) man. The distance of Billy Dixon's famous "long shot" was later precisely measured at 1,538 yards, about eight tenths of a mile.

That shot ended the actual Battle of Adobe Walls, though there was one more white casualty suffered within a few days. It was the restaurateur, William Olds. On July 1, having sighted a distant band of Indians from a hastily constructed watchtower, Olds hurried down the ladder to spread the news, fouled his gun on an obstruction, and accidentally shot himself through the head. He fell dead at his horrified wife's feet, and was quickly buried by the Rath store. The Indian band never approached the Walls.

The trading posts were abandoned soon after, as most of the clerks and hunters returned to Dodge with the Dixon group, but the site continued to be a camping ground for the ones who stayed. The buildings were abandoned altogether about six weeks later, when Lieutenant Baldwin rode through with his scouts and column of 6th Cavalry, allowing the Indians to return one last time to reclaim finally the bones of their dead. The hostiles burned Adobe Walls to the ground, even ripping up the timber pile foundations.

For them the Battle of Adobe Walls was a crippling defeat. Because they were unable to retrieve about a dozen of their dead and because later informants apparently reported as killed only those whom they personally knew to have been killed, the total number of Indian dead is usually given as nine to fifteen. Actually it went much higher, probably at least 70 killed and wounded. In 1876 Chief Whirlwind of the Cheyennes admitted the death of 115; a scout with the Baldwin expedition reported at least 30 Indian graves dotting the buttes surrounding Adobe Walls. The true figure will never be known.

The Indians' frightful losses notwithstanding, the Battle of Adobe Walls was the beginning, not the end, of the great 1874–75 Indian War. Stung by their humiliation at the Walls, the hostile warriors made one final, desperate, bloody attempt to salvage their way of life, terrorizing the plains of the Southwest for months. The large war party splintered, and the smaller groups ravaged the prairies, burning and pillaging a vast expanse of Texas, Oklahoma, Kansas, New Mexico, and southeastern Colorado. The weather, as if in response, turned deathly hot, as hardly a drop of rain fell the rest of the summer. Plagues of locusts devoured the plant life, leaving only bare, baked earth to reflect the sun's searing heat, as secondary streams and then the major rivers withered within their banks and soon disappeared entirely, all bringing to mind Isa-tai's prophecy of the preceding spring: "I tell you there will be a great dry time this summer."

VI. Lone Wolf's Revenge: The Lost Valley Fight

Estimates of the number of Kiowas who actually fought at Adobe Walls dip as low as a half dozen individuals, all of them chiefs or noted raiders: Lone Wolf, Satanta, Bird Bow, White Horse, White Shield, and Howling Wolf. After Adobe Walls these six—for it is indeed doubtful that there were more—repaired to the Indian Territory to join in their tribe's annual medicine dance, held the first week in July about fifty miles northwest of the agency, "at the end of the bluff," in what is now Greer County. The Sun Dance was already under way when the Kiowa warriors rode into the encampment, and the Comanches and Cheyennes, extremely anxious to win over the bulk of the Kiowas to the war, sent sizable delegations with them to speak in their councils.

The Kiowas had postponed the resolution of the war issue until the Sun Dance, and now required a big smoker to thrash out a policy, to the undoubted frustration of the war-ready Comanches. Though they had been allies for at least three quarters of a century, each tribe maintained a markedly distinct method of deciding policy, and occasionally became somewhat irritated at each other over this difference. Unlike the individualistic Comanches, who seldom met for longer than needed to take a vote and then did each man as he pleased anyway, the Kiowas held lengthy discussions, and loftily considered their Comanche allies to be impetuous and indeliberate. The Comanches, for their part, huffed that the Kiowas "talk too much."

This was easily the most important showdown between Striking Eagle and Lone Wolf, and as the council progressed one Kiowa chief after another elected the peace road. Among them were

Dangerous Eagle, the influential brother of once-imprisoned raider Big Tree, and also the noted war chief of earlier fame, Stumbling Bear. An army physician had recently cured the chief's little boy, who had been deathly ill, whereas no doctor had been present at the death on January 10 of his infant grandson. Having experienced such a demonstration of the white man's medicine, Stumbling Bear needed little urging from his younger cousin Striking Eagle to keep him in the right path. Another weighty "nay" fell as Chief Sun Boy, the same who had traveled to Washington and whose being named after the god-founder of the tribe gave him his special protection, joined the Striking Eagle faction. But probably the most decisive blow was struck against the war when Nap-a-wat, the Kiowas' primal medicine man, whom Haworth termed a kind of "High Priest, or Chief Medicine Man, without whose sanctioning favor they do not like to go into war," refused to sanction the Lone Wolf raid, and cast his lot with the peace faction.

Acutely sensitive to the importance of this council, and sensing the argument going against him, the aggrieved Lone Wolf attempted to win over the young men of the tribe by hinting that, in the fight with Lieutenant Hudson, Tau-ankia and Guitain might not have been killed if their companions had shown a little more bravery. But the usually effective technique of verbal abuse, which four years earlier had goaded even Striking Eagle into leading a raid, backfired in this instance; most of the young warriors were deeply insulted and would have nothing more to do with their bereaved principal chief or his proposed revenge raid.

In the end, when Striking Eagle struck camp on July 9, fully three fourths of the Kiowa tribe followed him back to Haworth and the agency, a spectacular victory for the elegant young peace chief. Aside from individual dissidents, only two full camps were convinced to join the war, those of Lone Wolf and Swan. The latter man, Swan, or Maman-ti (Walks-in-the-Sky), was one of the most mysterious and ominous characters of the Kiowa tribe. He was a fierce and popular war chief, a feared Do-ha-te, or medicine man, and atop that, an Owl Prophet, a seer who advised his people on the strength of messages given him by the inflatable skin of his medicine owl. It was Maman-ti who planned most of the Kiowas' raids and even led some, rather than Lone Wolf or Satanta or others who gained the notoriety. Hence, his reputation is one of being the power behind the chiefs, whereas he actually was an influential leader in his own right.

One other important event occurred before the Sun Dance broke up: the renowned Satanta, by this time over sixty years old and chastened by his two years in the Huntsville Penitentiary, abdicated his chieftainship and retired from the Kaitsenko warrior society, giving over his medicine lance to a reputable warrior named Ahto-tain-te (White Cowbird). In the coming raid the aging chief did not accompany Lone Wolf, but returned, to his credit, back to the agency.

After Striking Eagle and the bulk of the tribe set off for the agency, Lone Wolf still had difficulty getting warriors to agree to make the raid with him, and the whole operation threatened to dissolve in discouragement. The next afternoon, however, the revered Maman-ti agreed to be war leader, and quickly the raiding party swelled to about four dozen braves. The two hostile villages feasted and danced for the rest of the day, and in the evening a messenger from Maman-ti told them to assemble after dark before the Do-ha-te's tipi, which sat off by itself on a hill above the camp. The Owl Prophet would make medicine.

When night came the people gathered as summoned, and they sat down in front of Maman-ti's tipi and waited quietly; the hooting of an owl could be heard within. When the Do-ha-te came out he predicted that the revenge raid would be a success, no Indians would die, and at least one scalp would be taken. But they could not wait for morning: They must leave that very instant. At once the two villages broke into an exultant pandemonium, as the men gathered up their paint and selected their best war ponies, and the women ran down to saddle them. Other important Kiowas who rode with Lone Wolf and Maman-ti that night included Red Otter, Lone Wolf's brother and the father of the fallen Guitain. His participation in the raid was a radical departure from his normal behavior; one would suspect that he took part only because to fail to avenge his own son would have been an unspeakable disgrace. Red Otter had not fought at Adobe Walls; in fact, he spent the night of June 26 visiting Agent Haworth at Fort Sill.

Other members of the raid were Pago-to-goodl (Lone Young

Man), a brother of Kaitsenko initiate Ahto-tain-te, and himself an established member of that elect society, and also, curiously, a brother of peace chief Sun Boy. Participating also were Do-hauson (Little Mountain), the nephew and namesake of the famous chief of earlier days, and three apprentice medicine men of the Do-ha-te: Sankey-dotey (Medicine Feather), Do-ha-san, and Ho-an-t'agia. Riding as well were Mamay-day-te, who had been with Tau-ankia and Guitain at the time of their deaths; Tah-bone-mah, later famous as the army scout I-See-O, and his elder brother Tape-day-ah (Standing Sweathouse), also a close friend of the slain nobility and himself a member of the on-de aristocracy. Also, Qui-tan, a Mexican captive named Esteban who had become Big Bow's brother-in-law; Set-kop-te (Mountain Bear), a Cheyenne-Pawnee adopted into the Kiowa tribe at the age of twelve; Eonah-pah (Trailing the Enemy), twice over the son-in-law of Satanta, and a survivor of Custer's massacre on the Washita, of which he was the only Kiowa participant; and Tsen-tonkee (Horse Hunt or Hunting Horse), the youngest of the war party, who was participating in his first raid.

By midnight everyone was prepared, and they lit out southward. As they came upon the Red River about noon the next day they stopped to kill some buffalo they happened across, and then entered Texas at a much-used ford just east of the panhandle meridian. North of the present site of Quanah, Texas, they discovered a hill covered by a prairie dog town, and here they established their base camp. The worn horses were hobbled to keep them from wandering, as the braves mounted fresh ones, and the spare hardware was hidden. Nobody stayed behind to guard the cache, which was unusual, and the whole group pushed south again. After crossing the Big Washita the Kiowas killed some cattle, which they cooked by heaving entire carcasses onto a bonfire of mesquite, and the meat not immediately consumed was taken along with them for a second meal; before sunset they had covered another thirty miles, camping east of where Seymour, Texas, is now located.

Again the Do-ha-te made medicine. This time he predicted that, next day, the Indians would kill one, maybe two whites, and the ones who counted coup on them would be riding gray ponies. Last, he said, Tsen-tonkee, the young warrior who was involved in his first raid, would distinguish himself, and would get a bay horse as a trophy. The Do-ha-te then ordered the warriors to put on their war paint and be ready by sunup.

Accordingly, each brave began to apply the war paint to his body, using the colors and designs peculiar to his family, a custom not unlike that of European families displaying their coats of arms. Do-hauson II prepared the emblem of his famous family, painting his chest and back with blue dots on a yellow field, the same design as was emblazoned on his war shield, and black streaks running out from the corners of his eyes. Tahbone-mah was painted cerulean splashed on a light blue background. Tsentonkee, for whom Maman-ti had foretold a distinguishing role, colored his body white, with crimson stripes. The Do-ha-te himself, and his three apprentices, all shared the same magic emblem of the Owl Prophet: a blue owl on back and chest, set against a field of white. Three of the men very properly did not wear paint: Lone Wolf and Red Otter, the fathers of the slain young men, and their companion, Mamay-day-te. Still deep in mourning, their chests and backs were bare. Lone Wolf's (and probably Red Otter's) hair, hacked off in grief seven months before, fell unbraided and loose in the wind. The war horses were decorated, their tails and manes plaited through with bright cloth, and last, the war bonnets were donned by those distinguished enough to merit them.

When all were ready the warriors set out again, crossing the "Salt Prairie" between Cox and Flattop mountains, the scene of the Warren Wagontrain Raid, for which Satanta and Big Tree served time in the Huntsville Penitentiary. While there, the Kiowas visited the hilltop grave of a Comanche named Ord-lee, who had been killed in the Wagontrain Raid. Some of them later told Wilbur Nye that, after they had unscrambled the stones over the skeleton and stood around looking at it, the wind picked up, whistling through the brush, frightening them.

The superstitious Indians had little time to consider the phenomenon, as one of them spied four whites riding near the base of the hill, and the Indians all mounted up and gave chase. The four whites were cowboys: James C. Loving, whose ranch was a few miles to the east; W. C. Hunt; I. G. Newcomb; and Shad Damron. Knowing better than to run straight for the ranch, the four cowboys decoyed to the west until they struck a patch of sharp, rocky ground, where they circled around and then rode home. The ruse worked, as the Kiowas gave hard chase until they too came to the roughs where, upon discovering that their ponies' unshod feet were becoming lacerated on the jagged rocks, they let the men go. The Indians then shot several nearby calves and shod their ponies protectively in the fresh rawhide. The Indians were still on the high ground which forms part of the divide between the Brazos and the West Fork Trinity rivers when, before they had finished doctoring their horses, they saw some distance to the north a group of about two dozen white men, all wearing white hats, riding very fast along Salt Creek, following the Kiowas' trail. The Indians quickly mounted and rode up a draw in the hills that was known to the whites as the Lost Valley, then separated to obliterate their trail, and waited.

The riders in white hats were Texas Rangers, members of the newly formed "Frontier Battalion" of Major John B. Jones. The recently organized force owed its existence to Texas' governor, Richard Coke, a tremendous, bushy-bearded bear of a man who had seized power in a paramilitary coup d'état a few months before. At the time Coke evicted the carpetbag Reconstruction government and returned power to the Democrats, the Texas Rangers had been in decline for many years. During the Civil War they were virtually nonexistent, while many of the former Rangers organized under Benjamin Franklin Terry as the 8th Texas Cavalry, called themselves "Terry's Texas Rangers," and acquitted themselves well in Tennessee and Kentucky. When E. J. Davis came with Reconstruction, that governor revamped the organization as the Texas State Police, a force to which the people developed a vitriolic dislike for their enforcement of scalawag law and disregard for majority will.

After Coke's coup, however, the State Police force was swept away with every other vestige of the hated Republicanism. In his inaugural speech Coke called attention to the Indian menace on the frontier. During the Civil War the federal troops had deserted the Confederate border posts and gone east to fight, leaving the pioneer settlements on the edge of civilization to defend themselves as best they could, with what little aid the rebellious state could provide. The Indians, who after the Council House Fight of 1840 hated the Texans as much as the Mexicans, were quick to discover the state of affairs, and from 1860 to 1865 their war parties flailed away at the frontier, shoving the encroaching line of Texas at least 150 miles back to the southeast. After the war Davis' State Police had so aroused the hatred of the people that the governor found it necessary with disconcerting frequency to impose martial law on communities or whole counties, to protect the rights of seemingly everybody but white Democrats. Thus Indian fighting was left to federal troops, since returned, and they made some progress here and there—the most significant probably being the 1872 campaign against the Quahadi and Kotsoteka Comanches, the first time those tribes had ever felt the might of the United States. Nevertheless, there was a general realization on the part of most Texans that they would have to bear a large share of the protection themselves, and Coke called for the revival of the Texas Rangers to do the job.

The Texas Legislature so responded to Coke's call on April 10, 1874, by formally resurrecting the Rangers, banned for nine years, first by the federal military dictatorship and then by the carpetbag governor. Appropriating three hundred thousand dollars, they created two separate units: the Special Force, to operate in southwestern Texas against *bandidos* and other outlaws, and the Frontier Battalion, to protect the fuzzy, 400-mile-long boundary between the farthest outposts of Texas civilization and the heathen Indians of the still unsettled and partially unexplored plains to the northwest. The Frontier Battalion was specified to contain six companies of Rangers, each with 75 men, a total of 450 troopers. Their function, simply stated, was to serve as "Indian exterminators."

John B. Jones of Corsicana, a remarkable man from many standpoints, was selected to command the Frontier Battalion and given a major's commission. He was of slight build, about five feet eight and 140 pounds, and extremely handsome, his finely lined face framed by jet-black hair and drooping mustache. Quiet, erudite, traveled, and experienced by fighting with Terry's Texas Rangers, one historian called him the most underrated of the Rangers' many famous officers. From the time he received his commission he needed less than one month to organize five companies, and by the second week in July the Frontier Battalion was at its full strength, each company responsible for guarding a segment of the border country that stretched from the Red River to southwest of the Nueces River—about 40,000 square miles of lawless frontier. From the beginning Jones established the policy of riding a circuit up and down the defense line, exerting his "firm but gentle" control over the 450 undisciplined and often incorrigible Rangers.

July 12 found him visiting the camp of Captain G. W. Stevens, one of his company commanders, about two miles from the site of Graham, Texas, on Salt Creek, where Jones had recently moved it to facilitate its operation. Jones and his escort of twenty-five had ridden in about ten o'clock the preceding night, after a forced march of some sixty miles; Jones had been alerted that Indians might be coming on a raid, and he wanted to be positioned to deal with them. Early in the morning of the twelfth a half-dozen scouts were sent out to try to locate the suspected raiding party.

Among the six were an officer, a Lieutenant Wilson, and Major Jones' cousin, Walter Robertson of D Company. They had ridden out only a few miles before encountering the anticipated Indian trail, very large and very fresh, on the east side of Salt Creek. Leaving the other five Rangers to sit tight until he returned, Lieu- tenant Wilson galloped back to Stevens' camp with the news and the urgent request that Jones and Stevens "bring every available man," and at once the three officers and about sixteen Rangers, some of Stevens' company and some of Jones' escort, which included some men of all six companies, took up the chase. By the time they reached the scouts the latter had been waiting for about an hour and a half, and once united, the force, in all about twenty-five strong, then continued down Salt Creek. The confident Kiowas had made no attempt to disguise their tracks, so the Rangers were able to follow it easily, and moved very rapidly.

Now, while it must be admitted that Jones and his men were brave, tough, and hard-fighting individuals, they suffered from one overwhelming disadvantage: They had no experience whatever at fighting Indians. In fact, this very engagement was to be their baptism of fire: Only one of them, Major Jones, had ever been in action before; the rest, recruited only in the immediately preceding weeks, were as green as spring grass, and straightaway Lone Wolf and Maman-ti drew them into a trap that any seasoned veteran of Indian warfare would have seen and countered. But the Rangers heedlessly galloped along Salt Creek for a distance of fifteen miles, passing and noticing the wooden monument that had been erected at the site of Satanta's Wagontrain Raid of three years previous; they were concentrating on the freshening trail, scarcely guessing they might be observed, until about halfway between Jacksboro and Belknap they came upon the ridge of the Western Crosstimbers, rising prominently like a forested coastline above the grass. The landscape in the hills was extremely rough and broken, the rocky hills separated by rugged watercourses and dry washes, the sheltered slopes heavily wooded with post oak and scrub. The Indians' trail led directly into one of these huge ravines, known as the Lost Valley, where it intersected the trail of another war party of equal strength, making the tracking Rangers believe they were up against maybe a hundred Indians, so outnumbering them by a margin of four to one. That was not the case, however: Two days before, on July 10, a war party supposed to be Comanches had ridden down and killed an employee of James Loving's named Keith. In fact, the Lost Valley was a favorite escape route of raiding Indians; another young man, a herder named Walker, had been killed there on June 4, although Indian guilt is not proven.

As the hiding Kiowas watched the Rangers draw nearer, two of them, Maman-ti and Atah-lah-te (Loud Talker, or also Feather Head, see photo 42), dashed out into the mouth of the valley so the Rangers would chase them back and clinch the trap, but evidently they were not seen. The maneuver was unnecessary, as Jones and his men unhesitatingly entered the rough valley. Jones immediately discovered that the Indians' trail fanned out and disintegrated up into the heights, and he was then tricked into committing the cardinal sin of Indian warfare: He split his meager command into still smaller groups to try to rediscover a main trail.

One of the Rangers, Ed Carnal of Jones' escort group, was scouting "by my own hook" at the edge of the timber, but before he had gone far into the valley he suddenly looked up from the ground and beheld the first Indians he had ever seen. "I was very much astonished," he wrote later, "and reined up my horse and sat looking at them." For a few seconds he couldn't believe they were Indians; there were too many of them. He knew the Loving ranch was only a few miles away, so maybe they were ranch hands out like themselves in search of raiders. Carnal came to his senses when he spied their war lances; they were still some distance away, and hadn't seen him, but instead of backing away and reporting their location to Major Jones, Carnal in his inexperience brashly unholstered his pistol and fired at them to warn the other Rangers. How many Indians were in this group is not known—whether it was only a part of the Lone Wolf party or the full fifty. But since when he gave himself away they all turned and bore down on him in a mob, whooping and waving their lances, Carnal may be forgiven his estimate of three hundred.

The Kiowas had taken refuge in the rocky high ground, and when Ed Carnal fired his revolver the moment had come for them to spring the trap. Carnal had been left behind as the other Rangers entered the Lost Valley, and now he raced out onto the flat, mesquite-covered valley floor, pressing his body flat against his horse's side, riding straight for Major Jones, Captain Stevens, and about half a dozen others with them. By the time Carnal reached them with the Kiowas hard on his heels, Jones had managed to collect enough of his force to space them out and hold the Indians temporarily at bay. Thus far the Rangers had progressed about a half mile into the Lost Valley, to the point where it doglegs from northwest to northeast to follow Cameron Creek. Their position smack in the middle of the valley, far from the timber or any other cover, prompted Captain Stevens to volunteer what is now an almost amusing understatement: "Major, we will have to get to cover or all be killed."

The only cover anywhere near was an arroyo about a hundred yards long and four or five feet deep that lay back to the south, but as the Kiowas quickly had the small squad of Rangers surrounded, the only way to reach it was to fight their way through. This was successfully attempted, though in this initial encounter three of the Rangers were hit. Lee Corn was badly wounded in the shoulder, his arm "nearly shot off." Thereafter, Corn, in the company of another Ranger named Wheeler who got cut off from the rest of the group, reached the south bank of Cameron Creek, off to the north, where they lay isolated and hidden throughout the day. George Moore was shot below the knee and would remain a cripple for life. It was probably Moore who, as Hunting Horse described, shot Red Otter's horse as he led the charge into the Indians, but who was then himself dismounted, and limped off into the bushes and back to the arroyo. Seeing the Indians scatter before them, Jones and his men overshot the shallow arroyo and pursued the Kiowas to a ridge on the southwest side of the valley, but when the Indians attained the slopes they suddenly turned and counterattacked, forcing the Rangers to pull up short, then turn tail and retreat to the narrow wash.

The third casualty, William Glass, had lagged behind the others in turning back to the ravine; he was cut down far from the cover and lay motionless. Everyone else thought he was dead, so nobody stopped to pick him up, and years later Hunting Horse recalled how the Indians saw Glass fall and tried to get close enough to scalp him: "We could see the leader of the whites motioning his men to fall back. One of them was slow. Tsen-au-sain shot him down. 'I got one,' he shouted. But nobody was able to touch the fallen enemy to make coup. . . . We could see the man lying there in plain sight. The heads of the other Rangers could be seen sticking up from a dry streambed. Nobody dared go close enough to make coup.

"Red Otter got desperate. He called for volunteers. Not a warrior spoke up. I remembered the prophecy of the medicine man. It was my chance. I said I would go with Red Otter. Red Otter ran forward and took position behind a large tree. He signaled for me to join him. . . . The bullets were throwing bark in our faces. Then we ran to another tree. But the bullets came thicker. . . ."

Jones' Rangers had a clear view of Red Otter and Hunting Horse, as the trees they used for cover in approaching Glass, both about two feet thick, were closer to the white men than the concealed Indians by at least a hundred yards. Within a few moments of his being shot, Glass regained consciousness and saw the two Indians sneaking closer. Terrified, he somehow summoned the strength to begin crawling toward the ravine, screaming, "My God, my God, don't let them get me!" When Major Jones called for volunteers to carry him in, three men ran out and rescued him, as the others covered them with an intense fire at the two Indians. This last fusillade drove Red Otter and Hunting Horse back to the other Kiowas, and their chance for coup was missed, but the

Rangers' bravery in rescuing Glass netted them nothing, as he died shortly after being carried into the ravine.

From the time of the first ambush at about two o'clock, the Rangers had been shooting only with revolvers; none of the carbines were equipped with magazines, and the fighting had been too thick and fast to keep reloading the rifles. Some of the ex-farmhand Rangers showed signs of cracking in their first Indian engagement, but Jones managed to keep them relatively calm with his example. The major was proving himself a genuinely admirable commander, once he survived the initial blunder of dividing his force. Not seeking refuge in the arroyo with his men, Jones calmly strode back and forth on the east side of the ditch, positioning them, giving them encouragement, awing them with his nerve as at one point, with Indian bullets thrashing the branches about him, he leaned almost nonchalantly against an oak tree to get a steadier sighting through his field glasses.

Before long some of the Kiowas circled around behind the ravine and began firing down from the timbered slopes at the rear of Jones' line. Off his guard only momentarily, Jones led two volunteers, William H. Lewis and Walter Robertson, to an exposed ridge about 150 yards from the arroyo, bare of vegetation except for a large old oak tree. Stationing his men under the tree, from where they could cover the east side of the ravine, Jones departed with the instructions, "Boys, stay here until they get you or until the fight is over."

During a breather in the skirmish Lieutenant Wilson scrambled up to see if they were all right. Robertson and Lewis had been under intense fire for some hours, the Indians' bullets stripping away large patches of bark from their tree. Robertson recalled that on reaching them and discovering them safe, Wilson sat down under the tree, cursing forcibly at the Kiowas, when Lewis admonished, "Lieutenant, you ought not swear like that. Don't you know that you might be killed at any moment?"

Wilson agreed, fanning himself with his hat and resting from his exertion, when suddenly more Indian fire clipped off a dead limb that struck Wilson across the head as it fell. "By God, boys," he exclaimed, "I'm shot, sure as hell!" As mentioned, only Major Jones had been under fire before.

The stalemate continued, and as the afternoon wore on, the

Rangers' suffering from heat and thirst increased tremendously. The Kiowas had completely cut them off from Cameron Creek, which though practically dry contained a deep waterhole about a half mile to the north, and Major Jones had very properly given strict orders that no one was to separate himself from the group to try to retrieve water for the others, in spite of the fact that, as one of them wrote later, "there is nothing to equal the thirst created from inhaling the explosion of fresh gunpowder." As the ordeal became more grim, Ed Carnal noticed one young Ranger—he couldn't have been more than eighteen—dig a hole in the dusty wash to about arm's depth and pack his mouth with wet sand to reduce the swelling. Eventually the suffering became unbearable, and two men of Stevens' company, Mel Porter and David Bailey, announced they were going to the creek to bring back water; they grabbed up several canteens, then were on their horses and gone before anyone could stop them.

The fire had begun to slacken some from the ridge to the southwest, but not because the Indians were abandoning the fight. The Kiowas had correctly guessed the Rangers' situation, and a large number of them had circled to the west and divided, one group concealing themselves in another ridge just northwest of the waterhole, waiting for someone to attempt reaching water, and the second group had hidden in the brush of the creekbank above the waterhole, to cut off retreat. As the other Rangers watched with intense anxiety, Mel Porter, with the canteens, reached the waterhole first by about fifty yards, leaped from his horse onto the bank, and began filling the canteens. As the interminable seconds passed it appeared that they might not be killed after all, but their slowly kindling hopes were dashed as not less than two dozen Indians ambushed them from the creekbank thicket on the west. Screaming and blasting their guns, Jones' men tried to warn Bailey and Porter, but it was too late.

Bailey spurred his horse back to the south, trying to regain the dry arroyo. Had he circled to the east he might have outrun the Kiowas, but as they had him cut off at a right angle, he never had a chance. His horse faltered, and he was instantly surrounded and finished. The Kiowas said it was Do-hauson the Younger who speared Bailey from his horse, and Mamay-day-te who got first coup by touching him. When Lone Wolf rode up, the old chief dismounted, at long last to have revenge for the loss of Tau-ankia and Guitain. With his brass hatchet-pipe hacked Bailey's head into mush and gutted him with a butcher knife. Then, recalled Hunting Horse, "Everyone who wanted to, shot arrows into it or poked at it with their lances." Freed from his mourning, Lone Wolf made a speech over the corpse, thanking the braves for their help in avenging his son and nephew and then, to honor their friend Mamay-day-te's bravery, made him a gift of his name, Lone Wolf.

At the same time as Dave Bailey was being ridden down and killed, Mel Porter had jumped on his horse and attempted a getaway to the north, but two Kiowas, Quototai and Tahbone-mah, chased after him and gained steadily. As they closed in on him, Porter turned around and emptied his revolver at them, finally flinging the weapon at them in frustration, just as Tahbone-mah knocked him from the saddle with his lance and made off with his horse. Porter escaped by diving into the waterhole and disappearing, swimming underwater downstream. When he came back up for breath the two Indians pursued him again, but unknown to either Porter or the Indians, Porter when he surfaced had stumbled onto the creekbank hiding place of Wheeler and Lee Corn who, momentarily thinking Porter an Indian, blazed away at him as fast as they could. The two Kiowas thought the barrage was directed at them so, contenting themselves with Porter's strong bay horse, returned to their group. Later on, Tahbone-mah gave the animal to Hunting Horse, curiously fulfilling Maman-ti's prophecy.

Wheeler, Corn, and Porter waited for nightfall to cover them before making their way downstream to the Loving ranch, about two miles east. There they were joined later by the rest of Jones' command; sneaking away in the middle of the night, all but the wounded were afoot, since the Indians succeeded in shooting nearly all their horses. William Glass' body was strapped across an abandoned Indian pony. On their way to the Loving ranch the thirsty Rangers finally obtained some water, raking some six inches of scum from a small, stagnant pool. At Loving's some of the men ripped boards from a smokehouse wall to make a coffin for Glass, and they buried him next to the ranch hand named Keith who had been killed by Comanches two days before.

Once reasonably safe, the next step was to send for help at Fort Richardson at Jacksboro, about fifteen miles east through the rugged hills and draws of the Crosstimbers. Lee Corn, a resident of Jacksboro, was the only one who knew the territory, but he was too badly shot up to ride; however, his horse was one of the few to survive, and by giving him a completely loose rein and trusting the animal's homing instinct, one of the other Rangers was able to reach Richardson safely.

Everyone was still keenly on the lookout for Indians, but the Kiowas, after mutilating Bailey's corpse and singing victory songs, quitted the field and went home. Lone Wolf's revenge raid was a success, and so satisfied, they had no interest in pressing the attack, regardless of how great their advantage. This, combined with the fact that the war party returned to near Fort Sill and did not set off on a string of depredations, suggests that the Kiowas were merely taking an eye for an eye, and were not even yet committed to an all-out war to the death. But the damage was done, and the word would get out. The die was cast, and the two Kiowa villages of Lone Wolf and Maman-ti had willy-nilly consigned themselves to either taking their punishment immediately or continuing to fight indefinitely.

The Rangers returned to Lost Valley on the thirteenth, accompanied by troops from Richardson, and discovered Bailey's ghastly remains: "We came upon the body of the boy who had been killed. . . . His clothing was all gone and his body was terribly mutilated. He had been lanced and cut with Bowie knives until it was with difficulty one could recognize the remains as being those of a human. Even his head had been taken entirely away." Fourteen or fifteen arrows jutted from his body. The other Rangers, horrified by their first taste of Indian warfare, rolled Bailey into a shallow grave on the creekbank, scouted around for a while, then rode back to Jacksboro to refit.

VII. The United States Goes to War

After the fray at Adobe Walls the Cheyennes, unfamiliar with the Staked Plains, moved back to and raided in the area from their agency northwest all the way to southeastern Colorado. Fearing, however, that they might in the end have to seek refuge with the Comanches in the latter's hideouts on the Llano Estacado, they obtained from them a guide reputed to know the location of every waterhole in the region. The guide's name was Mule Smoking, but because of his unusually deep copper color the Cheyennes dubbed him "Black Comanche."

The stretch of plains north and west of the Cheyenne-Arapaho Agency was, as the buffalo hunters were certainly aware the preceding spring, the least protected on the entire southern frontier. On the Texas front there was a picket line of forts from north of the Red River to beyond the Pecos: Sill, Richardson, Griffin, Concho, McKavett, Stockton, and Davis. The Indian frontier in Kansas was watched over by the three closely linked forts—Zarah, Larned, and Dodge—and to the west, Fort Wallace on the Colorado border. But in the middle, with the exception of the small garrison at Camp Supply, there was nothing—not one regular outpost in the whole vast expanse of land bounded by Sill (Indian Territory), Dodge (Kansas), and Fort Bascom (New Mexico). There were some roads, though, and ranches, and among them the Cheyennes wreaked a furious havoc. Their raiding parties had actually been active since early June, in retaliation against the horse thieves from Kansas and the shooting of Little Robe's son, and first blood was drawn when three whites were cut down, ironically, not far from Medicine Lodge, Kansas. The warriors also sought prey along the road from Fort Dodge to Camp Supply,

attacking on June 19 a squadron of K Troop, 6th Cavalry, and D
Company, 3rd Infantry, which was escorting a paymaster. Two
days later about thirty Cheyennes assaulted Dodge's commander
Colonel C. E. Compton and the 6th Cavalry's G Troop, and A
Company of the 2nd Infantry, wounding one soldier and one civilian; more Indians attacked the same force on June 24, but this
time the army claimed four Indian dead.

On June 14 Miles' special deputy marshal, E. C. Lefebvre,
wrote him from Camp Supply that a survey party returning from
Adobe Walls had found and buried two dead hunters on the
twelfth, about fifteen miles from the hunters' settlement. Identifying the attacking Indians as Kiowas and Comanches, Lefebvre
commented, "The movement against the Buffalo hunters seemed
to have been well planned. The Indians divided themselves into
small parties and made simultaneous attacks on the different
camps." The marshal also wrote that Indians had run off his own
horses on the night of the eleventh, and he would return to
Darlington as soon as he could.

Agent Miles' news was a week behind the times when he first
heard of all these incidents, and he had no idea what was transpiring at Adobe Walls when on June 27 he scribbled hastily to
Friend Haworth, "My wife writes me back from Wichita that the
Indians made a raid on 'Medicine Lodge' in Kans. on the 17th
inst killing three men. . . . Also one man killed between Fort
Dodge and Camp Supply. There is 'no use talking.' *Some of our
Indians are on the warpath.* I think they will confine their raids
principally upon the Buffalo Hunters. . . ." If John D. Miles had
expected the worst, his situation at the end of June did not
miss it by far; only three friendly Cheyenne chiefs remained at the
agency—Little Robe, White Shield, and Old Whirlwind—and
among them they controlled less than three hundred Indians. The
rest were at war. The chief Gray Beard and his village were absent
and hostile, as were Heap-of-Birds and Minimic (Eagle Head), a
noted chief-medicine man. All the Dog Soldiers were at war, too,
and also, finally, the fearsome war chief Medicine Water, whose lot
it was to commit one of the most famous depredations in the history of the South Plains. Stone Calf was absent and presumed to
have defected to the hostiles, but those at the agency of course

had no way of knowing all that had befallen the unfortunate old chief; his village, though, was undeniably as hostile as any.

On July 2 one William Watkins was killed about thirty miles north of Darlington, and on the third a grain-laden wagon train on the road to Fort Sill via Darlington and Anadarko, the site of the Wichita Agency, was wiped out. The three drivers were killed and scalped, and wagonmaster Patrick Hennessey, who had been warned not to try the journey, was evidently taken alive. Chained to a wagon wheel and buried under his oats and corn, the Cheyennes burned him to death. Long noted only for its brutality, contemporary letters give a new significance to the Hennessey killings: This was the wagon train that had been specially dispatched to provision the Kiowa-Comanche Agency, in response to Haworth's desperate pleas for food for the Indians. It now appears evident that the Cheyennes, who were unable to talk most of the Kiowas into war at the Sun Dance a few weeks previous, unwittingly contributed to the later defection of many of the "friendly" Kiowas in August by keeping Haworth's stock of rations at hopelessly low levels.

To Agent Miles it must have seemed that the Cheyennes, who had within a few days struck all around his Darlington Agency, had gone mad with vengeance. Though as devout a Quaker as any, he realized that the situation was out of hand; fearing for his and his employees' lives, he determined to send for troops. The nearest post was Fort Sill, about seventy-five miles to the south, and on the night of July 3 Miles gave a small, fast sorrel horse to Johnny Murphy, a young worker at the agency, and sent him to Fort Sill, where he arrived about daybreak on Independence Day.

Murphy explained their plight to Sill's commander, Lieutenant Colonel John W. "Black Jack" Davidson, who immediately ordered out his M Troop of black 10th Cavalry to march to the Cheyenne-Arapaho Agency. Murphy himself waited for dusk, then made a flying return to Darlington, getting there, exhausted, on the morning of the fifth. His brave ride was for naught, however, because while still at Sill he saw Colonel Davidson receive another stringent plea for troops, this one from Agent Jonathan Richards at Anadarko, saying that a combined Comanche-Kiowa attack on the Wichita Agency seemed inevitable. The Anadarko

Agency was in the Military Department of Texas and was Davidson's immediate responsibility; Darlington, protected ostensibly by
the Department of the Missouri, was not. The colonel had no
choice but to countermand his own orders, sending out a messenger to overtake the M Troop and redirect them to proceed no farther than Anadarko. To Davidson, who in one day received nerv-
ously worded notes for aid from two of the Indian Territory's
agencies for the Plains Indians, while he himself watched over the
third and most unruly, it must indeed have seemed that the whole
frontier had ignited overnight.

When the winded but unharmed Murphy galloped back into
Darlington on the fifth with the sobering news that no help was
coming from Sill, he found that Agent Miles was not there; he had
gone for still more aid. Though troops were garrisoned at Camp
Supply, a hundred miles up the North Canadian, Miles had left
the night before with some agency workers to try to get through to
Caldwell, Kansas, the nearest telegraph station, to summon more
help. On their first day out Miles and his men, riding north-
northeast, came upon the Hennessey wagon train disaster, the
wagonmaster's charred body still chained to a rear wheel of his
wagon, smoldering. The site had been previously discovered by
Ed Mosier, whose ranch was in the area; he had buried the other
three teamsters, but before getting to Hennessey he became frightened by some distant Indians and fled. The Miles party did bury
him, though, and on reaching Caldwell, just across the border,
wired the military for additional troops, and also sent an account
of the situation to the Indian Commissioner.

After stopping in Caldwell, Miles went on to Lawrence to
confer with Superintendent Hoag on the tenth, successfully con-
vincing the even more pacifistic Hoag of the need to unleash
troops on the hostile Cheyennes. Also in Lawrence, however, were
meeting the Executive Committee of the Society of Friends, the
supervisory body of the Quaker Indian administration. Pious and
well-meaning but hopelessly ignorant of the Indian situation, they
condemned Miles for his "warlike" attitude and demanded his res-
ignation. Summarily, Miles defied them, and the Committee had
not the coercive power to force the issue. The same day, July 10,
Miles continued on to Leavenworth to meet with General Pope,
carrying with him a letter from Hoag to Pope asking for army pro-

tection for supply trains. Rations were needed at Sill to keep the Comanches and Kiowas at peace, and the intervening Cheyennes must not be allowed to burn the food. Before returning to Darlington, Miles arranged for a shipment of food to be sent to his own agency; which he estimated should arrive there in twelve days.

The army's reaction was swift, as a strong column moved out from Fort Dodge to the beleaguered Darlington, which Miles had left in the protection of Old Whirlwind, and Pope ordered out three cavalry troops to patrol the length of the Darlington-Wichita road, increased the troop strength at Camp Supply, and stationed more men in the vicinity of Medicine Lodge. These were just stop-gap measures, however. Once word of the new Indian uprising reached the East and its massive scale became apparent, no one in the War Department doubted that a full-scale campaign was the only way to deal with it, notwithstanding the fact that the Indians had caught the army in a state of dangerous unpreparedness: On June 16, 1874, a Congress still reeling from the staggering debts of the Civil War had actually reduced the strength of the standing army of the United States to 2,161 officers and 25,000 enlisted men.

In more historical terms the coming war meant the end of President Grant's five-year-old "peace policy," a realization that the battle-hardened campaigners of the Civil War greeted with nothing less than jubilation. Not only did most of them believe that war was ultimately the only medium in which the Indians could be handled, but it also presented a vast opportunity for promotion. To truly understand the eagerness of some officers for a campaign, it must be realized that the close of the Civil War brought more than peace; it brought wholesale reduction in the size of a huge army, and therefore a wholesale slaughter in the officers' ranks, which saw even major generals reduced to mere colonels, and that coupled with the realization that in peacetime the only avenue to promotion lay in the death, retirement, or promotion of superiors. Given the domineering personalities and insatiable ambitions of most of the hungry young line colonels, and given the fact that in the post-Civil War army there were billets for only eleven general officers (General of the Army Sherman, commanding, Lieutenant General Sheridan, three major generals, and six brigadiers), the often savage competition for the coveted positions seems not only understandable but inevitable.

After the Civil War the territory of the United States was divided for the purpose of military administration into a structural hierarchy of jurisdiction, and it was within this postwar framework that the Red River War was to be prosecuted. The primary units were the Military Divisions, each comprising hundreds of thousands of square miles, each—with the exception of Sheridan's —commanded by a major general. Each Division was segmented into Military Departments, commanded by brigadiers, and within each Department were scattered the various forts, camps, and bivouacs from which the troops would strike. The Indian conflagration on the South Plains was contained wholly within the million-square-mile Military Division of the Missouri, commanded from Chicago, Illinois, by the indomitable Lieutenant General Philip H. Sheridan. Quick-tempered, decisive, every inch a pugilist, "Little Phil" had after the Civil War descended upon New Orleans to rule the Fifth Military District of the conquered South. President Andrew Johnson, attempting to "bind the nation's wounds" as Lincoln would have done, was horrified at Sheridan's boot-heel regime, and in 1869 ordered him to trade commands with the then head of the Missouri Division, Winfield Scott Hancock, whose monumental arrogance and stupidity had two years previously brought about the war that bears his name. The Missouri Division headquarters in Chicago became Sheridan's bailiwick for the next fourteen years, until he succeeded Sherman as General of the Army in 1883.

Of the four Departments within the Division of the Missouri, the war had ignited within two: the Department of the Missouri, containing in all Missouri, Kansas, the northern Indian Territory, Colorado, and New Mexico; and the Department of Texas, consisting of all that state and the southern portion of the Indian Territory.

The Kiowa-Comanche Agency at Fort Sill was by 1874 considered to be within the Department of Texas, Brigadier General Christopher C. Augur commanding from his headquarters at San Antonio. That city, set like a jewel in the verdant Texas Hill Country, amid juniper-forested hills and hardwood river bottoms, harboring one of the largest concentrations in all North America of limestone caverns and gushing crystal springs, seemed far removed indeed from an ugly, dust-caked plains war, but it was the command center for a far-flung network of isolated forts that guarded the Mexican frontier on one side and the wild Indians on the other. The department commander, General Augur, was a thoroughgoing professional, with a countenance almost frightening in severity. Deep-set, penetrating eyes were underscored by heavy, wrinkled bags. The thinness of the white hair on his head was more than recompensed by a woolly mustache that completely hid his mouth, and fantastic, straight-combed flaring sideburns that nearly brushed his epaulettes when he turned his head. Unspectacular in his work but immensely capable, he took orders from his superiors as readily as he gave them to his subordinates. For four years previous to coming to Texas in 1872, Augur had commanded the Department of the Platte, sparring with the mighty Red Cloud and his hordes of Sioux warriors. He seldom took the field himself, but showed great skill in managing campaigns while giving his field commanders enough autonomy to "show their stuff."

The Cheyenne-Arapaho Reservation, on the other hand, by 1874 was defined to be within the Military Department of the Missouri. Augur's counterpart, commanding from Fort Leavenworth, in the northeast corner of Kansas, was Brigadier General John Pope, paunchy, conceited, and never at a loss for words in the verbal duels in which he constantly found himself. On station at Leavenworth for four years, Pope was as touchy and controversial as Augur was stolid and imperturbable. Still mentioned unkindly as the man who lost Second Manassas in 1862, Pope had since then become increasingly belligerent at the merest hint of criticism. Although certainly no coddler of Indians, Pope considered himself an expert on their situation, which more or less he was, by army standards anyway, and at least he saw that the 1874 uprising was not of their own making. It was Pope who had refused troops to rescue the Dodge City buffalo hunters from their plight at Adobe Walls; subsequently he gave his view of the settlement's illegality in his annual report: "A trading post [without] any permit or license from the Indian Bureau, or any other United States authority, was established by some persons doing business in Dodge City, at Adobe Walls, in the Pan-Handle of Texas, and

far beyond the limits of this department, to trade with the
Cheyennes and Arapahoes, and such other Indians as might come
there, but mainly to supply the buffalo hunters, whose continuous
pursuit and wholesale slaughter of the buffalo, both summer and
winter, had driven the great herds down into the Indian Reservations. This trading post sold arms and ammunition, whiskey &c.,
not only to the hunters, but to the Indians. . . . When the
Cheyennes made their attack upon this trading post . . . the proprietors made an application, through the governor of Kansas, not
for the protection of life, but to enable them to keep up their trad-
ing-post and the illicit traffic. . . . As I did not consider it proper
or right to defend such traffic, I declined to send a force for any
such purpose, and the traders, it is understood, left there and
brought back their goods."

Such a stance aroused the unbridled hatred of the buffalo hunters, their business backers, and, of course, the expansionist frontier newspapers, all of whom heaped on him vituperation on a
scale that would have strained the patience of the most temperate
men. "The merchants and business men of Dodge City," wrote J.
T. Marshall for the Kansas *Daily Commonwealth,* "have survived
the anathemas of General Pope, who seems to think they are fit
subjects for total extermination. If the general would take the
trouble to visit the frontier, and become acquainted with the real
facts, he would find that the business men of Dodge, or any other
town, are in no manner responsible for the outbreak. They are
shrewd, go-ahead business men, and the imputations of the general are unwarranted, to say the least."

Articles like this contributed nothing to alleviating Pope's
almost irrational sensitivity to criticism, but they constituted only
one of his problems; from the first few days in which a war strategy was being mapped, Pope found himself in a bad-tempered
squabble with Sheridan which began over he knew not what. On
July 15 Sherman telegraphed some very general instructions to
Sheridan on preparing for the campaign, which Sheridan answered
belligerently, "I coincide with you fully that Gen'l· Pope should
make the sixth (6th) Cavalry take the offensive. I asked him to do
so about a week ago, but he asked further time. He is so taken
with the idea of defense that he does not see the absurdity of using

Cavalry in that way. I will make him use his Cavalry on the offensive. . . ."

Sheridan's wire did a tremendous disservice to General Pope, showing a lack of regard for the department commander's overall situation. Pope's whole southern and western frontier had exploded in his face; he was still reacting to that situation, and his frame of mind was not helped when on July 7, Sherman himself wired him, "The Kiowas and Comanches . . . are reported to have risen and started for the settlements of Kansas," and then authorized him to waylay the 6th Cavalry, then en route to Arizona, and use them as best he could to protect himself. And Sheridan wondered why Pope was thinking defense! Pope's first responsibility was to protect the settlements and keep the roads open, and he had had no time to formulate a general offensive. He was not "taken with the idea of defense"; he saw very well that the only way to defeat the Indians was to pursue the marauders back to their reservations, but when he tried to get Superintendent Hoag's permission to do so, he was refused. Pope, on the one hand refused permission for an offensive operation against the Indians by the Indian Office, and then castigated by his superior officer because he did not do it, even though no official plan or policy had yet been handed down, asked for specific instructions.

Sheridan saw the request for clarification only as a stall for time, however, and when his communications criticizing Pope were leaked and printed prominently in the Kansas newspapers, Pope's patience was ready to break. When Pope complained, though, Sheridan stood firm, and even attacked Pope's refusal to bail out the buffalo hunters at Adobe Walls, writing that regardless of "the character of these men . . . you should have used the troops for the protection of life and property, wherever it might have been."

At this point General Sherman intervened to separate them, and from that time their argument cooled off. Sheridan's fulminations against his department commander were based on confusion, ignorance, and a quick tongue. Actually Pope had been suggesting to Sheridan that the most effective way to defeat the Indians would be a re-enactment of Sheridan's own 1868 "Winter Campaign," when the hostiles could be caught off the reservations in the cold with no grass for their ponies. Somewhere in the confusion that escaped Sheridan, but there was virtually no difference between his view and Pope's, and once this was straightened out, the two generals got on somewhat better.

The actual specifics of the plans of action in commencing the war effort—the real nuts and bolts of the campaign—were those of General Sheridan, and they played heavily on the geography of the Indians' secluded hideouts.

The only two major streams that drain eastward down and off the Staked Plains are the Canadian, with her tributaries, and the Red, with hers. But although the two river systems flow in close proximity to one another, a description of the landscapes through which they course could easily place them on different continents. The headwaters of the Canadian's tributaries, rising in the north of the Staked Plains, are typified by the area of Adobe Walls: grassland, dry but with lush forage and dense gallery forests along the streams, clear springs erupting from gravel banks and hillocks in the river valleys, filling clear pools from which flow the many small creeks of the region. The whole area supported incredible populations of game.

At the latitude of the Canadian, the Low Plains rising slowly from the Gulf of Mexico nearly reach the altitude of the Staked Plains, allowing the Canadian a relatively gentle transition from high country to low. Traveling south, however, the transition between the two becomes more and more abrupt, as the Llano Estacado maintains its altitude over the slowly descending Gulf Plains, until the two regions are separated only by the "Cap Rock," a series of massive rocky buttes and cliffs rearing at times nearly a thousand feet above the low prairies, the bluffs vaulting upward suddenly and breathtakingly to the table-flat Staked Plains. Into this spectacular escarpment the four prongs of the Red River have bitten deeply into the edge of the high plains, their waters periodically transformed from brackish trickles into raging torrents by thunderstorms of awesome intensity, scouring the normally dry washes with walls of grit-laden water. Over the aeons the forks of the Red have eroded massive canyons back into the Cap Rock, revealing rock layers up the sides of red, brown, white, and ochre often hundreds of feet thick, ringing the precipitous walls and treacherous scree slopes. The floodplains of the canyon floors, greened with juniper and mesquite and cottonwood, were yet rough, broken by gravel hills and small buttes composed of material slower to wash away than the surrounding sediments, as well as by rockfalls from the upper walls.

Mightiest of these canyons is the Palo Duro, carved by the Main (Prairie Dog Town Fork) Red River; over a thousand feet deep, the main canyon is ringed by a tortuous series of baffling subsidiary washes, all with treacherous sandstone scree slopes of footing so bad they are comparable only to mountains of marbles. The broken canyons were a nightmarish place to contemplate having a military action, but they were an excellent place to seek refuge. Traditionally it was to the crumbling fastness of the Cap Rock— to Palo Duro and the lesser but still formidable canyons like the Tulé to the south—that the Plains Indians retired when pressed by troops. Now it was Sheridan's strategy that the army should converge on the edge of the Staked Plains from every point of the compass to drive them out: harry them, summer and winter, giving them no time to rest or hunt, burning their villages, capturing their horses, violating their last refuge until the warriors, cold and debilitated, encumbered by their women and children, broke and surrendered to whatever terms the government should offer.

As Sheridan envisioned and the orders were finally issued, five separate expeditions would converge on the desolate place: first, Colonel Nelson A. Miles would strike southward from Fort Dodge with a force of 6th Cavalry and 5th Infantry; second, Major William Redwood Price would stab eastward from Fort Bascom, New Mexico, across the Staked Plains, with his 8th Cavalry; third, Colonel Ranald S. Mackenzie would sweep northward from Fort Concho with his crack 4th Cavalry; fourth, Colonel George P. Buell, would move northwestward from Fort Griffin with his 11th Cavalry; and fifth, battle-seasoned Lieutenant Colonel John W. Davidson would strike westward from Fort Sill with his 10th Cavalry.

The columns were to operate with virtually no restrictions; the boundaries between the two departments, and between the reservations and unrestricted lands, were not to be observed; the Indians were to be ridden down wherever they could be found. Sheridan outlined his plans to Sherman, and left it to the latter to "get as much coverage as you can . . ." with the bureaucrats in Washington. The two generals held identical opinions on Indian policy: Both thought that all Indian affairs should be administered by the War Department; neither sympathized with the peace policy, and they saw the coming war not only as a chance to teach the Indians a final lesson but also as a vindiction of their long-standing convictions.

The long-range policy of the war was worked out finally among General Sherman, War Secretary Belknap, Interior Secretary Delano, and Indian Commissioner Smith. Their package, as mechanically approved by President Grant, provided first for the safety of noncombatant Indians caught in the war zone. Those Indians who were known not to have been raiding, and who also professed their faith to the government, would be enrolled and allowed to intern at their agencies, not to leave, and would escape punishment. They would remain under the care and governance of their agents, but those who had been raiding, and those who failed to enroll and neutralize by a certain date—in fact, all Indians caught outside the designated internment camps—would be subject to attack. The plan also provided that the Indian Office would relinquish control of the unenrolled and therefore hostile Indians to the military, which was already looking about for a suitable fortress in which to imprison the chiefs and ringleaders after the war was ended.

The time span for all the planning was incredibly short: It took only ten days from the time Sheridan sketched his plans for Sherman, to the adoption of an official strategy, but it was important to begin operations before the raiders could slip back into the agencies to pass themselves off as friendly. And when all the necessary orders were issued by July 25, it was indeed official: The United States was at war.

VIII. Internment: The Anadarko Fight

Back at Fort Sill, meanwhile, a second, completely different war was raging, this one between Agent James M. Haworth, desperately struggling to retain control of his Kiowas and Comanches, and the commandant of Fort Sill, Lieutenant Colonel John W. "Black Jack" Davidson, who was pulling out all the stops to have the agent discredited and removed. The two men had assumed their duties at almost exactly the same time—late March 1873—and had conflicted immediately, and in the intervening sixteen months their antipathy toward each other had degenerated into a war of nerves and bureaucratic memoranda, the agent and his superiors complaining of Davidson's lack of co-operation in making the peace policy a success, Davidson stopping short only of criminal slander in his attempts to have Haworth dismissed as incompetent. Through a century of historical commentary Davidson's argument has held sway, thanks largely to promilitary historians like Wilbur Nye, and Haworth's reputation has never recovered. But contemporary letters and documents just do not support that version of the story, in addition to the fact that, as Haworth remained at Fort Sill until 1878 and was later promoted to Superintendent of Indian Schools, his career could not have been the dismal failure that Nye and others depict.

The two men probably could not have gotten along well in the best of circumstances. Haworth was a pacifist, intent upon civilizing the Indians by respecting their human dignity and letting them realize the virtues of the way of life he advocated. Davidson had fought Indians since before the Civil War; he drank, swore, and held to the Sherman-Sheridan persuasion that the peace policy was a mistake, an aberration that General-become-President

Grant had let slip through in a momentary lapse of concentration. Their war had started with Haworth's first official directive: He dismissed the military garrison-bodyguard which the previous agent, Lawrie Tatum, had maintained, and sent them back to the fort, about a mile north. Davidson denounced the act as reckless and suicidal, and made up his mind that, far from being a co-administrator and helpful resource, Haworth was a child with matches—a brainless fool who would be an endless drain on his attention and nerves. The Kiowa chiefs, for their part, thanked their new agent, not only for removing the armed soldiers, whom they regarded as an obvious threat, but also for the gesture of his trust in them, and they set up an all-Indian guard around the agency stores to prevent their being plundered by any other hungry or desperate Indians. Of course, all the Kiowas, even Lone Wolf, were walking on eggs to behave themselves until Satanta and Big Tree were released from prison in Texas, so their smiling protestations of friendship would seem understandably politic if not completely sincere, but the excellent relationship that Haworth established with the crucial peace chiefs—Striking Eagle, Horseback, Asa-toyah-teh, and others—in the first weeks of his administration no doubt helped limit the spread of war when it came a year later.

In January 1874, Haworth and Davidson collided over the issue of "an open bar," which had been operating on the agency grounds with the colonel's blessing and serving liquor to nonmilitary whites like Fort Sill's post interpreter Horace Jones, an exceptionally frequent visitor. Haworth wanted it shut down, charging that drunken white civilians had been stealing from Indians. Davidson called Haworth a liar, but the agent won the battle at least temporarily, as he reported the saloon closed to civilians before the end of the month.

In reporting this and other situations to Indian Commissioner Smith, Cyrus Beede wrote, "Col. Davidson manifests his open hostility to the President's *Indian Policy* by recommending that as an initiatory step in the treatment of these Indians, they receive at the hands of the military 'a good thrashing.'" Davidson's reply to that charge was incredible; he did defend himself, but with no pretense of a denial: "I have many personal friends among the chiefs of both tribes here, but . . . the sooner they receive such a thrashing the better it will be for them."

If Haworth seemed to Davidson a bungling impediment to be swept out of the way, then after this last episode the converse was equally clear to the agent: He now had to protect his Indians not only from buffalo poachers, horse thieves, and food suppliers who continually welched on their contracts, but now also he must shield the Indians from a predatory warmonger lurking within the fort who would sooner exterminate than feed them. Although Haworth stayed out of Davidson's way as much as possible, he refused to budge from the protection of his Indians. "It seems to me from his actions," he wrote angrily of Davidson, "that he is determined to bring about an unpleasant feeling between our respective departments, which I very much regret, but shall throw the responsibility on him. . . . I very much desire to avoid any difficulty or conflict of authority with him, but am not willing to yield the dignity of my department."

As far as the peaceful Indians at the agency themselves were concerned, Haworth never really doubted their loyalty, but neither did they suffer as silently as before. When they came in for rations on June 27 he was moved to report that they yet "made great complaint . . . of the terrible destruction of the buffalo by hunting parties, who are reported to be killing them by the thousands, and leaving the bodies to rot on the plains."

In addition to their hunger, the horse thieves, and their impossible position of having to constantly prove themselves to a skeptical and thankless military, the peace Indians were beset by still another complication to stretch their nerves and test their resolve for peace: They had suddenly to face the threat of raids from the hostile portions of their own tribes. After the Quahadi-sponsored Sun Dance in late May, rumors swept through the camps of the Fort Sill Indians that the hostiles were going to raid the agency and force the Indians there to join the war, after they had killed the leaders of the Comanche peace faction, Horseback of the Nokonis and Isa Havey of the Penatekas.

By the time the fight at Adobe Walls occurred, Davidson was surer than ever that Haworth should be kept in the dark about military plans and actions. When the colonel received an authorization on June 25 to pursue raiding Indians even onto their reservations, Haworth—probably more by design than oversight—was not furnished his customary copy, and was reduced to petitioning Davidson to send him one. The murder of a cowherder on July 13, eleven miles from Sill, paired with news from Darlington that hostile Cheyennes were contemplating a raid on the fort, convinced Davidson that the time had come to take full charge. On July 17 he placed the Fort Sill Kiowas and Comanches under a kind of house arrest, ordering Haworth to concentrate their camps on the far side of Cache Creek, about a mile east of the post, and shortly thereafter banned them from entering the fort except when accompanied by the interpreter. Haworth was at least as enraged at the usurpation of Indian control as he was at the danger it created. The Kiowas in particular were a primitive and superstitious people; they feared enumeration and confinement with a dread that can scarcely be appreciated. Now suddenly they were to be penned up, counted, their names written down, and as if that weren't enough, they were forbidden to see what the soldiers were doing. They thought they were going to be killed.

Moreover, Cache Creek was a poor choice of area to confine the Indians, as there was no grass there to graze the large pony herds. When Lone Wolf had returned from Texas after avenging Tau-ankia, he had camped there. But when he heard that the soldiers wanted to know where he'd been and the agent wanted to see him immediately, he and his camp had bolted for the Keechi Hills; they had left their fires going as a decoy, resulting in a range fire that destroyed the grazing. Another fault with the Cache Creek camp—and one which has escaped latter-day notice—was that the only water supply for the Indians staying there was the creek itself, which was so polluted after its passage through the fort and stables that the post surgeon had issued orders forbidding the soldiers to drink from it. (Incidentally, post commanders had never at any previous time permitted Indians to camp on the stream *above* the fort, as the resulting sewage would have jeopardized the garrison's health). Finally, Cache Creek below Fort Sill panned out into a malarial sump which gave the post its unfavorable reputation for sickness. The Indian camp was on the banks of this sewage-ridden, mosquito-infested sink, but Striking Eagle and his followers moved in obligingly.

When the official orders arrived from Washington on July 26 to enroll and intern those provably peaceful Kiowas, Comanches, and Katakas, Davidson's hand was considerably strengthened, in that it removed Haworth from responsibility for hostile Indians but did not clarify whose word would go in defining who was hostile and who was not. Davidson was quick to claim the prerogative; on the twenty-seventh he assembled the agency Indians and announced to them that Agent Haworth would commence to enroll them on the thirty-first; all the Indians who wanted to be interned would have to be in by August 3, a period of only four days. When Haworth heatedly insisted that in their present frame of mind no registration could be done in that amount of time and furthermore there might be innocent Indians who could not be informed in enough time for them to reach Cache Creek by the deadline, Davidson snapped that it could be done in two days and turned responsibility for the operation over to Captain George K. Sanderson, 11th Infantry, thus removing Haworth from the picture almost entirely. To the two officers it was of utmost importance to seal off the friendly villages at once, because they believed that Haworth was deliberately allowing the Cache Creek camp to become a "City of Refuge," a sanctuary that once the raiding hostiles reached, they were beyond punishment.

Davidson's and Sanderson's criticism of Haworth was not justified; Lone Wolf's flight from the agent should have told them that much. Haworth was aware and concerned that marauders had begun infiltrating the internment camp during the nights, and was doing all he could to stop it. "The camp," he wrote, "though started as I believe in good faith, has in some degree become a city of refuge to those who have been committing depredations." He then notified Striking Eagle and Sun Boy in the most authoritative voice he could that "all such persons must at once leave the camp," lest the whole tribe be punished with them. Subsequently he went even further, telling the Kiowas that only those who interned and stayed out of the war would thereafter be issued rations. It was a gutsy thing to do, considering that when Davidson had assembled the Kiowas and laid down the terms of enrollment, his harshness had come within a hairbreadth of driving even Striking Eagle into the hostile camps. "I thought I loved the white man," scowled the leading peace chief, "but now I am not sure who I love more, the whites, or those of my people not here." Haworth could do no more, short of surrendering the whole of the Kiowa tribe to Davidson's "thrashing."

The colonel, for his part, saw Haworth's plan for rationing only the enrolled Indians as a deliberate attempt to foil him in separating the raiders from the peaceful by luring hostile and friendly alike into the internment camps, using the food as bait. Although some historians maintain that Haworth secretly conspired with Superintendent Enoch Hoag to sneak known raiders, specifically Lone Wolf, into the peace camps, Hoag sent out a blanket directive to Haworth, Miles, and Richards on July 21 ordering, "Agents will cooperate fully with Commanding Officers both to Secure protection of the Innocent & punishment of the Guilty. . . ." Particularly concerning Lone Wolf, Commissioner Smith himself instructed Haworth, "Make no terms with Lone Wolf without previous authority from this Office . . . they must now submit to the authority of the Government, and . . . the Government will no longer consult their notions and superstitions."

With Haworth effectively out of the way, Sanderson began the enrollment on schedule, and encountered no problem in registering the Penateka Comanches, as well as the camps of the Nokoni chief Horseback, and the Yapparika chiefs Cheevers (He Goat) and Quirts Quip (Elk Chewing), though the latter three villages contained only thirty braves and their families. Haworth still protested that too rigorous a prosecution of the enrollment would panic even the most peaceful Kiowas and scatter them beyond the agency's protection; Horseback had come to him one night with the information that the Kiowas' fear had in no way diminished. The Nokoni chief warned him not to try entering their camp to register them—it would not be safe.

Sanderson was to begin the enrollment of the Kiowas the next day, but Haworth, bright enough to realize he had a very large tiger by a very short tail, stayed home, an act no doubt as much of protest as sensibility, but one that led to the charge of cowardice. Sanderson insisted, but when he led his men to the Kiowa camp he quickly realized he had taken his life in his hands. A renegade war party had slipped into the village shortly before he arrived; their ponies were still tied up to fight, and there was excitement over the display of a fresh scalp. At once Sanderson sought out

Striking Eagle to help in the registration, but when the chief obligingly went through the village trying to gather warriors to enroll, they ignored him almost to a man. Sanderson then conveniently loaded the burden of registration on Striking Eagle, telling him to bring the peaceful to the agency on the next day to enroll, and departed the vicinity with all the haste consistent with a calm demeanor to take up the registration of the placid Katakas.

Later, Sanderson agreed with Haworth not to press the Kiowas, understandable enough after his harrowing adventure, and in addition to delaying their enrollment, conceded to them that they would not be required to come in to roll call every day, as was previously planned, but only once each Thursday, when they came in for rations.

The Katakas willingly consented to the internment, and the most reluctant Kiowas finally gave in on the sixth and registered, though they did so only after a show of dissatisfaction bordering on defiance. Sanderson wanted to arrest the old war chief, Woman's Heart, for being "particularly insolent," but thought better of it when Haworth assured him "there would be trouble" if he did. At this time Colonel Davidson received word that Chief Iron Mountain was coming in with his band of thirty-two Yapparika warriors, including three minor chiefs, Yellow Moon, Prairie Fire, and Ho-weah (Clearing in the Woods). When they arrived on the eighth the internment was ended, but Davidson left no doubt that he believed the entire procedure a farce. His often sarcastically worded report of the loyalty of those Indians who interned failed to mention that the genuinely hostile element had shot Ho-weah's horses when he told them he would not fight.

On the eighth Sanderson was able to report for the southern reservation that of all the Indians who were supposed to be there, all the Katakas were present and accounted for, as were nearly all the Kiowas, including, to Davidson's disgust, Satanta, Big Tree, Woman's Heart, and others whom he considered at best marginally sincere. Missing from their ranks, however, were the two camps of Lone Wolf and Maman-ti, and also, curiously, Big Bow. Although Big Bow was present for the registration and Striking Eagle himself had earlier vouched for his good intention, so sure was Davidson of Big Bow's guilt in recent raiding that Davidson specifically forbade Sanderson to enroll him under any circumstances.

For the Comanches, Sanderson had a complete attendance only of Penatekas. All the Kotsotekas and Quahadis were at war; so too were many of the Yapparikas and nearly all of the Nokonis. Prominent absences among the chiefs were Wild Horse and Black Horse (Quahadi), Quanah Parker (Nokoni, but with the Quahadi), Tabananica and his brother-in-law White Wolf (Yapparikas), and Mow-way (Push Aside, the Kotsoteka).

When the spurious enrollment, the purpose of which Friends Hoag and Haworth had, in Davidson's opinion, successfully sabotaged, was completed on the eighth, the colonel knew it was only a matter of time before his "friendly" wolves would shed their sheep's clothing and begin raiding around Fort Sill. On August 19 they struck at Signal Hill, the site of an abandoned observatory and weather station a few miles west of the fort. A small party of civilians was camped inside the empty building, and when early in the morning one of them went down the north slope to fetch water from a small spring, he was met and overcome by three Kiowas— Elktongue, Snakehead, and Afraid of a Bear—with four or five Cheyennes. The very next day a number of Satanta's warriors, Kah-tia-son among them, all certified as friendly, rode out of the Cache Creek camp and after about three miles came upon and killed two more white men, throwing one body in the creek. It was never recovered. In the afternoon, eight miles south of the fort, more Indians killed two cowboys named Steve McKibbon and John Collier, employees of a Texas rancher.

To make matters worse, Davidson had been caught with most of his soldiers away from the fort; they were on patrol down to the Red River. So now, like a baited bear snapping at dogs, he sent out small squads of troopers in all directions, but the Indians invariably stayed one jump ahead of them and slipped away safely. The buffalo soldiers would merely go out, bury the dead, and return empty-handed to Sill.

Several days after the deadline had passed, the Comanche chiefs Isa-nanica (Hears a Wolf), Little Crow, Black Duck, and Big Red Meat, by then listed as hostile, communicated to Davidson that they, too, wished to enroll. Only Isa-nanica was admitted, and then with the proviso that he be disarmed; Davidson turned away all the others, who had allegedly participated in the Battle of Adobe Walls. Hardly outdone, though, Big Red Meat, the conservative Nokoni chief who controlled about sixty lodges, promptly moved his camp about thirty miles north-northeast to the Washita River, to the Wichita Agency at Anadarko, ordering Acting Agent J. Connell to provide rations for his village.

Connell was really an agency clerk filling in for longtime agent Jonathan Richards, who was away temporarily, but it wanted no experience for Connell to realize that he was in an extremely precarious position. Although Richards had enrolled all the friendly tribes of his agency—Pawnees, Delawares, Wichitas, and the six Caddoan tribes—with no mishaps, an ominous specter suddenly appeared in the person of Lone Wolf, still fresh and belligerent from the Lost Valley fight with the Texas Rangers. He was joined, in addition, by virtually all the Kiowas not under the personal sway of Striking Eagle—that is, the neutral and the marginally peaceful—the same ones who, with their certificates of enrollment folded within their clothing, had in the previous two days killed not less than five white men. Connell's problems were increased with the presence as well of a great many hostile Comanches: the Yapparikas of Tabananica and Isa Rosa, Mow-way's Kotsotekas —all had come east after Adobe Walls. Even Wild Horse and his legendary Quahadis had reportedly made a rare descent from the Staked Plains and were now lurking in the vicinity of the Wichita Agency. The arrival of Black Duck, Little Crow, and Big Red Meat, with the latter's hostile Nokonis, was enough to make Connell take stock of his situation from a military standpoint. He found it next to hopeless; the Wichita Agency was so poorly arranged for purposes of defense that about every feature of its layout could only be of benefit to attackers.

Located as it was on a broad flat near a south-turning bend in the Washita River, one man, Thomas Battey, the Quaker schoolteacher to the Kiowas, had praised the setting as "one of the richest and most beautiful valleys of the south-west." The agency's stables, school, and Connell's residence were all backed up against a high bluff north of the stream, rendering them especially vulnerable to attack from the heights. Moreover, the bluff was about a mile from the river, the post's only water supply, heightening the danger of an effective siege. The commissary, on the other hand, was off by itself, near the river, where it could easily by cut off and surrounded. Off to the northwest was the agency sawmill, and agency trader William Shirley's store was on the bluff toward the northeast. The scattered establishments were guarded only by Captain Gaines Lawson's single company of 11th Infantry.

Upon the arrival of Big Red Meat, Connell conferred quickly with Lawson, and they agreed there was only one thing to do: call Davidson to come rescue them. At once Lawson dispatched an orderly, who reached Fort Sill at six in the evening. Davidson received him as he was taking his ease on the veranda of the commandant's quarters, enjoying a drink in his shirt sleeves, just as he might have done in his native Virginia; at ten that night he rode out of Sill leading four companies of the 10th Cavalry for Anadarko. After a forced march of fourteen hours they arrived at the Wichita Agency at midday Saturday, August 22; Indians who lived south of Anadarko raced into the agency with word that Davidson was coming with many troopers, setting off a string of curious events. Up at the sawmill the foreman, a young man named Findlay Ross, suddenly spied Indian women and children scurrying north along the river toward the hills and safety; not long after, one of Lawson's men directed Ross to evacuate the sawmill and get to the agency buildings with his employees. When the colonel rode into the agency two hours later, the hostile chiefs ordered their braves to mount up for a fight.

Saturday was a particularly bad day for an action at Anadarko: It was issue day, and virtually all the friendly tribes had come in to the commissary for their rations. There too were the Penateka Comanches who, though registered at Sill, were still administered by the Wichita Agency (and were, until 1878). Perhaps sensing that the troopers would be hesitant to fire in such close proximity to agency Indians, Big Red Meat had his village camp only a couple of hundred yards from the commissary buildings, his sixty tipis almost mingling with those of the Penateka Comanches. Davidson grudgingly acknowledged the maneuver, noting in his report that the Nokonis had "squatted down under the shield of the Friendly Tribes." On his arrival Davidson summoned the Nokoni chief to his presence and personally delivered his ultimatum: The period of internment had passed. Big Red Meat and his camp were hostile, and now they must surrender to him and let themselves be disarmed and taken to Fort Sill. It took some amount of urging by Penateka chiefs Tosawi and Asa-toyah-teh to get Big Red Meat to give in to Davidson's terms, but the Nokoni chief, who undoubtedly noted the strength of Davidson's force, did submit in the end and agreed to surrender. Davidson thereupon sent forty soldiers under his regimental adjutant, Lieutenant Woodward, to seize their weapons and bring them in, while also sending Captain Lawson and his infantry company to the sawmill to prevent any Indians from escaping northward up the river.

Once in the Nokoni camp, however, Woodward discovered that, although the Indians were willing to give up their guns, they intended to keep their bows and arrows to hunt with, which in fact they had traditionally been allowed to do. Woodward insisted on taking all the weapons, and when the discussion grew unfriendly a messenger was dispatched to Davidson for instructions. Several Kiowas were loitering in the vicinity, and while Woodward and the Comanches were awaiting word from Davidson, the Kiowas started to tease and shame the Comanches. The situation became increasingly tense, and the Kiowas, among them warriors from the bands of Lone Wolf, Satanta, Woman's Heart, Double Vision, Red Otter, and Poor Buffalo (and probably a few of the chiefs themselves), sneered that the Nokonis were women for surrendering to a few buffalo soldiers without any attempt to resist. They should fight like warriors; if the soldiers got the best of them, the Kiowas would join in.

Big Red Meat, his pony's bridle held by troopers to see that he didn't escape, withstood little taunting before he shrieked a war whoop, somersaulted from his horse, and bolted, fleeing afoot toward the brush, the troopers immediately opening fire on him. The Indians later claimed that Big Red Meat had seen an Indian with whom he wished to consult, hailed him with the yell, and ran to meet him. That seems unlikely, since observers said that the chief flagged his blanket at the troopers' horses to startle them, but whatever the case, the Anadarko fight had begun; the Kiowas and Comanches all shot back, opening a brief but furious firefight. Within a few minutes the flat grounds of the agency were hazy from thousands of puffs of powdersmoke but, amazingly, there were no casualties, except for one excited warrior who bruised himself in a fall from his pony.

High atop the bluff, schoolteacher Mrs. John Coyle had been enjoying lunch with agency trader William Shirley and several others, and as the excitement began, the children grabbed field glasses and ran upstairs, affording them a panoramic view of the fracas. Mrs. Coyle and the other women followed upstairs, and for a while the battle provided a pleasant afternoon's diversion. But when the shooting got too close Shirley determined to ride down to the agency to ask for troops to protect his store, a couple of hundred yards west of his residence, and so ordered a black houseboy down to the corrals to fetch his horse. The servant dashed across the front yard, but before he reached the top of the bluff he was, to the spectators' horror, shot and felled just beyond the yard. The Indians who shot him had tried to escape the fight by fleeing up the Washita but, finding their way blocked by Lawson's infantry at the sawmill, were forced to scale the bluffs. They didn't stop to finish the young black, and throughout the day he lay there crying piteously for help. The people in Shirley's house could hear him above the clamor in the valley, but none would risk themselves to pull him to safety.

On hearing the gunshots, and seeing that the main part of the action was taking place in Big Red Meat's village, Lawson left his station at the sawmill and led his men, shooting, out of the timber and toward the camp, as Davidson had directed he should, if a fight started. The Indians, attacked now from two sides, fled to the safety of the cliffs, but immediately reformed and charged back at Lawson. The infantry held firm, however, and when Lawson could report to Davidson that the Nokoni camp was deserted, the colonel formed his cavalry in a line facing the village, ready to ride in and lay it waste. As he started to close on it, though, the Kiowas, who had promised Big Red Meat to help him if he got into trouble, took cover around the post commissary and, much to Davidson's surprise, opened fire on the exposed rear of his line. Almost immediately several horses were hit and two troopers wounded, and the colonel had little time to consider his alternatives—he could see Indians in Tosawi's camp on his right, the woods of the riverbottoms on his left, and now the commissary behind him. For the moment, he was a sitting duck. He and Lawson had cornered Big Red Meat only to be outflanked by the Kiowas, and Davidson had to think fast or be cut to ribbons, yet he could not shoot back without risking the death of any number of agency Indians, all of whom, having come in unsuspecting to draw their Saturday rations, were now running away or diving for cover wherever they could find it.

Seeing movement in the Penateka camp on his right, Davidson wheeled his formation to volley-fire into it. But Big Red Meat's reason for camping next to the Penatekas bore itself out as, with bullets whistling through his camp and ripping through his people's tipis, the friendly old Chief Tosawi, openly exposing himself to the fight, leaped onto a pony and galloped toward the soldiers, imploring, "No shoot there! Him Penateka house; him mighty good friend!"

Therefore, Davidson directed his men to ride for the dark woods of the riverbank, there to dismount and conceal the horses, then come back out afoot after the friendly Indians had all fled or taken cover. Advancing cautiously out of the woods, the cavalry troops suffered another man hit as they drove the Kiowas from the commissary, which the Indians were about to burn down. None of the Kiowas was ready to give up the fight, though, as many of them crossed the Washita and rode downstream about a quarter mile to occupy the large and productive farm of the famous chief of the Delaware Indians, Black Beaver. Davidson pursued and routed them with a charge, but could not capitalize on that, having to race instead back to the agency to protect the people there, when he learned that Kiowas, probably the same ones who had shot Shirley's houseboy, had circled back and were looting and vandalizing the trader's store.

Back at Black Beaver's farm, the chief's son-in-law, E. B. Osborne, along with two men named Ed Barrett and Charlie Lawson, left the safety of the house to go warn several men whom they knew were tending cattle and cutting hay on Delaware Creek, some four miles away. The three men found no one, but before they could regain the house, the Kiowas, who by this time had bullied a few Caddoes into joining them, attacked. Osborne and the others tried to flee on their horses, but as they were about to be overtaken they took cover in a shallow depression and shot back. Osborne's horse was killed, and as he tried to take cover barely managed to turn his horse around before being shot in the back of the head, and slumped dead from his horse.

The Kiowas did not stop to try to rescue his body, but the death of Chee-na-bony thoroughly incensed the Comanches. Many of their war leaders wanted to fall upon the lone company of buffalo soldiers in trenches across the Washita and fight them head on, but at this point one of the senior Wichita chiefs, Buffalo Good, intervened. He said there had been enough fighting; the Kiowas and Comanches had taken many goods and a few scalps, and it was time for them to leave. Some of the war chiefs objected indignantly, but when somebody suggested that the Wichita Agency might be connected to Fort Sill by the mysterious "singing wire" over which messages could be sent, and that more soldiers might at that moment be on the way, all agreed to desert the place —the Kiowas and Comanches up the river, the Wichitas, Caddoes, and the rest down the river.

To cover their getaway the Indians lit extensive grassfires north of the compound, hoping the husky north wind would blow them into the agency and fire the buildings. Davidson foiled them with counterfires, but the Indians made good their escape in the confusion, as Davidson's counterfires raged out of control in the wind and threatened for a while to burn down the agency anyway.

Although Davidson suspected that renegades remained in the close vicinity of the agency for some time, as indeed some of the Comanches may have done, the Kiowas actually rode up the Washita to Poor Buffalo's Cobb Creek camp to decide what to do next. The Anadarko fight was over; six white men had been killed, in addition to Shirley's black houseboy and Davidson reported the injury of four of his men and six horses. Unsure of the Indians' losses, he placed them at fourteen "shot off their horses." The immediate result of the melee was, for the agents, administrative chaos which was the potential ruination of the army's scheme to clear the plains of friendlies before annihilating the hostiles. The minor peace tribes at Anadarko had fled for their lives when the first shots rang out, and now had to be gathered in once more, but in addition, and much more seriously, runners from these tribes carried messages to the Kiowas, Comanches, and Katakas who were encamped under Haworth's protection at Fort Sill, crying breathlessly that the troopers were slaughtering the Indians at

1. Quahadi Comanche camp, 1872; man sitting at left is He Bear, or Bull Bear (Parra-o-coom)

"The buffalo is our money. It is our only resource with which to buy what we need and do not receive from the government. The robes we can prepare and trade. We love them just as the white man does his money. Just as it makes a white man feel to have his money carried away, so it makes us feel to see others killing and stealing our buffaloes, which are our cattle given to us by the Great Father above to provide us meat to eat and means to get things to wear."

2. Columbus Delano, Secretary of the Interior

"In our intercourse with the Indians it must always be borne in mind that we are the most powerful party. . . . We are assuming, and I think with propriety, that our civilization ought to take the place of their barbarous habits. We therefore claim the right to control the soil they occupy, and we assume that it is our duty to coerce them, if necessary, into the adoption and practice of our habits and customs. . . . I would not seriously regret the total disappearance of the buffalo from our western prairies, in its effect upon the Indians, regarding it rather as a means of hastening their sense of dependence upon the products of the soil."

3. Tabananica (Sound of the Sun), a chief of the Yapparika Comanches

"I have kept out on the plains because the whites were bad. Now you come here to do good, you say, and the first thing you want to do is pen us up in a narrow territory. Ugh! I would rather stay out on the plains and eat dung than come in on such conditions."

4. Billy Dixon

5. Bat Masterson

6. Josiah Wright Mooar

7. John Wesley Mooar

"During the fall and winter of 1872 and 1873 there were more hunters in the country than ever before or afterwards. Thus came the high tide of buffalo hunting. More were killed that season than in all subsequent seasons combined. I feel safe in saying that 75,000 buffaloes were killed within sixty or seventy-five miles of Dodge. . . . We had to make hay while the sun shone. . . ."

8. Dead buffalo on the plains, early 1870s

"During this autumn [of 1872], when riding along the north bank of the Arkansas, there was a continuous line of putrescent carcasses, so that the air was rendered pestilential and offensive to the last degree. The hunters had formed a line of camps along the banks of the river, and had shot down the buffalo, night and morning, as they came down to drink."

9. Skinning a buffalo on the Texas Plains, 1874

"[The buffalo hunters] have done more in the past two years . . . to settle the vexed Indian question than the entire regular army has done in the past thirty years. They are destroying the Indians' commissary. . . . Send them powder and lead, if you will; but, for the sake of lasting peace, let them kill, skin, and sell until the buffaloes are exterminated. Then your prairies can be covered with speckled cattle and the festive cowboy, who follows the hunter as a second forerunner of an advanced civilization." *General Philip H. Sheridan, 1875*

10. General John Pope, commanding the Military Department of the Missouri

"A trading post [without] any permit or license from . . . any United States authority, was established by some persons doing business in Dodge City, at Adobe Walls, in the Pan-Handle of Texas, and far beyond the limits of this department . . . mainly to supply the buffalo hunters, whose continuous pursuit and wholesale slaughter of the buffalo . . . had driven the great herds down into the Indian Reservations. . . . When the Cheyennes made their attack upon this trading post . . . the proprietors made an application, through the governor of Kansas, not for the protection of life, but to enable them to keep up their trading post and the illicit traffic. I declined to send a force for any such purpose. . . ."

11. General Philip H. Sheridan, commanding the Military Division of the Missouri

". . . Regardless of the character of these men. . . . You should have used the troops for the protection of life and property, wherever it might have been."

12. Rath Hide Yard, Dodge City, c. 1874; Charlie Rath (inset)

"The merchants and business men of Dodge City have survived the anathemas of General Pope, who seems to think they are fit subjects for total extermination. If the general would take the trouble to visit the frontier, and become acquainted with the real facts, he would find that the business men of Dodge . . . are in no manner responsible for the outbreak. They are shrewd, go-ahead business men, and the imputations of the general are unwarranted, to say the least."

13. Háhki oomah (Little Robe), a chief of the Southern Cheyennes

"Your people make big talk, and sometimes make war, if an Indian kills a white man's ox to keep his wife and children from starving; what do you think my people ought to say when they see their [buffalo] killed by your race when you are not hungry?"

14. Buffalo hunters' camp, Texas Panhandle, 1874

"The Cheyennes all seem in excellent humor and good spirits, except on the encroachment of buffalo hunters—and intimate trouble unless the whites are kept out."

"The Kiowas and Comanches make great complaint . . . of the terrible destruction of the buffalo by hunting parties, who are reported to be killing them by the thousands, and leaving the bodies to rot on the plains. . . ."

15. John D. Miles, Cheyenne-Arapaho Indian Agent

"We now have at this Agency over 500 lodges of Cheyennes and Arapahoes. . . . Our coffee, sugar, & bacon is exhausted, and the beef contractor is *considering whether* he can furnish any more beef. . . . We cannot afford to let these people leave the Agency just at this time. They could not find buffalo nearer than 150 miles, and that in the direction of western Texas, just the place that we do not want them to go. . . . It is *very important* NOW that these people be *fed!*"

16. James M. Haworth, Kiowa-Comanche Indian Agent

"I believe the Indians are peaceably disposed, but the want of something to eat at the very commencement of the raiding season seems to me most suicidal. . . . The shortness of our rations has had a bad effect upon all. I think it a great mistake in the government to allow the Commissaries, at the Agencies of the Wild Indians, to get out of supplies . . . to tell them in the face of an empty Commissary, if you go away I won't feed you, would only have made them laugh."

17. Big Bow, a chief of the Kiowas

"We come in from our camps on issue day, to get our rations, only we find little here. We carry that home, divide around among the people. It is soon gone, and our women and children begin to cry with hunger, and that makes our hearts feel bad. A white man's heart would soon get bad to see his wife and children crying for something to eat, when he had nothing to give them."

18. Enoch Hoag, superintendent of the Indian Territory agencies

"The Indians in the Indian Territory undoubtedly are impelled to these acts of hostility. . . . They should have been more liberally subsisted, and protected from Buffalo hunters—Whiskey Sellers, and Thievish outlaws. . . . designing white men, frequently living amongst them and gaining their confidence . . . are encouraging the depredators, for the purpose of provoking an Indian War, securing possibly to themselves as a result, employment at high salaries as scouts."

19. Little Robe

"On or about March 11, horse thieves from Kansas stole 43 ponies from the herd of Little Robe. . . . The Chiefs are very much provoked and discouraged . . . and express the fear that, should nothing be done . . . and another raid be made upon them, that it will be impossible for them to restrain their young men from making a like raid on the frontier of Kansas."

20. Ado etta (Big Tree), a Kiowa war chief   21. Set-tain-te (Satanta, or White Bear), a leading chief of the Kiowas

"It is a well-known fact that there is a gang of [white] desperadoes . . . who make a regular business of horse stealing and other desperate deeds. . . . passing readily for Indians when it suits their convenience to do so. . . . They [then furnish] telegrams and newspaper paragraphs,—anonymous, of course, but giving the authority of Major or Captain Someone, who has lately arrived from such a place and reports so and so,—giving the details of their own deeds. Sometimes the Indians thus reported on the war-path have been sick in their own lodges, on their own reservation, or running buffalo hundreds of miles from the scene of the reported depredation.

"This has lately been the case with Satanta and Big Tree, whose doings in Texas since their release have furnished hundreds of paragraphs for the newspapers, while to my certain knowledge the latter was at home, sick in his lodge, and the former enjoying—after two years' confinement in prison—the pleasures of the buffalo chase, on territory assigned for the purpose."

22. Téné-angopte (Striking Eagle), a chief of the Kiowas

"I long ago took the white man by the hand; I have never let it go; I have held it with a firm and strong grasp. I have worked hard to bring my people on the white man's road. Sometimes I have been compelled to work with my back towards the white people so that they have not seen my face, and they may have thought I was working against them; but I have worked with one heart and one object. . . . Five years I have striven for this thing."

23. Gui-päh-go (Lone Wolf), principal chief of the Kiowas

"I want peace—have worked hard for it—kept my young men from raiding—followed the instructions Washington gave me to the best of my knowledge and ability. Washington has deceived me—has failed to keep faith with me and my people—has broken his promises. And now there is nothing left but war. I know that war with Washington means the extinction of my people, but we are driven to it. We had rather die than live."

24. Nap-a-wat

. . . a sort of High Priest, or Chief Medicine Man, without whose sanctioning favor [the Kiowas] do not like to go into war."

25. Qua-nah (Fragrance) Parker, a war chief of the Nokoni Co-manches

"That time I was pretty big man, pretty young man and knew how to fight pretty good. I had a friend killed by the Tonkaway on Double Mountain Fork Brazos. That made me feel bad— We grew up together, went to war together. We very sorry [for] that man. Tonkaway kill him, make my heart hot. I want to make it even. . . ."

26. Isa Rosa (White Wolf), a chief of the Yapparika Comanches

"You pretty good fighter Quanah but you not know everything. We think you take pipe first against white buffalo killers. You kill white buffalo hunters, make your heart good— After that you come back, take all the young men, go to war, Texas!"

27. Kobay-o-burra (Wild Horse), after 1874; first chief of the Quahadi Comanches

28. Isa-tai (Wolf Shit), a Quahadi Comanche medicine man

"Isa-tai make big talk that time. He says, 'God tell me we going to kill lots white men—I stop bullets in gun—Bullets not pierce shirts. We kill them all, just like old woman. God told me the truth. . . .' "

Anadarko. The Fort Sill Indians, visions of previous massacres in their minds, stampeded in a body for the prairies—even the Kiowas' champion of peace, Striking Eagle, leaving the Cache Creek haven deserted, and leaving Haworth the job of gathering them in again before Davidson's and the other columns could give them their "thrashing."

Although Striking Eagle and the friendly bands returned to Fort Sill within a few days, there is in retrospect, something unsettlingly medieval about the Anadarko fight, as though the refusal to enroll Big Red Meat and his band was a revival in the purest sense of the concept of "outlawry." Big Red Meat and his men did not want a fight; if they had, they would not have surrendered their guns first, but the deadline for internment had passed, the peaceful gathered in, and the gates slammed shut in the raiders' faces. They had to take their punishment. It has the flavor almost of gladiators being thrust into an arena and the grilles bolted behind them; there was nothing for the Indians to do now but roam the plains, which the army had cleared for action, and wait for the troopers. Now, for the first time, the army felt it had a clear signpost as to precisely whom they were to fight, and as the five strike forces began to form up at Forts Dodge, Bascom, Concho, Griffin, and Sill, no doubt remained in anyone's mind— certainly not the Quaker agents'—that the army meant, as General Sherman put it, to "settle this matter at once."

IX. The Great Dry Time: The Miles Expedition and the Battle of Red River

For the enrollment at the Cheyenne Agency at Darlington, Agent John D. Miles had a much less complicated situation with which to deal: all the Arapahoes were for peace, and almost all the Cheyennes were for war. To protect the agency, the Arapahoes, and the small village of friendly Cheyennes, General Pope detailed Lieutenant Colonel Thomas H. Neill to the premises with a detachment of 6th Cavalry.

Neill's troops, however, were not part of Pope's offensive strategy. The first expedition to form and move against the Indians was the one assembling at Fort Dodge, commanded by one of the most complex and controversial officers in the history of the army, Nelson A. Miles, Colonel of the 5th Infantry and breveted Major General. The youngest of four children born to a poor farm family near Westminster, Massachusetts, in 1839, Nelson Miles had exhibited a military demeanor from early childhood. His family was a martial one from the time ancestor John Myles in 1675 laid down his Bible to fight in King Philip's War, and as the family farm would be inherited by the eldest son, the army seemed the only alternative for the boy Nelson. The family was too poor to finance any higher education for him—West Point was out of the question—so at sixteen Miles traveled to Boston to find work, and wound up clerking in a crockery store. Determined to rise above that level, the youngster attended night school, sat in on lectures at lyceums, and received instruction with some friends from a French veteran in military drill and tactics.

At the outbreak of the Civil War Miles used a thousand dollars he had managed to save, borrowed twenty-five hundred more, and formed a regiment of volunteers, quickly being elected and commissioned a captain. It was here that Miles got his first lesson in political survival: On the eve of the regiment's departure for the South, Miles found his captaincy revoked by the governor of Massachusetts on the grounds that Miles, twenty-one, was too young to command that many troops. Miles was recommissioned a lieutenant, and the captaincy was used to help along a political friend of the governor's. Miles was powerless, possessing utterly no influence to fight the situation. Seething with indignation, Miles throughout the war collected friends—powerful friends; not seeking them for friendship's sake, he assembled them, like an arsenal, for his future advantage.

From his first action in the war Miles astounded his superiors with his iron nerves and ability. He was slightly wounded at Chickahominy and Petersburg, and was nearly killed twice—shot through the throat at Fredericksburg and in the abdomen at Chancellorsville. By the close of the war he was twenty-five years old, a Major General of volunteers.

The glories that Miles won during the war, both by personal risk and by cultivation and cunning use of important friends, helped shape a personality that the country would one day try its best to forget. Miles' never attending West Point was held against him, a fact that he bitterly and vocally resented. Although tall and devastatingly handsome, he was utterly devoid of tact, diplomacy, or even basic social graces. In his vaunting ambition, Miles disparaged almost every other officer in the corps, concentrating on those who stood in the way of the few promotions that were to be had, eventually alienating all but one, another "boy wonder" of the Civil War, Colonel George A. Custer. But still Miles gained connections, not the least of which was a fortunate marriage into the Sherman family, making him the nephew of a United States senator and the General of the Army. On the postwar Indian frontier the only way to win recognition was to kill Indians, and by 1874 Miles had languished nine long years without a command. Once ordered to lead an expedition he left no doubt that he would thrill the nation with feats of bravado rivaling those of his days as a corps commander. He also took pains to insure that the nation would be correctly informed of his exploits, as one of his scouts, J. T. Marshall, was a traveling correspondent for the anti-Indian (and anti-John Pope) Kansas *Daily Commonwealth.* The hyper-sensitive Pope was doubtless not anxious to manage Miles as a field commander, as Miles' reputation was notorious: Miles was brilliant, vain, able, pompous, disrespectful and even jeering of the accomplishments of others (especially superior officers), indisputably brave, self-righteous and consumptively ambitious, the closest thing (Custer excepted) to a European-style martinet in the American army.

Miles was mercilessly critical of Pope for not giving him total command of all the forces in the field, remarking savagedly on what unusual gift Pope possessed to run the war from Leavenworth, five hundred miles away; it was a particularly cruel barb to Pope, who knew Miles held him personally accountable for the failure at Second Manassas and never pretended to respect his Department Commander. From the outset Miles was resolute and determined that his force should be the first to reach the battle zone at the edge of the Staked Plains, and that once there he would assume overall command of the other units that fell within his range, whether or not their commanders agreed. Miles had correctly diagnosed a serious flaw in Sheridan's war scheme, that five separate expeditions would operate simultaneously in the same territory, but with no designated supreme commander. Miles in the simplest terms regarded Davidson as a flop, Price as a fool, and Mackenzie as brash and unstable. As far as Miles' future was concerned, it was particularly important to beat Mackenzie to the fight, as the tough and experienced colonel of the 4th Cavalry was his greatest rival to fill the next opening for a new brigadier. A few days before leaving Dodge, Miles received an outline of Mackenzie's intended movements, and noted with satisfaction, ". . . we will be in the field quite as soon as the troops from that Department."

The Miles command as finally organized consisted of eight troops of 6th Cavalry (A, D, F, G, H, I, L, M) arranged in two battalions, commanded by Major James Biddle and Major C. E. Compton, respectively; four companies of 5th Infantry (C, D, E, I), under command of Captain H. B. Bristol; and an artillery detachment (one Parrot 10-pounder and two 10-barreled Gatlings), under Lieutenant James W. Pope, also of the 5th Infantry.

The force of scouts that accompanied the troops was a ragtag collection of buffalo hunters, newsmen, and friendly Indians. Among the plainsmen were Joe Plummer, who had a personal score to settle with the Indians, and not surprisingly, Billy Dixon and Bat Masterson. A few days before departing, one Thompson McFadden, a veteran scout who had served Carr, Crook, and Sheridan, applied to Miles for a position. McFadden had been off the trail for five years and was out of money; when he offered his services, Miles took him on readily. The colonel had no great regard for buffalo hunters generally, but he needed scouts who knew the country, and the hidemen were eager to volunteer for what most figured to be a few weeks' lark at government expense. As Miles wrote his wife, Mary, "I find no trouble in getting all that class of men I want, and though they are a rough set of individuals they will be valuable for what I want them for." The scouts were issued supplies and horses, and on the ninth of August —the day after his thirty-fifth birthday—Miles held a target practice to test their marksmanship, and appeared pleased when the buffalo hunters steadily spattered targets a thousand yards away. To supplement the seventeen white scouts, twenty Delaware Indians were rounded up from their reservation near Coffeyville, Kansas; their leader, Falling Leaf, was a noted chief then over seventy years of age. To command the whole woolly outfit, Lieutenant Frank D. Baldwin of Miles' own 5th Infantry was imported from his station at Newport Barracks, Kentucky.

The force moved south in a configuration of three columns, to cover as wide a front as possible and prevent any Indians they came across from slipping back behind them. Compton's four cavalry troops and thirty-one of Baldwin's scouts (all the Delawares and eleven plainsmen) were in the van, leaving Dodge on the evening of August 11. Almost at once Baldwin took a dislike to the young cavalry officers of Compton's force. "[They] are not entering into the spirit of the expedition," he wrote in his diary, "and it looks to me as though they merely went along because they were ordered and only intend to do as little as possible. Darn such men —they might as well be left at the rear for they only occupy room. . . ."

The first evening they camped on Crooked Creek at a point called Walkers Timber, twenty-seven miles from Dodge, and during the night two more of Baldwin's scouts, A. J. Martin and

Thompson McFadden, overtook them with dispatches from Colonel Miles, who intended to follow in a couple of days. On the fourteenth, two of Baldwin's Delawares, who were riding at the edge of the columns as flankers and lookouts, stumbled across some buffalo hunters skinning a day's kill; the hidemen shot at them but missed. After the hunters lumbered off with their hides, though, the Delawares returned to butcher a carcass, bringing the meat back to camp. That night the force camped at a spring about a mile and a half north of the Cimarron River, and the next day split into two groups. Major Compton and the bulk of the men, guided by scout David Campbell, continued downstream on the North Canadian to Camp Supply. Baldwin and his scouts, with Lieutenant Austin Henely and eighteen troopers of the 6th Cavalry (a total of fifty-three men), were to go on an extensive scout, upstream on the North Canadian to Palo Duro Creek, thence following the buffalo hunters' trail along the Palo Duro and then overland to Adobe Walls, finally downstream on the Main Canadian as far as the Antelope Hills, where Baldwin would link up again with Colonel Miles.

Miles himself, at the head of the infantry and artillery, set out from Dodge on August 14, largely duplicating Compton's route to Camp Supply, a distance of ninety-seven miles. In the five days it took them to reach this destination they made no contact with hostiles, but the oppressive weather that the men had marked from their rail cars on the journey to Dodge now struck home with a fury. Twelve miles out on their first day they crossed Mulberry Creek, which contained no water, but they did find water in Bluff Creek, twenty-two miles out, and camped. More accurately, it was Miles' setter, Jack, who found the water, and created a stir among the soldiers when they discovered his wet fur. Next day they crossed Bear Creek, also dry, and on the sixteenth they reached the Cimarron and observed its broad, sandy bottom shining in the sun—"dry as a bone," wrote McFadden, although the troops were mystified by the "Red holes," huge, hundred-foot-deep sinkholes fed by alkali springs.

"The season," wrote Miles, "was . . . one of intense heat, the whole . . . portion being parched, blistered, and burnt up in a universal drouth." The men in the columns suffered terribly; of the many pet dogs who had left Dodge, only two (one of them

Miles' Jack) survived to reached Camp Supply. "The heat," continued Miles, "even for the month of August, [was] unusually intense," and to make the ordeal even less bearable, what little vegetation was not withered by the drought was consumed by a plague
of locusts, the progeny of the infamous infestations of 1873.

Through this searing hell the columns advanced, and as Miles
continued on to Camp Supply, the Baldwin group marched to
Adobe Walls in heat no less withering, their nerves frayed by the
knowledge that hostile Indians were watching them steadily every
mile. On the sixteenth the Delaware flankers sighted eleven
renegades in the course of the day's march. The next day the column slogged in the sandy trail through large numbers of buffalo
for twelve and a half hours, reaching Palo Duro Creek at 1:20
P.M. and continuing up it until nearly six o'clock, camping finally
after a day's pull of thirty miles. That night some of the plains-
men-turned-scouts commandeered and herded into camp thirteen
head of cattle; Baldwin consented to the butchering of one for
fresh meat. At ten o'clock a fierce windstorm blew up, nearly
stampeding the horses, and as a telling comment on the avidity
with which the buffalo hunters pursued army life, Baldwin noted
in his diary, "All men turned out except J. H. Plummer and C. E.
Jones who had to be ordered a second time. These 2 men will be
discharged at first opportunity." Some of the men, Baldwin among
them, got sick that night, the result of a surfeit of fresh meat and
of drinking the rancid water of the region.

The Baldwin column reached Adobe Walls the next day after a
grueling trek of fifty miles. "One of the hardest marches I have
ever made with troops," wrote Baldwin, "more especially for want
of water." Signs of Indians were prevalent, and the men were constantly alert for a sudden skirmish, but spring-fed West Adobe
Walls Creek, with its abundant grass and timber, offered a much-
needed and greatly appreciated respite.

The buffalo hunters who stayed at Adobe Walls after the battle
of June 27 to July 1 had constructed some appreciable fortifications. Baldwin also noticed that those hunters who remained had
decapitated the twelve or thirteen dead Indians whose corpses the
other warriors were unable to recover, and spiked the bodiless
heads onto the corral gateposts as decoration. Colonel Miles, certainly no coddler of Indians, later remarked disgustedly that the

incident only bore witness to "the depravity of these men." J. T. Marshall, Miles' scout, newsman, and cheerleader, felt no such disgust. "Twelve Indian heads, minus hair, feathers and other *thum mim,* now adorn the gateposts of the corral," he wrote. "The collection is diversified by the *caput* of a Negro, who was killed among the Indians with a can of yeast powders in his hand. He didn't raise worth a cent after that."

Baldwin had arrived at the Walls just in time to halt a second Indian attack. The hostiles held a numerical advantage, but gave away their presence when they rode down and killed a hunter named Huffman (or Hoffman), who had wandered away from the camp to collect wild plums by the river a few hundred yards away. Billy Dixon and one other man, both unarmed and hiding in the bushes, praying the Indians wouldn't see them, witnessed the incident. This was Dixon's and Masterson's first visit to Adobe Walls since its general abandonment, and earlier in the day as Dixon was looking the place over his dog Fanny, lost since the battle, bounded out of the brush, leading a string of pups.

Within moments of Huffman's death, Lieutenant Henely was leading his company of 6th Cavalry in chase. The Indians were unaware that soldiers had arrived and, declining the fight, set fire to the prairie and retired to the southwest. Baldwin therefore turned his men around and headed downstream on the Canadian, taking with him all the hunters he found at the Walls, as they adamantly refused to stay in the area any longer. The command encountered a small group of hostiles at the mouth of Chicken Creek, but again the Indians, believed to be Cheyennes, chose not to stand and fight, although the scouts believed they wounded one before all could get away. Baldwin continued downriver to link up again with Miles' main force.

Camp Supply, Indian Territory, sat at the junction of the North Canadian River and Wolf Creek. Miles rested his men there but briefly before pressing onward again on the twentieth, upstream on the Wolf, and then toward the southwest along Commission Creek, guided by Ben Clarke, the same man who interviewed Big Bow the previous February. Clarke was an able frontiersman and particularly impressed Miles with his knowledge of the country; also joining the force was Amos Chapman, the twenty-five-year-old post interpreter at Camp Supply. On reaching a point near the

Canadian about twelve miles west of the Antelope Hills, Miles bivouacked to wait for Baldwin to join him, sending up rockets nightly to aid his Chief of Scouts in locating him. The rendezvous was effected on the twenty-fourth, and Baldwin used the opportunity to keep his word in discharging Joe Plummer and C. E. Jones, ditching two others as well and replacing these four with Clarke and Chapman, plus two more hunters from Adobe Walls, Ira G. Wing and I. J. Robinson. As Miles continued south-southwest, Baldwin's scouts swung wide again, to the west, twenty miles upstream on the Washita, south overland to the Sweetwater, thence downstream to rejoin Miles. It was on the Sweetwater that Baldwin struck the trail of a large Indian party; he communicated this information to Miles when the latter reached the Sweetwater on the twenty-seventh. The strike force was moving very rapidly, Miles driving forced marches of twenty-five miles per day across the broken, eroded edge of the Llano Estacado. That they were close on the Indians' tail was certain, as the hostiles continually scorched the prairie in their wake, igniting vast range fires to deprive the cavalry mounts of grazing.

The suffering of the men in the relentless heat, as daily the temperature was measured in excess of 110 degrees, was indescribable. The streams were nearly all dry, and what water they did find in isolated pools in the watercourses was stagnant and so polluted with gypsum, alkali, and salt that it was utterly undrinkable. Deposits of the mineral gypsum blanketed vast areas at the base of the Staked Plains, exposed by the eroding away of the edge of the high country, and all the waterholes were filled with the unpalatable "gyp water," sickening the men who fell headfirst into the slime-covered pools before testing the water. Hoping to make the vile liquid potable they even tried boiling coffee with it, only to find it still too bitter to swallow.

Now Miles quickened the column's pace, as on the twenty-seventh the Indians' trail freshened and grew larger, Baldwin estimating their number at three thousand, probably an exaggeration. On the twenty-eighth they found increasing amounts of abandoned baggage, indicating they were closing the gap, and Miles, leaving two companies of troops to protect the bulk of the supply train, rushed ahead with his army, encumbered only by two ambulances and five ammunition wagons. They covered sixty-five miles in two days, "an . . . incredible accomplishment in such a country."

On the morning of the thirtieth Miles ordered camp struck at four o'clock, an hour earlier than usual. Giving his scouts a two-mile head start, he again took up the chase. The weather this day was no more tolerable than those previous, and as early as half past seven the scouts began to suffer from the heat. Riding first southwest up a rugged cedar ravine, they soon emerged from the broken terrain onto a tableland several miles wide, bordered on the south by the crumbling buttes and escarpments of the Cap Rock. Scout McFadden, riding on the left of the line, suddenly spied a tiny spring bubbling from the base of a cedar tree, only a few yards before the parched sand sucked it back. He leaped from his horse, breathing a prayer of thanks, and fell prone on the ground, drinking (he estimated) about a gallon before he ran out of breath. Only then did he discover, to his horror, it was "more salty than the stream upon which we had camped, with the addition of something bitter as quinine and puckering my mouth like a green persimmon. These bitter springs are a peculiar feature of the country." Almost as an afterthought, he added, "I don't think I've uttered another prayer today."

The Indians' trail, very fresh now, led upward through a narrow cleft in the bluffs, but just as Baldwin's scouts reached it the hostiles, which the men correctly guessed were Cheyennes, ambushed them, laying down a withering curtain of fire from their places of concealment. There were fifty to seventy-five of them at first, probably left to fight a rear-guard action to hold up the pursuit. Though marveling at how well the Indians had hid themselves, Baldwin and his men returned the fire and dug in, as did Falling Leaf's Delaware trackers. Miles later credited that the old chief "exposed himself conspicuously, riding back and forth encouraging his braves."

Soon the cavalry arrived at a gallop; Major Compton's battalion took a position on the right of the scouts, Major Biddle's force of equal strength on the left. When the infantry and Lieutenant Pope's gatling guns and ten-pounder were added to the line, Miles ordered the formation to advance. All the officers, wrote Miles, acted with courage and gallantry; one of them, Captain (later General) Adna Chaffee, exhorted his men with a wry utterance now famous: "FORWARD! If any man is killed I will make him a corporal!" The Cheyennes, evidently surprised that a whole army was being thrown against them, broke, gave ground, and regrouped time after time, following the line of the Cap Rock for over twenty miles, grimly and savagely contesting every foot of what Miles called "the roughest ground that I had until that time seen men fight upon."

Throughout the fight the scouts were in the lead, and Baldwin's greatest problem in controlling them was to prevent them from racing so far ahead of the main command that the Indians could cut them off momentarily and maul them. Miles' casualties were unbelievably light, only one soldier wounded, but one of the Delawares, Young Marten, was injured in an incident that throws a telling sidelight onto Miles' verbose but selective battle reports and later reminiscences. As Scout McFadden noted in his diary, "Myself and the Delaware being the farthest out, [the Cheyennes] aimed to cut us off, but by a quick flank movement, we regained the little band of scouts who had dismounted. . . . They came so close, however, that they hurled a spear at [the Delaware]; but slightly missing its aim, the staff of the spear which was six feet long, knocked him senseless from his horse which they ran against, knocked him completely from his feet. I dismounted and commenced firing into them. . . . My Delaware friend soon scrambled to his feet and looked around in a dazed sort of way, looking for his horse and wondering no doubt how it all happened . . . his wound on the head was slight."

When making his report of the battle to General Pope, Miles noted curtly that "Our loss was very slight, only one Sergeant and one Delaware Indian wounded," but failed to mention why the Delaware was unable to escape. The Cheyennes could have easily killed the scout but spared him, content to seize his horse, which the hostiles later told George Bent was a very scrawny one, as well as his saddle and bridle, which they described as cheap and worn. The White Chief, they said, "ought to be ashamed" for giving his Indian soldiers such miserable nags to carry them to the front of the battle. The implication was, of course, that Miles did not particularly care what happened to the Delawares and was abusing them in their zeal to prove their loyalty to Washington. If Miles

was indeed aware of the facts of the matter, his prolific pen was
curiously dumb on this account.

Throughout the heat of the day the Miles force pursued the Indians across the Main (Prairie Dog Town Fork) Red River,
powder dry in the drought, a red, sandy wasteland a half mile
wide, shimmering in the sun. The only pool of water the men
found was so fouled by alkali and gypsum that no one could drink
it. On crossing the river Miles found burning lodges and more
abandoned utensils, unmistakable signs that the Cheyennes were
fleeing and scattering out onto the Staked Plains. By evening their
chase had brought them to the rugged canyon of Tulé Creek—not
really a stream but a dry wash that contains water only when carrying flood runoff. His soldiers utterly exhausted, Miles here
beheld a ghastly phenomenon he had never before experienced:
Many of his troops, their tongues swelling for want of moisture,
slit open veins in their arms and sucked the blood.

Finally Miles ordered his men to camp and rest, and the next
morning the soldiers climbed out of Tulé Canyon after great labor,
but on reaching the lip of the Staked Plains discovered that the Indian trail split and branched until it became untraceable. The
Cheyennes had vanished, and further pursuit was useless. Abandoning the chase, Miles wrote to Mary, "This is a terrible country
to operate in. I have had every obstacle but intense cold to con-
tend with—heat, dust, sand, canyons, ravines, mountains, bluffs
and a scarcity of water." Later on Miles continued charac-
teristically, "Added to that, I find altogether too many incompetent and inefficient officers who have no interest in their duties."
One exception to that generality was Chief of Scouts Baldwin, who
concurred in Miles' judgment of the other junior officers, and to
whom Miles had taken a great liking. But as to the others, they
were "worse than useless. They had rather gamble and drink at a
post than serve in the field."

Miles was also very nearly out of supplies, and if he ran out of
food here his whole operation would have collapsed. However, a
withdrawal would only have left the Indians in control of that part
of the country, and what was worse, leave them to Mackenzie or
Davidson. Therefore Miles determined to stay where he was, and
ordered his supply train back to Camp Supply to replenish

provisions, banking on the hope that it would return before his troops started slaughtering cavalry horses to prevent starvation. To guard the train from possible Indian attack he sent with it one company of his infantry and a few cavalrymen, under command of Captain Wyllys Lyman, 5th Infantry.

The indecisive fight along the edge of the Cap Rock had cost Miles astonishingly little, one white and two Delawares wounded in all. Scout Marshall wrote the *Daily Commonwealth* that the Cheyennes left twenty-five dead on the field, a wild exaggeration probably put forward for propaganda purposes; the official reports claimed only two or three Indian dead. Later on, General Sheridan, in his annual report to the War Department, summarized the engagement very simply: "Colonel Miles encountered the Indians near the headwaters of the Washita River, and kept up a running fight for several days, the Indians steadily falling back until they reached the hills . . . where they made a bold stand, but were promptly routed, and pursued in a southwesterly direction across Main Red River and out onto the Staked Plains, losing heavily in men, animals, and baggage." Long accepted to be the close of the whole incident, it now appears that this was not the whole story.

It is well worth noticing that, up to this point, all the history of the Battle of Red River is traceable to white, military sources—namely, Miles, Sheridan, Marshall, and McFadden. Even ignoring any ingrained prejudices in their accounts—and that is impossible —it is obvious and apparent that the Indians have not been heard from. In 1876, however, as Wright Mooar was passing through the Indian Territory on his way to Texas, he stopped and obtained an interview with the Cheyenne chief, Whirlwind. Although Old Whirlwind was demonstrably present at Darlington at numerous given times throughout the war, the elderly chief confided, or alternatively, lied, to Mooar that he was with the Indians at the Battle of Red River. Not published, apparently, until 1933, and then in an obscure journal now defunct, Whirlwind's account of the fight agrees exactly with the army's in chronology, but is dead opposite to Sheridan's in conclusion. Whirlwind, scathingly contemptuous of Miles' ability at Indian fighting, commented acidly, "Miles no good. Me lead 'um on long trail, round and round.

Braves make big trail for him to follow, then slip back behind and scalp stragglers and shoot up rear.

[Mooar]: "Where did you lead him?"

"Palo Duro Canyon."

"Where next?"

"Got 'um down in breaks on gyp water. Soldiers got sick. Braves get on bluffs and throw rocks at 'um. Too sick to move." When Mooar asked him why he and his braves didn't kill them, the chief grunted that Washington would only have sent more. Concerning Miles' patriotic, if in this instance ill-advised, habit of thundering artillery salutes to the raising and lowering of the flag at dawn and dusk, Whirlwind's wry comments display Indian humor at its most devastating:

"Sundown, [Miles] shoot 'um big gun—BOOM—tell every Indian for fifty miles where he camp. Every morning shoot 'um big gun—BOOM—tell every Indian fifty miles he still there. Umph. Heap big bull."

The problem of whom to believe in this argument is an interesting problem of historical analysis. Evidence exists for either argument that Whirlwind was or was not present, but there is no denying that most white accounts badly overstate the importance of the engagement; whereas Marshall bragged of the ascertained deaths of twenty-five, the Cheyennes confided to their trusted half-breed interpreter, George Bent, that the only Indian to die was the Comanche guide, Mule Smoking, killed by shrapnel from Pope's ten-pounder. Although their material losses were in fact considerable, the Cheyennes were not defeated by this fight, and Miles, chained to his present position by chronic supply problems, sat fuming and immobile for days, unable to pursue, eventually pulling back to find Lyman and the supply train.

X.   Medicine Water: The Lone Tree Massacre and the German Kidnapings

The primary reason for Miles' moving his force south in staggered segments was to cover as wide a front as possible, forcing the hostile Indians to flee before him. The plan failed: At least one Cheyenne war party slipped through his phalanxes and terrorized the frontier of southwestern Kansas for weeks, and Fort Dodge, stripped to a garrison with its commander, Major C. E. Compton, absent with Miles, could do little to stop them. The Cheyennes were led by a theretofore obscure war chief named Medicine Water—predacious, evidently not a man of great intellect, but a fierce and cunning war leader. With him was his wife, Mochi (Buffalo Calf Woman); a large woman, no more civilized than her husband and no less hard, she bore the singularly honored distinction of being a Warrior Woman, taking full part in Medicine Water's raids, to the adulation of the other Cheyenne women. Medicine Water was her second husband; her first, along with the rest of her family, was killed at Sand Creek ten years before. With these two were one other woman, smaller and more timid and sensitive than Mochi, and a war party of about twenty or twenty-five braves. Mostly they remain unidentified, but one was apparently Yellow Horse, the son of another minor chief, Sand Hill.

Exactly when and how the Cheyennes slipped through Miles' three big columns and widely scattered scouts without even a trail being discovered is not explained. But so sure was the army of the success of its plan that when on the way south, in Meade County, Kansas, just north of the Indian Territory border, a party of government surveyors requested a detachment of troops be left to guard them from possible Indian attack, the commanding officer refused them. Not only had he no authority, he said, but there were no Indians in the area, anyway.

The surveyors were two of a series of eight teams engaged in completing the general public survey of Kansas' public lands. One outfit was led by Captain Oliver Francis Short, forty-one, originally from Ohio but then a resident of Leavenworth. He was among the first surveyors to begin platting the Kansas Territory in the 1850s, and had worked at one time or another in virtually every region of the state. A religious man and abolitionist, his career almost came to an early end a few times at the hands of the proslavery forces during the time (1857–58) he owned and edited a free-state newspaper, the Atchison *Squatter Sovereign*. His wife, Frances, had accompanied him on at least one survey expedition, in 1863, having to ride over sixteen hundred miles, and had always maintained a lively interest in his profession. Short's second in command was Captain Abram Cutler, of Lawrence, who like Short had been active in the frontier military and politics. He had sat in the free-state legislature in Topeka, served in various militia forces, and in 1861 had joined the 10th Kansas Volunteer Infantry.

The second team of surveyors was led by Captain Luther A. Thrasher, forty-one, of Iola, Kansas, originally from Lynchburg, Virginia. During the Civil War he had served in three different Kansas volunteer regiments, becoming an efficient quartermaster. After the war he helped survey some public roads, surviving one Indian attack. A man of many interests, he subsequently organized and accompanied a cattle drive from Texas and served for a time as quartermaster of the 19th Kansas Volunteer Cavalry before retiring to Iola to be principal of the public schools.

With the contracts let on July 8, Short began preparing to get into the field. He departed Lawrence on July 28 for Dodge City, where he was joined on August 4 by his crew: his sons Daniel Truman and Harry C., Captain Cutler, an assistant named Shaw, and several workers, students attending Kansas University. Captain Thrasher and his party joined them soon after, and the whole survey party, twenty-two strong, headed southwest to Meade County, on the Indian Territory border, their goal to measure off nearly two thousand miles of section lines. The expedition established their main camp about six miles south-southwest of the future site of the town of Meade, in a broad vale that contained in the center a spring-fed pond that supported a single giant cottonwood tree, a noted landmark known as the "Lone Tree." The site was ideal: Grazing was good, rocks were abundant for marking cornerstones, and the men sank a well and capped it with a pump, supplying excellent water in the midst of the drought-baked wilderness. The surveyors were aware of the Indian unrest, and decided that, as they would often be widely separated, in case of attack whoever was in trouble would ignite a range fire in the brittle, tinder-dry grass as a distress signal. This plan risked confusion, as natural grass fires were a regular occurrence, but it was the best means available.

By the time the teams were ready to move out, the camp was beset by some personality conflicts, and as it more or less devolved upon Short to smooth things over, he directed his son Harry to remain in camp as referee. Short spent Saturday the twenty-second readying gear for a week's excursion, and wrote a letter to his wife. Sunday he read his Bible and washed clothes. With him on his trip he would take his son Daniel, aged only fourteen; his assistant James Shaw, a fifty-one-year-old farmer; Shaw's son J. Allen, about eighteen; and a couple of Allen's friends from the university, John H. Keuchler, about eighteen, and Cutler's nephew Harry C. Jones, in his early twenties. Some buffalo hunters drifted through the Lone Tree camp on Monday morning, agreeing to mail Short's letter to Frances, and after that three teams, Short's among them, rumbled off to begin work. It was the last time the Short group was seen alive.

About midday the following Wednesday, the twenty-sixth, S. B. Crist, of Captain Thrasher's half of the expedition, spied the Short wagon standing, deserted, near the east bank of Crooked Creek, about three miles from camp. He could see no men, nor any stock moving about. Apprehensive, he told Thrasher, who rounded up three more of his men to ride out with him to investigate. Herding some oxen before them to hitch to the deserted wagon, the heavily armed party came upon the sickening spectacle of a full-blown Indian massacre.

Short and Shaw, their two boys, Harry Jones, and John Keuchler were all dead, laid out in a row on the ground, systematically mutilated. Keuchler's and the two Shaws' skulls were smashed, Jones and the Shorts were scalped, Oliver Short's compass smashed into his forehead. They were still clothed, their pockets pulled inside out in the search for valuables. Their pet dog was dead; the still-hitched oxen had been butchered, their hindquarters carried away for food. Grimly Thrasher's men counted twenty-eight bullet holes in the Short wagon; eight slugs lay in the water barrel.

With careful tracking Thrasher and his men discovered that the attack had begun some 3½ miles to the west; Short and his crew tried to make a run for the main camp, and had gotten this far before the Cheyennes managed to kill the oxen and strand them. The trail was littered with gun shells and gear tossed from the wagon to make more room. His distinctive boot tracks showed that James Shaw was the last one to die.

Cutting loose the dead oxen and rehitching the Short wagon, Thrasher and the others carried the six bodies back to the main camp, wrapped the remains in tent canvas, and buried them about sundown in a single, shallow grave a hundred yards southeast of the Lone Tree landmark. The victims' initials were carved on rude headstones for later identification. The morning after the burial another party of hunters passed through the Lone Tree camp, telling the surveyors that they had seen a band of twenty-five Cheyennes several miles to the west. When the Indians moved on, they left behind the strange gadgets for which they had no use, and thus were recovered Short's chains, gear, and some personal papers. Much later, Daniel Truman Short's horse was recovered from Medicine Water's camp, about one hundred miles west of Camp Supply.

Later in the day, with nerves understandably frayed, an argument broke out between Captain Thrasher, now the ranking officer in the camp, and Captain Cutler, who had been Short's second in command, as to who was to have final authority over the expedition. The very military Thrasher saw a crisis situation in which only one leader could be tolerated; Cutler, who had cosigned Short's contract, firmly claimed control of Short's men. When neither man proved willing to acquiesce, the expedition was canceled and returned to Dodge City.

After the Short massacre Medicine Water and his band ranged generally to the west and north. The actual extent of their depredations on this foray will never be determined, due first to the probability that other, unidentified war parties were working the same territory at about the same time, and second that, just as before the war, many murders committed by whites were deliberately disguised to throw the blame on Indians. In the succeeding weeks, several dozen individual murders were credited to marauding Indians in southwestern Kansas, southeastern Colorado, and northeastern New Mexico, but about the only other incident that can be ascertainably laid to the Medicine Water band occurred on September 11, when they overtook the lone wagon of emigrating pioneer John German.

Originally a Georgia farmer from the Blue Ridge country in the northwestern part of that state, German's move to Colorado was the culmination of ten long years of dreaming and backbreaking labor. Freed from a Union prisoner-of-war camp at the end of the Civil War, he had returned home to find his fertile valley devastated, and so decided to make a new life for himself, his wife Lydia, and their growing number of children. Colorado became the goal when he received a milk-and-honey-type letter from a friend there, stringently urging him to pull up stakes and go, and for five years the Germans saved money from their little farm in Georgia—five years just to buy a wagon and team and some supplies—but once they acquired them they left the Blue Ridge country on April 10, 1870.

The Germans' seven children saw their first locomotive train in Cleveland, Tennessee, but only three weeks after leaving Georgia they ran out of money, in Sparta, Tennessee, and took odd jobs until they could leave again in August. This time they got as far as Howell County, Missouri, where settlers convinced German to stop short of his goal and live there among them. With relatives nearby, German sold his wagon and team for a cabin and 160 malarial acres, their home for 2½ years. Not content with the climate and his family's deteriorating health, John German moved again, working for his uncle in Stone County for four months to get traveling money, and the next leg of their journey took them as far as Elgin County, Kansas, where German and his son Stephen were employed for ten months plowing fields on the Osage Indian Reservation.

By this time the elder children were grown. Rebecca was

twenty, Stephen eighteen, Catherine seventeen, Joanna fifteen, Sophia thirteen, Julia seven, and Adelaide five. They and their mother were understandably tired of the incessant moving, but the elder German would be detained no longer, almost within sight of his goal. Over the rest of the family's protest they departed for Colorado on August 15, 1874. Their plan was to travel northwest until they struck the Union Pacific Railway, and then follow it west indefinitely. At Ellis City, however, some men advised German, because of the drought, to take the stage route up the Smoky Hill River to Fort Wallace, on the Colorado border, because there was no water along the railroad tracks, and the station masters would not sell him any. Accordingly they set out westward on the Smoky Hill Road, and finally on September 10 some travelers coming in the opposite direction informed them, to their joy, that they would reach Fort Wallace, and the Colorado frontier, the following day.

One can only imagine John German's thoughts as they camped that night. To come this far had taken ten grueling years of scrabbling to save every penny, working incessantly, and this time tomorrow they would be in Colorado, and even if not the end of the hard times, it would be the end at least of the uncertainty and the miserable, indefinable dissatisfaction. The sense of relief must have been overpowering. On the morning of the eleventh a heavy dew covered the prairie; getting an early start, Stephen was walking alongside the wagon, carrying one of the family's two ancient muzzle-loaders, their only firearms. It was still early when he noticed some pronghorn nearby and got his father's permission to try to bag one, but he had gone only a short distance on his stalk when a band of about twenty-five Indians suddenly swarmed out of a draw and attacked the Germans, and within a few minutes the crushing irony of their brutal deaths was over. Catherine had been nearby herding the family stock, but when the attack began she ran toward the others to help. "Running towards the waggon," she recalled, "I saw my poor father shot through the back and my mother tomahawked by a big Indian. An old squaw ran up and stuck an axe into my father's head and left it there." The eldest girl, Rebecca, tried to defend herself with an axe, but was soon knocked to the ground, raped, and killed. John, Lydia, Stephen, and Rebecca all fell in the first assault; the younger five daughters were rounded up as captives and watched horrified the scalping of the four bodies. Of her capture, Catherine later remembered, "As the savages neared me an arrow struck my thigh. A big burly Indian jumped off his horse, grabbed me and pulled out the arrow. He kicked me several times; then he put me on his large bay horse."

In the quest for scalps the Cheyennes rippped off the girls' bonnets to judge their hair, and it was fifteen-year-old Joanna who had the longest. "As I remember," recalled Catherine, "Joanna was sitting on a box that had been taken from the back of our wagon. Indians detained her there, while others led us four . . . to the front of the wagon. We heard the report of a rifle, and when we looked again . . . Joanna was dead." After ransacking the wagon for usable goods the Cheyennes set fire to it and quitted the scene, leading Kate, Sophie, Julie, and Addie German into bondage.

Several days later a Fort Wallace scouting party discovered the pathetic site and the charred wagon. In the dirt they found the German family Bible, thrown from the wagon during the looting and spared the flames. The nine names contained in it failed to tally with the five bodies recovered, and the surviving tracks showed pretty clearly what had befallen the four missing girls. For the next many weeks the goal of rescuing them was for the South Plains cavalry a *cause célèbre* that never quite had its equal in any other incident.

During the weeks of their captivity the German sisters were indeed treated with staggering cruelty. Addie and Julie suffered from exposure and malnutrition, but the elder two were even less fortunate—forced into concubinage and even gang raped, given bestial labors to perform, and harassed and abused by the Cheyenne women. Once, recalled Catherine, "I was stripped naked, and painted by the old squaws, and made the wife of the (first) chief who could catch me when fastened upon the back of a horse and set loose on the prairie. I don't know what Indian caught me." Although Catherine managed to establish a sort of empathy with the smaller woman of Medicine Water's band and even occasionally won some small favors from her, the chief's wife Mochi taunted them relentlessly in every small way imaginable: she "seemed delighted to see us tortured or frightened. Once when

I was roasting a piece of liver over the campfire, [she] snatched it from the stick which held it and ate it just before I had finished cooking it."

In time Medicine Water steered his group back to the south, and eventually Catherine and Sophia were separated from their two smaller sisters when the latter were traded to Gray Beard, in whose possession they continued to be neglected and starved, being regarded at best as a potential but unnecessary source of income through ransom. The separation became even wider when Gray Beard led his band down the east side of the Staked Plains, while Medicine Water with some other groups traveled down the west side, possibly crossing at one point or another into eastern New Mexico.

In the final analysis, Medicine Water's depredations in Kansas were allowed to happen because Nelson Miles had left too few men to garrison the forts of the region, taking the huge majority of the available fighting force with him on the campaign. But more fundamentally, Miles had broken one of the most cardinal rules of Indian warfare. When Oliver Short's surveyors asked for a small detachment to guard them, they were refused on the grounds that no Indians could have slipped through Miles' lines. Two days after the Shorts' and the other surveyors' corpses were found, General Augur, commanding the distant Department of Texas, took the trouble to remind his field colonel, Mackenzie, of the importance of the canon, "A commander against hostile Indians is never in such imminent danger as when fully satisfied that no Indians can possibly be near him."

29. Red Moon, a Cheyenne war leader

"My wife writes me back from Wichita that the Indians made a raid on 'Medicine Lodge' in Kans. on the 17th inst killing 3 men. . . . Also one man killed between Fort Dodge and Camp Supply. . . . There is 'no use talking,' *Some of our Indians are on the warpath.* I think they will confine their raids principally upon the Buffalo Hunters. . . ."

30. John B. Jones, Major of the Frontier Battalion of the Texas Rangers

"The Indians ambushed us as we rode into the valley, cutting us off from water, and we had to fall back to a ravine. One of the men, William A. Glass, was slow in following the others to the streambed, and was cut down. The other Rangers thought he was dead and didn't stop for him. We saw two warriors sneaking toward him, darting from one tree to another for cover. Glass regained consciousness and saw them coming for him, and began crawling toward us most piteously. 'My God,' he screamed, 'my God, don't let them get me!' The Rangers in the ravine began shooting at the savages to drive them off."

31. Tsen-tonkee (Hunting Horse), a Kiowa warrior

"We could see the leader of the whites motioning his men to fall back. One of them was slow; Tsen-au-sain shot him. 'I got one,' he shouted. . . . We could see the man lying there in plain sight. The heads of the other Rangers could be seen sticking up from the dry streambed. Nobody dared go close enough to make coup.

"Red Otter called for volunteers. Not a warrior spoke up. I remembered the medicine man's prophecy; it was my chance. I said I would go. He ran forward, behind a large tree. He signaled for me to join him. I ran forward . . . the bullets were throwing bark in our faces. Then we ran to another tree. But the bullets came thicker. Red Otter said it was too dangerous. . . ."

32. Colonel Nelson A. Miles, 5th Infantry

"Colonel Miles encountered the Indians near the headwaters of the Washita River, and kept up a running fight for several days, the Indians steadily falling back until they reached the hills . . . where they made a bold stand, but were promptly routed, and pursued in a southwesterly direction across Main Red River and out onto the Staked Plains, losing heavily in men, animals, and baggage."

33. Minninewah (Whirlwind), a chief of the Cheyennes

"Miles no good. Me lead 'um on long trail, round and round. Braves make big trail for him to follow, then slip back behind and scalp stragglers and shoot up rear. . . . Sundown, [Miles] shoot 'um big gun—BOOM—tell every Indian for fifty miles where he camped. Every morning shoot 'um big gun—BOOM—tell every Indian for fifty miles he still there. Umph. Heap big bull."

34. Tape-day-ah, a Kiowa warrior, wearing otter fur cap of the on-de aristocracy

"The next hill was grassy and had a few low mesquite trees on top. We could see from there without being seen. It was lucky for us that this was so, for there in front of us, about a mile and a half away, was a line of wagons guarded by soldiers! There were twenty or thirty white-topped wagons, each drawn by four mules, coming slowly in single file. . . .

"Sai-au-sain said, '. . . you go back to the village with the news. We will stay here to watch the enemy. Tell the chiefs to bring up a big crowd of warriors.' "

35. Captain Wyllys Lyman, 5th Infantry

36. William F. Schmalsle, scout

"Sir: I have the honor to report that I am corralled by Comanches, two miles north of the Washita, on Gen'l. Miles' trail. . . . I consider it injudicious to attempt to proceed further, in view of the importance of my train. . . . Communication with Gen'l Miles is closed. Scout Schmalsle very properly will not return.

"I have only a small pool of rain water for the men which will dry up today; I have but twelve mounted men.

"I think I may properly ask quick aid. . . ."

37. Lieutenant Frank D. Baldwin, 5th Infantry

"The Indian captive being an undesirable companion, and an encumbrance, the question of disposing of him had to be seriously considered and at once. We concluded that the best thing to do was take him along on foot, so we made the lariat more secure around his neck. . . . We continued downriver until dark swimming the river eleven times, often having to help the horses across with rope, as it was running bankfull. Indian was made to swim . . . with one of us at the other end of the rope about his neck. It was amusing to witness his strenuous efforts to keep the rope as loose as possible and on emerging from the water he would wipe his face and cry out 'Me good Commanche, Me good Commanche.' "

38. Tsen-tain-te (White Horse),
Kiowa

39. Mow-way (Push Aside),
Kotsoteka Comanche

40. Minimic (Eagle Head),
Southern Cheyenne

All Courtesy the Smithsonian Institution

41. Man-yi-ten (Woman's Heart), Kiowa

Kiowa warriors

42. Left to right, Chief Poor Buffalo, Kaw-tom-te, Short Greasy Hair, Silver Horn, and Feather Head

43. Do-hauson the Younger, in war shirt

44. Tau-ankia (Sitting in the Saddle). Lone Wolf's son. Killed December 1873

45. Eonah-pah (Trailing the Enemy)

"As we left the wagon train we heard the sound of gunfire to the southwest. Riding in that direction about three miles below the Washita we found that some of the Kiowas had surrounded a party of five or six white men, several of whom were soldiers. The Indians seemed to be having a lively time. . . ."

46. Upper Palo Duro Canyon, looking southeast toward the Mackenzie battlefield

"Being subject to long periods of excessive heat and drouth, when its surface becomes impermeable to water, and then to sudden and most violent rainstorms, every considerable declivity is seamed and gashed by the floods . . . show[ing] the great washing away of the Staked Plains, which has evidently consumed ages of time. The Red River appears to have cut its course through the dead level plains, making deep and precipitous cañons. . . ."

United States Signal Corps Photo (Brady Collection)

47. Colonel Ranald S. Mackenzie, 4th Cavalry

"Col. Mackenzie struck the Indians on main Red River at mouth of Canon Blanco, on morning of Sept. twenty-eighth (28th) and destroyed five small camps and captured fourteen hundred horses and mules, of which he killed over one thousand. His loss three horses slightly wounded, four dead Indians found on the field—his camp on October first was on Tule Creek. . . ."

48, 49. Catherine German (left) and Sophia German, captives of Medicine Water

"As the savages neared me an arrow struck my thigh. A big burly Indian jumped off his horse, grabbed me and pulled out the arrow. He kicked me several times; then he put me on his large bay horse. . . . The Indians removed our bonnets to see if we had long hair, which would make good scalp locks. My hair was short. As I remember, Joanna was sitting on a box that had been taken from the back of our wagon. Indians detained her there, while others led us four sisters to the front of the wagon. We heard the report of a rifle, and when we looked again . . . Joanna was dead."

50. Adelaide German (left) and Julia German, taken shortly after their rescue from Gray Beard

"Lieut. Baldwin [has] recaptured . . . Addie and Julia German, aged respectively five and seven years. . . . The poor little innocents were nearly naked and in a famishing condition when they were Providentially picked up by the troops. . . . The little creatures had been treated most cruelly by their savage captors and were so weak and emaciated as to be scarcely able to stand on their feet. . . . They are now with Gen. Miles' command and will be tenderly cared for."

51. Medicine Water, a Cheyenne war chief

52. Mochi (Buffalo Calf Woman), wife of Medicine Water

"In view of the terrible crimes charged against 'Medicine Water' I have to request that every effort be put forth to secure his capture.— The information that we get from every source places this man at the head of the twenty-two Cheyennes who murdered the *Short party,* and also the Germaine family."

"The large squaw, whom I called Big Squaw, seemed delighted to see us tortured or frightened. Once when I was roasting a piece of liver over the campfire, Big Squaw snatched it from the stick which held it and ate it just before I had finished cooking it. . . . [This was] the woman who chopped my mother's head open with an ax."

53. Stone Calf, a Cheyenne chief, and his wife

"It has been currently reported in the newspapers . . . that Stone Calf a Cheyenne chief was one of the chiefs who outraged the German girls —It is but justice to him that this statement be corrected. . . . We have the girls' statement clearing him of such charge, And further that he (Stone Calf) was first in advocating their release, and that he has always treat[ed] her kindly."

54. Indian prisoners arrive at Fort Marion

55. Hach-i-vi (Little Chief, Southern Cheyenne), on the way to prison, May 10, 1875

". . . the roofs and walls of every casement are dripping with water, and in places covered with a green scum, while all the cells have a musty, sickening odor. . . . A short time in such confinement will destroy the general health of the prisoners under my charge."

*Courtesy the United States
National Park Service*

**56. Lined up in prison: left to
right, Chief Heap of Birds
(Cheyenne), Hummingbird,
Mountain Bear, unknown, Zo-
tom, Chief White Horse (all
Kiowas)**

Courtesy the Smithsonian Institution

**57. Black Horse, second chief
of the Quahadi Comanches,
poses in Fort Marion**

"This is not a good place to advance them. They are simply objects
of curiosity here. There are no industries worth noting. They can
polish sea beans and Alligator teeth
with professionals, and have earned
. . . over three hundred dollars at it,
but they have glutted the market.
They might learn to make Palm
Hats. . . ."

58. Lieutenant Austin Henely, 6th Cavalry

"I attacked at daylight, on the north fork of Sappa Creek, a party of sixty Cheyennes, which I believe to be some of those who have not been at the agency. I cut off twenty-seven from their ponies, and demanded their surrender. My demand was answered by a volley of rifles, upon which I attacked them, and after a desperate affray they were all killed."

XI. The Anadarko Renegades: The Battle for Lyman's Wagon Train and the Battle of Buffalo Wallow

At the time Medicine Water took the German sisters captive, Colonel Miles was beginning to realize, if he hadn't before, how tenuous was his situation and how easily the Indians could cut off his sorely underprovisioned units and, if not destroy him, at least put him in an extremely embarrassing predicament. Miles had not been able to bully Pope into detailing more men for protecting his rear, and already Miles suspected that the Cheyennes he had been pursuing were circling back behind him. In the first week in September the thing occurred that he feared most and wanted least: A great number of Kiowas, fugitives from the Anadarko fight and the declared prey of Black Jack Davidson's "thrashing," camped on the extreme upper Washita River, chopping Miles' line of supply and communication as surely as if they had severed it with a ceremonial hatchet-pipe.

After the fight and looting at the Wichita Agency, these Kiowas had retired to Poor Buffalo's camp on Cobb Creek to consider their next move. Pressed by the fear that Davidson was in hot pursuit with his buffalo soldiers, they decided to flee at once to the headwaters of Elk Creek, several hours distant to the west, not resting until they reached it safely. They rode all night, up the Washita to where that stream swings to the north, then overland due west, getting to Elk Creek about midmorning on Monday. When they stopped there to rest and eat some jerky, they were caught off guard and drenched by a crackling, booming thunderstorm, the lightning bolts stabbing the ground so nearby that the Indians could smell the acrid burning.

The thunderstorm was a local one and had no effect on the overall drought, which went on unabated. After the squall line blew past the wet, shivering Kiowas rode upstream until they found a buffalo herd in a valley near a small waterfall at the head of the creek. Many of the animals were killed, and enough meat jerked to last some length of time. Still they were nagged by the problem of what to do about peace or war, and finally decided that, if any of them should go back to Fort Sill, they should tell Striking Eagle that they still followed him; they were not going far, and would come back if he wished. Satanta and Big Tree, who had been paroled the previous autumn on the condition that the Kiowas should cease all raiding forever, were with this band. As one old Kiowa later remembered, the message to Striking Eagle "reminded Satanta and Big Tree that they had promised to be good when Washington . . . let them out of prison last year. If they were caught now taking part in an outbreak, it would go hard with them."

While the buffalo were being cut up, the two leading chiefs of the war faction, Maman-ti and Lone Wolf, called a council by the low waterfall to decide once and for all which way to go. Satanta's and Big Tree's conditional paroles were probably already forfeit, but nevertheless they wanted to go back to Fort Sill and stay out of trouble. Maman-ti and Lone Wolf, probably realizing that they needed the other two chiefs' influence to hold their movement together, prevailed upon Big Tree and Satanta to remain, at least for the time being. Before the council reached any decision, Big Bow rode into the camp with news. Having been refused registration papers at Sill during the internment, he left there to go south and west, as he had told Ben Clarke he would do if he did not get satisfaction at Sill. He told the assembled Kiowas that from the head of the White River in Texas north along the Cap Rock he had seen a large number of army scouting parties, and said it would not be good to go there. Instead they would do better to ride back downstream on Elk Creek till they came to a rugged canyon on the east side they knew about, and hide there for a time. Lone Wolf and Maman-ti wanted to ride at once for the edge of the Staked Plains and hide in the canyons along the Cap Rock, their traditional refuge, but they were outvoted. Therefore, leaving behind Maman-ti's seventeen-year-old nephew Botalye, and another young man named Ke-soye-ke (Blue Shield) to guard their rear, and sending two others to scout far to the northwest, the camp struck out south, obliterating their trail as they went with tree branches. The first ford the villages came to was impassable with high water from the recent storm, but the second—and the last one available—was crossed safely. No soldiers were in pursuit, so Botalye and Blue Shield rejoined their people that evening in the canyon downstream.

That night another council was called, to decide what to do next, and when some of the chiefs sided with Big Bow in favor of sitting tight, Maman-ti, insistent on going to the Staked Plains, brought forth his sacred owl and made a prophecy that the Kiowas would be safe if they hid in Palo Duro Canyon, on the Main (Prairie Dog Town Fork) Red River. Whether the Do-ha-te made this convenient prophecy in sincerity or did it deliberately, to get his way, is indeterminable, but it had the effect of escalating his quarrel with Big Bow over what to do into more general terms: a confrontation between one of the Kiowas' most potent medicine man-prophets against the tribe's most notorious scoffer. Big Bow could hold his own against any man, but once Maman-ti's mystic owl entered the picture, Big Bow, whose irreverence for magic had made him more or less a loner among the superstitious Kiowas, lost the argument. The next morning the Kiowas left to go upstream on the North Fork Red and the Sweetwater to west of the head of the Washita, thence overland southwest to Palo Duro Canyon.

Once again Blue Shield and Botalye were left behind to watch over the rear of the village but, seeing no one except a few Mexicans whom they figured were Comancheros, the two young men followed later in the day, coming eventually to where the Kiowas made their camp at a large spring west of the head of the Washita.

The Kiowas of course had no idea of their strategic advantage, that by camping at that particular place at that particular time, they threatened catastrophe to Miles' whole expedition; Miles in fact did not even know they were there—yet. But when the colonel received the dispatch on September 6 advising that a war party of an estimated two hundred Cheyennes had been seen to his rear, he got worried enough about the fate of his supply train, which he had sent back to Camp Supply for provisions, that he decided to send out scouts to locate it and make certain of its safety. Summoning his Chief of Scouts, Lieutenant Baldwin, who had become his most trusted aide, Miles told him of the situation and what had to be done. Baldwin quickly volunteered to go himself, and then "volunteered," army style, scouts Lem Wilson, William F. Schmalsle, and Ira G. Wing, all buffalo hunters, to accompany him. When each man had copies of the dispatches securely tied to his underwear, and the group prepared to set out, an amusingly touching scene developed as one of Baldwin's friends, Captain McDonald, secreted a packet in Baldwin's saddlebag with the advisory, "Frank, enjoy this. It's the last drop in the camp." With that the four men left about eight in the evening for what was, as recorded in Baldwin's diary, one of the most harrowing and dangerous scouts of the war, fraught with more breathcatching narrow escapes from death than most men experience in a lifetime.

Before they were an hour out of camp they saw unmistakable signs that the Indians were trailing them. As day began to break the scouts left the road and picked their way through the broken ravines of the edge of the Cap Rock, at one point wading their horses several hundred yards up a stream and then emerging on bare rock, trying to throw the Indians off, but the ruse failed. After sunrise the scouts hid in an isolated canyon for breakfast, but before their bacon was cooked, one of the men standing lookout yelled, "They are coming!" Baldwin claimed that two Indians were killed in the firefight, one of the corpses rolling to within twenty feet of the tiny cookfire, "too dead to partake of our abandoned breakfast, as we all remarked at the moment." Escaping with only the loss of the pack horse, the four men decided that rather than fleeing up or down the canyon and still be prey to ambush, they should scramble straight up the ravine slope, banking that once they gained the level of the Staked Plains, where hostile movements could be seen at a great distance, their superior marksmanship would keep the Indians at a respectful distance. They estimated the number of renegades on the ravine wall at twenty, whom they were obliged to charge straight through, revolvers blazing. Their nerve in this maneuver took the Indians somewhat aback, giving Baldwin and his scouts a badly needed head start, but the hostiles maintained a sort of moving siege, feinting and attacking frequently over the next five hours, until it began to rain.

The rain on September 7, which had begun intermittently a couple of days before, was significant, because the oppressive drought, which had dominated the weather for three months, was beginning to break all over the South Plains before a violent succession of overwhelming thunderstorms and northers, and whereas the drought and locusts had severely afflicted the plant cover, the gullywashing rainstorms quickly turned vast expanses of the sun-baked ground into impassable mire. This rain continued, heavy and soaking, all that day and through the night, but Baldwin and his scouts dared not stop again. Their horses had not eaten since leaving Miles' camp and were badly exhausted, so to spare them for an emergency, the group dismounted and sloshed through the mud on foot. A couple of hours after daylight on September 8, Lem Wilson, who had been leading about fifty yards in front, suddenly signaled the others to stop. Wilson had seen a loose pony in a ravine they were about to cross, and needed to investigate. Crawling in the mud up to the rim of the wash, he peered over the edge and saw a small group of hostiles huddled in the draw from the storm. Giving the Indians a wide berth, they reached Gageby Creek about noon. Out of danger for the moment, Ira Wing shot a buffalo, part of which they ate raw after soaking it in Baldwin's whiskey, not risking the discovery of another cookfire.

The horses got in several hours' grazing while the exhausted men rested, and the next day as they approached the divide between the Washita and Gageby Creek, they saw far away a large camp, undoubtedly the supply laden train that Captain Lyman was guarding. The scouts kept out of sight in the draws as they neared it, in case there should be any Indians between it and themselves, finally riding out onto a ridge overlooking the encampment only when they were practically upon it. Then suddenly they realized, to their unutterable horror, that it was not Lyman's train at all. It was a large village of renegade Indians; the scouts had from miles distant mistaken the tipis for the army's similarly conical field tents. Breathlessly backing out of sight, the four men turned and retreated downriver, which they figured would lead them safely around the southeast end of the camp, but before long they encountered a mounted Indian at the head of a small side ravine. Unable to shoot him because the noise would alert the nearby camp, the scouts trained their guns on him, and he surrendered quietly. Casting a rope about their prisoner's neck, Baldwin and the others tied him to his saddle, discovering in the process that he was not an Indian but white; he had fair skin and bright red hair.

The white Indian was Tehan (Tehanna, or Texan), captured as a boy and named for the place of his origin. He had been adopted into the Kiowa tribe and showed promise of becoming a skilled fighter, and was, in fact, the foster son of the owl prophet Mamanti. Although Tehan did not tell the scouts of his high station and pretended to welcome his "rescue," the whites did not trust him and continued to treat him exactly as they would any other captured Indian.

Baldwin's men continued down the ravine, believing it would lead them away from the hostile camp, but to their surprise it snaked around and emptied directly into the Kiowa village. It had been raining heavily again for some hours with intermittent hail, chilling the scouts who had lost their warmer clothing either on the dead pack horse or elsewhere along the trail. Protected from the elements only by their blankets, which they had tied around their waists and thrown over their heads, the disheveled whites were scarcely recognizable in the storm. They had doubtless been seen by somebody in the village anyway, so the only thing to do was suck in their breath and trot straight through the renegade encampment as though they were themselves Indians and nothing were wrong. Luckily the village was practically deserted, as they saw only two Indian women, chopping wood; nevertheless, two of them kept their concealed revolvers trained on the captive to deter him from attempting an escape.

Successfully clearing the camp, the scouts continued downriver, not daring to get out of the meager growth of bottom timber, confining their movements to narrow game trails, which time and again crossed the flooding stream. After fording the river the first time, Ira Wing's horse fell from exhaustion; they were still too near the village to shoot it so, forcing the white Indian captive from his pony, which Wing then mounted, they made Tehan kill the floundering animal with a hatchet and then, the rope still secure around Tehan's throat, dragged him along behind. Baldwin's own recollection of the incident does not, sadly, reflect creditably upon an otherwise highly praised officer: "The Indian captive being an undesirable companion, and an encumbrance, the question of disposing of him had to be seriously considered and at once. We concluded that the best thing to do was take him along on foot. . . . River was running bankfull. We continued downriver until dark swimming the river eleven times, often having to help the horses across with rope. Indian was made to swim and by no unusual merciful efforts, assisted by one of us at other end of rope about his neck. It was amusing to witness his strenuous efforts to keep the rope as loose as possible and on emerging from the water he would wipe his face and cry out 'Me good Commanche,' 'Me good Commanche.' "

Before long they crossed the Camp Supply trail and, continuing up it, finally reached Lyman's wagon train very late in the night of September 9, or the wee hours of September 10. Through a system of couriers Miles had arranged for another caravan to move south from Camp Supply to meet Lyman's thirty-six wagons on the Canadian and transfer supplies there, the rendezvous to take place on September 5. Lyman reached the place on time, but when he found no train from Camp Supply waiting for him, he sent a six-man detachment to go there to find out what happened. Lyman himself continued slowly north on the trail, and on the next day one of the civilian wagon teamsters, a man named Moore, who had gone hunting, was killed and scalped by Indians, evidence enough that Miles was not sweeping the hostiles before him like a broom. Finally taking on the load of supplies, Lyman formed his single infantry company on either side of the train and his dozen or so cavalry fanning out in front, and began his return march. The drought-breaking storms that lashed the plains also hampered his movements, but for two days, at least, no Indian attacks occurred, although a couple of hostile scouts were observed, overlooking the three dozen wagons from far in the distance.

Baldwin rested only briefly at the wagon train, soon continuing on with his dispatches to Camp Supply, accompanied by two of his scouts, Ira Wing and Lem Wilson. Baldwin left scout Schmalsle in Lyman's train to report back to Colonel Miles, as well as the red-haired white Indian captive, whom Baldwin believed Miles would wish to interrogate.

Long before this time, however, the Kiowas had noticed Tehan's absence. He had originally left the village to search for some lost stock, and when he did not return in a reasonable time several warriors mounted to look for him, among them his foster cousin Botalye. About ten miles from the camp Botalye encountered another group of searchers, who told him Tehan's trail disappeared in the midst of the tracks of shod horses; there was no doubt he had been captured, and they had abandoned the search. Botalye refused to give up on his cousin, however, and riding on, he soon caught up with two more Kiowas, who instructed him enigmatically to ride on to the next rise and look around. Later he accused that they had seen something dangerous, and wanted him to do the dirty work of finding out what it was; but not understanding at the time, he did their bidding, being joined before he reached it by two other Kiowas, who accompanied him up the hill. Botalye years afterward related the sight from the top:

"The next hill was grassy and had a few low mesquite trees on top. We could see from there without being seen. It was lucky for us that this was so, for there in front of us, about a mile and a half away, was a line of wagons guarded by soldiers! There were twenty or thirty white-topped wagons, each drawn by four mules, coming slowly in single file, preceded by ten to fifteen cavalrymen spread out ahead. About twenty-five walk-soldiers were marching in a single file on either side of the wagons. In the morning light we could plainly see the blue of their uniforms.

"Sai-au-sain said, 'Botalye, you go back to the village with the news. We will stay here and watch the enemy. Tell the chiefs to bring up a big crowd of warriors.' "

Botalye did so, discovering that the village had pulled up stakes and was moving. His news so excited the camp that one of the chiefs (accounts differ whether it was Maman-ti or Poor Buffalo) sternly ordered the women, who had begun whooping to encourage the warriors, to be silent or they would cause some of their deaths. Very quickly all the proper medicine was made to go into battle; Maman-ti inflated his owl to make a prophecy, inviting the spectators to bring gifts to the magic bird to ensure a successful raid. This was after all the way medicine men made their living, and everyone, with the exception of the disbeliever Big Bow and some of his followers, contributed.

By eight in the morning the large war party had surrounded the wagon train, and began firing at long range. The dozen cavalrymen were kept busy chasing small clusters of hostiles away from the train, and its forward progress continued for about twelve miles, until it reached the steep ravine of Gageby Creek, not far above its mouth on the Washita. Lyman successfully forded Gageby, but just as he emerged at about two in the afternoon the hostiles suddenly acted concertedly and rushed him from all directions. He formed his wagons as quickly as he could into a protective corral, but in the first assault the Indians very nearly breached his defenses, and for a time the fight was very close indeed. An experienced infantry sergeant named DeArmond was shot and instantly killed, and the officer who was outranked only by Lyman himself, Lieutenant Granville Lewis, was severely wounded when shot through the left knee, and it was feared he would die of shock. A civilian wagon master named Sandford was mortally wounded while lugging ammunition to the cavalrymen in the van.

The infantry and cavalry held their lines, however, and the Kiowas and Comanches settled down to their usual strategy of laying siege. Previously they had been cutting all kinds of capers, yelling insults at the soldiers, showing off their feats of horsemanship for the troopers and for themselves. Younger warriors who still needed to prove their bravery made daring individual charges at the wagons, to the whooping acclaim of the others. One almost suspects that they realized their raiding days were coming to a close, and were making the most of the opportunity to enjoy themselves at the bluecoats' expense. "The excitement," recalled Botalye later, "was grand."

When the fighting fell off about sundown, Lyman had the infantry dig protective rifle pits, ringing the train with them, and curiously, the Indians did the same thing, to be able to snipe at the train at their leisure. Clearly, Lyman was going nowhere for some time. It had not been raining during the day, and with the train cut off from the streams, the men's water began to run low, bringing on some amount of suffering from thirst. With night to cover them, though, a small party ventured outside the perimeter to reach a waterhole about a quarter mile away. The captive Tehan, who had evidently been ingratiating himself to his rescuers, offered to help get the water, but once out from under the watch of the troops, he scurried off into the night and was never seen again. Tehan returned to his Kiowas, wearing an outfit of new clothes that the soldiers had given him, and advised them the bluecoats had very little water, and they should maintain their siege.

Their vigil over the wagon train lasted all the next day; the hostiles cut off the waterhole, intently driving back all attempts to reach it. Lyman had no doctor in his company, and the wounded were beginning to lapse into a dangerous condition. The only thing left to do was try to slip a messenger through to Camp Supply to send help. Hastily Lyman scribbled a message to Lieutenant Colonel W. H. Lewis, commandant at Camp Supply; the note was brief and understandably a little disjointed, but rather elegantly phrased, considering the hair-raising danger in which Lyman found himself:

> In the field near Washita River
> 3 o'clock, P.M., Sept. 10th, 1874

Commanding Officer
Camp Supply

Sir:

I have the honor to report that I am corralled by Comanches, two miles north of the Washita, on Gen'l. Miles' trail. We have been engaged since yesterday morning, having moved since first firing, about 12 miles. I consider it injudicious to attempt to proceed further, in view of the importance of my train, and the broken ground ahead. It was nearly stampeded yesterday. Communication with Gen'l. Miles is closed. My scout very properly will not return.

Lt. Lewis is dangerously wounded through the knee and I think he will die if he has no medical assistance. The Assistant Wagoner McCoy is mortally wounded, I fear. Sergeant DeArmon, Co. I, 5th Infantry is killed, a dozen mules disabled.

I think I may properly ask quick aid especially for Lieut. Lewis, a most valuable officer. I have only a small pool of rain water for the men which will dry up today.

I estimate the number of Indians vaguely at several hundred (as Lieut. Baldwin did), whom we have punished somewhat.

Scout Marshall, who left Camp Supply, I am told, has not reached me.

I have but twelve mounted men—West made a pretty charge with them yesterday.

> Very respectfully
> Your obedient servant,
> (s) *W. Lyman*
> Capt. 5th Infantry
> Commdg. Train Guard

There remains some unresolved confusion on the dates involved —those in Lyman's correspondence, for instance, do not match those in Baldwin's diary, but however confusing, the discrepancies do not appear to be of critical importance. The message was entrusted to scout Schmalsle, who was one of the less prominent buffalo hunters turned scouts, and evidently not held in the highest regard by the others. He was a small man, though, and when put on a fast horse, he stood the best chance of getting through. Having volunteered for the mission, he left after dark on what was probably the night of the eleventh, and only barely got away with his life. The Indians saw him trying to sneak through and gave chase, and at one juncture Schmalsle's horse stumbled in what must have been a prairie dog hole. Schmalsle managed to stay in the saddle, though he lost his rifle. With the Indians hard upon him he raced into the middle of a large buffalo herd, stampeding them, and that succeeded in throwing the Indians off the trail, but Lyman and his men had no idea whether he survived until he reached them again on the fourteenth, with a relief column from Camp Supply.

The day after Schmalsle left, September 12, the Indians saw signs that a great many soldiers were in the very near vicinity, and the warriors were beginning to worry for the safety of their nearby families. Therefore they began to drift away from Lyman's train, except Botalye, who in an often-related episode set out to prove his bravery. Still too young to be respected as a warrior, he was also half Mexican, and therefore the object of some upper-class discrimination. Determined to establish himself, Botalye mounted his pony and, against the chiefs' warnings, slung himself over on the horse's side and charged straight through Lyman's line of trenches, shot up the camp, and raced back to the other Indians. The chiefs praised his bravery but advised him not to try such a stunt again. In response Botalye repeated his death-defying maneuver, and when again he returned unscathed, the chiefs repeated their warnings: He had proven his prowess to all; there was no need to get killed for nothing. Heedless, Botalye charged the wagon train a third time and then still a fourth. The soldiers' bullets hit his saddle, ripped through his robe, even clipped the feathers from his hair, but he was completely unharmed, and the others were struck dumb by his audacity, incredible even for an Indian. Satanta praised him, "I could not have done it myself. No one ever came back from four charges." Botalye's chief, Poor Buffalo, in a sort of field promotion, commemorated his bravery by bestowing on him a new name: Eadle-tau-hain, which means, literally, "He Would Not Listen to Them."

Two days after sending out Baldwin and his small detachment of scouts, Miles entrusted yet another bundle of dispatches to a different group, consisting of scouts Billy Dixon and Amos Chapman, the half-breed interpreter of Camp Supply, and four regulars of the 6th Cavalry. Impressing upon them that the messages were of importance, Miles offered them as large an escort as they wished, but the scouts believed that their number should be kept to a minimum, and no additional troops were assigned. Traveling usually under cover of darkness, they made it safely as far as the divide between Gageby Creek and the Washita River, but there, just about sunrise, they topped a slight rise in the landscape and found themselves confrontedly staring directly at a very large party of over a hundred Kiowas and Comanches who had grown tired and discouraged with the action at the wagon train and were retiring to the south to secure the safety of their nearby families.

Sensing prey much easier to bring down than that just abandoned, the Indians quickly split and thinned out, completely encircling Dixon and the others, stranding them with not so much as a bush for cover. The couriers dismounted to make themselves less conspicuous, preparing to make the best fight of it they could. One private was given all the horses' reins to hold, but within moments he was shot in the lungs; dropping his gun, he crumpled in his tracks and lay motionless. With the horses uncontrolled the Indians found no difficulty in stampeding them, gaining possession at the same time of the messengers' spare clothing. The lack of horses left the whites utterly vulnerable, crouching on the ground, depending only upon their marksmanship (and Dixon's, at least, was formidable) to keep the Kiowas and Comanches at a distance. Dixon himself was so far untouched, to his lifelong amazement, especially since his bloused cashmere shirt was laced through with bulletholes.

If the war party had closed in the first moments the six scouts could have been finished off with ease, but at some cost to themselves, and that they did not do so suggests that this fight—like Botalye's breathtaking dashes past Lyman's firing lines—was at least as much a quest for coups and honor as it was a case of the enraged Indians venting their fury on the enemy. And an attempt at coup did not count if the Indian were injured. Dixon theorized that the hostiles had merely decided to have a little fun with them before taking their scalps: "The Indians seemed to feel [so] absolutely sure of getting us . . . that they delayed riding us down and killing us at once, which they could easily have done, and prolonged the early stages of the fight merely to satisfy their desire to toy with an enemy at bay, as a cat would play with a mouse before taking its life."

Dixon's assessment appears to be not far from the truth of the matter, as Botalye, who had been among the last to leave the wagon train fight, later remembered, "As we left the wagon train we heard the sound of gunfire to the southwest. Riding in that direction about three miles below the Washita we found that some of the Kiowas had surrounded a party of five or six white men, several of whom were soldiers. The Indians seemed to be having a lively time, and one of them, a young fellow named Pay-kee, had had his horse shot from under him."

It was obvious from the start that the men could not last much longer exposed as they were in the open. When about four hours after first firing Amos Chapman was finally hit, shattering his left knee, Dixon was the only uninjured man left in the party, and he determined to make use of what scant cover there was. Some distance away lay a buffalo wallow, a shallow depression in the plain that the bison had scooped out to a diameter of about ten feet which, when filled with rainwater, furnished a mudbath to the animals. The sandy soil had absorbed the previous rains, leaving the wallow dry; it was the only possibility of cover within sight, so Dixon dashed a zigzag course for it, the bullets kicking up dirt around him, and reached it safely. At his call three of the others reached it also, and immediately began deepening it with their knives, throwing up sandy breastworks as fast as they could. The two men still out were the private who had been shot first and was believed dead, and Chapman, who was crippled. Amos Chapman knew many of his assailants personally, and his frame of mind was not improved as, holding his useless and painful leg, he heard some of the Indians taunting, "Amos? Amos! We got you now, Amos!" Those in the wallow were not aware of the nature of Chapman's wound, but when he called to them that his leg was broken, Billy Dixon sprinted out to rescue him, only to be driven back repeatedly. When Dixon finally reached him he picked him up, piggyback, girdling Chapman's legs around his own body, laying the shattered limb across the good one, and carried him to the wallow safely.

During this time there was activity on the Indians' side of the fight as well. During the hottest part of the fray a messenger arrived from Striking Eagle by the name of Kop'e-to-hau (Mountain Bluff). Before making the decision to move to Palo Duro Canyon, this band of Kiowas (with the exceptions of Lone Wolf's and Maman-ti's camps) had sent word to Striking Eagle that they would come in at his call, and now the peace chief commanded their return. The Indians who had surrounded the buffalo wallow tried to get the envoy to take the white flag and piece of paper guaranteeing safe passage he had brought and show them to the troopers who, the Indians feared, were closing the gap from the wagon train. But Mountain Bluff, a middle-aged Mexican who had been adopted into the tribe, succumbed to the excitement; he "wanted to smell some powder first."

"We worked hard with him," recalled Botalye, "but finally had to let him join the fight."

By three in the afternoon the white scouts had been pinned down in the heat, without water, for about nine hours, and were suffering intensely from thirst. But by midafternoon the legendarily fickle plains weather was coming to their rescue, as they saw a violent squall line off in the west, with rain pouring from the bottom of the lightning-sheeted black clouds. When the storm reached them it quickly deposited a couple of inches of water in the bottom of the hole, which, though tainted with mud as well as blood from their wounds, the men were grateful to drink. However, Dixon and his companions soon realized that they had traded one form of misery for another: With their protective heavy clothing lost with the horses, they lay in their mudhole and shivered in the merciless cold of the norther. Later Dixon recalled how, with the loss of his coat, he lost also the only picture he had of his mother, which he had kept in one of the pockets. With the advent of the inclement weather the pressure from the Indians let up noticeably, a fact that has been used as evidence that the warriors, out principally for a lark, would break off a fight merely because the weather became unpleasant. While that is probably true in some degree, it was not entirely the case here, as many of the Kiowas and Comanches were turning their attention to still another target.

Major William Redwood Price had marched east from Fort Bascom, New Mexico, on August 28; he sent his supply train with one cavalry troop under Lieutenant H. J. Farnsworth on a course almost due east, while he with the other three 8th Cavalry companies headed east, and after an uneventful march of ten days crossed Miles' southgoing trail on the sixth of September. When he finally rendezvoused with Miles the next day, the colonel promptly turned him around and sent him northeast, to try to locate his and Price's own supply trains. As Price approached the Washita from the south on the morning of the twelfth he was swept by a soaking rainstorm, and when it cleared about midday, Price beheld a long column of mounted figures, which he thought to be a troop column, moving right to left, westward, across his front.

On discovering they were not soldiers but hostile Indians, Price at once set about attacking them, and of all the clashes of the Red River War this one was somewhat unique in its balance. Price's three companies numbered 110 men, roughly equal to the number of Indians involved. That the Plains Indians would fight in the middle of the day against a force of mounted cavalry of at least their own strength was highly irregular, but they did it for the same reason they had begun to pull away from the wagon train fight. Their families were nearby and, in view of the large numbers of white soldiers in the countryside, in constant danger; the Indians had been trying to get away. When the combined force of Kiowas and Comanches lined up on the afternoon of September 12 to fight Price, their women and children were scurrying away, barely beyond earshot of the gunfire, struggling to lug the heavy lodgepoles and camp equipment across the rapidly deepening streams. Price would have to be held up until they were safe.

Price had with him one mountain howitzer, which was useless because the ammunition had gotten waterlogged in the rainstorm, and the horses that pulled the caisson through the mud were about to drop from exhaustion. Detailing his officer of the day, Lieutenant Fuller, to take a platoon of twenty men to guard the field piece, Price ordered the rest of his force to prepare for battle. If the howitzer had been serviceable it would have made things go very badly for the Indians, and it was just their good fortune that it had become a liability. Price intended to charge headlong at the Indians, who had drawn up in a broad battle line on a steep ridge in front of him, and on arriving there sweep to the left and clear them from the high ground. It was a good plan, but unknown to Price the hostiles had been working out some stratagems of their own, a fact that also contributes to the uniqueness of this particular skirmish. As Price later admitted, they had "selected their own ground," and when they were ready to begin the fight—that is, after their families had crossed a nearby creek to get away—one of the Kiowas' more respected war chiefs, Set-maun-te (Bear's Paw), separated himself from the group and cantered up the left side of the soldiers' line, drawing their attention. When he was within range they began shooting at him, but failed to hit him, and with this feat of bravado completed, Set-maun-te galloped back to the Indian line. Then a lone Comanche rode up from a half-hidden draw toward two officers in front of the rest of the soldiers. Evidently believing he wanted to talk, the officers holstered their sidearms, whereupon the Comanche shot at them, drawing more fire from the bluecoats as he raced back to the others. He was

unhurt, though his pony was shot in the shoulder. The purpose of
these Indian theatrics is difficult to guess; they could have been
stalling for more time to get their families farther away. Set-
maun-te and the Comanche could have been drawing attention to
themselves to cover some hidden maneuver, or they could simply
have been taking an opportunity to show off, or any combination
of factors. But whatever the meaning, Price soon tired of the game
and ordered the charge, only to discover at last the Indians' battle
plan.

Instead of breaking and running before him, they diverged into
smaller groups and very vigorously attacked Price's flanks and
rear, putting the major in a very surprised and suddenly defensive
position. One group of Indians was zeroing in on the disabled
howitzer, the warriors dismounting and taking cover in ravines,
working their way closer to the detail that guarded it, and Price
was forced to lead a small detachment himself to secure the piece.
The major was obviously impressed by the Indians' stamina,
crediting that they "fought very stubbornly, and during the first
hour and a half of the fight were very bold, exposing themselves
by rapidly riding on every side of us and firing at short range."
When their families were finally out of immediate danger the Indians withdrew, leaving no dead on the field, letting Price believe
that he "drove" them for six or seven miles before they split up
and scattered. But the major unquestionably gained in his first encounter a healthy respect for his adversary, and allegedly a not
very soldierly aversion to meeting them again.

As the afternoon wore on back at the buffalo wallow, Dixon
and the others began to run low on ammunition, and someone
mentioned that the dead private's revolver and ammunition belt
should be recovered. Pressure from the Indians was slight at this
point, and one of the troopers, Private Rath, made the trip in
safety. But when he crawled back into the hole and told the others
that Smith, the private, was still alive, the next time Dixon went
out with Rath to carry him in. Smith's condition was frightful.
"We could see that there was no chance for him," Dixon wrote in
his memoirs. "He was shot through the left lung and when he
breathed the wind sobbed out of his back under the shoulder
blade." Near the wallow one of the Indians had discarded a
willow switch that he had been using as a makeshift quirt, and

using this implement, a silk handkerchief was stuffed into the hole in Smith's back.

At nightfall Dixon cleaned the guns with the willow switch, while the others began to bed down on springy tumbleweeds that Dixon and Rath had gathered to keep the wounded off the soggy ground. As the men talked over their situation it was decided that someone should try to reach help, even though the nearest post was Camp Supply, about seventy-five miles distant, and they had no idea of the location of the troops in the field. Rath and Dixon were the two ablest ones, but the wounded were unwilling to part with the sureness of Dixon's marksmanship should the Indians renew their attack. Rath therefore set out into the dark of a new moon, but returned within two hours and sadly announced he could not locate the Camp Supply trail. During the night Private Smith, who had lain begging for someone to finish him and end the pain, died in his sleep and was laid outside the hole, a handkerchief over his face.

In the morning there was no choice left but for Dixon to try to reach help, and before he covered a half mile he struck the trail to Camp Supply, and after another two miles along it saw a large formation of men about two miles distant, coming toward him. Hiding in a growth of tall grass until he could determine that they were whites and not Indians, he stood up and boomed two shots from his buffalo rifle to attract their notice, and two troopers came riding out to meet him. The force was Major Price's; he had linked up with Lyman's train and was escorting the supplies south to Miles' needy command.

Dixon described the horrible condition of his companions, and Price sent out his surgeon and two soldiers to the buffalo wallow to tend to them. Price detained Dixon himself, though, as he wanted to hear the details of the fight, and Dixon agreed when the surgeon assured him that they could follow his directions to the wallow. After several hundred yards it was apparent that they were going too far to the south, obliging Dixon to fire his buffalo rifle and motion them to the proper heading. Three shots had been fired in all, all heard by the wounded, stranded, and desperate scouts. They interpreted them in one way: Dixon had been killed, and now the Indians would close in and finish them. Readying their guns to sell their lives as dearly as possible, they spied three men on horses riding toward them, and opened fire the instant they were within range. One shot dropped the horse of one of the two soldiers escorting the surgeon. Dixon ran up and got the situation back in control, but so thoroughly piqued was the doctor at being shot at while on a mission of mercy that, in spite of the horrible scene that greeted him, he treated none of the wounded, but just looked them over. When Price heard of the incident he, too, became disgruntled over the loss of a "fine" horse. A couple of the scouts were too badly wounded to be moved but, incredibly, Price just left the men in their hole. He left no detail to protect them; they were out of ammunition, and the troops had none of the proper kind, and Price refused to spare any additional arms for them. He did assure them, however, that he would let Colonel Miles know of their needs, and some of the soldiers charitably left them a little dried beef and hardtack.

Miles, when he heard of their plight, had them rescued at once, as he had been forced to retire farther to the northeast to reach his supply train, and was in the vicinity. "Severely censuring" Price for his handling of the affair, Miles movingly recommended that all six men receive the Congressional Medal of Honor: "The simple recital of their deeds," the citation closed, "and the mention of the odds against which they fought; how the wounded defended the dying, and the dying aided the wounded by exposure to fresh wounds after the power of action was gone; these alone present a scene of cool courage, heroism, and self-sacrifice which duty, as well as inclination, prompts us to recognize, but which we cannot fitly honor."

All the Medals of Honor were awarded, but in Dixon's and Chapman's cases, were revoked years later because they were not officially enlisted in the army. One technicality of the buffalo wallow fight does tend to mar its heroism, though. Practically all accounts of the battle, and particularly Billy Dixon's own memoirs, claim a large number of Indian dead—as many as two dozen; Amos Chapman later confided to interpreter George Bent that the six scouts killed not one of the Indians who had pinned them down.

Though Captain Lyman did finally manage to reach Miles and replenish his supply stores, the flashy colonel was still in an extremely dangerous situation. His men were still chronically short on rations, and his lines of supply were badly overextended. In fact, it can be argued cogently that it was only the fortunate arrival of Price's 8th Cavalry and Lieutenant Lewis' relief column from Camp Supply that prevented the Anadarko renegades from eventually annihilating the Lyman train, and that Miles had indeed lucked out. In spite of Miles' incessant slights of General Pope's ability at running a campaign, Pope knew very well the logistical problems involved, and had literally "stripped his department" to keep Miles supplied. And Pope, the thin-skinned paranoid, had begun to strike back to defend his reputation, fuming to Sheridan on September 18, "He [Miles] seems to want wagons enough to haul supplies and half forage to great distances which it is impractical to furnish him and impracticable for him to get along with if he had them." The day before Pope had ordered the commander of the Camp Supply garrison to send word to Miles that there were no soldiers but his own to keep his supply lines secure and that Miles must protect the lines himself "if he has to move back to the Washita to do it." Pope was justified in making this directive, as the soldiers at Camp Supply, who Miles was demanding be given to him to patrol his route, were instead needed to keep the road open from Supply to Fort Dodge, and could not be spared for Miles. To all this Miles responded by complaining to his accompanying newspaperman, who never lost an opportunity to attack Pope, that he was hurt and completely baffled as to why the commanding general of the Department would hold him back and not even say why.

Also involved in the supply dispute was Miles' belief that General Pope's chief supply officer, General Stewart Van Vliet, was engaging in corrupt activity and skimming off supplies that should have been reaching him in the field, which led to his further belief that Pope was deliberately refusing to investigate Van Vliet in order to subvert the expedition. At one point Miles demanded Van Vliet travel down to him for a conference, or more accurately an examination; the Chief Quartermaster wisely replied that his health would not permit the journey, a refusal which Miles, of course, took as proof of his guilt.

Aside from the supply shortages, a second factor that should have entered Miles' calculations was that the Cheyennes whom he had fought across the Red River, after escaping out of Tulé

Canyon, had slipped back behind him and were threatening to help the Kiowas cut his supply line, isolate him, and maul his command. The obviously prudent thing for Miles to do would be retire back to the northeast, consolidate his gains, clear his supply lines, and wait to link up with Price, as indeed Pope had ordered him to do, and which the starving condition of his men eventually forced him to do. In spite of the fact that the Indians he was fighting were no longer in front of him but behind him, Miles was in a seething rage at having to pull back to the Washita, where he set up a base camp. Though Miles fumed, he never did address himself to exactly what he meant to accomplish by striking deeper into Texas, especially since the brilliant young commander of the 4th Cavalry, Ranald Mackenzie, was at that very time known to be entering the southern Staked Plains to subjugate the Quahadi Comanches and any other Indians with them.

Harsh indictment as it is, many now generally believe that Miles' object was simply to defeat the fierce Quahadis before Mackenzie could get a chance at them, thus snatching an important victory, with its attendant glory, from the hands of the one man who stood between him and a generalcy.

Whether or not that was the case, Miles remained hog-tied by continuing supply problems, and sat fuming in his supply camp on the Washita, waiting for the situation to improve. When he got Pope's letters ordering him to guard his own supply lines he called them "coldblooded," and poured out his feelings, both to William Marshall of the *Commonwealth,* and in letters to his wife, Mary. Then, in a typically Milesian gesture, he took it upon himself to enlarge his responsibilities still further. Once he linked up with Price and learned of the latter's less than stellar performance in not aiding the wagon train, Miles took personal charge of the four companies of the 8th, though not without a little trepidation at his own boldness. "Yesterday I assumed command of Price's command and gave him orders," he wrote Mary. "I don't know how General Pope will take it."

XII. The Mackenzie Column: The Battle of Palo Duro Canyon

At the same time as Miles was gathering his 5th Infantry and 6th Cavalry at Fort Dodge, the army's best Indian fighting force, the 4th Cavalry, began stirring in its headquarters at Fort Clark, on the Rio Grande downstream from the mouth of the Pecos, nearly six hundred miles from Fort Sill, with other units stationed fifty miles farther downriver at Fort Duncan, at Eagle Pass. By August 10 six companies (D, F, G, I, K, and L) were on the road to Fort McKavett, to the northeast, where they picked up companies A and H with two companies of infantry. At McKavett on the fifteenth they were also joined by C Company, 10th Infantry, from Kerrville, and the regiment's commanding officer, who had been in San Antonio plotting strategy with General Augur.

The Colonel of the 4th was Ranald Slidell Mackenzie, probably the army's premier example of the dashing young cavalry officer, with the contested exceptions of Miles and Custer. Not tall (about five feet eight), he had however considerably rounded out his once slim 130 pounds. Only thirty-four, Mackenzie's war record was brilliant, having been seven times breveted and six times wounded, including the loss of two fingers, which gave rise to his Indian nickname, Bad Hand, or Threefingers. Like Miles he had connections, though not so much by design as by earned recognition; his commander in chief, U. S. Grant, termed him outright "the most promising young officer in the army." Although unlike Miles, Mackenzie seemingly lacked ambition for pure advancement's sake, he was not without faults. For all his devotion, his war wounds and exposure had left him nervous, harsh, eccentric (he was forcibly relieved when he went mad in 1883), not very predictable, and easily aroused. He also wrote little: Where the

loquacious Miles left two autobiographies and volumes of correspondence, Mackenzie's pen was practically sterile, though his father had been a fine writer and a companion of Washington Irving. Mackenzie's field reports are a historian's bane, bare of color
or even basic details of his tactical movements, and were no doubt
a rich source of frustration to the army's record-keeping corps of
adjutants.

In response to the Warren Wagontrain Raid of 1871, it was
Mackenzie whom Sherman selected to lead a punitive force onto
the then practically untrammeled Staked Plains against the
Quahadi and Kotsoteka Comanches who, though they had noth-
ing to do with the Warren Massacre on the Salt Prairie, never-
theless needed in Sherman's view some demonstration of the gov-
ernment's power. Marching west from Fort Griffin, Mackenzie set
up a semipermanent supply camp below the Cap Rock at the
Mouth of Blanco Canyon, about forty miles due east of the site of
Lubbock, on a stream called Catfish Creek, or more recently,
Running Water Draw or White River, a major tributary of the Salt
Fork Brazos. Finally engaging the Indians on their home territory,
Mackenzie's force was badly beaten, the colonel himself admitting
disgustedly, "We didn't look worth a damn." Returning east to
supervise the removal and trial of Satanta and Big Tree, Mackenzie went back to the Staked Plains for another go in 1872, with
more success. On September 29 of that year he surprised and captured Mow-way's village on McClellan Creek, killed about twenty-
five, and captured over a hundred women and children, forcing
the Kotsoteka and Quahadi bands to go to the agency, many for
the first time, and to behave themselves pending the promised return of their families.

The 1874 campaign would be the third in four years for the 4th,
and their experience, combined with Mackenzie's harsh and raw
discipline of the soldiers, had whipped them into the standing of
the army's crack unit of Indian fighters. On September 17, 1874,
the command began to march for Fort Concho, a long distance
northeast, in Tom Green County, arriving there on the twenty-
first, the day before Davidson's melee at Anadarko, and the day
after Miles departed Camp Supply to engage the Cheyennes.
When they left for the campaign two days later and paused for
inspection by General Augur and Colonel Mackenzie, the

"Southern Column" consisted of well over six hundred men and officers: 4th Cavalry, Companies A, D, E, F, H, I, K, and L; 10th Infantry, Companies A, C, I, and K; 11th Infantry, Company H. The scouts under Lieutenant William A. Thompson included Sergeant John B. Charlton of F Company, 4th Cavalry (the same who had killed Kiowa Chief Satank in 1871), Fort Richardson's post guide Henry W. Strong, three other whites, a dozen Tonkawa Indians, some Lipan Apaches, and thirteen Seminole-Negroes. Also accompanying Mackenzie from Fort Concho as a scout was a man named Johnson, a half-breed Mexican-Lipan Apache, who had evidently sought out the colonel and asked for the job. One of the notorious "Mexican traders" who kept the plains tribes supplied with contraband, Johnson had in previous years been a gun runner in the upper Red River area, trading weapons to the Indians for buffalo robes and probably stolen Texas cattle. Although Mackenzie had reason to arrest the Comanchero and was doubtless tempted to, Johnson's shady activities had given him a thorough knowledge of the Llano Estacado, a territory still practically uncharted, and Mackenzie had no other scout who knew the region so well. Hence the colonel overlooked his stained past and took him on.

While Mackenzie went with General Augur to Fort Griffin in Shackelford County, northeast of the later site of Abilene, to make sure of his supply source, the Southern Column itself rode north-northwest to re-establish Mackenzie's old base camp on Catfish Creek, about 150 miles west of Griffin. Mackenzie was being much more careful in securing his supplies than was Nelson Miles, aided in the effort by his superbly efficient quartermaster, Captain Henry W. Lawton, who after dumping the first load of supplies brought from Concho, turned his wagons around and trekked back to Fort Griffin for more. Lawton had been enjoying a leave of absence, but voluntarily cut it short to join in the fight. While the troopers were engaged in refurbishing the camp and drilling, the Seminole-Negro scouts took the trail, as they had been directed at Concho, beginning the search for hostile Indian trails. At Fort Griffin General Augur was giving Mackenzie his final instructions: Pursue the Indians "wherever they go." If the hostiles ran for Fort Sill, he should follow them there, assume command of the post, and contain them. Mackenzie was delayed at Griffin on account of having no corn to feed his horses, but when he finally arrived at Catfish Creek on September 19 the Seminole-Negroes reported that they had discovered three different trails.

Mackenzie paused at his supply camp very briefly—less than a day—before striking out north for the Staked Plains, leaving a garrison of three infantry companies to guard the Catfish Creek depot and dividing his eight cavalry troops into two battalions. The first, consisting of Companies D, F, I, and K, was placed under a former Civil War general of volunteers, Captain N. B. McLaughlin; the second, comprised of A, E, H, and L troops, was given to Gettysburg veteran Captain Eugene B. Beaumont.

In keeping with his prediction of the nineteenth, that "I can't say exactly what my future movements will be any more than I anticipate moving north," Mackenzie marched out on September 20 to do exactly that, moving in a very general north-northwesterly direction, skirting the gigantic stairstep of the Cap Rock, scouting on and off the Staked Plains, following fresh Indian trails, smelling them out, as it were, to find where they were concentrated. The devastating drought was by this time completely broken, and much of the marching was done through a plain of deep, sticky mud; Lawton's supply train, the wagons buried at times up to the hubs in muck, struggled constantly to keep pace with the aggressive colonel.

On the twenty-second he approached the Cap Rock above Quita Que Creek, "a place of marshes, springs and small running streams," where he pitched a camp that was that night wracked by a dazzling thunderstorm. At one point during the deluge some of the officers had taken refuge under the wall of the Cap Rock when suddenly a part of the soggy massif gave way and collapsed near by, a continuation of the erosion process that had over the aeons carved all the canyons back into the Staked Plains. All the next day Mackenzie sat still, drying out, resting, gathering in his scouts and sorties, giving the supply train a chance to catch up. On the twenty-third he managed to proceed seven miles farther, slogging northward for five hours before cowing beneath a wild, howling, drenching, frigid norther. This storm spilled over into the twenty-fourth, when only three miles were covered, but the weather cleared at dawn on the twenty-fifth, and Mackenzie pressed on, twenty miles to Tulé Canyon with his two cavalry battalions, leaving his supply wagons to flounder along behind in the mud as best they could.

At dusk Henry Strong reported he had crossed an Indian trail to the east, not very large at 150 ponies, but he had left Thompson and his friendly Indians to investigate further. Just as darkness was falling, the chief of scouts arrived in the Tulé and advised that during their exhausting day-long scout of some 60 miles, his men had stumbled across numerous trails, the largest—about 1,500 ponies—pointing eastward. Without delay Mackenzie ordered Captain Beaumont's four troops of the Second Battalion to mount and give chase, leaving McLaughlin's First Battalion to rest in the Tulé. When a five-mile chase under a ghostly full "Comanche" moon (the third since Adobe Walls) netted them nothing, the colonel selected as a campsite a rugged side ravine that had been rather whimsically named "Boehm's Canyon" for his longtime associate, Captain Peter M. Boehm of E Company. The soldiers slept fully dressed and armed, the horses well guarded, but no attack occurred.

The next day, September 26, Mackenzie lay in, waiting for the Indians to make a move, waiting for Lawton to bring up the supply wagons, and waiting for McLaughlin to join him with the other four cavalry companies. In the afternoon Mackenzie shifted his position about five miles farther downcanyon, soon joined by McLaughlin. Mackenzie knew he must be very close; Indian signs were everywhere. A band of maybe a half dozen hostiles had shot at McLaughlin's force as they moved down the Tulé. About half past nine the ex-Comanchero Johnson rode in with the news that he had seen buffalo running fast, as if hunted. Scouts said hostiles were gathering all around and must attack during the night.

Two years previous, Mackenzie's successful sacking of Mowway's village was largely spoiled by the Comanches' retaking of their large horse herd, nabbing as well several cavalry horses, including Mackenzie's own. This time he was ready for them. Every single animal was tethered by inch-thick rope to its individual iron stake driven deep into the ground. Each had been hobbled and even "cross-sidelined," one foreleg roped to the opposite back leg. Clusters of skirmishers were planted at strategic places, and a guard stood duty every fifteen feet around the camp.

The attack came at ten o'clock, in force, as about 250 hostiles

charged straight for the horse herd, the brunt of the attack falling
upon battalion commander Beaumont's own A Company. A night
attack in force by Plains Indians was remarkable and unusual, but
the special medicine, if there was any, availed nothing. Thwarted
by the well-laid defenses, the Indians began the classic circling
maneuver, trying to figure out some way to panic the horses; by
the time they withdrew a half hour later they had wounded three
cavalry mounts. Their own losses were never determined by the
whites. While the renegades were still firing intermittently, the
cavalrymen noticed strange noises filtering down into the ravine,
indistinguishable at first, but soon clearly identifiable as Mackenzie's supply train, squeaking and rumbling through the mud. Completely untouched and in spite of the commotion unaware of the
fighting, the supply unit rumbled into the camp about midnight.

By two in the morning all the Indians had retired to cover toward the north, giving Mackenzie's men a fitful breather, but at
dawn the Indians reappeared on a high ridge, an estimated three
hundred strong, shooting at long range. When the bullets began to
land too close, Mackenzie sent out Thompson's scouts and Captain Boehm's E Company to break up the Indian force, and there
followed an incident that offers perhaps more comment on the low
esteem in which the white soldiers held their friendly Indian
guides than does the wounding of Nelson Miles' Delaware. The
entrenched hostiles refused to stand up to a mounted charge, and
so sprinted for their ponies and galloped up the ravines to escape.
By a fortunate shot one of the Tonkawa guides named Henry shot
the pony from beneath a finely dressed Comanche, who plopped
limply to the ground. Henry, sensing a scalp and honor from the
white soldier-chief, rapidly closed on the Comanche, only to have
him spring up at the last instant, wrestle him from his horse, and
begin beating him with his bow. Whether he simply had no other
weapon to use on the hated Tonkawa or simply wished not to spill
another Indian's blood (even a collaborator's, as frequently happened) is not known, but throughout the desperate grappling
Henry screamed for aid from a cluster of nearby troopers, shriek-
ing, "Why you no shoot? Why you no shoot?" For several seconds
the soldiers enjoyed a hearty chuckle, until one of them leveled his
rifle and leisurely killed the Comanche, the only confirmed hostile
Indian death. Henry was allowed the scalp, but that did not com-

pletely mitigate his humiliation and enraged bewilderment at his treatment.

Once driven from their cover, the Indians fanned out on the muddy table of the Staked Plains into an impressive battle line a mile across, but suddenly broke off the engagement and retired, disappearing "as completely as if the ground had swallowed them." Now it was Mackenzie who was ready to take the offensive. Sometime during the night one of the scouts, probably Johnson, reported that during his explorations he had uncovered the central hostile Indian encampment, in the upper reaches of the main Palo Duro Canyon.

There is an alternate story of the discovery of the Palo Duro villages, that during Mackenzie's march to the north he had snared a number of the ubiquitous New Mexican Comancheros, among them the inimitable José Piedad Tafoya, one of the most celebrated of them all, who "knew the plains from the Palo Duro to the Concho by heart." Tafoya was known to have been trading actively but surreptitiously with the Comanches for at least nine years—that is, from the date that New Mexican cattle trading with the Comanches had been banned. He admitted that his success was due in part to the complicity of the commandant at Fort Bascom. A flourishing trade developed, with the Indians stealing cattle in Texas from the Loving, Goodnight, and many other ranches, trading them for goods to middleman Tafoya, who then got them to New Mexico, where the cattle helped hold down the price of beef. The volume of the trade mushroomed, and the site of the transactions between Tafoya and the Indians was usually the canyons at the edge of the Staked Plains. When Mackenzie finally got hold of the old bootlegger, Mackenzie very understandably demanded that Tafoya guide the army to the Indians' hideout, but Tafoya, familiar enough with how Indians dealt with stool pigeons, responded with a bewildered "*¿No sabe?*" Mackenzie then, reportedly, propped up a wagon tongue, cast a noose over the high end, and stretched Tafoya's neck until he remembered his English and divulged the secret of their location. When Charlie Goodnight told this story to Quanah Parker four years later, that chief vowed to kill Tafoya if he ever saw him again, which he never did. Although Mackenzie himself credited Johnson with the discovery, it is not impossible that Mackenzie simply failed to report his near execution of a civilian without trial. On October 7 a Mexican wagon train was in fact overtaken; several Comancheros were caught and arrested later in the winter, and in the colonel's seldom-examined letterbook he does make mention of an ill-defined arrangement with "Jose Piedad a Mexican Indian Trader," so just about anything is possible. One should perhaps recall here that Mackenzie's father, a naval commodore, once hanged without trial a midshipman who happened to be the son of the Secretary of War.

Whatever the source of Mackenzie's intelligence, he was by his third campaign canny enough in the fine points of Indian fighting to approach it properly. The retreating hostiles' trail led southwest, but Mackenzie knew they were holed up in Palo Duro, to the north, and were leading him away from their most vulnerable liabilitiés, their women, children, and homes, burdens with which the whites' "warrior society" were not encumbered. He also knew that the Indians were watching him to make sure he followed. Therefore he marked time, marching for hours leisurely up the Tulé to its head, which was also the most convenient exit, and then went into camp at sundown, giving every indication to the decoying Indians that he intended to gullibly follow on their trail on the morrow.

As soon as darkness covered him, however, Mackenzie dropped all pretenses and moved in for the kill. With Johnson leading, the column altered course ninety degrees to the right, abandoning the Indians' trail, and moved swiftly to the northwest, toward Palo Duro. The forced march was kept up all night, and about four in the morning of September 28 they again crossed the Indian trail, made barely an hour before, also heading toward the canyon, and Mackenzie knew he had succeeded in fooling them into thinking they had fooled him, and so believing their ruse had worked, were returning to their hideout. Realizing now he was very close to the canyon, Mackenzie halted his men to wait for daylight before attacking.

The scouts and eight cavalry troops mounted again just before dawn, and very soon saw on their left the Cañon Blanco, an upper arm of the Palo Duro, and just afterward, its depth still gloomy, "like a dark blotch on the prairie," the yawning pit of the main Palo Duro. Peering over the sharp ledge, Mackenzie and his men could make out in the murky depths an entire forest of miniscule tipis, they and their attendant horse herds so distorted by distance that one of the Seminole-Negroes gaped, "Lor' men, look at de sheep and de goats down dar." The limestone cap of the cliff wall fell sheer away, in some places for hundreds of feet, and the force had to snake slowly up the canyon rim for a mile or so before finding a narrow, cliff-hanging trail, threading and switchbacking its way down into the dark canyon. In the time spent finding it Mackenzie feared he had lost his best advantage, surprise; dawn had broken, sharp, beautifully clear and cold, and the command was plainly visible etched against the brightening sky. Nevertheless, on reaching the head of the trail Mackenzie turned to his chief of scouts and ordered with measured poise, "Mr. Thompson, take your men down and open the fight."

The Tonkawas and Seminole-Negroes led the way down the dizzy trace, with A and E Companies close behind. The path was much too steep and tortuous to negotiate while mounted, and the men descended the trail afoot in single file, leading their horses, literally running and sliding headlong down into the canyon. Lieutenant Charles Hatfield of E Troop recalled that they had covered about 150 yards in this fashion when an Indian sentry, perched on a lookout near the trail, caught sight of them. Instantly the brave fired his rifle and signaled by waving his red blanket, and "disappeared immediately afterwards in a marvelous manner." The warrior can be identified with some certainty as Red Warbonnet (or Older Man, Kya' been), a little-known, minor war chief who had been wounded at Satanta's Salt Creek Massacre in 1871. Red Warbonnet's village was the farthest downstream and the closest to the advancing Mackenzie. The Indians later said that he fired two shots, but, instead of riding through the camps spreading the alarm, ran to his tipi to put on his war paint.

If at any time during the whole Red River War one fateful mistake could be said to have cost the Indians every chance at victory or at least a negotiated peace, it was this. Mackenzie was banking all on surprise; his men were vulnerable, laid bare as they scrabbled down the cliff face, and if only the Indians had been warned of them, a very few braves could have in a very short time slaughtered the greater portion of the United States 4th Cavalry. As it happened, the Kiowas far up the canyon did hear the reverberating rifle shots but, believing a baffled Mackenzie was stalled miles to the south, trusting in Maman-ti's prophecy that they would not be harmed within the embrace of Palo Duro, and certainly not suspecting that their Comanchero supplier—if indeed it had been Tafoya—had sold them out, they figured that one of the Indians was shooting at a deer or something, and rolled over and went back to sleep.

When the advance units reached the spot where the lookout had been stationed, they stood on the ledge and beheld the great secret winter encampment of what was certainly a large portion, if not a majority, of the Indians who remained hostile to the government. The nearest village, directly under them, where "a stone could easily have been pitched into it," consisted of about forty tipis, just at the outlet of the Cañon Blanco. Hatfield noted that the lodges appeared no larger than coins, while some of the soldiers still mistook the Indian ponies for sheep and even chickens. The huge encampment contained in all hundreds of lodges, the clustered villages following the winding course of the Main (Prairie Dog Town Fork) Red River for over two miles up the mighty canyon. According to the later testimony of the Comanche Mumsukawa, who was present that morning, the most prominent of the Comanche chiefs in Palo Duro was O-ha-ma-tai, and the Cheyenne villages were under Chief Iron Shirt. Wild Horse's and Quanah Parker's Quahadis were not present, but were far to the south.

The Kiowas, by comparison, were under Maman-ti's lead, and could not have been in the canyon more than a week. After the wagon train fight, the brush with Price, and the excitement at the buffalo wallow, the hostile Kiowas retreated back to the southeast all the way to the head of Elk Creek, Indian Territory, to evade the columns of soldiers. Beset by a relentless succession of thunderstorms, the story is told how, at Elk Creek, the Kiowas received (erroneous) word that more troops were coming and that they must mount up and flee at once. But one miserable young Indian refused; he had just gotten his puddle warm, he said, and nothing could make him leave. But shortly thereafter all the Indians were driven from the soggy ground by an unbelievable army of crawling tarantulas, evidently escaping high water, forcing the Indians to spend the night "like roosting turkeys" on their ponies, blankets draped over their heads as protection from the rain. The superstitious Kiowas were petrified by the occurrence, and fled back to the west, dodging the crisscrossing columns of soldiers, making their way safely into Palo Duro Canyon at last. By the time the scouts and first troops reached the floor of the canyon, formed into a skirmish line, and began a gun-blazing charge through the first camp, the alarm had finally spread across the whole area, and the Indian camps dissolved in turmoil. Braves by the hundreds were rounding up their war ponies and spurring them to the upper reaches of the canyon to take cover and fight. Women and children, panic-stricken, were fleeing in the same direction, up the canyon, laden with whatever they could carry in their hands. There was no time to lash together travois to carry away large items. Pack mules, hastily loaded and then abandoned as the bluecoats neared, stampeded wildly through the villages, dragging their half-tied bundles behind them. Within minutes after the pandemonium began, the string of villages lay utterly deserted, and an entire winter's store of food, supplies, and most importantly, forage for the ponies, fell into Mackenzie's hands.

Fighting a rear-guard action to cover the getaway of their families, the routed braves took cover on the broken cliff faces and sniped at the advancing troops to slow them down, and managed to hit and seriously wound one of Mackenzie's men, a bugler with the unfortunate name of Henry E. Hard, shot through the stomach. A couple of cavalry horses were also shot, but aside from that, the Indians were completely bested, and began to take casualties themsêlves. At one point during their flight up the canyon, Chief Poor Buffalo was discovered behind a huge rockfall, singing the song of his warrior society over the body of Red Warbonnet. The lesser chief had fallen early in the fight, shot in the head; he was not scalped, but his killers had cut off a finger to obtain a large silver scoop ring. Informants later recalled how several big strong women were assembled before Red Warbonnet's mother was told of the loss; the Kiowas carried Kya' been's body to the top of the cliffs, where they danced to honor him, then buried him in one of the rocky clefts. Elsewhere, one of the Tonkawa's women came upon a badly wounded warrior who had been left behind; she killed him after calling him numerous insulting names. One other hostile was also killed, a total of three during the battle.

Mackenzie's part in the fight was extremely personal and active: He was everywhere. Leaving McLaughlin's battalion stationed on the rim as a reserve, Mackenzie himself led Beaumont's other two companies, H and L, to the bottom, formed them up, and charged as a second wave through the villages. Indian snipers were high on the bluff, from where they could not be dislodged, and Mackenzie discovered that Captain Gunther of H Company had sent up a platoon to clear them out. Knowing "not one man would live to reach the top," he ordered them back to their company and chewed Gunther out for the stupid move. Almost simultaneously a private named McGowan had his horse shot from under him, leaving the soldier tugging insistently at his saddlebags, which were pinned under the horse's body. "McGowan," yelled the colonel, "get away from there or you will be hit!" The private first moved as if to obey, but when Mackenzie turned away, he went back for his saddlebags. Mackenzie ordered him again and then a third time, demanding, "I told you to go away from there. Are you going?" McGowan replied that he needed his ammunition (and tobacco), and Mackenzie let him finish. After a group of hostiles took cover on a canyon wall flanking the companies and opened fire from a new direction, one of the soldiers began to lose spirit and muttered, "How will we ever get out of here?" Mackenzie overheard him and answered sternly, "I brought you in; I will take you out."

Knowing that the key to defeating the Indians lay not so much in killing them as in getting their horses and stranding them afoot, Captain Beaumont raced his company like an arrow, straight up the canyon for over two miles, not getting pinned down like the rest. When he returned, his men were herding between fourteen hundred and fifteen hundred head of Indian ponies that they had succeeded in capturing, a disastrous loss for the warriors. When McLaughlin brought down three of his four companies to help mop up the action and clear the remaining hostiles from the area, the fighting began to tail off, until by afternoon Mackenzie was ready to start destroying the captured villages.

During the latter stages of the rout, when the camps lay deserted but before Mackenzie gave the order to burn them, the wives of the Tonkawa scouts lost no time in looting them of anything that might be useful. Lieutenant Albee's tally of their bonanza gives some indication of the damage inflicted on the fleeing hostiles: "There are bows and arrows, shields, lances, quivers, buffalo robes with and without hair, highly decorated and painted, new blankets just from the reservation . . . stone china, kettles, tools and implements of every description down to a pair of tinners shears; the best breech loading arms, with plenty of metallic cartridges, one mule being found packed with 500 rounds, and another with lead and powder kegs, bales of calico and turkey red, sacks of Minneapolis and Osage Mission flour, groceries of all kinds in profusion."

Also found in the villages were two forlorn scraps of paper on which, in one observer's words, "comment is unnecessary":

Office Kiowa and Comanche Agency
I. T., 4 Mo. 9, 1874

Long Hungry is recognized as a chief among the Cochetethca Comanche Indians, and promises to use his influence for good among his people, while continuing to conduct himself in a friendly and peaceable manner. I ask for him kind treatment by all with whom he may come in contact.

J. M. Haworth
United States Indian Agent

No. 13—Kiowa and Comanche Agency
I. T. August (month) 6, 1874

Wah-lung, of Sun Boy's band of Kiowas, is registered and will not be molested by troops, unless engaged in acts of hostility, or away from his camp without special permission.

J. M. Haworth
United States Indian Agent

Although only three Indians were killed in the Battle of Palo Duro, the devastating loss of supplies and above all their ponies broke the back of at least these Indians' resistance. In exchange for the army's loss of 14 horses and mules killed, Mackenzie discovered that he had netted a haul of 1,424 head. He cut out just over 350 of the healthiest animals for his own men and scouts to use; he had promised forty to the scout who should find the Indian camp, and had other debts to pay the Seminole Negroes and Tonkawas for making their lengthy and extremely hazardous scouts. Mackenzie disliked the idea of paying his scouts with horse bribes. "I do so," he reported in an apologetic defense of the practice, "because it is the only way that it is practicable for me to get such dangerous work out of the men."

In disposing of the remaining captured horses, Mackenzie knew that these hostiles, just like Mow-way's Kotsotekas and Quahadis two years before, could and would steal them back within days. Therefore he had the rest, over a thousand head, led to the rim of the canyon and methodically shot down by a firing squad.

When that was accomplished Mackenzie circled the head of the canyon before moving slowly back south. Although General Augur had closed his last briefings with him with the enjoinder, "Make reports by every opportunity and give as much detail as possible," during his long march out of Catfish Creek Mackenzie had been, to put it mildly, lax in maintaining contact with either his superiors or the other units in the field. It was his "style" as a soldier, when given an assignment, to perform it in a magnificent manner, but in return he expected his commanders to trust his capacity and his judgments, without his being required to waste time on impeding progress reports. Unfortunately, while no one doubted Mackenzie's ability to deliver, the lines of communication even at their best were so poor that the high command had only the vaguest and most belated notion of what was transpiring in the field. Mackenzie's "notorious" silences, therefore, if they did not create administrative chaos, certainly did nothing to alleviate the nerve-wrecking infrequency of field reports.

On September 28, just as Mackenzie's men were picking their way down the precipitous walls of Palo Duro, Colonel John W. Davidson, operating at the edge of the Staked Plains, detached five companies to search the headwaters of the Red to "ascertain if anything could be heard or seen of Col. McKenzie." They found nothing. In a report ten days previous to this, General Pope had informed his superior Sheridan in Chicago that he knew nothing of the movements of either Mackenzie or Davidson—or, for that matter, Buell. Of course, those three field commanders were of the Department of Texas and would report to Augur, not Pope, but communications in the field were so bad that on October 12 Colonel Miles, who was at that instant a distance of one day's forced march to Mackenzie's northeast, wrote petulantly to Pope, "Since taking the field I have not been fully advised of the movements of the troops from Texas, which I am expected to cooperate with; if anything is known of their movements, I hope the same may be furnished me by telegraph and couriers."

Word of Mackenzie's victory was finally flashed over the wires on that day, October 12, from San Antonio, the Department headquarters, and thence to the army's central command, which had been moved from Washington to St. Louis to be nearer the scene of the fighting.

XIII. The Wrinkled-hand Chase

The summer-long drought that had caused such intense misery to Miles' soldiers in the field also made its presence felt at Fort Sill, and Agent Haworth's outgoing letters substantiate Miles in reporting its severity. On August 8: "I believe it has been forty-six days since any rain of consequence fell in this country." On August 17: "The long continued drouth with the prevailing hot winds has made the vegetation as dry as the frosts of fall . . . during the last 10 days the mercury has stood as high as 107°, several days reaching 111° and 112° in the shade." On September 5: "The hot dry weather still continues. The Indians say the Qua-ha-da Medicine Man made Medicine so strong it will be a long time before we have any rain."

Although the drought mercifully broke the day the last letter was dispatched, the temperature was not the only thing that had been rising all summer, as Haworth's no-holds-barred feud with Lieutenant Colonel Davidson had not only continued but intensified mightily. Davidson was much too military not to stay on the offensive against the agent, and about a month after the close of the enrollment he used the opportunity of a visit by his Department Commander, Brigadier General Augur, to so foully disparage Haworth that General Augur was moved to sit down immediately and write the Division Commander, Lieutenant General Sheridan, about the matter: "Lieut. Col. Davidson, 10th Cavalry, and other reliable officers, who have been stationed here a number of years, assure me that the charges [of Haworth's incompetence] can be sustained. . . . My own acquaintance with Mr. Haworth, is very limited and would not justify me, in making complaint of him. I am perfectly satisfied however, that he is not fitted for his position here, and fear that, through his weakness and indecision, he may do something that, under the circumstances, cannot be permitted. . . . [Lieutenant Sanderson] tells me that Mr. Haworth hardly ever sees his Indians, and has no influence or control over them, except such as he purchases by certain issues of sugar and other articles specially desired by them. . . . the Agent here should be a man of force and ability, and practical common sense; familiar with these Indians and not afraid to do his duty." The letter is actually a reflection more on Augur than on Haworth, being merely an example of a brother officer taking another's word without any doubt, qualification, or attempt to hear the other side.

By 1874 Sill had earned the reputation of being one of the finest and best-equipped forts in the army. Not the stockaded blockhouse usually pictured today as a frontier post—few forts were—Fort Sill covered a section of land consisting of a large, square parade ground surrounded by buildings of locally quarried stone, built with army labor at no expense to the government. The structures on the north and east sides were the officers' quarters, on the west were barracks, and behind them, the cavalry stables. The south line was more barracks and the post headquarters, and south of them, storehouses, the forge, and warehouses. A short walk to the southeast lay the post corral, about 150 feet square, ringed after its initial completion with eight-foot stone walls to protect the supplementary stock from horse thieves and Indians. Laced with shooting loopholes and containing a deep well, the corral was also intended as a sort of *donjon* that could be defended should the open post fall to hostiles. A small redoubt overlooked approaches from the southwest, and off to the northwest lay the ten-thousand-dollar post hospital, the only structure that required a government appropriation.

The highest temperature officially recorded at the post during the drought was 106 degrees, and Colonel Davidson took advantage of the dry months to patiently lay in precious supplies for his campaign. Because of chronic unrest at Anadarko the commitment to launch Davidson's drive was delayed until the first week of September. Marching orders issued on the fourth indicated his expedition would include the 10th Cavalry's Companies B, C, H, M, and K, under Major George W. Schofield; the 11th Infantry's

Companies D, E, and I, commanded by Captain Wikoff; Lieutenant Pat Kellihan, 25th Infantry, with a section of mountain howitzers and forty rounds of shells; and Lieutenant Richard H. Pratt, 10th Cavalry, with forty-four Tonkawa Indian guides and trackers. Davidson directed that his force should travel light, and ordered the quartermaster to pack food, ammunition, and some forage, but ". . . no tents beyond one for the officers of each company, and ten (10) for each company, will be carried, no cots, mattresses, tables or chairs will be allowed . . . baggage will be limited to the necessary changes of clothing." On September 10 Davidson turned command of Fort Sill over to Lieutenant Sanderson, and leaving him Companies E and F of the 10th for a garrison, took the field.

When Davidson was finally ready to move he mounted 610 fighting men, but from the beginning of the uprising he had maintained smaller detachments in the field. As early as May 2 Lieutenant Quincy O. M. Gilmore, with a small squadron of 10th Cavalry, attacked what he assumed to be a war party, but claimed no casualties inflicted. Once on the march it took Davidson twelve days to reach Nelson Miles on the upper reaches of the Sweetwater and hold a conference. The thrashing that Davidson had promised for Haworth's Indians, however, turned out to be mostly bluster; having effected the death of only one Indian, a lost Kiowa named Little Chief on September 17, he returned to Sill to resupply on October 8 without having fought a major engagement.

Operating conjunctively with Davidson, Lieutenant Colonel George P. Buell marched from Fort Griffin with six troops of cavalry, one from the 10th and five from the 9th, and two companies of infantry. He too had been active since the beginning of Indian troubles the previous winter; as late as July 21, Buell and two other officers, with nine soldiers and nine Tonkawa scouts, had attacked a war party in Palo Pinto County, Texas. The result was indecisive, as the troops claimed no Indians killed and only one pony captured.

With all five columns finally in the field, and particularly after the Indians' disastrous rout and eviction from their hideout in Palo Duro Canyon, it became apparent that Sheridan's plan of reenacting his 1868 campaign was going to pay off in a big way. Of the operations so far, and of the chronic supply problems,

Sheridan wrote, "All of these columns were pushed out much sooner than was desirable, (especially that of Col. Miles and Major Price), but I deemed it necessary that we should take the field at once, to prevent hostile Indians from forcing out those of their tribes who had made up their minds to remain at peace, and also, to prevent the accumulation of winter supplies from the buffalo herds. As these hostile Indians have their families and stock with them and as Col. Miles has given them little time to hunt for the last six or eight weeks, and as all of our columns are now in the field, we may hope for good results soon." Sheridan would not be disappointed.

For the Indians, the wet discomfort and exposure that began at the siege of Lyman's wagon train proved to be only the first and merest hint of what they were to suffer throughout the fall. For weeks on end, line after line of booming thunderstorms rolled across the South Plains; with every raid by the soldiers the Indians lost more food and supplies, and more lodges. The army gave them not a moment's peace to hunt and make new equipment from the buffalo. As the soggy weeks dragged on, the Indians' enthusiasm for the war lessened steadily, until what had begun for some of the younger warriors as an adventurous lark turned into a devastating series of abject routs which the Indians, constantly pounded by the frigid northers with hardly any days to dry out, miserably and aptly named the "Wrinkled-hand Chase."

One of the first casualties of the Wrinkled-hand Chase was a surprise and, for the army, the occasion for an almost hand-rubbing gloat. On October 4, 1874, Lieutenant Colonel Thomas H. Neill, commanding the garrison of troops protecting the Darlington Agency, dashed off this significant message to General Pope:

> Headquarters Cheyenne Agency
> Indian Territory, October 4th, 1874

To The
Assistant Adjutant General
Department of the Missouri
Fort Leavenworth, Kansas
Sir:

I have the honor to report that Satanta with twenty-five lodges of Kiowas, consisting of 145 men, women, and children (37 warriors, 40 squaws, 66 children, and 2 old men) came into this camp and surrendered themselves. I desarmed them of 13 rifles, 3 pistols, 18 bows, and four lances, all the arms they had; placed Satanta and Big Tree under close guard as hostages, and placed the rest in camp as prisoners. They are too numerous to be kept under close arrest.

Neill also informed the department headquarters that "A party of 104 Kiowa and Comanche lodges, say 500 souls in all, came into Ft. Sill, they were disarmed, enrolled, and turned over with the other Kiowas there." Satanta's band had heard of this previous surrender, and hoped to be given similar terms. "Woman's Heart is amongst the Kiowas who are prisoners here," continued Neill. "I have written to find out what part he took in the fight at Wichita. . . . We hear that Poor Bull [Poor Buffalo], with his party of Kiowas, will come into Ft. Sill, as soon as his ponies are fat enough."

At his surrender Satanta claimed, as he always did when he surrendered, that he had not gone to war and had not committed any depredations against the whites. As rendered by an interpreter, on this occasion he gave Neill the following alibi: "When the fight commenced at the Wichita Agency, all were excited; I packed up and left, and took no part in the fight; soon after, I left the Kiowas and Comanches, who have gone to the Staked Plains, and remained at the headwaters of the Washita with the party now with me. . . . I have done no fighting against the whites, have killed no white men, and committed no depredations since I left Fort Sill." Of course, Neill could hardly be expected to believe such assertions from the most famous raider on the plains, but this time, Satanta claimed, he had proof, as he handed over his certificate of registration from Fort Sill, dated August 6, 1874. Big Tree as well could prove that he had enrolled, but Neill was not in the least persuaded, and wrote to Sill for more information.

As soon as they heard of Satanta's surrender, Superintendent Hoag and Agent Haworth, conscious of how far the chief had gone out of his way to stay on the peace road, began laboring for his release, but this time it was the army who had the drop on the Quakers. Within a day of his surrender Satanta found himself back in chains, being hauled back to Texas in a prison wagon. Actually, the army found him guilty only by association, suspecting (by chance rightly) that he had been at the wagon train fight, and so assuming he had taken an active part, an unsubstantiated assertion that certainly was not the inevitable case. Satanta's mistake lay in letting himself be persuaded to remain with Lone Wolf and Maman-ti as long as he did, letting the latter use him and Big Tree to lend respectability to their movement, the same trap he had escaped in early June at the Sun Dance, when Lone Wolf tried to enlist him in the Tau-ankia revenge raid. But Satanta's personal involvement or innocence was not the central issue in returning him to the Huntsville prison. In fact, "The question as to whether Satanta himself became hostile or not," wrote General Augur, "was not considered." The conditions that attended his parole in the autumn of 1873 stipulated that he should be reincarcerated if any of the Kiowas ever again went to war regardless of his personal stance, and it was on this general pretext, as well as the army's overall perception of him as a bad influence to his tribe, that Satanta was sacked out of the way in the Piney Woods of southeastern Texas for the rest of his life. Big Tree, on the other hand, was thought of as a salvageable character, and was soon released.

Neill's letter of October 4 also gave some indication of what groups remained hostile, the information apparently gained by interrogating the prisoners. Neill reported that two Kiowa chiefs, Lone Wolf and "Tahoos," had gone to the Llano Estacado with the war parties of seven Comanche chiefs, of whom Neill obtained the names of five: the Yapparikas Isa Rosa (White Wolf) and Tabananica (Sound of the Sun), Medicine Man, Mow-way's Kotsotekas, and Wild Horse's Quahadis. Since Neill registered the opinion, endorsed by General Pope, that these were the Anadarko renegades, it is probable the Big Red Meat (Tanima-Nokoni) was one of the unnamed chiefs.

As Satanta was packed off to prison, the Wrinkled-hand Chase continued with dreadful consistency. On October 9 Colonel Buell, with five companies of the 11th Infantry, struck and destroyed a small Kiowa camp in the southwestern Indian Territory. Following the trail northward, two days later he sacked another of 75 lodges, and on the twelfth he put to the torch a village that he claimed numbered 475 tipis, all identified as Kiowa. However, either a large number of other Indians were with the Kiowas or Buell grossly exaggerated their number, as the hostile portion of the Kiowas could not possibly have put together that many lodges; the population indicated by 550 tipis is 3,300 Indians, about 2½ times the size of the entire tribe. All the villages had been freshly abandoned and Buell raced northwest after the fleeing hostiles all the way to the Canadian, where he finally overextended his supply lines and had to backtrack to his supply camp, northwest of Fort Griffin, Texas.

On October 13 Major Price and his 8th Cavalry, taking orders now from Nelson Miles, attacked a war party on Gageby Creek, just inside the Indian Territory boundary, and on the seventeenth, Captain Adna R. Chaffee of Miles' command, with I Company of the 6th Cavalry, surprised an Indian camp five miles north of the Washita, destroying it without loss to himself.

Meanwhile, Colonel John W. Davidson's second expedition was having considerably more success than the first, and October 24 was a particularly busy day for the buffalo soldiers. Only five days out of refitting at Fort Sill, they had traveled as far as Elk Creek when Major Schofield, leading three companies of the 10th, surprised a Comanche camp and took it intact. Unwilling to run any farther in the interminable mud, the beaten Comanches surrendered under a white flag, netting Schofield 69 warriors, 250 women and children, and some 2,000 horses. At about the same time Captain Lewis H. Carpenter, with two more companies of the 10th, struck a much smaller Kiowa camp. The Indians scattered, but were driven in to surrender at Sill four days later. They numbered 20 braves, about 50 women and children, and 200 ponies, upping Davidson's total haul to about 400 Indians and 2,200 head of stock. Among the leaders captured were Yapparika brothers-in-law, Tabananica and White Wolf, Little Crow, and the catalyst of Anadarko, Big Red Meat.

Another big chief gave up the fight on October 20, as the Cheyenne Dog Soldier leader White Horse surrendered to Colonel Neill at Darlington. Badly worked over by Mackenzie at Palo Duro, the poor and ill-equipped band totaled 12 men, 13 women, 1 old man, and 134 ponies.

By the last week in October, Nelson Miles had sat simmering in his Washita base camp since the first of September, finally being forced to do what all the other commanders had been doing all along: carefully garnering enough supplies to mount major expeditions. His scouts and skirmishing parties had been out constantly, and Miles got word that many of the remaining hostiles had taken refuge in the western Staked Plains, closer to the New Mexico line. Probably sensing that this would be one of his last chances to make a decisive strike, Miles formed a campaign to swing far to the west, driving the hostiles back eastward, where Major Price would be waiting for them with his (or, more appropriately, Miles') four companies of 8th Cavalry.

Colonel Mackenzie, too, was not idle after his triumph at Palo Duro. Rounding the head of the canyon at the first of November, on the third he crossed some Indians at Las Lagunas Quatro, in a brief fight killing two and taking nineteen prisoners, before returning to his base at Catfish Creek. Thereafter he limited his operations to the southern portions of the Staked Plains.

Finally on November 6, the Indians took some measure of revenge for their previous setbacks, as about one hundred warriors of Gray Beard's Cheyennes surprised and ambushed Lieutenant H. J. Farnsworth and twenty-five men of H Company, 8th Cavalry. The troopers had left the main bivouac on the Washita on the third to make a lengthy scout to the south, and had trekked as far as the breaks at the head of McClellan Creek, south of the later site of Pampa, when Gray Beard pinned them down and dealt with them severely. Four troopers were wounded; two, Rufus Hibbard and William Densham, were killed, and, in the desperation of the fight, abandoned to the Cheyennes, as Farnsworth retreated northward for aid from the Washita base. Price rode south to the rescue with two companies of the 8th, finding and burying the dead men's scalped, gashed, and gutted remains before returning to the Washita on the twelfth.

Two days after the fight, though, on November 8, Gray Beard and his band paid the price. With Miles operating in the western part of the Staked Plains, Lieutenant Frank D. Baldwin, 5th Infantry, was escorting the empty wagon train back to the Washita camp for more supplies. Approaching the head of McClellan Creek from the west, Baldwin accidently came upon Gray Beard's vulnerable link, his village. Baldwin had with him only one troop of mounted cavalry, D Company of the 6th, and some infantry, and the twenty-three empty wagons, an insufficient force for rushing a camp this size. But, using the ingenuity and raw nerve for which Miles found him so praiseworthy, Baldwin drew the supply wagons into two parallel columns and apportioned his infantry among them, placing at least one sharpshooter in each, turning them into primitive sorts of tanks. Then, flanking them with his scouts and cavalry, he gave the order to charge. The surprised and unnerved Indians broke and stampeded out onto the Staked Plains, able to salvage only few of their possessions. The camp was identified as that of Gray Beard when one of the men recognized his tipi. As reported later at Darlington, other chiefs in the camp included Heap of Birds, Lean Bear, Medicine Water, Sand Hill, Red Moon, Left Hand Bull, the Dog Soldier chief Bull Bear and, incredibly, Old Whirlwind, who was supposed to be quietly sitting out the war at the agency.

For his courage and resourcefulness in leading the gutsy raid, Baldwin was awarded his second Congressional Medal of Honor. Although he undoubtedly deserved recognition for this action, it was not learned until later that the Cheyennes could not have fought if they wanted to: They were out of ammunition.

In one of the abandoned lodges the soldiers found, so weak from malnutrition, exposure, and abuse that they could barely walk, two small white girls about seven and five years of age: Julia and Adelaide German. Back at the Washita base camp the children were the objects of the tenderest solicitation. "The poor little innocents were nearly naked and in a famishing condition," raged J. T. Marshall in his news correspondence. "They had been once left alone on the wild prairie to be devoured by wolves or suffer another equally horrible death by starvation. For a whole week, while in this lonely condition, their only food was wild grapes and the few grains of corn they picked up in the [abandoned] camps of the soldiers." Also recovered from the deserted village, before it was destroyed, were two fresh scalps, almost undoubtedly those of the two soldiers whom Farnsworth had lost on the sixth.

Baldwin and his giddy outfit chased after Gray Beard's band for ten to twelve miles, and although Baldwin found himself outpaced, he drove the hostiles straight into Major Price and the 8th

Cavalry. But Price, who was at one point within one mile of the fight, inexplicably did not move to the attack. Instead he loosed his stock to graze for several hours, then marched away from the action. Maybe Price had his reasons, and maybe he actually chose not to fight, but when Miles heard of the incident he was speechless with rage. In the preceding weeks Miles had come to the conclusion that Price was guilty of letting the Kiowas slip through his fingers by failing to ride to the aid of Lyman's wagon train sooner than he did (although to do so, Price would have had to disobey Miles' own orders, which were themselves of specious validity). But now Miles considered the major more than a nuisance and an obstacle; he was a liability that had to be gotten rid of, and Miles handled the sensitive question of relieving an expedition commander in a typical fashion. Accusing Price of dereliction, he wrote, "I have placed the little gentleman in arrest, ordered him to Camp Supply and will prefer charges against him." No formal charges could ever have been made to stick, but the important gain was that Price was once and for all out of Miles' hair, and the latter assumed personal control of the 8th Cavalry.

If Price failed to pursue Gray Beard's band, however, John W. Davidson took up the chase with spirit. With a large force he ran them as far back northwest as the Cap Rock, where he himself pulled out of the rout, but sent Lieutenant Pratt's scouts and 120 buffalo soldiers, hand-selected from several companies and commanded by Captain Charles D. Viele, to keep after them. After an initial defeat near McClellan Creek, the winded Cheyennes continued to outrun all pursuers, and Viele gave up the chase at the Canadian River, after two days and 96 exhausting miles.

Meanwhile, back in the Washita supply camp, Miles had returned, and detailed his surgeon, Dr. Powell, to escort the sadly emaciated German sisters back to Kansas for recuperation. As the two girls were orphans and utterly helpless, Miles, to his great credit, arranged for his wife to take them into their house. When Dr. Powell returned to the field he gave Miles a photograph of the girls he had taken in Leavenworth, showing them in their "improved condition." Miles kept the picture for two months, at which time he would have occasion to put it to good use.

Not all of Davidson's forces were committed to the Gray Beard chase, as B Company of the buffalo soldiers fought an indecisive engagement on the eighth at Laguna Tahoka, far to the southwest. And still the rains came, laced more and more frequently with snow and stinging ice storms of the coming winter.

Toward the end of November the army began to wind down its operations and began to issue orders rescinding companies of soldiers from the battle zone, considerably altering the plan to keep major forces in the field during the colder months, the envisioned re-enaction of Sheridan's "winter campaign" of 1868. The decision was made in view of the growing number of hostile surrenders, the failure of supply sources, and the weather, which suddenly turned so consistently cold that cavalry horses were freezing to death while staked to picket lines. One ice storm raged for four days, from November 15 to 19, slamming Davidson's command with the loss of more than ninety horses frozen to death, and twenty-six men incapacitated with severe frostbite. As a last exercise for the 8th Cavalry before having to send them home, Colonel Miles dispatched them north to sweep the countryside around the Canadian. With Major Price safely tucked away in Camp Supply, Miles placed in charge of the 8th Captain Charles A. Hartwell, the expedition leaving the Washita cantonment on the twelfth. On November 29 the Hartwell column engaged about fifty hostile Cheyennes at the head of Muster Creek; as that stream is a small feeder of the Canadian, it seems to point to the Indians as being a part of Gray Beard's village. Hartwell pursued them for twelve miles, but the hostiles escaped at dusk into Palo Duro Canyon, losing, according to the captain, two dead and two wounded.

A few days later, on December 2, Sergeant Dennis Ryan of Miles' command, with a patrol of 20 men of I Company, 6th Cavalry, chased some unidentified Indians about 10 miles, destroying their abandoned property and killing or capturing 50 ponies.

Black Jack Davidson returned with his column to Fort Sill on November 29, but he kept patrols out, and on December 5 Captain Alexander S. B. Keyes, with I Company of the buffalo soldiers, attacked a Cheyenne camp on Kingfisher Creek and netted a considerable haul: Twenty-six Indians—13 warriors and 13 women—were taken prisoner.

Mackenzie was already out of the panhandle picture, so when Buell returned to Fort Griffin in the first week in December, from that time, with the single exception of Miles' cantonment at the edge of Staked Plains, the howling blizzards roared unchecked over the frigid, desolate country, and the Wrinkled-hand Chase ground to an ice-sheeted halt.

XIV. The Collapse of Indian Resistance

Throughout the winter minor operations were continued. Ranald Mackenzie kept a few scouts out on the southern Staked Plains constantly, and on December 18 a 10-man patrol under Lieutenant Lewis Warrington attacked a small band of 15 unidentified hostiles—probably Comanches—claiming two killed, one wounded, and one captured. Mackenzie dissolved his expedition shortly after.

On the twenty-eighth Captain A. S. B. Keyes of Davidson's command struck again, dogging a Cheyenne band for 80 miles, all the way to the North Fork Canadian, before the whole village gave up the flight and surrendered. Keyes captured 52 Indians with their herd of 70 thin ponies.

Though he had been ordered to lay in and only keep scouts in the field, the headstrong Colonel Nelson Miles had other ideas. "I am quietly waiting here for supplies," he wrote Mary on December 2, "and as soon as they are received, I intend to make one more movement towards the head of Red River, with a hope of driving out the Indians that may have taken refuge in that region or of making it uncomfortable for them, even if I cannot capture them." The fate of the elder two German sisters weighed heavily on his mind, as he added, "And possibly we may be able to do something for those poor white girls who are still in their hands."

Miles despised "that most disagreeable camp," his supply base on the Washita, and when he was resupplied he sortied on December 14, west and then south. "I have with me only one company of cavalry but shall take other troops as circumstances require." Miles' whole command had now shrunk to only three

companies of cavalry and three of infantry, and he was furious
that his expedition was disintegrating before he had completed his
job to his satisfaction. The week before Christmas, more information came into his camp regarding Kate and Sophie German,
whose rescue Miles now considered a primary goal. "I know the
chief who has one or both of them," he wrote indignantly without
identifying him. "He offered to trade them to some Mexicans for
squaws."

By the third week in January Miles had almost completed his
uneventful trek across the alternately frozen or boggy Staked
Plains, having marched south as far as the Tulé, then east downstream all the way to Fort Sill, and finally back to his base via
Camp Supply. By now he reasoned that those Indians who
remained hostile, deprived of most of their food stores, with what
few ponies they still had weak from hunger, must be ready to surrender. Calling in some of his Indian scouts to go out to find the
hostiles, he dictated his ultimatum of surrender. Then Miles took
out the photograph of Adelaide and Julia that surgeon Powell had
given him, turned it over, and dashed off the following message:

Headquarters Indian Territory Expedition.
In the field, January 20th, 1875.

To the Misses Germaine: Your little sisters are well, and
in the hands of friends. Do not be discouraged. Every
effort is being made for your welfare.
(s) Nelson A. Miles, Colonel and Brevet-Major
General, U. S. Army, Commanding Expedition

By this time the beleaguered Cheyennes had fled far to the west,
and were found almost in New Mexico, encamped on a feeder
stream of the Pecos River. The tracker who carried the photograph and message succeeded in slipping it furtively to one of
the elder sisters, giving them their first indication of what had
become of Addie and Julie since their separation. The head chief
of the large band was identified as Stone Calf. He had found his
tribe on returning from exile in Mexico, and had begun to regain
some of his following. When told that peace was conditional upon

the girls' safety, Stone Calf moved them into a lodge next to his own for their protection.

Up at the Cheyenne Agency, meanwhile, information from other sources was beginning to trickle in about the missing German sisters. On December 20 Davidson's Captain Keyes captured a Cheyenne named Big Moccasin. When that prisoner was transferred to Darlington he attempted to improve his standing with the whites by pointing out two members of the notorious Medicine Water's band, Limpy and Bear's Heart, who had surrendered in anonymity on the nineteenth, and who now were placed under a strong guard. By this time Colonel Neill, commanding the agency garrison, had heard from enough sources that Catherine and Sophia German were being held by Cheyennes to the southwest to justify sending out his own messenger to demand their release. The Indian selected for the job was named Little Shield, who, although it was undiscovered until a few days later, had also been involved with Medicine Water in the German and Short massacres.

During the two days following Christmas, 12 Cheyennes surrendered in Darlington—six men (including Tall Bull, a leading Dog Soldier chief), two women, and four children. The beaten Indians said they had broken off from Medicine Water's band after repeated futile attemps to "talk him in." From them Agent Miles learned the identity of the German sisters' captors. One of them was the property of Long Back, a lesser chief of Stone Calf's band, and the other of Wolf Robe, a leading warrior of Gray Beard's band. Though the sisters were at least alive, the groups who held them were still "a great way off" on the Staked Plains. Miles also learned that another group that surrendered on December 20 was "jumped" by troops while coming in to the agency, and one of the young warriors, Big Head, the nephew of Chief Minimic, was killed.

Also around the first of the year Neill received instructions that all Indians who could be proven guilty of any serious crime committed any time within the previous two years should be arrested pending a general disposition of the prisoners of war. The army, clearly, was taking the opportunity afforded by the war to rid the tribes of all individuals considered harmful influences, regardless of whether they had fought in the uprising. Included on Neill's list of suspects were three Arapahoes: Packer, for the 1873 murder of agency employee Leon Williams; White Bear, for shooting with intent to kill employee F. W. Williams, also in 1873; and Crow Man, for the 1874 killing of worker John F. Halloway, the son of the agency doctor. During the year of war the Arapahoes had won praise for their steadfastness in maintaining peace among themselves, and Agent Miles feared deeply that to march into their camps now and arrest some of them for past transgressions would cause an emotional uprising among them, but still he backed Neill up: "My opinion is," Miles wrote, "that it will require a strong force to prevent the loss of life at this Agency when the Arapahoe arrests are made [but] it is the only humain policy to be pursued, by making individuals responsible for their crimes." No trouble occurred, however, when the arrests were made, but Crow Man later escaped and fled north, supposedly to the Red Cloud Agency.

Meanwhile, increasing numbers of hostiles defected and came in. On January 20 three braves arrived from Gray Beard's camp; they informed Agent Miles that Stone Calf was still a great distance off to the southwest, and they confirmed that the two elder German girls were in his camp. They further added to Miles' store of information on the girls, adding that Long Back had bought his captive from a member of the Medicine Water band, a son-in-law of Stone Calf named Black Moon. Additionally, the three warriors stated that Little Shield had arrived with Colonel Neill's demand for the captives' surrender, but the ultimatum was scorned by Heap of Birds, Gray Beard, and the other war chiefs. "Let them send a few more times," they quoted Gray Beard as saying, "and we can make peace on our own terms."

The informants said that the hostile elements were greatly encouraged by the slackening of military activity that attended the end of the Wrinkled-hand Chase, and they had sent raids to Old Mexico to get horses with which to renew the war in the spring. One Mexican wagon train had been massacred in the quest for horses; another raiding party had gone to Texas under Cloud Chief and returned successful. Other war parties recruited included one by Sand Hill's son, Yellow Horse, who intended to return to the headwaters of the Red River, and another by Minimic's son Howling Wolf, who intended to steal horses from the Wichita Agency. The informants said that the mass of

Cheyennes were suffering terribly from exposure and frostbite and had few supplies, but the most intractable war chiefs, Medicine Water, Medicine Arrows, and White Antelope, were going to make a run for it, northward, to join with the Northern Cheyennes.

On February 10 four more Cheyennes came in and identified themselves as part of the Medicine Water group: Gray Eyes, Mad Wolf, Cedar, and Red Eagle. At the same time, some 50 more Indians—nine men, 20 women, and 20 children—surrendered at Darlington, telling Miles that Stone Calf was following them in with almost all the remaining hostile Cheyennes. Skeptical because of the information on new war parties, Miles wrote, "I shall believe it when I *see them.*"

Exactly two weeks later, however, the old chief Stone Calf rode into Darlington with an entourage of 15 warriors and announced his intention to surrender all that part of the tribe that followed him. On learning of the proximity of the German sisters, Colonel Neill dispatched an ambulance to bring them in at once, writing a thankful end to their 5½-month captivity. Stone Calf proved as good as his word, as on March 6 he surrendered 820 Indians, including Gray Beard, Heap of Birds, Lean Bear, High Back, Red Moon, Dog Soldier chief Bull Bear, Eagle Heart, and Bear Shield. Also in the mass of starving and miserable Indians were the former owners of Kate and Sophie German, Long Back and Wolf Robe, and the chief Medicine Water, who had abandoned his scheme of running north. The latter man was arrested two days later and placed in chains.

"The surrender on the 6th," wrote Neill the following day, "was a very beautiful sight. Stone Calf in front with a white flag was followed by a line of three divisions of Indians on foot, a center and two wings: they halted, threw down their arms in line on the ground, and then sat down on the ground. The behavior on this occasion was orderly and decorous." But if Stone Calf thought his long ordeal was, at last, over, he was wrong: Once more he would be shamed. Neill, who knew nothing of Stone Calf's peaceful inclinations and resulting fall from power and exile from the tribe, and the chief's courtesies to and personal protection of the German girls, regarded the old man as merely one more hostile leader who had been beaten into submission. Thus, when Stone Calf brought in the more than 800 Indians to surrender, Neill told him abruptly that he, Neill, knew they were surrendering in bad faith and hiding some of their weapons. "I told Stone Calf the count of men and arms was unsatisfactory, that I wanted all the men, women, and children, and all the arms, and was going to have them." Stone Calf, realizing he had been double-crossed by some of his own braves, who had hidden caches of weapons without telling him, and then left alone to face Neill, must have been mortified. In an emotional council that night the elderly chief demanded to know whether or not they followed him; they capitulated, and the next day the surrender was accepted.

If the surrender of the Cheyennes had struck Colonel Neill as a "very beautiful sight," that tribe's agent, remembering how hard and with what frustration he had tried to forestall the war, was sickened by the spectacle of its conclusion, reporting to the Indian Commissioner, "A more wretched and poverty-stricken community than these people presented after they were placed in the prison camp it would be difficult to imagine. Bereft of lodges and the most ordinary cooking apparatus; with no ponies or other means of transportation for wood or water; half-starved, and very little to eat, and scarcely anything that could be called clothing, they were truly objects of pity; and for the first time the Cheyennes seemed to realize the power of the government, and their own inability to cope successfully therewith."

Agent Miles did not himself question Sophie and Kate German on the details of their sordid captivity, discreetly letting his genial and popular wife, Lucy, conduct the interview. To her Sophie confided that she had been taken to wife by two masters—her original captor, and Wolf Robe, to whom she had been traded. Catherine, however, had been less fortunate, and Miles' outrage was difficult to control as he slashed away a barely legible report that her final master, Long Back, had made money by farming her out as a prostitute. "While Long Back who held possession of Catherine had not himself treated her brutally," he seethed, "yet he had permitted his Lodge to be visited regularly by the young *Bucks* of the tribe—He no doubt realizing a *pecuniary benefit* ————" The Cheyenne women, he continued, who used her for performing camp drudgeries, would deliberately send her out for wood, knowing full well that she would be assaulted from one to a half dozen times before she could get back. He vaguely estimated the number of Kate's rapists at "perhaps fifty or perhaps one hundred." Also during that winter, recalled Kate later, "I nearly froze. The snow was very deep, and I had nothing to keep me warm but a blanket. Both feet were frozen, and my nails came off from my feet."

After hearing all the German girls' story, Miles realized also how utterly wrong everyone had been in assuming that the elder chief, Stone Calf, had gone over to the hostiles, using as proof his absence from the agency. Hastening to exonerate the old man, Miles wrote, "It has been currently reported in the newspapers . . . that Stone Calf a Cheyenne chief was one of the chiefs who outraged the German girls—It is but justice to him that this statement be corrected. . . . we have the girls' statement clearing him of such charge, And further that he (Stone Calf) was first in advocating their release, and that he has always treat her kindly."

Large as was the Stone Calf surrender, they still were not the last of the Cheyennes out. "We have reliable information," wrote Miles shortly after, "that a party of young *Bucks* are now camped . . . thirty to fifty miles from this Agency, waiting to hear the fate of the party who have just surrendered." They had, he continued, retained the best weapons and ponies to attempt a desperate escape if the ones who gave up were not kindly treated. They were few in number, however, and under the lead of one or two Dog Soldier chiefs succeeded in escaping to join the Northern Cheyennes. For the rest of that tribe, the war was over.

The army's prosecution of the war on the northern front never did prevent the white Kansas horse thieves from continuing to ply their trade. Several head were stolen from Miles' agency Indians on October 24, 1874. Colonel Neill allowed Miles to use military guide-interpreter William F. Morrison to recover them, but only on the strict condition that the Indian Office would pay all Morrison's expenses. The scheme was successful, although Miles' report of it makes clear that even yet the Indian Bureau had not formulated a policy for paying such debts. "Through the efforts of Morrison," wrote Miles, "17 Head of the ponies were recovered in western Kansas & three of the thieves *severly* handled by the troops from Dodge. —From what funds shall this bill be paid?" Miles' problem of feeding the peaceful Indians had not significantly improved, either, as on January 19 he had to allow the Arapahoes and friendly Cheyennes to leave the agency, guarded by some of Neill's troops, for a buffalo hunt. By March of 1875 his double-underscored and emphatically punctuated letters pleading for food had almost ceased to have meaning; on the eighteenth of that month he wrote Commissioner Smith in Washington, "Referring to the items of *Coffee & Sugar* for the Arapahoe & Cheyenne Indians I have to inform that these two articles of supplies are entirely exhausted." As far as rations were concerned, only one thing had changed in the preceding year: In the spring of 1874 the Cheyennes still possessed the option of war. In the spring of 1875, having experienced the impossibility of resistance, the beaten Indians abjectly resigned themselves to their squalid existence.

One other noteworthy set of circumstances surrounded the final capitulation of the Cheyennes: the vigor with which the different army officers scrambled to claim the credit for it. Lieutenant Colonel Neill and Colonel Miles had both sent out messengers demanding the surrender, and each man was quick to place the laurel wreath on his own head. Usually it is Miles who gets the credit now; not only did he have troops in the field that posed a greater threat to the Cheyennes than Neill, he also left two autobiographies describing his part in the campaign. Neill, however, did actually receive the surrender. Finally, when Black Jack Davidson got wind that Stone Calf's band was crossing the northern part of his district on the way to Darlington, he, too, tried to get some of the action, announcing that he was going out to intercept the hostile Indians, give them one of his thrashings, and impound them. Neill would have none of that, however, and threatened even to send a force down to arrest Davidson if he tried any such move! Evidently, Neill and Davidson had been nursing a feud over a long period; higher authority finally separated them, and Davidson was not involved in the Cheyenne surrender.

The origin of the hostility between Neill and Davidson has never been made clear, aside from the general strain of competition. Other evidence suggests, however, that Neill was an extremely difficult man to work with. In one instance Neill, impervious to Agent Miles' ever-deepening frustration in trying to feed and clothe the friendly Arapahoes and Cheyennes, worried about his own supply shortages (which were less than anyone else's), and shortly after the Stone Calf surrender informed Miles in an elaborately worded communiqué that he had "the honor to make formal written demand" that Miles suddenly take over the care and feeding of Stone Calf's 800 destitute Indians, whom Neill was holding in a prison camp two miles from the agency. The letter, which in less tragic circumstances would have been ludicrous, took Miles completely off guard. In a flustered reply the agent informed Neill that Indian Department care of officially hostile Indians was illegal under the latest Indian Appropriation Act, aside from the fact that the army's general orders the previous July had removed him from any responsibility for hostiles, and claimed control for the army. Hostile Indians had not figured in Miles' ration plans, and for him now to contemplate the care of over eight hundred renegades while the friendly Arapahoes and Cheyennes were maintained only marginally above starvation, was ridiculous in the extreme. Though an arrangement was finally worked out, the besieged and overworked agent sent copies of the whole exchange to Superintendent Hoag, begging for a clarification of his position, and then took a brief leave of absence to rest from a year of nerve-fraying work.

During the weeks of maneuvering in effecting the surrender of Stone Calf, Colonel Davidson had returned to Fort Sill and had determined to talk the remaining Kiowa and Comanche hostiles in peaceably, with the crucial help of Striking Eagle, and also Big Bow, who had slipped into the fort under cover of night and traded his help in the endeavor for amnesty for himself. The prisoners Big Red Meat and Tabananica also agreed to help in the effort, as did the friendly Yapparika chief, Cheevers. Emissaries were sent out to negotiate, and the policy paid a huge dividend on February 26, as on that date the Kiowas' principal chief, Lone Wolf, in the company of Maman-ti, Poor Buffalo, Do-hauson the Younger, and Red Otter, with over 250 Kiowas, all laid down their weapons and turned over to Davidson what pathetically little stock they had salvaged from the Palo Duro nightmare—some 400 head.

In March, Davidson and his 10th Cavalry were assigned new duties in Texas, and the command of Fort Sill and the Indian cap-

tives there was assumed by Ranald Mackenzie, the victor of Palo
Duro, and his battle-hardened 4th Cavalry. The move was part of
a general reorganization, by which all the Indian Territory was
placed under a single commander, Mackenzie, and unified within
General Pope's Department of the Missouri. Mackenzie wisely
pursued Davidson's line of persuasion, and on April 18, 1875,
Mackenzie received the surrender of Mow-way, the Kotsoteka
chief, and his band of 200. When White Horse followed him on
the nineteenth, only the Quahadis remained hostile to the government. They had not been among those trapped in Palo Duro, and
were still far away, roaming their traditional haunts somewhere on
the Llano Estacado. Determined to talk them in without further
bloodshed, Mackenzie sent out four messengers to negotiate: Sergeant Charlton and two friendly Comanches, with the delegation
led by Dr. J. J. Sturms, the husband of a Caddo woman and
respected by hostile and friendly Indians alike.

Within weeks of his arrival at Fort Sill, Mackenzie was
confronted by two serious problems of totally different natures.

First, he discovered that Nelson Miles, incensed that Mackenzie
and not himself should receive command of the whole Indian Territory, had been intriguing against him in Kansas, attempting to
get half of Mackenzie's regiment transferred to himself, so he
could share in the command. The plan, which Miles doubtless
bullied General Pope into endorsing, called for Mackenzie to retain control of Fort Sill and the garrison at Darlington, while
Miles stepped in to command Camp Supply and a new cantonment on the upper Sweetwater, which later became Fort Elliott.
Against a Price or a Pope, Miles could usually get his way, but
Mackenzie bristled. Writing Division Commander Sheridan, who
was in New Orleans for a brief stay, Mackenzie urgently requested
Sheridan to detour to Fort Sill on his way back to Chicago, to settle things. In a very long and emotional letter, Mackenzie
protested, "I dislike writing this letter very much. . . . I have no
word to say against Colonel Miles on the contrary I regard him as
a very fine officer. [But] I am not in the slightest degree jealous of
him. I regard him not as my Superior in any way and in some particulars I am sure he is not my equal." Mackenzie had been
promised authority in the Indian Territory and had, with Augur
and Sheridan, laid plans on that premise, plans that if Miles sud-

denly strode into the picture would have to be scrapped to allow him his proper slice of the input. "While I like Miles," continued Mackenzie, "I think that this ought not be done and was very much hurt by even such a proposition being made." Mackenzie had always been the darling of the high command, whereas Miles' reputation as a grasper had become ingrained into the circles of the officer corps. In Mackenzie, Miles had met his match, and for the time being Miles backed down and sought easier prey.

The second great dilemma that Mackenzie had to wrestle was, as at Darlington, the care and feeding of several hundreds of starving, destitute, and sometimes naked Indians. The total war that Mackenzie had waged in the Palo Duro, and Buell on the lower forks of the Red River, which encompassed the burning of all the Indians' worldly possessions taken in the debilitating routs of the Wrinkled-hand Chase, had left the former renegades in sickening want. But in spite of their utter dependence on the government to care for them, the Indian Office continued to neglect friendly and hostile alike. So disgusted was Mackenzie with the rations that the agent had to feed the loyal Indians that he ordered them fed, along with the prisoners of war, out of the post commissary, a startling reversal of Neill's policy at Darlington.

Working with the beaten Indians meant additionally that Mackenzie would have to work with James Haworth. During the uproar that attended Haworth's battles with Colonel Davidson and then General Augur, Mackenzie had added his name to the list of those calling for Haworth's removal as a bungling incompetent. As the spring of 1875 dragged on into summer, however, and Mackenzie perceived for himself the impossible odds that Haworth had been laboring against for over a year, Mackenzie began slowly to change his mind. Later on Haworth won a deserved vindication from Davidson's slanders as Mackenzie, writing General Pope that "I feel there is a heavy responsibility resting on me to try and act rightly for these Indians," bitterly attacked the Indian Department for their callousness and bureaucratic ineptitude. "In all this matter," he added, "the Agent is in nowise to blame but some higher authority whom I do not know[.] And as I[,] once quoting the opinions of others, spoke unfavorably of Mr. Hayworth I wish, to say that so far as my observation exceeds he is doing what he is able and doing right."

Near the middle of May, word was received from Texas that one final action had been fought there. It involved a Comanche later identified as Black Coyote, his wife, and a few braves with them, who had reportedly been released from the reservation to go hunting and were found near Jacksboro, Texas—whether on a raid or as part of their hunt is unknown. On May 8 Major John B. Jones of the Texas Rangers' Frontier Battalion, whom Maman-ti and Lone Wolf had trapped and mauled the previous July, with a force of about twenty men pursued the Comanches into the Lost Valley, believing that the Comanches had stolen stock from the Loving Ranch. He crossed the Indians' trail "just where I entered the valley last summer, when in pursuit of Lone Wolfe and his party." This time, however, there was no massive ambush by fifty warriors led by wily war chiefs. Instead, Jones and his men gave hot pursuit for about five miles before overhauling seven Indians, of whom they killed five in a running battle. The Indians, noted Jones, were in possession of the most up-to-date firearms, and fought with extraordinary valor—two of them continuing to battle after being shot from their horses. "One of those killed was a squaw," he reported, "but handled her six-shooter quite as dextrously as did the bucks. . . . Another was a half-breed or quarter, spoke broken English, and had curly auburn hair. . . . One of them had the scalp of a white woman fastened to his shield."

Jones mentioned in his letter that he was very pleased with the performance of his Rangers, particularly because they did not pause to scalp the four warriors and woman as they fell, but "continued the rout without stopping till the last Indian in sight was killed." Jones could not claim, however, that no scalps were taken after the fight. As Ed Carnal related, "We rangers, as well as Indians, fought under the black flag. We asked no quarter and gave none. When we fell into their hands they scalped us and frightfully mutilated our bodies, frequently cutting and hacking us to pieces. We didn't do as bad as that but scalped them just the same. Indian scalps in ranger camps were as common as pony tracks."

Late in the night of May 13 Dr. Sturms and his party returned to Mackenzie from their negotiations with the renegade Quahadis. The whole band, led by Wild Horse and Quanah Parker, had been found on the western side of the Staked Plains, isolatedly pursuing their ancient way of life, apparently clinging to their traditional wish to be left alone. In a series of hard talks, Sturms laid down the conditions of surrender. Undoubtedly he told them that Fort Sill had a new soldier chief, the Three-fingered "Kinzie," who had captured their women and children in 1872 and then returned them unharmed when the Comanches gave in to him. If they surrendered now, Sturms told them, "Kinzie" would neither harm nor punish them, but if he had to come get them, he would do to them what he had done to Maman-ti's village in the Palo Duro. From experience the Quahadis knew that Mackenzie could deliver on that threat, but they also knew he had been honorable in vigilantly protecting their captured families from a mass lynching by the good citizens of Jacksboro. After three days of debating and stalling, the Quahadi Comanches gave in. "Unless something unforeseen takes place," reported Mackenzie jubilantly on the fifteenth, "the entire Qua-ha-dee band will come in and their intention is I am confident to give up in good faith." Somewhat dubiously he added that guarding the remnants of the Indians' pony herds would be a serious drain on his manpower. "I shall have to keep large herds of these horses at night in corrals with rail fences," he wrote, "and unless they be heavily guarded the Horse Thieves will get many of them." The ubiquitous horse thieves were still prowling the countryside around the fort and agency.

On May 25 Mackenzie modified his estimate of the pending surrender. "Unless there is an unforeseen accident," he reported to Pope, Sturm's "success will be much greater than I anticipated when I sent him. It will be a wonderfully rich surrender." On June 2, 1875, the last of the Quahadi renegades—some four hundred of them—with Quanah Parker in the lead, filed quietly into Fort Sill, where they threw down their arms and gave up fifteen hundred ponies.

The Red River War was over.

XV. Prison

Although the last of the Quahadis did not surrender until June, for the rest of the Indians the war was over by mid-April, and the question of how to dispose of the worst murderers and "ringleaders" had to be considered then. As finally formulated, the policy fixed that once selected the culprits would be transferred to Florida to be imprisoned in Fort Marion, more familiar as the ancient Spanish Castillo de San Marcos, whose hulking gray limestone ramparts loomed over the balmy coastal town of St. Augustine.

At Fort Sill, when it came time to pick and remove those leaders adjudged culpable, Colonel Mackenzie offered the detail of overseeing them to Lieutenant Richard H. Pratt of Davidson's 10th Cavalry, whom the latter had placed in general charge of incoming prisoners in late 1874. A big, burly man over six feet tall and every inch a soldier, a capricious fate had repeatedly spared Pratt an early death, granting his attainment of the age of thirty-four. As a small boy in upstate New York he was stricken by smallpox, becoming so ill that an undertaker was summoned to measure him; the calling card of that terrible visitation still pocked his rugged face. After being apprenticed to a tinsmith, young Pratt was quick to volunteer for duty in the Civil War; at Chickamauga a stray cannonball missed cutting him in two by scant inches—his horse saw the spent missile coming and stopped in fright—and on two other occasions mounts were shot from under him.

A veteran of Indian fighting, Pratt remained assigned to Sill, when Davidson and the rest of the 10th were transferred to Texas in March. The duty of guarding the Indian prisoners appealed to him, and he lost no time, once he cleared the idea with Mackenzie, of writing Division Commander Sheridan, requesting that he be assigned to them permanently: "If, in the care of these Indians east, the Government requires an officer of my rank, I want to go, because I have been down here eight years and am hungry for a change.

"I know all the leading Cheyennes from a one year duty at Camp Supply, 72 & 73—Having had charge of Indian prisoners here since Dec. and having sought out the offences for which the Kiowas and Comanches are sent away, besides having been amongst them since 67. I am well acquainted with the disposition &c of our batch."

Concerning the care that the warriors could expect at Pratt's hands, the letter spoke ominously, echoing Sheridan's own sentiments: "I am sorry to hear their is a possibility that none of the[m] will be tried. Lone Wolf and five others, of those from here, can clearly be tried and convicted on acts committed since the war began, August 22, last, and charges have been sent in against them. . . . Some of them ought to be tried and executed here in the presence of their own people." Pratt displayed some amount of knowledge in the legal machinery involved in executing Indian chiefs, telling Sheridan he was familiar with the "Modoc case" in California, where four headmen of the Modoc Indians were hanged and decapitated in similar circumstances; in Pratt's opinion, the rule of law applied by the Attorney General in that case could and should be made applicable to the Plains Indians.

All that notwithstanding, none of the chiefs were put to death, and it was not this passage but the final one of the letter that intimated Pratt's famous destiny as a compassionate and able Indian reformer: "Most of the *young men* going up have been governed by the leadership of the chiefs, much as soldiers are, and are not so culpable as at first seems—As . . . [they will] return to their people sooner or later, much can and should be done for them while under this banishment." Sheridan favorably recommended him to War Secretary Belknap, and before long the shackled savages were Pratt's sole responsibility.

The Fort Sill prisoners were housed in two locations, the few more influential chiefs isolated in the post guardhouse; the rest, varying in number from eighty to over one hundred, were penned within the walls of a small, unfinished icehouse. There, once a day, an army wagon would roll up to the gate, and an attendant would throw chunks of raw meat over the wall. "They fed us," said one of the prisoners later, "like we were lions."

When the time came to select which ones would go to Florida, Pratt rather high-handedly instructed Striking Eagle, the leader of the Kiowa peace faction, to pick those of his tribe to go. But with this latest directive the peace chief's famous patience finally broke: He refused. He had done his best to shepherd his people, lovingly and gently, toward the advancements of the white man's road. To turn on them now and name who must be sent away and locked in little rooms would only cost him his influence in the tribe, undoing in a single stroke his five years' labor.

Pratt would brook no resistance from any Indian, however, and —inexcusably in many minds—engaged in tribal political chicanery to get his way. For some time a rivalry had been developing among the Kiowas over who would head the peace faction, with Striking Eagle's leadership being increasingly challenged by the subchief Dangerous Eagle, a brother of Big Tree. Striking Eagle, for all his good intentions toward the whites, still grasped only the most simplistic understanding of their ways and was tragically susceptible to victimization by the nuances and subtleties of white politics. When Pratt pretended to back Dangerous Eagle's claims in order to pull Striking Eagle into line, the latter chief, apparently deserted by his white backers, abjectly gave in to Pratt's demands to preserve his authority, and agreed to select the prisoners. It was a decision that cost him his life.

Hoping to raise as little furor as possible in naming the exiles, Striking Eagle limited the number of influential Kiowas to the barest minimum of the most notorious raiders: Lone Wolf, Maman-ti, White Horse, Woman's Heart, and one somewhat lesser-known figure, Bird Chief, a buffalo medicine man, were the notables to be imprisoned. Big Bow, having been prevailed upon to bring in additional hostiles, was exempted. The peace chief then filled in the ranks as much as he could with men of little account —delinquents, the unpopular, Mexican captives, and the like, until he had an acceptable quota of twenty-seven convicts.

Among the Comanches the thankless task was given to the sick but tractable old Nokoni chief Horseback, whom Agent Haworth named interim Principal Chief, undoubtedly for purposes of respectability. Horseback selected but nine men, and only one of them was of any note: Black Horse, second chief of the Quahadis. Whereas most of the Quahadis escaped punishment by holding out, Black Horse had come in with an earlier group, and now bore the brunt of the government's feeling against that band. The rest of what were generally conceded to be the treacherous war chiefs —Isa Rosa, Tabananica, Mow-way, and others—were released into the custody of friendly chiefs like Cheevers. Big Red Meat, who precipitated the Anadarko fight in August, had died in the icehouse pen on New Year's Day 1875. The Kiowas greeted the news that only nine Comanches were going to jail with a great deal of very justified protest. A much greater proportion of the Comanches had gone to war than the Kiowas, yet the Kiowas were required to give up four times the number of prisoners than the Comanches. But the count stood, and toward the end of April preparations were made for the removal to Florida. Rounding out the list of prisoners was the Caddo, Hu-wah-nee, who murdered E. B. Osborne during the Anadarko fight of August 22.

As the shackled warriors were finally led from the icehouse to the waiting wagons on April 28, Striking Eagle rode up on a lovely gray, a gift from one of Fort Sill's officers, telling his tribesmen they would not be held for long, that he loved them and would work for their release. Among the prisoners, however, sentiment had been understandably rising against him, and some of the arrested warriors had been putting pressure on the owl prophet, Maman-ti, to hex Striking Eagle and "pray him to death." The Do-ha-te finally consented, saying even as he did so that he himself would die for using his power to kill another man. When Striking Eagle rode up to bid them farewell, Maman-ti made his final prophecy: "You think you have done well," he glowered. "You are free, a big man with the whites. But you will not live long; I will see to that." It was a self-fulfilling prophecy, as a few days later, on May 5, the gallant Striking Eagle keeled over dead, the victim, according to the post surgeon, of strychnine poisoning. Striking Eagle's last words: "I have taken the white man's road, and am not sorry. Tell my people to take the good path."

As with the August registration, the process of selecting which prisoners would go to Fort Marion was much less complicated at Darlington than at Sill. The method was also considerably less just. Agent Miles was absent on leave, but Colonel Neill's handling of the affair was recorded by a horrified Acting Agent J. A. Covington. After stipulating that the Indian Department was in no way involved in the affair, Covington wrote that on April 6 Neill had the former hostiles drawn up in a line and an effort made to identify particular Indians against a list of known depredators. "Considerable time was consumed," he reported, and "night came on before the list was completed and Genl. Neil, in order to get his complement of prisoners . . . ordered eighteen struck off from the right" of the line to fill the quota. This selection, protested Covington, was made "irrespective of name, rank, or character. . . . That a number of apparently innocent parties were selected, there can be no doubt." Neill's interpreter, a Mexican named Romeo, later told George Bent that Neill was visibly drunk during the entire process.

Among the Cheyenne prisoners were many of the chiefs not consistently identified with the Little Robe peace party: Gray Beard, Minimic, Heap of Birds, Medicine Water, and others. Also selected was the only woman to be sent to Florida, Medicine Water's wife, Mochi, whom Sophia German concertedly identified as the "woman who chopped my mother's head open with an ax." Catherine German too went down the lineup of prospective convicts, identifying as many of her rapists as she could remember. Rounding out the list were the two wanted Arapahoes, Crow Man having escaped.

At two o'clock in the afternoon of the same day, a small guard detail commanded by Captain Andrew S. Bennett of the 5th Infantry's B Company stood watch over a group of the Cheyenne prisoners while the agency's blacksmith, a Negro named Wesley, fitted their chains for the long trip to Marion. Observers said the shame was excruciating to the warriors, especially after some of their women sat down close by and teased them. But when it came the turn of a young brave named Black Horse to be shackled, he kicked the blacksmith over as the latter was fitting his leg irons, fought loose, and bolted for the nearby Cheyenne village. When he continued his flight after the guards ordered him to stop, the detail leveled their rifles and opened fire. Black Horse was hit and felled at once but, even more ominously, the men had fired in the direction of the Cheyenne camp, and some of their bullets ripped through the Indians' tipis.

The encamped Cheyennes, after Sand Creek and the Washita, were not strangers to first surrendering and then being slaughtered in their villages by soldiers; the Cheyennes prepared to fight, and in a few horrible seconds Neill realized he had serious trouble on his hands. The Indians had been stripped of their guns but still had some bows and arrows, and some of the braves in the Indian encampment sent a spray of arrows back at Bennett's guard detail, hitting and gravely wounding one of the soldiers. Neill now had no choice but to order up a cavalry troop to help Bennett's men, but when the Indians saw the line of mounted soldiers forming up they fled in wild-eyed terror for the bush, and in a few seconds the camp of from 100 to 150 warriors, with some women and children, lay deserted and starkly silent. The Cheyennes fled to a pronounced sandy hill by the south bank of the North Fork Canadian, where they dug up a cache of guns and ammunition that they had hidden away before surrendering. They had not, apparently, told Stone Calf about the arms in the night powwow when he upbraided them for their duplicity, and no doubt they suddenly felt justified at having deceived the white victors.

The first group of soldiers to follow the Cheyennes to the hill was Captain William A. Rafferty's M Company, 6th Cavalry, assigned to Darlington after the dissolution of Nelson Miles' command. At Rafferty's order the men held their fire, dismounted, and walked cautiously toward the hill. The Indians, too, held their fire, but only until the soldiers were very close, when the concealing bushes erupted in a barrage of noise and smoke. Rafferty, learning for the first time that the Indians had firearms, retreated hastily. Soon Captains Stevens T. Norvall and A. S. B. Keyes arrived to reinforce Rafferty with M and D Companies of 10th Cavalry buffalo soldiers, detailed to the Cheyenne Agency from their base at Fort Sill. The enraged Cheyennes held firm, however, against the combined assaults of three cavalry troops. When Colonel Neill rode up at about two-thirty and boldly ordered another mounted charge into the Cheyenne positions, Norvall and Keyes demurred, informing him from their first experience that the difficult ground between themselves and the Cheyennes rendered such a maneuver extremely hazardous.

Neill deferred to their judgment for the time being, and instead ordered up a Gatling gun, whose revolving barrels poured rounds into the entrenched Indians from four hundred yards' distant. When that was done Neill again ordered the men forward, this time afoot. Rafferty's M Troop advanced, but was beaten back when he received no aid from either company of 10th Cavalry. Once more Neill sprayed the Indians with the Gatling gun, and resolutely ordered all the men to charge. Again, incredibly, the Cheyennes turned back the troops, and with nightfall Neill broke off the engagement, preparing to charge at dawn with every man he could muster. His losses by this time amounted to a shocking nineteen men wounded, in addition to three horses dead and six hit. One soldier, Private Clark Young of M Company, 10th Cavalry, lay dying; three others of the nineteen were wounded seriously.

The next morning Neill's men stormed the sand hill, without resistance; the Cheyennes had escaped during the night, under cover of a crashing thunderstorm, their trail heading north across the river. In their flight, Neill reported, they had abandoned seven bodies on the hill, one woman and six braves. At once Neill ordered out two cavalry companies in hot pursuit and flashed the news to General Pope in Leavenworth, who relayed it to the commander of Fort Wallace, Kansas, Major H. A. Hambright of the 19th Infantry. Fort Wallace lay on the Smoky Hill River, near the Colorado border, the narrowly missed goal of the German family the preceding September. It was the most advantageous station from which to intercept the new renegades, but it had no cavalry units assigned, and Hambright had to send for help to Fort Lyon, Colorado. But when forty soldiers of H Company, 6th Cavalry, arrived led by Second Lieutenant Austin Henely, he sent them out speedily, allocating them two supply wagons and rations for fifteen days.

Lieutenant Henely and his men rode out eastward from Wallace, downstream along the south bank of the Smoky Hill, crossing the trail of the northbound Indians on April 20, exactly two weeks after the breakout. The trail was not as large as he might have expected, because many of the runaways had quickly returned to Darlington under an amnesty promised by General Pope. The trail was a small one, ten or twelve lodges, but the troops veered north across the river to pursue them anyway, only to discover that, after it crossed the Kansas-Pacific railroad tracks not far from Monument Station, the trail split and vanished—a method of throwing off pursuit that the Plains Indians mastered to perfection generations before Henely was born. The young lieutenant was forced to begin a general search by moving to the upper reaches of the Solomon River, where he hoped to pick up the trail again, and arrived in the region late on the twenty-first. He found no sign of Indians there, however, and the following day he set out for Beaver Creek, a tributary of the Republican River, to the northeast.

It was still morning, however, when the soldiers met three hunters on the prairie: Henry Campbell, Charles Shroder, and Samuel B. Srack. They informed Henely that Indians, undoubtedly the ones he was after, had ransacked their camp on the previous day, and were at that very time bivouacked on the North Fork of Sappa Creek, a minor feeder stream of the Beaver, less than a day's march away. The hunters agreed to guide Henely and his men to them, and true to their word, crept up on the unsuspecting Indians after nightfall.

In a well-handled cavalry maneuver the next morning Henely handed the Cheyennes their most crushing defeat of the war in terms of persons killed. About half the renegades escaped to join the Northern Cheyennes. The rest, twenty-seven in number, Henely cut off from their horses and trapped in a shallow sink near the creek, and when he demanded their surrender the angry, scared Indians answered with a rifle volley and cries of "Go 'way John, bring back our ponies." Henely then opened his attack, and against a loss of two dead to himself, every one of the Cheyennes was eventually picked off—nineteen braves and eight women and children, more than were lost in any other engagement of the war. When General Pope heard of the victory he considered that it wrote a finish to the Indian wars on the South Plains, and issued special orders citing the young lieutenant's prowess, boasting in part, ". . . the skill and good judgement of Lieut. *Henely* in his management of the fight, as evinced by the results——nineteen warriors left dead on the field, and only two of his own men killed . . . cannot be too highly praised. It is believed that the punishment inflicted upon this band of Cheyennes will go far to deter the tribe from the commission of such atrocities in the future as have characterized in it the past."

A great deal of controversial and emotional material has been written about the Sappa Creek "Massacre," some of it comparing Austin Henely to Chivington and Custer, but if there is any immediate responsibility to be borne for the tragic and needless affair it is not Henely's but Colonel Thomas Neill's, for his calloused and grossly unjust method of selecting the Fort Marion prisoners. Shortly after the humiliating lineup Neill soothed an enraged Covington that he intended to correct the rolls at a future date, but he never got around to it and glossed over the whole incident by categorizing each of the eighteen unfortunate Indians in his official reports as "ringleaders" and sent them to prison with Kate German's rapists and the rest. In the duplicate Indian Bureau list of prisoners, however, Covington, and after him Agent Miles, coldly and stubbornly insisted on the designation, "No particular charge." The key to all this is, if the young Cheyenne Black Horse, who touched off the stampede when he kicked over the blacksmith and ran, was among those eighteen probable innocent who were condemned, then he must have fled, not from a defeated warrior's humiliation, as the traditional history has it; rather he was running, desperately and confusedly, from a punishment he knew he did not deserve. Two new bits of evidence suggest this may actually have been the case. First, nowhere in the Indian Bureau letter file is Black Horse identified as being wanted for a particular crime, contrasted with Medicine Water, Long Back, and many others who were; second, an old photograph in the collection of the Oklahoma Historical Society depicts a young Indian man named Oakerhater, circumstantially identified as the same Black Horse, with three classmates at the Carlisle Indian School in Pennsylvania, indicating that after he recovered from the wounds received during his escape attempt he became a bright and accomplished scholar, not indicative of the wild-eyed raping savage type.

The question of the Sappa Creek fight remains open, but more and more it appears to have been not the tragic result of an ignorant Indian's attempt to flee from the unknown, as much as the result of one officer's arrogance and stupidity. Black Horse's name was stricken from the roll, which again would likely not have been the case were he a wanted man, and all the Indian prisoners— seventy-seven in all—were rounded up to begin the long trip to Florida. As the Pratt train passed through Leavenworth the Cheyenne war chief Minimic requested General Miles to assume responsibility for his son, Howling Wolf, about twenty-two years old, and teach him the white man's road. Miles of course refused to take him. "I appreciated the sentiment," he wrote, "but at the same time I realized the futility of trying to accomplish any good results with but one Indian." As the train rolled through the Deep South another Cheyenne chief, Gray Beard, was foiled in a suicide attempt, but was shortly after shot and killed trying to effect an escape.

Although the Captain of Army Engineers in the South had telegraphed Washington that "Fort Marion is ready" to receive the Indian prisoners, Lieutenant Pratt, when he arrived in St. Augustine at five in the afternoon on May 21, discovered for himself how well prepared the old bastion really was to house the convicts: It was a stinking sieve. "The roofs and walls of every casement are dripping with water," he wrote, "and in places covered with a green scum, while all the cells have a musty, sickening odor. . . . A short time in such confinement will destroy the general health of the prisoners under my charge." He went on to ask for tar paper and whitewash, even offering, owing to his own "practical knowledge," to direct the Indians in applying the material themselves. Pratt's prediction was accurate, as before they had a chance to get accustomed to the new surroundings, several of the prisoners died of various illnesses, among them, ironically, the Kiowas' owl prophet, Maman-ti, who foretold his death as punishment for hexing Striking Eagle. Although Maman-ti was suspected of taking an accomplice to secure the prophecy against Striking Eagle, the medicine man's own death appeared to be from natural causes, whether spiritually induced or otherwise.

As time passed the prisoners gradually settled into a routine at the fort, but Pratt became increasingly less satisfied with the lack of effort to improve them—educate them or at least teach them useful trades that they could spread among their own people when they returned. "This is not a good place to advance them," he complained. "They are simply objects of curiosity here. There are no industries worth noting. They can polish sea beans and Alligator teeth with professionals, and have earned . . . over three hundred dollars at it, but they have glutted the market. They might learn to make Palm Hats. . . ." But aside from that they were merely wasting away at the direction of a vengeful government.

Finally, near the end of June 1875, precisely one year after the buffalo guns boomed at Adobe Walls, the following incredible letter arrived on the desk of the Commissioner of Indian Affairs:

THE GREAT ATLANTIC COAST LINE
Washington, D.C., June 29, 1875

W. J. Walker
Genl. Eastern Passr. Agt
P. O. Box 582

Hon. Sir:

A Guide to Florida under the auspices of the Atlantic Coast Line is now being prepared for the benefit of those contemplating a trip South next winter.

We are also preparing short sketches of many places of interest in Florida and we desire, if consistent with your official duty, to have photographed some of the prominent Indians now incarcerated at the Old Fort (Marion) at St. Augustine, Florida—all expense necessary thereto to be paid by this line. I therefore respectfully ask your assent, and hope for an early and favorable consideration to my request.

Very respectfully
(s) W. J. Walker
Genl. E. P. Agt.

To the Honorable
Commissioner of Indian Affairs.

The mighty chiefs and warriors, who for months had held the South Plains from central Kansas to central Texas in a blood-spattered reign of terror, had become tourist attractions for the polite society of the Eastern Seaboard.

NOTES

Notes, Chapter I
page 1
Katakas . . . or Gattackas, more frequently called Kiowa-Apaches, from the mistaken notion that they were an eastern race of the desert-dwelling Apaches. Though their language stock was Athapascan, the same as the Apaches, the two are no more closely related than that. The Katakas have been closely associated with the Kiowas from the earliest times; on the frontier, the latter tolerated them more or less as "poor relations," calling them "Semat": thieves (Leckie, *Conquest*, p. 11), or "weasel people" (Mooney, "Kiowa Indians," p. 245). In the 1870s they numbered probably three hundred to four hundred individuals, and are usually dealt with as a subtribe of the Kiowas. They were of sufficiently little importance in the Red River War to do so here. In the Medicine Lodge Treaty they are called simply "Apaches" (Kappler, *Laws and Treaties*, p. 982); in Haworth's correspondence he usually refers to them as "Esa-que" Apaches, after one of their head chiefs, Esa-que (or Dego, Pacer, or Peso).

page 2
prisoners of their culture . . . For a more detailed analysis of this phenomenon, see Farb, *Man's Rise*. He devotes one chapter to considering very perceptively the problem of what he calls "The Make-Believe Indians."

page 3
razed the Spaniard's San Saba Mission . . . For a more specific account see Dunn, "Apache Mission."
dozens of the executives . . . One accessible list is that in the *Texas State Almanac* of 1972–73, p. 612. The governors of the area comprising later New Mexico are a still separate list.
As Thomas Battey observed . . . Battey, *Life*, pp. 276–77. Among the Cheyennes it was a "great crime" to kill even captives once they had been sheltered in a lodge (Hyde, *Life*, p. 26).

page 4
Mexicans reportedly offered . . . Wharton, *Satanta*, p. 60 ff.

"an exterminating war . . ." from the Lamar papers, quoted in Leckie, *Conquest,* p. 13.

page 6

an agreement of friendship . . . Buntin, "Removal," p. 62.

Kiowas' first treaty . . . Kappler, *Laws and Treaties,* p. 489.

make certain the pacification . . . See also Foreman, "Texas Comanche Treaty."

Washington . . . The term "Washington" came to be used by the Indians as a personification of federal authority.

page 7

made a separate peace . . . The federal government tried to patch up this *faux pas* with the Fort Atkinson Treaty of 1853, but that agreement soon dissolved in resentment and misunderstanding. Annuities were canceled, and the Kiowas and Comanches were back where they had started (Buntin, "Removal," p. 74).

"The white man grows jealous . . ." Jones, *Medicine Lodge,* p. 156. Wharton, *Satanta,* incorrectly attributes this speech to Satanta, as does Rister, "Satanta." Rister notes his source as the Austin *Tri-Weekly Republican* of December 17, 1867.

referred to in common . . . Mooney, "Cheyennes," p. 372.

page 8

"A smothered passion for revenge . . ." William Bent in Commissioner of Indian Affairs, *Annual Report for 1859,* pp. 137–38.

John Chivington's massacre . . . For more details see Mellor, "Investigation."

"The particulars of this massacre . . ." House of Representatives Executive Document No. 97, 40th Cong., 2nd sess., pp. 8–9.

page 9

Senate amendments . . . Garfield, "Defense 1864," p. 151.

"There are three chiefs . . ." Wharton, *Satanta,* p. 77.

"cannot be tolerated for a moment . . ." Utley, *Regulars,* p. 119.

"We go prepared . . ." Ibid., pp. 119–20.

page 10

"If the lands of the white man are taken . . ." House of Representatives Executive Document No. 97, 40th Cong., 2nd sess., p. 6.

page 11

"hereby set apart . . ." Kappler, *Laws and Treaties,* p. 978.

last-minute verbal persuasions . . . Jones, *Medicine Lodge,* p. 182.

"If it results in the utter annihilation . . ." Utley, *Regulars,* pp. 150–52.

page 12

Custer was vehemently attacked . . . see Jones, *Medicine Lodge*, p. 76.

page 13

aide-de-camp to General James A. Garfield . . . Vail, *Memorial*, p. 14. Additional distrust on the part of orthodox Quakers stemmed from the pragmatism of Haworth's theology; for ten years after moving to Kansas he had associated with the Methodist Church, there being no meeting of Friends closer than Lawrence.

page 14

less than twenty-five hundred individuals . . . In 1870 Dr. William Nicholson, making a tour of the Indian Territory Agencies, enumerated 300 Katakas, 1896 Kiowas, and 3742 Comanches (Nicholson, "Tour"). This figure, as well as Battey's estimate of 1600 Kiowas, are too high. See Mooney, "Kiowa Indians," p. 236, and Nye, *Carbine*, p. 17.

a wriggling motion of the hand . . . Debo, "Comanches," p. 51 n.

Isa-havey (Mikly Way) . . . The Comanche name actually means "Wolf Road," which was their term for the gray streak in the sky that is the visible galaxy (Nye, *Raiders*, p. 296). Chief To-sa-wi (Toshaway, or Silver Brooch), who was so prominent at the Medicine Lodge encampment, had evidently declined somewhat in influence at Fort Sill and stayed at the Wichita Agency.

Asa-toyah-teh (Striding Through the Dusk) . . . This name is almost universally translated "Gray Leggings." I use the name that appears on his tombstone in the Fort Sill Cemetery.

Tabananica (Sound of the Sun) . . . Richardson (*Barrier*, p. 346 n.) translates this name as "My Name is Sun," or "Named Sun," evidently on the premise that it derives, not from *Nan'-a-ca* (to hear), but rather from *Nan'-i-käh* (I am called). Wallace and Hoebel (*The Comanches*, p. 314) translate it as "Voice of the Sunrise"; still others as "Hears the Sunrise" and "Rising Sun." Sound of the Sun, used here, is the name that appears on the chief's headstone in the Otipoby Comanche Cemetery at Fort Sill.

page 15

"I have kept out on the plains . . ." Richardson, *Barrier*, p. 356. An account of the Alvord Council is contained in the New York *Herald* of Sept. 8, 1872.

Mow-way (Push Aside) . . . This chief was called "Shaking Hand" or "Hand Shaker" until Nye corrected this in *Raiders*, p. 298. Little information survives about the second chief of the Kotsotekas besides his name: Ka-wirts-a-mo (Long Hungry), Letter, Haworth to Richards, July 8, 1875.

"I was promised lots of things . . ." Richardson, *Barrier,* pp. 282–83 n.; Wallace and Hoebel, *The Comanches,* p. 314.

band had numbered some two hundred . . . Battey, *Life,* p. 113.

page 16

as early as 1868 . . . Griswold, "Fort Sill," p. 3.

Pe-arua-akup-akup . . . Nye, *Carbine,* p. 204.

reputedly the bravest fighter . . . Vail, *Memorial,* p. 91.

a well-defined plateau . . . For a more detailed description of the Staked Plains, see Rathjen, "Physiography," and Bryan, "The Llano Estacado."

page 17

six warrior societies . . . One of the societies, the Rabbits, was for young boys; four were of secondary prominence: the Headdresses (or Tsetanma), Black Feet, Berries, and the Shepherds (of the last of which Big Bow was lifetime leader). Most prestigious was the Big Horse or Kaitsenko, whose membership was limited to the very few bravest fighters in the tribe (Lowie, "Societies," pp. 844–48). Jane Hanks ("Law and Status," p. 9) says there were five societies.

about five feet ten . . . Capps, *Raid,* p. 145. This was large for an Indian, but such was Satanta's magnetism that contemporary witnesses are almost unanimous in crediting him a height in excess of six feet.

Warren Wagontrain massacre . . . For an outstanding analysis of this incident see Capps, *Raid.*

Téné-angopte (Striking Eagle) . . . This chief is much more commonly referred to as "Kicking Bird," the result of an early mistranslation of the sign language. I use the more accurate interpretation of Henry M. Stanley, a correspondent who covered the Medicine Lodge camp (Taylor, "Kicking Bird," p. 296 n.).

bitter and often ugly confrontation . . . Battey, *Life,* p. 103.

page 18

more than fifty troopers . . . Taylor, "Kicking Bird," p. 309.

"tough and reckless" . . . Nye, *Raiders,* p. 228.

page 19

Nap-a-wat (No Moccasins) . . . Nye and even Battey identify No Moccasins (or No Shoes) not as Nap-a-wat, but rather as "Tohaint." Becker ("Comanche Indian") identifies a prominent medicine man as "Nappy-wat, or No Shoes," but does not clarify whether he means a Comanche or Kiowa. The photograph of "Na-pa-wa" in the photo archives of the Oklahoma Historical Society is in the Kiowa file; it appears to be an original print, but does not offer a translation. It appears in this book next to Lone Wolf's.

little obstacle to peace . . . "From this time [the end of the 1868 war] to the spring of 1874 the Cheyennes were peaceful, wishing only to be left alone and dealt with according to treaty stipulations" (Hyde, *Life*, p. 353).

Notes, Chapter II
page 21
"the grandeur and dangers . . ." Branch, *Hunting*, p. 152.
James White . . . White is mentioned only by Branch, of all authors on Mooar.
page 22
the figure for the three years . . . Dodge, *Plains*, quoted in Miles, *Recollections*, p. 159.
page 23
"In the autumn of 1868 . . ." William Blackmore, in Introduction to Dodge, *Plains*, pp. xiv–xvi. Following Blackmore segments are from the same source.
"During the fall and winter . . ." Bard, *Life*, pp. 109–10.
page 25
"to settle the vexed Indian question . . ." Gard, *Hunt*, p. 215.
Tallies were kept . . . Wharton, *Satanta*, p. 99; Guggisberg, *Man and Wildlife*, pp. 30–31.
moved south yet again . . . Mooar, "Buffalo Days," Part II, p. 44.
page 27
"Major, if we cross . . ." Ibid.
"Boys, if I were a buffalo hunter . . ." Ibid.
page 28
"Each outfit would take a wagon . . ." Gard, *Hunt*, p. 135.
keep track of the Wheelers' outfit . . . Joe Wheeler was one of the first hunters to fall to the Indians that winter. See Gard, p. 136.
"The camp bed of a frontiersman . . ." Mooar, "Buffalo Days," Part II, p. 10.
page 29
"once took 120 hides . . ." Mayer, *Harvest*, p. 35.
Other top scores . . . Hyde, *Life*, p. 356 n.
"Killing more than we could use . . ." Mayer, *Harvest*, p. 35.
2,000 foot-pounds . . . Ibid., p. 36.
"I killed 6,500 buffaloes . . ." Gard, *Hunt*, p. 124.
rather grim article . . . Mayer, *Harvest*, p. 46; Rossi, "Buffalo," p. 16.

page 30
"*A sack of flour . . .*" Branch, *Hunting,* p. 159.
page 31
a Cheyenne woman . . . According to Quanah Parker's son White
Parker (Atkinson, *Texas Indians,* p. 161 n.) the word "squaw" was
not Indian in origin but white, and was used in derogation. It is not
used narratively in this text.
"*They's a lot of them Kiowas . . .*" Sandoz, *Hunters,* p. 179.
"*shoot their way through . . .*" O'Connor, *Masterson,* p. 37.
page 32
young greenhorn from Illinois . . . This and the later exploit of
Fairchild are found in Sandoz, *Hunters,* and O'Connor, *Masterson,*
and some original memoirs. If they aren't true, they ought to be.
page 33
an old, abandoned trading post . . . The most detailed description of
this post is found in Hyde, *Life.*
page 35
"*the Indians threatened . . .*" Harrison, "Damage Suits," p. 48.
page 36
an estimated two hundred . . . Ibid., p. 56.

Notes, Chapter III
page 38
"*They are all very poor . . .*" Letter, Miles to Hoag, Feb. 10, 1874.
"*In our intercourse with the Indians . . .*" Secretary of the Interior,
Annual Reports for 1872 and 1873.
"*The testimony satisfies us . . .*" House of Representatives Executive
Document No. 97, 40th Cong., 2nd sess., p. 6. Wharton *Satanta,* p.
83 ff.) gives an account of the Box affair. Curiously, Striking Eagle
was one of the leaders of the Box raid. Morris Taylor ("Kicking
Bird," pp. 298–300) speculates that the army ignored this trans-
gression of Striking Eagle's because he represented the single
greatest hope for peace with the Kiowas.
page 39
"*What you think now? . . .*" Battey, *Life,* p. 258. Other Kiowas in the
delegation were Lone Wolf and Gui-kati (Wolf-Lying-Down), both
of whom were hostile in the 1874 war. Woman's Heart, Red Otter,
Do-hauson the Younger, and Stumbling Bear were originally slated
to go but did not (Mooney, "Kiowa Indians," p. 190).
page 40
"*One of the strongest causes . . .*" Miles, *Recollections,* p. 157.

"distinct treaty stipulation . . ." Ibid. Rations were not specifically provided for by the Medicine Lodge Treaties (Buntin, "Removal," p. 77; Utley, *Regulars,* p. 149; and Kappler, *Laws and Treaties,* pp. 977–89). Rations were separately voted the Indians on the assertion of their agents that the reservations were too small to subsist the tribes, and feeding the Indians was the only way to avoid new raids (Buntin, "Removal," p. 75). Five hundred thousand dollars was approved for this purpose in July 1868, but not given to the Indian Bureau. It was to be administered by General Sherman, of all people (Utley, *Regulars,* p. 141).

"I believe the Indians are peaceably disposed . . ." Letter, Beede to Hoag, Mar. 30, 1874.

page 41

peaceful intentions . . . Letter, Haworth to Hoag, Feb. 20, 1874.

"Our sustenance is getting very low . . ." Letter, Haworth to Smith, Apr. 8, 1874.

"The shortness of our rations . . ." Letter, Haworth to Beede, June 29, 1874.

"Big Bow said the Agent had sent for him . . ." Letter, Clarke to Brooke, Feb. 17, 1874.

"This week's issue will exhaust our supply . . ." Letter, Haworth to Hoag, Apr. 20, 1874.

"Issue day is almost here . . ." Letter, Haworth to Hoag, May 6, 1874. When the army itself had care of the Indians (up to 1869), there was even then never enough money to feed the Indians "for any length of time." One agent, Colonel W. B. Hazen, when he received no answer to his requests for additional food, bought more on his own volition, on the credit of the United States (Buntin, "Removal," p. 78). Under army control, "Often there was no sugar or coffee, the meal or flour was musty, the tobacco rotten, and the beef stringy and inferior to the buffalo . . ." Also, "Torrential rains" interfered with the delivery of rations to Haworth at Fort Sill (Richardson, "Comanche Indians," pp. 25–26).

page 42

"We come in from our camps . . ." Quoted in letter, Haworth to Hoag, May 8, 1874. In spite of the disappointment, Striking Eagle vouched a week later that he believed Big Bow still desired peace (letter, Haworth to Hoag, May 13, 1874).

"If I had supplies on hand . . ." Letter, Haworth to Hoag, May 21, 1874.

laboring under . . . a personal tragedy . . . Vail, *Memorial,* p. 61.

White Horse hatched at least two plots . . . Ibid., pp. 59–61.

head chief of the . . . *Dog Soldiers* . . . Care should be taken not to confuse the Cheyenne Dog Soldier White Horse with the Kiowa war chief of the same name.

page 43

"We will soon be out of rations . . ." Letter, Miles to Hoag, Mar. 21, 1874.

"500 lodges . . ." This is the rough equivalent of three thousand people.

"Our coffee, sugar, & bacon is exhausted . . ." Letter, Miles to Hoag, Mar. 31, 1874.

"They must be treated well . . ." Letter, Miles to Hoag, Apr. 4, 1874.

"It is very important . . ." Letter, Miles to Hoag, May 12, 1874.

page 44

"No matter what . . ." Ibid.

"If bad men among the whites . . ." Kappler, *Laws and Treaties,* pp. 977, 983.

enforcement . . . *meant the United States Army* . . . Letter, Delano to Smith, Nov. 23, 1874.

Little Robe . . . *journeyed to Washington* . . . Hyde, *Life,* p. 354.

authority to direct federal marshals . . . Letter, Delano to Smith, Jan. 30, 1874.

Two deputy marshals . . . Letter, Miles to Hoag, Jan. 10, 1874.

"to patrol that portion of Kansas . . ." Letter, Williams to Delano, Nov. 12, 1874.

page 45

claimed he had no authority . . . Letter, Delano to Smith, Nov. 23, 1874.

no power to arrest offenders . . . Letter, Williams to Delano, Nov. 23, 1874.

"The Chiefs are very much provoked . . ." Letter, Miles to Hoag, Mar. 28, 1874.

Indians knew the precise identity . . . Letter, Bent to Miles, May 6, 1874.

Bent too, . . . *lost his horse herd* . . . Hyde, *Life,* p. 355.

page 46

"This matter must have attention . . ." Letter, Miles to Hoag, Apr. 16,

"I do not apprehend . . ." Letter, Hoag to Smith, Apr. 23, 1874.

"How are we to rid this country . . ." Letter, Miles to Hoag, Apr. 16. 1874.

Brooke refused them . . . Letter, Lefebvre and Talley to Tough, Dec. 31, 1874. It does seem, however, that Brooke's troops were used in the February arrest of the eleven poachers (Berthrong, *Southern Cheyennes*, p. 381). After that one time, though, the troops were apparently permitted to intervene only when criminal statutes were violated (Ibid., p. 383 n.) and there were no criminal provisions for game poaching.

Martin . . . literally settled in . . . Letters, Lefebvre to Miles, May 15, 1874 and ff.

page 47

"That Indians committed this crime . . ." Letter, Compton to Assistant Adjutant General, Department of the Missouri, June 19, 1874.

"Since the Indians have camped . . ." Letter, Haworth to Smith, Sept. 26, 1874.

"I might as well make no effort . . ." Letter, Haworth to Hoag, Feb. 23, 1875.

page 48

"Instead of real Indians . . ." Letter, Haworth to Hoag, Dec. 27, 1873.

"On one occasion the sheriff . . ." Battey, *Life*, p. 239.

"It is a well-known fact . . ." Ibid.

page 49

"foolish water . . ." In contemporary correspondence I am unable to find the term "fire water," usually ascribed as the Indians' name for whiskey; they called it "foolish water." The Comanche word for it was *Bosah-pah*, meaning "crazy water" (Becker, "Comanche Indian," p. 331).

"then whiskey is plenty . . ." Letter, Miles to Hoag, June 13, 1874.

"This country . . . was given by Washington . . ." Vail, *Memorial*, pp. 48–49.

Comancheros had made it too profitable . . . Comanche trade with the Comancheros had flourished at least by the mid-eighteenth century. The Goodnight-Loving cattle trail was established in 1866, and by 1870 its cattle rustling trade was "enormous" and a prime source of revenue for the Comanches (Haley, "Comancheros," pp. 157–60).

page 50

Charlie Rath, in particular . . . Taylor, "Kicking Bird," p. 300.

up to ten thousand buffalo robes . . . Griswold, "Fort Sill," p. 4.

"under instructions from his employers . . ." Letter, Haworth to Smith, May 15, 1874.

page 51

attacked by Lieutenant Colonel George P. Buell . . . This battle took place on February 5 (Crimmins, "Fort Elliott," p. 45).

about two weeks after this . . . Letter, Haworth to Hoag, Feb. 20, 1874.

Congress passed a law . . . Indian Appropriation Bill, 41st Cong., 3rd sess., Ch. 120, p. 556.

any longer an "independent nation . . ." This curious amendment was a child of compromise if ever there was one. For a good synopsis of its history, see Priest, *Stepchildren,* pp. 96–101.

page 52

Isa-tai (Wolf Shit) . . . The name "Isa-tai" has undergone an annoying series of euphemistic translations, stemming undoubtedly from Victorian considerations of delicacy and printability, probably the most polite of them being "Little Wolf" (Gard, *Hunt*), and "White Eagle" (Scott ms.). Probably the closest anyone has come to a true rendering is "Rear End of a Wolf" (Nye, *Carbine*), and "Coyote Droppings" (Wallace and Hoebel, *Comanches*). The Indians themselves were refreshingly free of such daintiness, and generally displayed a remarkably earthy humor in giving names. For instance, one famous Penateka chief of earlier days was cosmetically translated as "Buffalo Hump," of all things, when his name actually had to do with priapism, and thus would have been more accurately rendered as "Erection That Won't Go Down," or more simply, "All Day Hard-on." One of the early small bands of Comanches which later became absorbed into the others, had been called by the other bands "Maggoty Penises," on account of the prevalence of venereal disease caused by their extraordinary sexual license (Wallace and Hoebel, *Comanches,* p. 30). I have translated "Isa-tai" as simply as I have in order to initiate some amount of remedial effect.

Later on in the book, at the Battle of Adobe Walls, where Isa-tai was War Leader and Quanah his main support, it is an almost irresistible historical footnote to observe that the attack was led by Wolf Shit and Fragrance.

His medicine was strong . . . Richardson, "Comanche Indians," quotes the report of F. W. and J. W. Smith, which is located in the Central Superintendency letter file. Dated September 26, 1874, it also appears in the Kiowa Agency file.

"ascended above the clouds . . ." Richardson, *Barrier,* p. 373.

page 53

Comanches had never been assembled . . . Linton, "Sun Dance," p. 420, asserts that the Comanches practiced some form of medicine dance at "irregular intervals" from 1860 to 1878, though he never claims they were pan-tribal. The 1874 Sun Dance was unique and pan-tribal.

"They have a new Medicine Man . . ." Letter, Haworth to Hoag, May 5, 1874.

Haworth also sent a peace feeler . . . Leckie, "Red River War," from Commissioner of Indian Affairs, *Annual Report for 1874.* Also used in Battey, *Life,* p. 220.

page 54

"an invocation . . ." Wallace and Hoebel, *Comanches,* p. 320.

emphasis . . . on the buffalo . . . Battey, *Life,* pp. 168–72. A stuffed buffalo was also used in the Kiowa Sun Dance.

page 55

The first plan . . . Quirts Quip to Haworth, in Haworth to Hoag, letter of May 21, 1874. The cannibalism of the Tonkawas is established well enough in contemporary accounts. For a particularly grisly first hand description of one of their battles, see *Nine Years Among the Indians* by Herman Lehmann of Fredericksburg, Texas, who was captured by and adopted into both the Apache and Comanche tribes. The Penatekas did get word of this plan out of the camp, and the Tonkawas were spirited away to the protection of Fort Griffin, Texas (Mooney, "Kiowa Indians," p. 202).

"I had a friend killed by the Tonkaway . . ." Scott ms., pp. 5–6. I-See-O, in 1875 known as Tahbone-mah, said it was a nephew killed by whites. Since the Tonkawas often scouted for the army, it could have been either case, or not inconceivably both, involving two separate deaths.

"I work one month . . ." Ibid. Ordinarily when a chief got up a war party, he would tie a red flag and eagle feathers to a long pole and ride through the camps singing a war song; followers fell in behind (Debo, "Comanches," p. 44).

page 56

Quanah . . . set forth the second . . . plan . . . That it was Quanah's idea is claimed in Nye, *Carbine,* p. 190. See next note, however.

attack . . . the . . . buffalo hunters . . . How the Indians first got word of the hunting in Texas is a mystery. Walter Robertson ("Reminiscences," p. 100), a Texas Ranger of the Frontier Battalion, said first word came from Apaches who crossed through eastward for a visit, and scavenged the carcasses along the way. Big Tree later told Milburn C. Harper ("Railroad Agent," p. 293) that he and some others once made a scout to check on the white hunters and found over a thousand carcasses in one area. Nye (*Carbine*, p. 187) gives only secondary importance to the buffalo hunting *per se* as causing the war, at least among the Comanches and Kiowas, giving more weight to the general desire to avenge battle losses. However, that seems to be disputed by the Scott manuscript: when Quanah wanted to take a war party to Texas for that general revenge, the big chiefs told him to "take pipe first against white buffalo killers."

North Fork Red River . . . Leckie, *Conquest*, p. 196.

Yellow Horse . . . Trenholm, *Arapahoes*, p. 249.

of such religious importance . . . Richardson, *Barrier*, pp. 379–80.

page 57

"they should conclude . . ." Battey, *Life*, p. 306.

"a great dry time this summer . . ." Tilghman, *Quanah*, p. 83.

The leaders . . . "have a great many hearts . . ." Letter, Haworth to Hoag, June 8, 1874.

eighty mint-new . . . rifles . . . Ibid.

page 58

"I am at a loss . . ." Letter, Haworth to Hoag, May 21, 1874.

"this cloud will . . . pass away . . ." Letter, Haworth to Hoag, June 3, 1874.

Notes, Chapter IV

page 59

"Your people make big talk . . ." Branch, *Hunting*, p. 179.

"all seem in excellent humor . . ." Letter, Miles to Hoag, Mar. 16, 1874.

"The buffalo is our money. . . ." Striking Eagle to Haworth, in letter, Haworth to Hoag, June 8, 1874: tense changed.

page 60

Indians had attacked the camp . . . The identity of these Indians is a mystery. Most likely they were Cheyennes, as their war parties were the first out; it would seem probable that the main war party had not yet gone that far west, although smaller bands were operating in the vicinity before it got there (Leckie, *Conquest*, p. 189).

It was Amos Chapman . . . The events that occurred from the time of Chapman's arrival at Adobe Walls to the end of the battle are so well and often chronicled as to be traditional. Therefore I am noting those points only that are unique to one account, or unusually controversial.

page 61

Saturday, June 27 . . . While the contemporary accounts of Adobe
Walls all refer to June 27 as a Sunday, the twenty-seventh was actually a Saturday. There is no discernible reason for this discrepancy.

page 62

"Is your gun ready, Mooar?" . . . Mooar, "Buffalo Days," Part III,
p. 8.

page 64

Rath and Myers both cleared out . . . In 1892 Rath sued the federal
government and the Comanche and Kiowa Indian tribes to recover
his Adobe Walls losses. At that time, he swore and his coplaintiffs
agreed that he had left on May 20, as soon as his store was operating smoothly (Harrison, "Damage Suits," p. 47). Those not joining
Rath in his lawsuit were either silent or contradicted his story. It is
not impossible that Rath did indeed leave Adobe Walls on May 20
and came back, though the bad blood between Rath and several of
the hunters after the fight still makes Rath's protestations of innocence unconvincing.

Rath lost his suit. (I am unable to find any reference that the Indians ever sued to recover damages for the loss of the buffalo.)

about ten thousand buffalo hides . . . Harrison, "Damage Suits,"
p. 52.

page 65

the largest war party ever . . . Ellis (Pope, p. 262 n.) cites Berthrong
(*Cheyennes*, p. 385), saying "recent studies" show it is doubtful that
over three hundred were involved in the Battle of Adobe Walls.
Berthrong in turn cites Texan Joe Griffis, who claimed to be the
"Tehan" of Lyman's Wagon Train fight, which he almost certainly
was not, for the figures. Hoodle-tau-goodl (Red Dress), the daugh-
ter of Kiowa Owl Prophet Maman-ti and the real Tehan's foster
sister, told Wilbur Nye that Griffis was not Tehan (Nye, *Raiders*, p.
368), despite the fact that her letters to Griffis before she met him
indicate an initial belief in his authenticity (see Peery, "Mystery").
Hence Griffis is not a reliable source for the lower figure. Estimates
given by white buffalo hunters who were present vary from two
hundred to the traditional seven hundred.

On the other hand, Horace Jones, the heavy-drinking post interpreter at Fort Sill, who had lived with the Quahadis (Sheffy,
"Baldwin," p. 10), had told Col. Davidson that 200 to 250 Indians
were involved (letter, Davidson to Assistant Adjutant General,
Department of Texas, July 7, 1874). Lt. Frank D. Baldwin also

believed the attacking Indians numbered about 200, though he may have been influenced at least partly by Jones (Brown, "Expedition" ms., p. 2).

The number of Indians killed in the battle strongly indicates a larger force than this; also, a few accounts have the hostile women exhorting their men from the nearby buttes, if this were true the women could have been mixed in with the count. These and other factors considered, I would settle on a figure of about 500 Indians taking part in the raid.

"Isa-tai make big talk that time . . ." Scott ms., p. 7.

"Pretty soon we move Fort Elliott . . ." Quanah meant the site where Fort Elliott was later built. It was not fully established until 1876 (Oswald, "Fort Elliott"); Crimmins says June 5, 1875. Actually, Fort Elliott was constructed on the site of Nelson Miles' Sweetwater Cantonment (see p. 206), and thus had been in use since the 1874–75 winter.

page 66

"Black Beard say, 'All right . . .'" Very little information has come down about this evidently important figure. Battey never discusses him in detail, as the Quahadis were seldom near the agency, but he does mention him in passing as being a primal Quahadi chief, active in the slave trade (Battey, *Life*, p. 105).

Notes, Chapter V

page 67

slipped out his pistol . . . and pressed the trigger. . . . Mooar, "Buffalo Days," Part III, is subtitled "The Real Story of the 'Cracked Ridgepole' at Adobe Walls." Most accounts of the Battle of Adobe Walls do retain the story of the ridgepole cracking just as the Indians were gathering in the timber, but most of the accounts were either published before Mooar's article appeared (Branch, *Hunting;* Grinnell, *Fighting Cheyennes,* etc.) or make no mention in the bibliography or notes that Mooar's version was seen and rejected. Recent authors who opt for the pistol shot version include Gard, *Hunt,* and J. C. Dykes in Allred, Dykes, et al. (eds.), *Fights.*

Aside from the acceptance that the Mooar story has gained over the traditional version, common sense steers one away from the ridgepole's cracking. First, the law of averages is overwhelmingly against it, which probably accounts for a large part of its heretofore wide appeal. Second, the first ridgepole was 2½ feet thick, and after it "cracked" it left the buffalo hunters scratching their heads when none of them could find any visible flaw in it. Third, a perfectly cut substitute for it just happened to be lying in the woodpile. Fourth, Mooar was one of the few people at Adobe Walls who knew what was going on; it was John who sheltered Amos Chapman to prevent his lynching, so Wright was in a position to know if any oaths of secrecy were taken. Finally, although Mooar says in 1933 that Billy Dixon had kept his word until his death in 1914 not to tell the secret, Dixon's memoirs contain a tantalizing twist to the "ridgepole" story—that it cracked "with a sound like a gunshot."

page 68

"What the hell is that?" O'Connor, *Masterson,* p. 52.

slinging one arm through a loop . . . Debo, "Comanches," p. 43.

page 69

Yellow Fish and Tim-bo . . . This account appears in an unspecified newspaper clipping of 1941, located in the Adobe Walls file at the Panhandle-Plains Historical Museum in Canyon, Texas.

page 71

"Riding at full gallop . . ." Jones, *Medicine Lodge,* p. 150.

"Old Man" Keeler . . . For more on Keeler see Crane, "Keeler."

plucked up his friend's body . . . The death of a young Comanche at the door of one of the buildings is substantiated by Hyde, *Life,* p. 360, and others. Zoe Tilghman (*Quanah*) identifies the fallen Indian as Ho-we-a, certainly an error, unless she means a different Ho-we-a (Clearing in the Woods) than the Yapparika headman who interned on the eighth of August. It was Ho-we-a who on June 3 gave Haworth his first notice that the Comanches were off the reservation (letter, Haworth to Hoag, June 3, 1874).

page 72

an established avenue of restoring honor . . . for more insight into the philosophy of saving face from shame or despondence by dying in battle, see Grinnell, *Buffalo,* pp. 87–95.

Horse Road . . . identified in Hyde, *Life,* p. 360.

"One Comanche killed was a yellow nigger . . ." Scott ms., p. 9.

page 73

"They were all shooting at Keeler . . ." Crane, "Keeler," p. 103.

"I took some water . . ." Ibid.

page 75

Sai-yan (Rag-Full-of-Holes). Translated in West ms., p. 31 n. One other Indian casualty was So-ta-do. Nye believed this was the black bugler, equating So-ta-do with "Soldado," Spanish for soldier. Richardson (*Barrier,* p. 381 n.) and Wright (*Dodge City,* pp. 123–24) say that a Negro was one of the eleven bodies left unrecovered and subsequently mutilated, according to Porter, "Negroes," p. 162. Scout J. T. Marshall wrote that one of the heads on the corral gatepost was that of a black.

a Cheyenne named Hippy . . . Hippy was known well enough in later days around the Darlington agency. For more on him see Seger, *Early Days.*

"All Cheyennes pretty mad . . ." Scott ms., p. 9.

someone had killed a skunk . . . "For a member of a war party to kill and skin a skunk while on the way to attack was likely to nullify some of the most potent war medicine." Skunks possessed great power; warriors often rode into battle with skunk tails tied to their horses' tails, and some medicine men used skunk hides to hold sacred bundles (Wallace and Hoebel, *Comanches,* p. 203).

"a very strong medicine . . ." West ms., p. 32.

page 76

"two indians lay there dead . . ." Harrison, "Damage Suits," pp. 42–43.

Motivated by a consideration . . . This according to Adobe Walls carpenter Andy Johnson (Harrison, "Damage Suits," p. 54). R. M. Wright stated that one other man rode with Lease, and they were paid two hundred dollars each.

page 77

"justly earned all that may befall . . ." Ellis, *Pope,* p. 183. Pope's immediate superior, Lieutenant General Philip Sheridan, "respectfully disagreed" with Pope's analysis, blaming the advent of the war on the "restless nature of the Indian, who has no profession but arms, and naturally seeks for war and plunder when the grazing gets high enough to feed his ponies" (House of Representatives Executive Document No. 1, 43rd Cong., 2nd sess., p. 27).

"break up the grogshops . . ." Leckie, *Conquest,* p. 193. See also O. K. Dixon, *Life,* p. 180.

hunter Tom Nixon . . . for more on this man see J. W. Snell, "Diary."

page 78

the death of 115 . . . Mooar, "Buffalo Days," Part IV, p. 22.

30 Indian graves . . . Marshall, *Expedition,* p. 5. Although Scout Marshall had an insistent tendency to exaggerate, in 1897 I-See-O (Tahbone-mah) substantiated that, after Adobe Walls's abandonment, the Indians returned and buried the dead in the surrounding buttes; he gave a much smaller figure, however (Nye, *Medicine*, p. 180). On the other hand, Marshall's estimate of thirty graves is backed up by Ben Clarke, the Camp Supply scout: "After the hunters left the Indians came and gathered up the bones of their dead, wrapped them in robes and blankets & put them up in the hills on the south side of Canadian above Adobe Walls. Ben Clarke says thirty Cheyennes were killed." (Scott ms., p. 12).

Notes, Chapter VI
page 79
a half dozen individuals . . . These are the names given in Nye, *Carbine*, p. 191. Mayhall, *Kiowas*, p. 246, omits White Shield for White Skull. In 1897 I-See-O said there were "six or seven," not chiefs, but "crazy Kiowa" (Scott ms., pp. 10–11). On the other hand, Bat Masterson and others were sure that some of the Indians killed at Adobe Walls were Kiowas (Harrison, "Damage Suits," p. 58). One wonders, therefore, if perhaps the "six or seven" were indeed chiefs, and had other warriors from their own bands with them.
"at the end of the bluff," . . . Mayhall, *Kiowas*, p. 171.
already under way . . . Richardson, *Barrier*, pp. 379–80. For more on the Kiowa Sun Dance see Battey, *Life*, pp. 166–84; also, Spier, "The Kiowa Sun Dance"; and Nye, "Kiowa Sun Dance."
page 80
Stumbling Bear . . . His name is more accurately rendered Bear-Shoving-You-Down (Nye, *Raiders*, p. 218).
death on January 10. . . Battey, *Life*, p. 243.
Sun Boy . . . In Kiowa tradition, the tribe was founded when Sun Boy (Pai-talyi: Son of the Sun) descended from heaven and thumped on a hollow log, and the Kiowas marched out in response. Chief Sun Boy had a reputation as a capable warrior, though somewhat of a bully (Hanks, "Law and Status," p. 31).
a kind of "High Priest . . ." Letter, Haworth to Hoag, July 21, 1874.
page 81
Satanta, by this time over sixty years old . . . Satanta's age is unknown; his date of birth has been given as early as 1807, and as late as c. 1821. From all the contemporary accounts, and from examining some seldom published photographs, in which he appears as a more elderly man than in the well-known Soule photos, I would guess his birthdate at about 1812–14. A Scribner's correspondent

who talked with Satanta in 1873 states that the chief was then "more than sixty years old." (Rister, "Satanta," p. 96, n. 61 to *Scribner's Monthly,* Vol. VII, No. 4 [Feb. 1874]). Benjamin Capps (*The Warren Wagontrain Raid*) makes a case that Satanta abdicated from the Kaitsenko Society from the realization that it didn't matter who held the medicine lance. That well could be, but in a society as rigidly structured as the Kiowa, I can't help but think that advancing infirmity must have been a consideration before volunteering such a drastic demotion. See next note.

retired from the Kaitsenko . . . "If a member felt too old to go to war, he would [give his place to] a younger man, who was then obliged to become his successor. . . . the new member presented his predecessor with blankets or other property." (Lowie, "Societies," p. 848).

Ahto-tain-te (*White Cowbird*). . . . Ahto-tain-te was murdered by Texas Rangers in 1878 while on a deer hunt. Pago-to-goodl (Lone Young Man) led the revenge raid, the last Kiowa depredation in Texas.

Red Otter . . . Very little information survives about Red Otter (Apen-goodl). He was a chief in his own right, but did not get along well with Lone Wolf. Red Otter was imprisoned for a time after the war, but was not sent to Fort Marion.

page 82

Tahbone-mah . . . For more on Tahbone-mah, see Morris Swett, "I-See-O."

Set-kop-te . . . Information on Set-kop-te is from the caption of a picture of him taken in Fort Marion in 1875; data supplied the National Park Service by Mr. George Zotom Otis, Sr., the grandson of Zotom (Biter), another Fort Marion prisoner.

Eonah-pah . . . Nye, *Carbine,* p. 64.

son-in-law of Satanta . . . Nye, *Raiders,* p. 358; Battey (*Life,* p. 188) says he was the son-in-law of Lone Wolf.

participating in his first raid. Tsen-tonkee's tombstone in the Fort Sill Cemetery gives his date of birth as 1846; he died in 1953 at the age of 107. If this was his first raid and he was indeed that old, he got a very late start in raiding, being 28 at the time of the Lost Valley fight.

page 83

the colors and designs . . . These are given in Nye, *Carbine,* p. 194.

page 84

Richard Coke . . . For more on Coke see W. P. Webb, *Frontier Defense,* pp. 219–29.

vitriolic dislike . . . see Webb, *Frontier Defense,* pp. 219–29.

deserted the Confederate border posts . . . Day, James M. (ed.), *Texas Indian Papers,* IV, 1–90; also quoted in Leckie, *Conquest,* p. 18.

what little aid . . . Webb, *Frontier Defense,* p. 219.

page 85

war parties flailed away . . . Haley, "Comancheros," p. 165.

150 miles . . . Rister, "Fort Griffin," p. 16.

April 10 . . . Holden, "Defense, 1865–1889," p. 58 n.

three hundred thousand dollars . . . Sheffy (ed.), "Baldwin," p. 7.

"Indian exterminators." Holden, "Defense," p. 59.

page 86

"bring every available man . . ." Robertson, "Reminiscences," p. 101.

page 87

an employee . . . named Keith. The only secondary source to name Keith is Carnal, "Reminiscences." The death of one "Mr. Keith" appears in "List of Persons Killed or captured by Indians within the limits of the *Post of Fort Richardson,* Texas, during the 3rd Quarter, 1874," filed by the post commander, Col. W. H. Wood, on Sept. 30, 1874 (Taylor [ed.], *Campaign,* p. 16). Also reported killed in the same document were a Mrs. Huff and her two daughters, at Briar Branch, Wise County, Texas.

A herder named Walker . . . Letter, Haworth to Smith, July 2, 1874.

Atah-lah-te . . . the connection that Loud Talker is the same Indian as Feather Head is tentative, but similarity of Indian pronunciation makes it likely.

"I was very much astonished . . ." Carnal, "Reminiscences," p. 21.

page 88

"we will have to get to cover . . ." Robertson, "Reminiscences," p. 102.

page 89

"We could see the leader . . ." Nye, *Carbine,* pp. 198–99.

"My God, my God, don't let them get me!" Carnal, "Reminiscences," p. 22.

page 90

"stay here until they get you . . ." Robertson, "Reminiscences," p. 102.

"you ought not swear like that . . ." Ibid.

page 92

"Everyone who wanted to . . ." Nye, *Carbine,* p. 200.

made him a gift of his name . . . Mamay-day-te lived to old age, and when recognized as a leader he always went by the name "Chief

Lone Wolf," and was sometimes called "Lone Wolf II." He was an ancestor of Pulitzer Prize winner N. S. Momaday.

six inches of scum . . . Carnal, "Reminiscences," p. 23.

page 93

"We came upon the body . . ." Carnal, "Reminiscences," p. 23.

Notes, Chapter VII

page 95

unfamiliar with the Staked Plains . . . Hyde, *Life,* p. 361.

page 96

attacking on June 19. . . Crimmins, "Fort Elliott," p. 46.

about thirty Cheyennes . . . House of Representatives Executive Document No. 1, 43rd Cong., 2nd sess., p. 30.

"The movement against the Buffalo hunters . . ." Letter, Lefebvre to Miles, June 14, 1874.

"My wife writes me back . . ." Letter, Miles to Haworth, June 27, 1874.

page 97

letters give a new significance . . . Letter, Hoag to Smith, July 11, 1874 and enclosures.

black 10th Cavalry . . . In the racially segregated frontier army, two cavalry regiments, the 10th and 9th, and two infantry regiments, the 24th and 25th, were composed entirely of black enlisted men, directed by white officers. To the black troopers the Indians gave the name "buffalo soldiers," because their curly black hair reminded them of the fur on a buffalo's head. For a good history of the black cavalry see Leckie, *Buffalo Soldiers.*

page 98

After stopping in Caldwell . . . Topeka *Commonwealth,* July 11, 1874, clipping in Office of Indian Affairs letter file.

condemned Miles for his "warlike" attitude . . . Letter, Miles to Smith, July 18, 1874, and enclosures.

page 99

reduced the strength of the standing army . . . Garfield, "Army," p. 196; the specific War Department memorandum is found in Taylor (ed.), *Campaign,* p. 9.

page 101

within the Military Department of the Missouri . . . General Orders No. 66 of November 1, 1871, had included all the Indian Territory in the Department of Texas (Taylor [ed.], *Campaign,* p. 8). General Orders No. 4 of July 10, 1874, extended the Department of the Missouri south to the Main (South) Canadian River (Wallace [ed.], *Correspondence,* Vol. II, p. 77), and the remainder stayed under Augur's jurisdiction. Later on, the entirety of the Indian Territory was assigned to the Department of the Missouri (Mackenzie, *Letterbook*).

"A trading post [without] any permit . . ." House of Representatives Executive Document No. 1, Part II, 43rd Cong., 2nd sess., p. 30.

page 102

"The merchants and business men. . ." Marshall, *Expedition,* p. 5.

"I coincide with you fully . . ." Taylor (ed.), *Campaign,* p. 11.

page 103

on July 7, Sherman himself wired . . . Taylor's edition of War Department File 2815-1874 is not illumined with this important telegram. Sherman to Pope, July 7, 1874, turned up as an Office of Indian Affairs file copy.

asked for specific instructions . . . Ellis, *Pope,* pp. 182–85.

"you should have used the troops . . ." Ibid., p. 185.

page 104

geography of the Indians' secluded hideouts . . . Miles, *Recollections,* p. 165.

page 105

Forts Griffin and Richardson . . . Secondary sources have Buell starting from both places. Part of his command formed up at Richardson, but Griffin was his headquarters (Wallace [ed.], *Correspondence,* Vol. II, p. 80; Taylor [ed.], *Campaign,* p. 17). In addition to the active columns, troops at Fort Wallace, on the Smoky Hill River in extreme west-central Kansas, were put on alert to prevent hostiles from going north to incite the Northern Cheyenne and Sioux.

"get as much coverage as you can . . ." Taylor (ed.), *Campaign,* p. 11.

Notes, Chapter VIII

page 107

Haworth's reputation has never recovered . . . For representative comments see Nye, *Carbine,* pp. 203–4.

later promoted to Superintendent of Indian Schools . . . Letter, E. B. Tritle to author, Nov. 15, 1974.

page 108

set up an all-Indian guard . . . Vail, *Memorial,* pp. 32–35. Later on the Kiowas asked the military guard to return, after their food stores were threatened by hostile Cheyennes.

helped limit the spread of war . . . In fact, Haworth's impression on the Kiowas was such that James Mooney, doing anthropological work among those Indians more than twenty years later, had to observe that Haworth "is held in grateful memory by the Kiowa" (Mooney, "Kiowa Indians," p. 198).

Davidson called Haworth a liar . . . Letter, Davidson to Assistant Adjutant General, Department of Texas, Jan. 10, 1874.

reported the saloon closed . . . Letter, Haworth to Delano, Jan. 23, 1874.

"Col. Davidson manifests his open hostility . . ." Letter, Beede to Smith, Jan. 20, 1874.

"I have many personal friends . . ." Letter, Davidson to Assistant Adjutant General, Department of Texas, Jan. 10, 1874.

page 109

"It seems to me from his actions . . ." Vail, *Memorial*, pp. 55–56.

"made great complaint . . ." Letter, Haworth to Hoag, June 27, 1874.

rumors swept through the camps . . . Letter, Haworth to Hoag, July 14, 1874.

page 110

was not furnished his customary copy . . . Letter, Haworth to Smith, June 25, 1874.

only water supply for the Indians . . . Vail, *Memorial*, p. 30.

post surgeon had issued orders . . . Medical Reports, Old Files, Fort Sill.

page 111

Capt. George K. Sanderson, 11th Infantry . . . Letter, Davidson to Assistant Adjutant General, Department of Texas, Aug. 26, 1874.

"though started as I believe in good faith . . ." Letter, Haworth to Smith, Aug. 8, 1874.

only those who interned . . . Letter, Haworth to Smith, Aug. 8, 1874.

"I thought I loved the white man . . ." Letter, Haworth to Hoag, July 29, 1874.

page 112

"Agents will cooperate fully . . ." Letter, Hoag to Miles, Haworth, and Richards, July 21, 1874.

"Make no terms with Lone Wolf . . ." Letter, Smith to Haworth, Aug. 15, 1874.

page 113

"there would be trouble" . . . Letter, Davidson to Assistant Adjutant General, Department of Texas, Aug. 26, 1874.

Davidson received word that Chief Iron Mountain . . . Letter, Haworth to Smith, Aug. 3, 1874.

Prairie Fire . . . I have found little additional information on this chief; he died the following year (Vail, *Memorial*, p. 91).

hostile element had shot Ho-weah's horses . . . Letter, Haworth to Smith, July 28, 1874.

so sure was Davidson of Big Bow's guilt . . . Letter, Haworth to Smith, Aug. 3, 1874.

page 114

Little Crow . . . This leader was the son of the famous Yapparika chief, Ten Bears. Letter, Haworth to Hoag, Mar. 28, 1874.

page 115

Big Red Meat, the conservative Nokoni chief . . . Richardson, *Barrier*, p. 394, writes that "Red Food," while leading a Nokoni village, was himself a Tanima (Liver-eater) Comanche, one of the small bands that by this time were almost totally absorbed into the "Big Five." In 1874 Colonel Davidson still considered the Tanima band a viable unit (Letter, Davidson to Assistant Adjutant General, Department of Texas, Aug. 26, 1874).

the six Caddoan tribes . . . Originally from the Brazos River Valley in Texas these included the Caddo, Kichai (or Keechi), Ioni, Anadarko, Waco, and Tawakoni tribes (Bender, "Frontier 1851–60," p. 136 n.).

so poorly arranged for purposes of defense . . . Davidson's report Aug. 26, 1874, includes a good map of the area.

"one of the richest and most beautiful valleys . . ." Battey, *Life*, p. 25.

page 116

Penatekas . . . administered by Wichita Agency . . . This information is contained in an index to the National Archives file M-234, "Office of Indian Affairs, Letters Received."

"squatted down under the shield . . ." Letter, Davidson to Assistant Adjutant General, Department of Texas, Aug. 26, 1874.

page 117

The Indians later claimed . . . Richardson, *Barrier*, p. 385 n.

page 118

schoolteacher Mrs. John Coyle . . . For more on Mrs. Coyle see Nye, *Carbine*, p. 207. She is also mentioned *passim* in other local sources. William Shirley had established his Anadarko trading post as early as 1859 (Mitchell, "Anadarko," p. 390).

page 119

"No shoot there! . . ." Campbell, "Red Men," p. 648.

Black Beaver . . . An Indian explorer, Black Beaver had traveled extensively from Mexico to the Pacific Northwest, and guided such ex-

peditions as those of Capt. Randolph Marcy and naturalist John
James Audubon (Battey, *Life*, p. 51).

Back at Black Beaver's farm . . . Details of these encounters differ
considerably from one account to another. Probably closest to the
source was Anadarko's town historian, Rev. J. J. Methvin (*Lime-light*, pp. 37–39).

page 120

Kiowas and Comanches had fled . . . The best rendering of the Indians'
side of the fight is Nye, *Carbine*, pp. 206–10, and *Medicine*, p.
184 ff.

page 122

the mysterious "singing wire" . . . This is asserted in Nye, *Medicine*,
p. 186. If it is true, the fear of the telegraph was probably ground-less, as the first telegraph to reach Sill was installed in 1875, and
then from Fort Richardson, not Anadarko (Griswold, "Fort
Sill," p. 5).

fourteen "shot off their horses." Throughout the army correspondence
the cliché "shot off their horses" seems to have been little more than
the dramatic equivalent of "killed, wounded or clumsy, I don't
know." Although Nye (*Medicine*, p. 186) asserts that none of the
Indians stopped to pick up the body of Chee-na-bony, it must have
been recovered before the fight was over, as Davidson makes no
mention of it. If Davidson had found the chief's body he most cer-tainly would have confirmed one Indian dead. Chee-na-bony seems
to have been the only Indian fatality described, though Kiowas in
the 1890s told James Mooney that two of their number were killed
(Mooney, "Kiowa Indians," p. 205).

page 123

"settle this matter at once." Taylor (ed.), *Campaign*, p. 10.

Notes, Chapter IX

page 125

Battle of Red River . . . Because this fight took place in the extreme
lower reaches of Palo Duro Canyon, it is sometimes referred to as
the First Battle of Palo Duro Canyon, with Mackenzie's fight, far
upstream in the canyon proper, listed as the Second.

Nelson A. Miles . . . Further information on Miles may be obtained
from his two autobiographies, *Recollections* and *Serving the Re-public*, and two book-length biographies, Virginia W. Johnson's *The
Unregimented General* and Newton Tolman's *The Search for Gen-eral Miles*, neither of which, however, are very analytical.

page 126

J. T. Marshall . . . Scout Marshall's dispatches to the *Daily Commonwealth* were edited by Lonnie J. White and published by the Encino Press of Austin in 1971 as *The Miles Expedition of 1874–75: An Eyewitness Account of the Red River War.*

page 127

"we will be in the field . . ." Johnson, *Miles,* p. 49.

as finally organized . . . Miles, *Recollections,* pp. 164, 167.

one Parrot 10-pounder . . . Marshall, *Expedition,* p. 11.

page 128

Billy Dixon and Bat Masterson. . . . Other scouts who accompanied Baldwin were J. C. Leach, John Kirley, C. B. Nichols, A. C. Coburn, J. G. Dewalt, J. C. Frederick, C. E. ("Dirtyface?") Jones, David B. Shultz, David Campbell, William F. Schmalsle, J. T. Marshall, J. A. McGinty, and A. J. Martin (Brown, *Expedition* ms., p. 1).

Thompson McFadden . . . Scout McFadden also kept a diary of the campaign, found in 1969 in a San Diego, California, garage, and published in the *Southwestern Historical Quarterly,* edited by R. C. Carriker.

"I find no trouble . . ." Tolman, *Miles,* p. 43.

Delaware Indians were rounded up . . . Besides the chief Falling Leaf, other Delawares included George and Fred Falling Leaf, Ice and George Wilson, Charles Washington, John Kiney, Jim Coon, Elk Hair, Jacob Parker, Sam Williams, Lenowesa, John Silar, Young Marten, John and George Swannosh (or Swannock), Yellow Jacket, and Calvin Evert, (Brown, *Expedition* ms., p. 1).

"[They] are not entering into the spirit . . ." Brown, *Expedition* ms., p. 1.

page 129

Miles' setter, Jack . . . Johnson, *Miles,* p. 50.

"dry as a bone" McFadden, "Diary," p. 201.

mystified by the "Red holes" . . . Marshall, *Expedition,* p. 10.

"The season was . . . one of intense heat . . ." Miles, *Recollections,* pp. 163–64.

page 130

"All men turned out . . ." Brown, *Expedition* ms., p. 2.

"One of the hardest marches . . ." Ibid.

page 131

"the depravity of these men." Miles, *Recollections,* p. 160.

"Twelve Indian heads, minus hair . . ." Marshall, *Expedition,* p. 5.

page 133

"*an . . . incredible accomplishment . . .*" Miles, *Recollections,* p. 167.

"*more salty than the stream . . .*" McFadden, "Diary," p. 203.

"*exposed himself conspicuously . . .*" Miles, *Recollections,* p. 167.

page 134

"*FORWARD! If any man is killed . . .*" Ibid., p. 168.

"*the roughest ground . . .*" Ibid., p. 168.

"*Myself and the Delaware . . .*" McFadden, "Diary," p. 204.

"*Our loss was very slight . . .*" Taylor (ed.), *Campaign,* p. 24.

"*ought to be ashamed*" . . . Hyde, *Life,* p. 361.

page 135

"*This is a terrible country . . .*" Johnson, *Miles,* p. 54.

"*worse than useless. . . .*" Ibid., p. 55.

page 136

"*Colonel Miles encountered the Indians . . .*" H. R. Exec. Doc., No. 1 43rd Cong., 3rd sess., Serial 1635.

"*Miles no good. Me lead 'um on long trail . . .*" Mooar, "Buffalo Days," Part IV, p. 22.

Notes, Chapter X

page 139

The Lone Tree Massacre . . . Of all the actions of the Red River uprising this one has come closest to being entirely forgotten. The only secondary source to deal with it is Montgomery, "Surveyors." Also consulted in the present treatment were the E. D. Smith letters, contemporary newspapers (most also cited by Mrs. Montgomery), Mrs. Short's letters in the OIA files, written in an attempt to get monetary compensation for the loss of her husband and son, and William Blackmore's foreword to R. I. Dodge, *Plains.*

German Kidnapings . . . The best source for the captivity of the German sisters is of course Meredith, *Captives.* Grace Meredith was Catherine German's niece.

distinction of being a Warrior Woman . . . Sandoz, *Cheyenne Autumn,* pp. 85–86.

commanding officer refused them. . . . This was probably either Baldwin or Miles, but as neither officer thought it important enough to mention, the question stays open. If it was Baldwin he probably did not have authority.

page 142

compass smashed into his forehead . . . Letter, Frances Short to John D. Miles, Dec. 6, 1874.

page 144
"Running towards the waggon . . ." Dodge, *Plains,* p. 1.
page 145
"As the savages neared me . . ." Meredith, *Captives,* pp. 17–18.
"Joanna was sitting on a box . . ." Meredith, *Captives,* p. 20.
"I was stripped naked . . ." Dodge, *Plains,* p. li.
"seemed delighted to see us tortured . . ." Ibid., p. 25.
page 146
"A commander against hostile Indians . . ." Carter, *Border,* p. 476.

Notes, Chapter XI
page 147
After the fight and looting . . . This migration is detailed by Nye in both *Carbine* and *Medicine,* also "Excitement."
page 148
"reminded Satanta and Big Tree . . ." Botalye to Nye in *Medicine,* p. 187.
page 150
"Frank, enjoy this. . . ." Brown, "Scout" ms., p. 1.
"They are coming!" . . . Ibid., p. 2.
page 152
Tehan . . . See note for page 65. See also Peery, "Captive," and Methvin, *Andele.*
"The Indian captive being an undesirable companion . . ." Brown, "Scout" ms., p. 3.
page 153
thirty-six wagons . . . Leckie, "Red River War," p. 86.
page 154
"The next hill was grassy . . ." Nye, *Medicine,* pp. 189–90.
page 155
"The excitement was grand." Nye, "Excitement," p. 243.
page 156
"In the field near Washita River . . ." Taylor (ed.), *Campaign,* p. 31.
page 158
set out to prove his bravery. . . . All the Nye books mention it, also Mayhall, *Kiowas,* and others.
another bundle of dispatches . . . best account of following events is O. K. Dixon, *Life.*
page 159
"The Indians seemed to feel . . ." Bard, *Life,* p. 257.

"As we left the wagon train . . ." Nye, "Excitement," pp. 241–42.

page 160

"Amos? Amos! We got you now, Amos!". . . Leckie, *Conquest*, p. 214.

"We worked hard with him . . ." Nye, "Excitement," p. 242.

page 162

"selected their own ground" . . . Nye, "Excitement," p. 246.

page 163

"fought very stubbornly . . ." Ibid.

"We could see that there was no chance for him . . ." Bard, *Life*, p. 264.

page 165

"The simple recital of their deeds . . ." Miles, *Recollections*, p. 174.

Amos Chapman later confided . . . Hyde, *Life*, p. 362.

page 166

"stripped his department" . . . Ellis, *Pope*, p. 190.

"[Miles] seems to want wagons . . ." Taylor (ed.), *Campaign*, p. 41.

page 167

before Mackenzie could get a chance . . . Ellis, *Pope*, pp. 190–91; Utley, *Regulars*, p. 231.

"coldblooded" . . . Johnson, *Miles*, p. 55.

"Yesterday I assumed command . . ." Ibid., p. 59.

Notes, Chapter XII

page 169

"the most promising young officer . . ." Utley, *Regulars*, p. 216.

page 170

"We didn't look worth a damn." . . . Capps, *Raid*, p. 95.

page 171

enjoying a leave of absence . . . Wallace (ed.), *Correspondence*, Vol. II, p. 110.

"wherever they go." . . . Wallace, *Frontier*, p. 129.

page 172

"I can't say exactly . . ." Wallace (ed.), *Correspondence*, Vol. II, p. 93.

"a place of marshes . . ." Hatfield ms., p. 2.

page 174

sent out . . . E Company . . . Three enlisted men of E Company were awarded Congressional Medals of Honor for their part in Boehm's charge. Ibid., p. 198.

"Why you no shoot? . . ." Wallace, *Frontier*, p. 137.

page 175

"as completely as if the ground . . ." Carter, *Border,* p. 487.

"knew the plains from the Palo Duro . . ." Letter, Goodnight to J. Evetts Haley, Nov. 13, 1927, in Haley, "Comanchero Trade," p. 175. Others have questioned Tafoya's veracity concerning his near hanging by Mackenzie.

page 176

train was in fact overtaken . . . Wallace (ed.), *Correspondence,* Vol. II, p. 138.

"Jose Piedad a Mexican Indian Trader" . . . Letter, Mackenzie to Sheridan, Apr. 17, 1875, in Mackenzie *Letterbook.*

"like a dark blotch on the prairie" . . . Hatfield ms., p. 5.

page 177

"Lor' men, look at de sheep . . ." Wallace, *Frontier,* p. 139.

"Mr. Thompson, take your men down . . ." Ibid., p. 140.

"disappeared immediately afterwards . . ." Hatfield ms., p. 5.

The warrior can be identified . . . Nye, *Carbine,* p. 222.

page 178

"a stone could easily have been pitched . . ." Hatfield ms., p. 5

army of crawling tarantulas . . . Nye, *Carbine,* p. 221, also Momaday, *Way to Rainy Mountain,* p. 27.

"like roosting turkeys" . . . Nye, *Carbine,* p. 221.

page 180

"not one man would live . . ." Wallace, *Frontier,* p. 143; Carter, *Border,* p. 490.

"get away from there . . ." Carter, *Border,* p. 491.

"How will we ever get out . . ." Ibid.

page 181

"There are bows and arrows . . ." Hunter (ed.), "Battle," p. 181.

"Long Hungry is recognized . . ." Wallace (ed.), *Correspondence,* Vol. II, p. 118.

page 182

"it is the only way . . ." Ibid., p. 147.

"Make reports by every opportunity . . ." Ibid., p. 82.

"notorious" silences . . . Utley, *Regulars,* p. 240 n. During Mackenzie's 1872 campaign on the Staked Plains, when he overran Mowway's village, Indian survivors drifted back to Fort Sill and informed authorities there of what happened before Mackenzie made out a report of the affair (Richardson, *Barrier,* p. 363 n).

"ascertain if anything could be heard . . ." Taylor (ed.), *Campaign,* p. 71.

General Pope had informed . . . Ibid., p. 42.

page 183

"Since taking the field . . ." Ibid., p. 63; for Miles' position, see Leckie, *Conquest,* p. 211.

flashed over the wires . . . Wallace (ed.), *Correspondence,* Vol. II, p. 135.

Notes, Chapter XIII

page 185

"I believe it has been forty-six days . . ." Letter, Haworth to Smith, Aug. 8, 1874.

"The long continued drouth . . ." Letter, Haworth to Smith, Aug. 17, 1874.

"The hot dry weather still continues. . . ." Letter, Haworth to Smith, Sept. 5, 1874.

"Lieut. Col. Davidson, 10th Cavalry . . ." Letter, Augur to Sheridan, Sept. 9, 1874.

page 186

Sill had earned the reputation . . . For a good history of the early days of the post see Griswold, "Old Fort Sill," and Nye, *Carbine.*

highest temperature officially recorded . . . Medical History, Old Files, Fort Sill.

chronic unrest at Anadarko . . . Taylor (ed.), *Campaign,* p. 18; Letter, Davidson to Richards, July 20, 1874.

Marching orders issued on the fourth . . . General Orders No. 54, Sept. 9, 1874, Old Files, Fort Sill. Some of the notations in the Orders are illegible, but my deciphering matches Nye, *Carbine,* p. 188.

page 187

twelve days to reach Nelson Miles . . . Leckie, "Red River War," p. 89.

a lost Kiowa named Little Chief . . . Nye, *Carbine,* p. 220.

page 188

"All of these columns were pushed out . . ." Sheridan's report of Oct. 1, 1874 in Crimmins, "Fort Elliott," p. 52.

"I have the honor to report that Satanta . . ." Taylor (ed.), *Campaign,* p. 88.

page 189

"When the fight commenced . . ." Ibid.

page 190

"whether Satanta himself became hostile . . ." Ibid., p. 100.

for the rest of his life . . . On being told that he would never again be released, Satanta committed suicide on October 11, 1878, flinging himself from an upper-story window of the prison hospital (Capps, *Raid*, p. 187).

On October 9 Colonel Buell . . . Crimmins, "Fort Elliott," p. 49.

page 191

On October 13 Major Price . . . Crimmins, "Fort Elliott," p. 49.

Capt. Adna R. Chaffee of Miles' command . . . Ibid., p. 50.

a particularly busy day . . . Crimmins, "Fort Elliott," p. 50.

Only five days out of refitting . . . General Orders, Old Files, Fort Sill.

Among the leaders captured . . . White (ed.), "News Items," p. 78.

page 192

crossed some Indians at Las Lagunas Quatro . . . Ibid.

some measure of revenge . . . Marshall, *Expedition*, p. 39; see also Taylor (ed.), *Campaign*, pp. 102–3.

page 193

drew the supply wagons into . . . *columns* . . . Crimmins, "Fort Elliott," pp. 49–50; Miles, *Recollections*, pp. 174–75; Utley, *Regulars*, p. 233.

other chiefs in the camp . . . White (ed.), "News Items," p. 80.

Baldwin was awarded . . . Taylor (ed.), *Campaign*, p. 9 n.

out of ammunition . . . White (ed.), "News Items," p. 80.

"The poor little innocents were nearly naked . . ." Marshall, *Expedition*, p. 38.

page 194

"I have placed the little gentleman in arrest . . ." Johnson, *Miles*, p. 67.

Davidson took up the chase . . . Crimmins, "Fort Elliott," p. 50; Utley, *Regulars*, p. 233.

"improved condition . . ." Miles, *Recollections*, p. 175. This photograph, taken at Henry's Gallery in Leavenworth (White [ed.], "News Items," p. 88), is the one used in this book.

page 195

more than ninety horses frozen . . . Wallace (ed.), *Correspondence,* Vol. II, p. 173.

Capt. Charles A. Hartwell . . . Crimmins, "Fort Elliott," p. 51.

Cheyenne camp on Kingfisher Creek . . . Ibid.

Notes, Chapter XIV
page 197
a 10-man patrol . . . Crimmins, "Fort Elliott," p. 51.
Keyes of Davidson's command . . . Ibid.

"I am quietly waiting here . . ." Tolman, *Miles,* p. 53; Johnson, *Miles,* pp. 65–66.

"that most disagreeable camp" . . . Tolman, *Miles,* p. 54.

"I have with me only one . . ." Johnson, *Miles,* p. 69.

page 198

"I know the chief . . ." Ibid.

all the way to Fort Sill . . . Marshall, *Expedition,* p. 49.

"To the Misses Germaine . . ." Miles, *Recollections,* p. 176.

page 199

Captain Keyes captured a Cheyenne . . . Letter, Miles to Smith, Jan. 1, 1875.

12 Cheyennes surrendered . . . Letter, Miles to Smith, Dec. 29, 1874.

page 200

"it will require a strong force . . ." Letter, Miles to Smith, Jan. 3, 1875.

"Let them send a few more times . . ." Letter, Miles to Smith, Jan. 20, 1875.

Minimic's son Howling Wolf . . . This sortie was in spite of the fact that an October raid on Caddo horses at Anadarko had been repulsed, with the death of three Cheyennes (letter, Miles to Smith, Oct. 23, 1874).

page 201

four more Cheyennes came in . . . Letter, Miles to Smith, Feb. 10, 1875.

"I shall believe it when I see them . . ." Ibid.

an entourage of 15 . . . Letter, Miles to Smith, Feb. 24, 1875.

he surrendered 820 Indians . . . Letter, Miles to Smith, Mar. 9, 1875.

"The surrender on the 6th . . ." Taylor (ed.), *Campaign,* p. 191.

page 202

"I told Stone Calf . . ." Ibid.

"A more wretched and poverty-stricken community . . ." John D. Miles in Annual Report of Commissioner of Indian Affairs for 1875, quoted also in Mooney, "Cheyennes," p. 394.

"Long Back who held possession of Catherine . . ." Letter, Miles to Smith, Mar. 19, 1875.

page 203

"I nearly froze . . ." Dodge, *Plains,* p. li.

"It has been currently reported in the newspapers . . ." Letter, Miles to Smith, Mar. 19, 1875.

"We have reliable information . . ." Letter, Miles to Smith, Mar. 9, 1875.

one or two Dog Soldier chiefs . . . One of those chiefs, White Antelope, escaped with his band, and lived in the north for about a year before returning to Darlington and surrendering on May 30, 1876 (Taylor [ed.], *Campaign,* pp. 263–64).

"Through the efforts of Morrison . . ." Letter, Miles to Smith, Jan. 8, 1875.

page 204
"Referring to the items of Coffee & Sugar . . ." Letter, Miles to Smith, Mar. 18, 1875.

Neill would have none of that . . . Taylor (ed.), *Campaign,* pp. 176–77.

page 205
"the honor to make formal written demand" . . . Letter, Neill to Miles, Mar. 8, 1875.

page 206
part of a general reorganization . . . Wallace, *Correspondence,* Vol. II, pp. 158–59.

the husband of a Caddo woman . . . Zimmerman, "Mackenzie," p. 13.

"I dislike writing this letter very much. . . ." Letter, Mackenzie to Sheridan, Apr. 17, 1875. This and ff. are found in the colonel's *Letterbook,* deposited at the Gilcrease Institute in Tulsa.

page 207
"I feel there is a heavy responsibility . . ." Letter, Mackenzie to Pope, Sept. 5, 1875.

page 208
identified as Black Coyote . . . Nye, *Carbine,* p. 236.

"just where I entered the valley . . ." Webb, *Frontier Defense,* p. 317.

"We rangers, as well as Indians . . ." Carnal, "Reminiscences," p. 24.

page 209
"Unless something unforeseen takes place . . ." Letter, Mackenzie to Pope, May 15, 1875.

"I shall have to keep large herds . . ." Ibid.

"Unless there is an unforeseen accident . . ." Letter, Mackenzie to Pope, May 25, 1875.

the last of the Quahadi renegades . . . Leckie, *Conquest,* p. 231.

Notes, Chapter XV
page 211
Lieutenant Richard H. Pratt . . . For more on Pratt, see Eastman, *Red Man's Moses,* and Utley (ed.), *Battlefield and Classroom.*

page 212
"If, in the care of these Indians . . ." Taylor, *Campaign,* p. 279 ff.

housed in two locations . . . Guard Reports, Old Files, Fort Sill Museum.

page 213

"They fed us," said one . . . Nye, *Carbine*, p. 229.

buffalo medicine man . . . for more on that order, see Nye, *Carbine*, pp. 46–48.

page 214

"You think you have done well . . ." Nye, *Carbine*, p. 233.

"I have taken the white man's road . . ." Battey, *Life*, p. 317. According to Haworth's report of Striking Eagle's death, the chief had been in ill health for at least two days prior to his death, complaining of a pain in his chest like "someone tearing my heart out." On May 5 a Mexican servant gave him a cup of coffee, and he died suddenly after drinking it. In accordance with Striking Eagle's wish to be buried with his most cherished possessions, Haworth had constructed for him a coffin four feet deep and eight feet long.

page 215

Neill was visibly drunk . . . Hyde, *Life*, p. 365.

"woman who chopped my mother's head open . . ." Letter, Covington to Smith, Apr. 7, 1875.

a Negro named Wesley . . . Hyde, *Life*, p. 365.

Black Horse was hit and felled . . . When Neill reported the incident he stated, "He was shot and we have his body," therefore Black Horse is usually reported dead. Mari Sandoz (*Cheyenne Autumn*) says not, and most historians, like G. Derek West, "Sappa Creek," leave the door open. A close study of the agency letter file shows he was not killed: "The one man reported killed in my [last] letter was badly wounded but not killed." (Letter, Miles to Smith, Apr. 29, 1875). That does not necessarily make Neill a liar, as apparently he did indeed have one body, another Cheyenne named Good Heart (ibid).

page 218

"Go 'way John, bring back our ponies." . . . West, "Sappa Creek," p. 160.

"the skill and good judgement . . ." Eight Medals of Honor were awarded among Henely's men for this action, more than for any other engagement of the war with the exception of thirteen given for the defense of Lyman's wagon train. A total of thirty-five Medals of Honor were awarded during the Red River War (Taylor [ed.], *Campaign*, pp. 223–24, 226).

page 220

"I appreciated the sentiment . . ." Miles, *Recollections*, p. 179.

"The roofs and walls of every casement . . ." Taylor (ed.), *Campaign,*
p. 296.

page 221

"This is not a good place to advance them . . ." Ibid., p. 311.

"A Guide to Florida . . ." Ibid., p. 305. This scheme was approved
by the Commissioner, and also by War Secretary Belknap and Interior Secretary Delano.

Notes, Photograph captions
1. *Quahadi Comanche camp, 1872.* Striking Eagle to Haworth in letter, Haworth to Hoag, June 8, 1874: tense changed.
2. *Columbus Delano, Secretary of the Interior,* Secretary of the Interior, *Annual Reports* for 1872, 1873.
3. *Tabananica (Sound of the Sun).* Richardson, *Barrier,* p. 356.
4–7. *Billy Dixon, Bat Masterson, Josiah Wright Mooar, and John
Wesley Mooar.* Bard, *Life,* pp. 109–10.
8. *Dead Buffalo on the plains, early 1870s.* Dodge, *Plains,* pp. xiv–
xvi.
9. *Skinning a buffalo on the Texas plains, 1874.* Gard, *Hunt,* p. 215.
10. *General John Pope.* House of Representatives Executive Document No. 1, Part II, 43rd Cong., 2nd sess., p. 30.
11. *General Philip H. Sheridan.* Ellis, *Pope,* p. 185.
12. *Rath Hide Yard, Dodge City, c. 1874; Charlie Rath (inset).*
Marshall, *Expedition,* p. 5.
13. *Háhki oomah (Little Robe), a chief of the Southern Cheyennes.*
Branch, *Hunting,* p. 179.
14. *Buffalo hunters' camp, Texas Panhandle, 1874.* Letters, Miles to
Hoag, Mar. 16, 1874; Haworth to Hoag, June 27, 1874.
15. *John D. Miles, Cheyenne-Arapaho Indian Agent.* Letters, Miles to
Hoag, Mar. 31, 1874; May 12, 1874.
16. *James M. Haworth, Kiowa-Comanche Indian Agent.* Letters,
Beede to Hoag, Mar. 30, 1874; Haworth to Hoag, June 29, 1874.
17. *Big Bow, a chief of the Kiowas.* Letter, Haworth to Hoag, May
8, 1874.
18. *Enoch Hoag, Superintendent of the Indian Territory Agencies.*
Directive, Hoag to Haworth, Miles, and Richards, July 8, 1874;
letter, Hoag to Smith, July 10, 1874.
19. *Little Robe.* Letter, Miles to Hoag, Mar. 28. 1874.
20–21. *Ado etta (Big Tree), and Set-tain-te (Satanta, or White
Bear).* Battey, *Life,* pp. 239–40.
22. *Téné-angopte (Striking Eagle), a chief of the Kiowas.* Battey,
Life, p. 295.

23. *Gui-päh-go (Lone Wolf), principal chief of the Kiowas.* Nye, *Carbine,* pp. 174–75.

24. *Nap-a-wat, a Kiowa medicine man.* Letter, Haworth to Hoag, July 21, 1874.

25. *Qua-nah (Fragrance) Parker, a war chief of the Nokoni Comanches.* Scott ms., pp. 5–6.

26. *Isa Rosa (White Wolf), a chief of the Yapparika Comanches,* Ibid., p. 6.

27–28. *Kobay-o-burra (Wild Horse), after 1874 first chief of the Quahadi Comanches; Isa-tai (Wolf Shit), a Quahadi Comanche medicine man.* Scott ms., p. 7.

29. *Red Moon, a Cheyenne war leader.* Letter, Miles to Haworth, June 27, 1874.

30. *John B. Jones, Major of the Frontier Battalion of the Texas Rangers.* This caption is a composite of Carnal, "Reminiscences"; Robertson, "Reminiscences"; Webb, *Frontier Defense,* and material from Chapter VI.

31. *Tsen-tonkee (Hunting Horse), a Kiowa warrior.* Nye, *Carbine,* pp. 198–99.

32. *Colonel Nelson A. Miles, 5th Infantry.* House of Representatives Executive Document No. 1, 43rd Cong., 3rd sess., Serial 1635.

33. *Minninewah (Whirlwind), a chief of the Cheyennes.* Mooar, "Buffalo Days," Part IV, p. 22.

34. *Tape-day-ah, a Kiowa warrior.* Nye, *Medicine,* pp. 189–90.

35–36. *Captain Wyllys Lyman, 5th Infantry; William F. Schmalsle, scout.* Taylor (ed.), *Campaign,* p. 31.

37. *Lieutenant Frank D. Baldwin, 5th Infantry.* Brown, "Scout" ms., p. 3.

38–41. No caption.

42–45. *Kiowa warriors.* Nye, "Excitement," p. 243.

46. *Upper Palo Duro Canyon.* Miles, *Recollections,* p. 165.

47. *Colonel Ranald S. Mackenzie, 4th Cavalry.* Wallace (ed.), *Correspondence,* Vol. II, p. 135.

48–49. *Catherine German (left) and Sophia German, captives of Medicine Water.* Meredith, *Captives,* pp. 17–18.

50. *Adelaide German (left) and Julia German, taken shortly after their rescue from Gray Beard.* Marshall, *Expedition,* pp. 38–39.

51. *Medicine Water, a Cheyenne war chief.* Letter, Miles to Smith, Dec. 29, 1874.

52. *Mochi (Buffalo Calf Woman), wife of Medicine Water.* Meredith, *Captives,* p. 25.

53. *Stone Calf, a Cheyenne chief, and his wife.* Letter, Miles to Smith, Mar. 19, 1875.

54–55. *Indian prisoners arrive at Fort Marion, Hach-i-vi (Little Chief, Southern Cheyenne), on the way to prison, May 10, 1875.* Taylor (ed), *Campaign,* p. 296.

56–57. *Lined up in prison; Black Horse, second chief of the Quahadi Comanches.* Taylor (ed.), *Campaign,* p. 311.

58. *Lieutenant Austin Henely, 6th Cavalry.* Lawrence, Kansas, *Journal,* clipping in Office of Indian Affairs letter file.

BIBLIOGRAPHY AND FURTHER READING

I. Unpublished material

 1. *Letter files.* Collections of correspondence which were preserved from the Red River War period, which were consulted, included the following:

 A. In the National Archives Regional Depository at the Federal Records Center in Fort Worth, Texas, Publication ✗ M-234, "Office of Indian Affairs, Letters Received," from

 Central Superintendency, 1874 (Box 108, roll 64); 1875 (Box 108, roll 65);

 Upper Arkansas Agency, 1874 (Box 143, roll 882); (this agency was not officially designated "Cheyenne-Arapaho Agency" until 1875);

 Cheyenne-Arapaho Agency, 1875 (Box 110, rolls 119 and 120);

 Kiowa-Comanche Agency, 1874 (Box 122, roll 379); 1875 (Box 122, roll 380);

 Wichita Agency, 1867–75 (Box 145, roll 929).

 B. In the National Archives Records on permanent loan to the Oklahoma Historical Society at the Society's headquarters building in Oklahoma City, the letter files

 "Satanta and Big Tree"

 "Agents and Agencies"

 "Kiowas: Depredations"

 "Cheyennes: Depredations"

 Much, though not a majority, of the material contained in the collection of the Oklahoma Historical Society duplicates that found in the Regional Depository, because nearly all the letters of both the War Department and the Indian Bureau were secretarily copied at the time and distributed throughout the bureaucracy. Hence, much of the material found in the Indian Office letter files is military correspondence. However, the Oklahoma Historical Society collections do include intra-agency notes and memoranda absent from the regional collection.

C. "Old Files, Fort Sill." Of this collection, which was consulted by Wilbur Nye, Rupert Richardson, and others, very few remain deposited at Fort Sill. Because of the extensive duplication just mentioned, though, I doubt that much unique material was lost when they were transferred beyond my reach. Among those that do remain are:

"General Orders and Circulars, Fort Sill, Oklahoma, 1869–1879," Vol. 1. Fort Sill Museum.

"Guard Reports, Ft. Sill, 1874–75." Fort Sill Museum.

"Record of Medical History, Ft. Sill, Indian Territory, Feb. 1873–May 1880." Fort Sill Museum.

Very little military correspondence from this period has been edited and published. The only complete letter file to be so treated is Joe F. Taylor's work on the Adjutant General's Office File 2815-1874, a superb piece of source material. Ernest Wallace has edited several military letter files to extract General Mackenzie's correspondence, published in two volumes. One could only hope that the rest of this tremendous mass of letters and documents will also one day be similarly ordered and brought to print.

2. *Annual Reports.*
Secretary of War, 1873–75.
Secretary of the Interior, 1873–75.
Commissioner of Indian Affairs, 1870–75.

3. *Miscellaneous manuscripts.*
Baird, George W. *Papers:* Excerpts from the Diary of Lieut. Frank T. Baldwin. Kansas State Historical Society, Topeka, Kansas.

Brown, W. C. "Baldwin Indian Territory Expedition, From His Own Diaries." W. C. Brown Papers, Western Historical Collection, University of Colorado, Boulder, Colorado.

———. "Gen. Baldwin's Scout in Panhandle of Texas, Sept 6–9, 1874." W. C. Brown Papers, Western Historical Collection, University of Colorado, Boulder, Colorado.

Dixon, Olive K. *Papers.* Panhandle-Plains Historical Museum, Canyon, Texas.

Hatfield, Col. Charles A. P. "The Comanche, Kiowa and Cheyenne Campaign in Northwest Texas and MacKenzie's Fight in the Palo Duro Canon, September 26, 1874." (sic) Panhandle-Plains Historical Museum, Canyon, Texas. This was later published in the *West Texas Historical Association Yearbook,* Vol. V.

Mackenzie, Gen. Ranald S. *Letterbook.* Thomas Gilcrease Institute of American History and Art, Tulsa, Oklahoma. This seldom used piece contains much previously unpublished material.

McKinley, J. W. *Narrative.* Panhandle-Plains Historical Museum, Canyon, Texas.

Nohl, Lessing H. "Bad Hand: The Military Career of Ranald Slidell Mackenzie, 1871–1889." Ph.D. dissertation, University of New Mexico, 1962. Xerox University Microfilms.

Scott, Capt. Hugh L. Manuscripts on the sign language of the South Plains Indians: "The Battle of Adobe Walls." The Library of Congress, Washington, D.C. These unique accounts were given to Scott by sign and partly in broken English Comanche Chief Quanah Parker and Kiowa scout I-See-O in 1897. They were quoted extensively (and loosely) by Wilbur Nye in his books on the plains wars.

Smith, E. D. *Letters*. E. D. Smith to George W. Martin, Secretary of the Kansas State Historical Society, January 11 and 16, 1911. The originals were lost by 1937, but partial typescript survives. Kansas State Historical Society, Topeka, Kansas.

Smithsonian Institution, National Anthropological Archives. "Negatives of Kiowa Indians in Bureau of American Ethnology Collection, March, 1961, Chronologically Arranged." Contains biographical material on several Kiowas.

———. "Negatives of Cheyenne Indians in Bureau of American Ethnology Collection, May, 1962, Chronologically Arranged."

———. "Partial List of Negatives of Comanche Indians in Bureau of American Ethnology Collection."

West, G. Derek. "The Battle of Adobe Walls." Panhandle-Plains Historical Museum, Canyon, Texas. Later published in the *Panhandle-Plains Historical Review*, Vol. XXXVI (1963).

II. Published Documents

(Books)

Day, James M.; Winfrey, Dorman, et al. (eds.). *Texas Indian Papers, 1860–1916*. Austin: Texas State Library, 1961.

Kappler, Charles J. (comp.). *Indian Affairs: Laws and Treaties*. Washington, D.C.: U. S. Government Printing Office, 1904, Vol. II.

Taylor, Joe F. (ed.). *The Indian Campaign on the Staked Plains, 1874–1875: Military Correspondence from the War Department Adjutant General's Office, File 2815-1874*. Canyon, Tex.: Panhandle-Plains Historical Society, 1962.

Thorndike, Rachel S. (ed.). *The Sherman Letters, Correspondence Between General and Senator Sherman from 1837 to 1891*. New York: Charles Scribner's Sons, 1894.

Wallace, Ernest (ed.). *Ranald S. Mackenzie's Official Correspondence Relating to Texas*. Lubbock, Tex.: West Texas Museum Association, 1967, Vol. I.: 1871–73.

——— (ed.). *Ranald S. Mackenzie's Official Correspondence Relating to Texas*. Lubbock, Tex.: West Texas Museum Association, 1968, Vol. II.: 1873–79.

Webb, George W. *Chronological List of Engagements Between Regular Army of the United States and Various Tribes of Hostile Indians Which Occurred During the Years 1790–1898, Inclusive*. St. Joseph, Mo.: Wing Printing and Publishing Co., 1939.

(Articles)

Harrison, Lowell H. "Damage Suits for Indian Depredations in the Adobe Walls Area, 1874," *Panhandle-Plains Historical Review*, Vol. XXXVI (1963).

"List of Actions, etc., with Indians and Other Marauders, Participated in by the Tenth United States Cavalry, Chronologically Arranged—1867 to 1897," *Cavalry Journal*, Vol. X (1897).

"Record of Engagements with Hostile Indians within the Military Division of the Missouri, from 1868 to 1882, Lieutenant General Philip H. Sheridan, Commanding," *West Texas Historical Association Yearbook*, Vol. IX (1933).

Richardson, Rupert N. (ed.). "Documents Relating to West Texas and Her Indian Tribes," *West Texas Historical Association Yearbook*, Vol. I (1925).

Rister, Carl Coke (ed.). "Report of the Commissioner of Indian Affairs," *West Texas Historical Association Yearbook*, Vol. II (1926).

III. Diaries and Memoirs

(Books)

Babb, Theodore Adolphus. *In the Bosom of the Comanches*. Dallas, Tex.: John F. Worley Co., 1912.

Baldwin, Alice B. *Memoirs of the Late Frank D. Baldwin, Major General, United States Army*. Los Angeles, Calif.: Wetzel Publishing Co., 1929.

Battey, Thomas C. *The Life and Adventures of a Quaker Among the Indians*. Boston, Mass.: Lee and Shephard, 1875. A second edition was published, Norman, Okla.: University of Oklahoma Press, 1968.

Carter, Robert G. *The Old Sergeant's Story: Winning the West from the Indians and Bad Men in 1870 to 1876*. New York: Frederick B. Hitchcock, 1926.

————. *On the Border with Mackenzie: Or, Winning West Texas from the Comanches*. Washington, D.C.: Eynon Printing Co., 1935.

Conover, George W. *Sixty Years in Southwest Oklahoma*. Anadarko, Okla.: N. T. Plummer, 1927.

Dixon, Billy. *The Life and Adventures of Billy Dixon of Adobe Walls*. Guthrie, Okla.: Cooperative Publishing Co., 1914.

Grinnell, George Bird. *When Buffalo Ran*. Norman, Okla.: University of Oklahoma Press, 1966.

Keim, DeBenneville Randolph. *Sheridan's Troopers on the Borders: A Winter Campaign on the Plains*. Philadelphia, Penn.: D. McKay, 1885.

Lehmann, Herman. *Nine Years Among the Indians, 1870–1879*. Austin, Tex.: J. M. Hunter, 1927.

Marcy, Randolph B. *Border Reminiscences*. New York: Harper & Brothers, 1872.

Marshall, J. T. (White, Lonnie J. [ed.]). *The Miles Expedition of 1874–1875: An Eyewitness Account of the Red River War*. Austin, Tex.: The Encino Press, 1971.

Mayer, Frank H., and Roth, Charles B. *The Buffalo Harvest*. Denver, Colo.: Sage Books, 1958.

McConnell, H. H. *Five Years a Cavalryman: Or, Sketches of Regular Army Life on the Texas Frontier Twenty Odd Years Ago*. Jacksboro, Tex.: J. N. Rogers & Co., 1889.

Meredith, Grace E. (ed.). *Girl Captives of the Cheyennes*. Los Angeles, Calif.: Gem Publishing Co., 1927.

Miles, Gen. Nelson A. *Personal Recollections and Observations*. Chicago, Ill.: Werner Co., 1896.

————. *Serving the Republic*. New York: Harper, 1911.

Pratt, Richard H. (Utley, Robert M., ed.). *Battlefield and Classroom: Four Decades with the American Indian*. New Haven, Conn.: Yale University Press, 1964.

Seger, John Homer (Vestal, Stanley, ed.). *Early Days Among the Cheyenne and Arapaho Indians*. Norman, Okla.: University of Oklahoma Press, 1956.

Sheridan, Gen. Philip H. *Personal Memoirs*. New York: Charles L. Webster & Co., 1888.

Sherman, Gen. William Tecumseh. *Memoirs of Genl. W. T. Sherman*. New York: Charles L. Webster & Co., 1891.

Smith, Clinton L., and Smith, Jeff D. (Hunter, J. M., ed.). *The Boy Captives*. Bandera, Tex.: J. M. Hunter, 1927.

Strong, Capt. Henry W. *My Frontier Days and Indian Fights on the Plains of Texas*. n. p., n. d.

Wheeler, Homer W. *Buffalo Days: Forty Years in the Old West*. Indianapolis, Ind.: The Bobbs-Merrill Co., 1925.

Wright, Robert M. *Dodge City, The Cowboy Capital*. Wichita, Kans.: Eagle Press, 1913.

(Articles)

Beaumont, E. B. "Over the Border with Mackenzie," *United Service*, Vol. XII (1885).

Campbell, C. E. "Down Among the Red Men," *Collections of the Kansas State Historical Society*, Vol. XVII (1928).

Carnal, Ed. "Reminiscences of a Texas Ranger," *Frontier Times*, Vol. I, No. 3 (Dec. 1923).

Godfrey, Edward S. "Some Reminiscences, Including the Washita Battle, Nov. 25, 1868," *Cavalry Journal*, Vol. XXXVII (1928).

Harper, Milburn C. "An Early Day Railroad Agent," *Chronicles of Oklahoma*, Vol. XXXIII, No. 3 (Fall 1955).

Hobart, Mrs. T. D. "Pioneer Days in the Panhandle-Plains," *Panhandle-Plains Historical Review*, Vol. VIII (1935).

Keeling, Henry C. "My experiences with the Cheyenne Indians," *Collections of the Kansas State Historical Society*, Vol. XI (1909–10).

McFadden, Thompson (Carriker, Robert C., ed.). "Thompson McFadden's Diary of an Indian Campaign, 1874," *Southwestern Historical Quarterly*, Vol. LXXV, No. 2 (Oct. 1971).

Mooar, Josiah Wright (Hunt, James Winfred, ed.). "Buffalo Days," *Holland's Magazine*, Vol. LII, Nos. 1–4 (Jan.–Apr. 1933).

———. "The First Buffalo Hunting in the Panhandle," *West Texas Historical Association Yearbook*, Vol. V (1930).

———. "Frontier Experiences of J. Wright Mooar," *West Texas Historical Association Yearbook*, Vol. IV (1928).

Murphy, John. "Reminiscences of the Washita Campaign, and of the Darlington Agency," *Chronicles of Oklahoma*, Vol. I, No. 3 (June 1923).

Nicholson, William. "A Tour of Indian Agencies in Kansas and the Indian Territory in 1870," *Kansas Historical Quarterly*, Vol. III, Nos. 3–4 (Aug. and Nov. 1934).

Pratt, Richard H. "Some Indian Experiences," *Cavalry Journal*, Vol. XVI (1906).

Rister, Carl Coke (ed.). "Some Early Accounts of Indian Depredations," *West Texas Historical Association Yearbook*, Vol. II (1926).

Robertson, Walter. "Reminiscences of Walter Robertson, the Loss Valley Fight," *Frontier Times*, Vol. VII, No. 3 (Dec. 1929).

Sheffy, L. F. (ed.). "Letters and Reminiscences of General Theodore A. Baidwin: Scouting After Indians on the Plains of West Texas," *Panhandle-Plains Historical Review*, Vol. XI (1938).

Snell, Joseph W. "Diary of a Dodge City Buffalo Hunter," *Kansas Historical Quarterly*, Vol. XXXI, No. 4 (Winter 1965).

Tahan, "The Battle of the Washita," *Chronicles of Oklahoma*, Vol. VIII, No. 3 (Sept. 1930).

Thompson, Maj. W. A. "Scouting with Mackenzie," *Cavalry Journal*, Vol. X (1897).

Wheeler, T. B. "Reminiscences of Reconstruction in Texas," *Southwestern Historical Quarterly*, Vol. XLVI, No. 1 (July 1942).

White, Lonnie J. (ed.). "Kansas Newspaper Items Relating to the Red River War of 1874–1875." *Panhandle-Plains Historical Review*, Vol. XXXVI (1963).

Wright, Robert M. "Personal Reminiscences of Frontier Life in Southwest Kansas," *Transactions of the Kansas State Historical Society*, Vol. VII (1902).

IV. Biographies

(Books)

Anderson, Charles G. *In Search of the Buffalo: The Story of J. Wright Mooar*. Seagraves, Tex.: Pioneer Book Publishers, 1974.

Athearn, Robert G. *William Tecumseh Sherman and the Settlement of the West*. Norman, Okla.: University of Oklahoma Press, 1956.

Bard, Frederick S. *Life and Adventures of "Billy" Dixon of Adobe Walls, Panhandle, Texas.* Guthrie, Okla.: Cooperative Publishing Co., 1914.

Carter, Gen. William H. *The Life of Lt. Genl. Chaffee.* Chicago, Ill.: University of Chicago Press, 1917.

Dixon, Olive K. *The Life of "Billy" Dixon.* Dallas, Tex.: P. L. Turner Co., 1927.

Eastman, Elaine Goodale. *Pratt: The Red Man's Moses.* Norman, Okla.: University of Oklahoma Press, 1935.

Ellis, Richard N. *General Pope and the U. S. Indian Policy.* Albuquerque: University of New Mexico Press, 1970.

Hyde, George E. *Life of George Bent, Written from His Letters.* Norman: University of Oklahoma Press, 1968.

Johnson, Virginia Weisel. *The Unregimented General: A Biography of Nelson A. Miles.* Boston, Mass.: Houghton Mifflin, 1962.

Lewis, Lloyd. *Sherman: Fighting Prophet.* New York: Harcourt, 1932.

O'Connor, Richard. *Bat Masterson.* Garden City, N.Y.: Doubleday & Company, Inc., 1957.

Rister, Carl Coke. *Border Command: General Phil Sheridan in the West.* Norman: University of Oklahoma Press, 1944.

Seymour, M. *Indian Agents of the Old Frontier.* New York: D. Appleton & Co., 1941.

Tilghman, Zoe A. *Quanah, Eagle of the Comanches.* Oklahoma City, Okla.: Harlow Publishing Corp., 1958.

Tolman, Newton F. *The Search for General Miles.* New York: G. P. Putnam's Sons, 1968.

Vail, Rev. A. L. *A Memorial of James M. Haworth, Superintendent of United States Indian Schools.* Kansas City, Kans.: Press of H. N. Farey & Co., 1886.

Wallace, Ernest. *Ranald S. Mackenzie on the Texas Frontier.* Lubbock, Tex.: West Texas Museum Association, 1964.

Wharton, Clarence R. *Satanta, The Great Chief of the Kiowas and His People.* Dallas, Tex.: B. Upshaw and Co., 1935.

(Articles)

Becker, Daniel A. "Comanche Civilization, With History of Quanah Parker," *Chronicles of Oklahoma,* Vol. I, No. 3 (June 1923).

Buntin, Martha. "The Quaker Indian Agents of the Kiowa, Comanche, and Wichita Indian Reservations," *Chronicles of Oklahoma,* Vol. X, No. 2 (June 1932).

Crane, R. C. "Old Man Keeler," *West Texas Historical Association Yearbook,* Vol. IV (1928).

Crimmins, Col. M. L. "General Nelson A. Miles in Texas," *West Texas Historical Association Yearbook,* Vol. XXIII (1947).

Dorst, Capt. Joseph H. "Ranald Slidell Mackenzie," *Cavalry Journal,* Vol. X (1897).

Ellis, Richard N. "General John Pope and the Southern Plains Indians,

1875–1883," *Southwestern Historical Quarterly*, Vol. LXXII, No. 2 (Oct. 1968).

Hunter, J. Marvin, Sr. "John W. Mooar, Successful Pioneer," *Frontier Times*, Vol. XXIX, No. 12 (Sept. 1952).

Le Van, Sandra W. "The Quaker Agents at Darlington," *Chronicles of Oklahoma*, Vol. LI, No. 1 (Spring 1973).

Richardson, Rupert N. (ed.). "The Death of Nocona," *Southwestern Historical Quarterly*, Vol. XLVI, No. 1 (July 1942).

Rister, Carl Coke. "Satanta, Orator of the Plains," *Southwest Review*, Vol. XVII (1931).

Swett, Morris. "Sergeant I-See-O: Kiowa Scout," *Chronicles of Oklahoma*, Vol. XIII, No. 3 (Sept. 1935).

Taylor, Morris F. "Kicking Bird: A Chief of the Kiowas," *Kansas Historical Quarterly*, Vol. XXXVIII, No. 3 (Autumn 1972).

Thoburn, Joseph B. "Horace P. Jones, Scout and Interpreter." *Chronicles of Oklahoma*, Vol. II, No. 4 (Dec. 1924).

Wallace, Edward S. "General Ranald Slidell Mackenzie, Indian Fighting Cavalryman," *Southwestern Historical Quarterly*, Vol. LVI, No. 3, (Jan. 1953).

Wellman, Paul I. "Some Famous Kansas Frontier Scouts," *Kansas Historical Quarterly*, Vol. I, No. 4 (Aug. 1932).

Zimmerman, Jean L. "Colonel Ranald S. Mackenzie at Fort Sill," *Chronicles of Oklahoma*, Vol. XLIV, No. 1 (Spring 1966).

V. General Works

(Books)

Allred, Dykes, et al. (eds.). *Great Western Indian Fights*. Garden City, N.Y.: Doubleday & Company, Inc., 1960.

Atkinson, Mary Jourdan. *Indians of the Southwest*. San Antonio, Tex.: The Naylor Company, 1935.

———. *The Texas Indians*. San Antonio, Tex.: The Naylor Company, 1935.

Bedford, Hilary G. *Texas Indian Troubles*. Dallas, Tex.: Hargreaves Printing Co., Inc., 1905.

Berthrong, Donald J. *The Southern Cheyennes*. Norman: University of Oklahoma Press, 1963.

Brady, Cyrus T. *The Conquest of the Southwest: The Story of a Great Spoliation*. New York: D. Appleton & Co., 1905.

Branch, E. Douglas. *The Hunting of the Buffalo*. New York: D. Appleton & Co., 1929.

Brill, Charles J. *Conquest of the Southern Plains*. Oklahoma City, Okla.: Golden Saga Publishers, 1938.

Brown, John Henry. *Indian Wars and Pioneers of Texas*. Austin, Tex.: L. E. Daniell, n. d. (c. 1890).

Burton, Harley T. *A History of the JA Ranch*. Austin, Tex.: Von Boechmann-Jones Co., 1928.

Capps, Benjamin. *The Warren Wagontrain Raid.* New York: The Dial Press, 1974.

Carriker, Robert C. *Fort Supply, Indian Territory: Frontier Outpost on the Plains.* Norman: University of Oklahoma Press, 1970.

Catlin, George. *North American Indians.* London: Chatto & Windus, 1876.

Conger, Roger N., et al. *Frontier Forts of Texas.* Waco, Tex.: The Texian Press, 1966.

Cook, John R. *The Border and the Buffalo.* Topeka, Kans.: Crane & Co., 1907.

Dale, Edward Everett. *The Indians of the Southwest.* Norman: University of Oklahoma Press, 1949.

———. *Frontier Ways: Sketches of Life in the Old West.* Austin: University of Texas Press, 1959.

Deaton, E. L. *Indian Fights on the Texas Frontier.* Fort Worth, Tex.: Pioneer Publishing Co., 1927.

De Shields, James T. *Border Wars of Texas.* Tioga, Tex.: Herald Co., 1912.

Dodge, Maj. Richard Irving. *Our Wild Indians.* Hartford, Conn.: A. D. Worthington & Co., 1890.

———. *The Plains of the Great West.* London: Chatto & Windus, 1877.

Farb, Peter. *Man's Rise to Civilization.* New York: E. P. Dutton, 1968.

Frazer, Robert W. *Forts of the West.* Norman: University of Oklahoma Press, 1965.

Freeman, George D. *Midnight and Noonday: Or, The Incidental History of Southern Kansas and the Indian Territory.* Caldwell, Kans.: n. p., 1892.

Fritz, Henry. *The Movement for Indian Assimilation, 1860–1890.* Philadelphia: University of Pennsylvania Press, 1963.

Gard, Wayne. *The Great Buffalo Hunt.* New York: Alfred A. Knopf, 1959.

Glass, Maj. Edward L. N. *History of the Tenth Cavalry.* Tucson, Ariz.: Acme Printing Co., 1921.

Grinnell, George Bird. *The Cheyenne Indians.* New Haven, Conn.: Yale University Press, 1928.

———. *The Fighting Cheyennes.* Norman: University of Oklahoma Press, 1966; orig. New York: Charles Scribner's Sons, 1915.

Hagan, William T. *Indian Police and Judges.* New Haven, Conn.: Yale University Press, 1966.

Haley, J. Evetts. *Fort Concho and the Texas Frontier.* San Angelo, Tex.: San Angelo Standard Times, 1952.

Herr, John K., and Wallace, Edward S. *The Story of the U. S. Cavalry, 1775–1942.* Boston, Mass.: Little, Brown and Company, 1953.

Hoebel, E. Adamson. *The Cheyenne Indians of the Great Plains.* New York: Holt, Rinehart and Winston, 1960.

Hornaday, William T. *The Extermination of the American Bison: Report of the National Museum, 1887.* Washington, D.C.: U. S. Government Printing Office, 1889.

Hunter, John Marvin. *The Bloody Trail in Texas: Sketches and Narratives of Indian Raids and Atrocities on Our Frontier.* Bandera, Tex.: J. M. Hunter, 1931.

Hyde, George E. *Indians of the High Plains.* Norman: University of Oklahoma Press, 1959.

Inman, Col. Henry. *The Old Santa Fe Trail: The Story of a Great Highway.* New York: The Macmillan Company, 1897.

Jones, C. Douglas. *The Treaty of Medicine Lodge: The Story of the Great Treaty Council as Told by Eyewitnesses.* Norman: University of Oklahoma Press, 1966.

Kenner, Charles L. *A History of New Mexican-Plains Indian Relations.* Norman: University of Oklahoma Press, 1969.

Knight, Oliver. *Following the Indian Wars: The Story of the Newspaper Correspondents Among the Indian Campaigners.* Norman: University of Oklahoma Press, 1960.

Leckie, William H. *The Buffalo Soldiers: A Narrative of Negro Cavalry in the West.* Norman: University of Oklahoma Press, 1967.

———. *The Military Conquest of the South Plains.* Norman: University of Oklahoma Press, 1963.

Llewellyn, K. N., and Hoebel, E. Adamson. *The Cheyenne Way: Conflict and Case Law in Primitive Jurisprudence.* Norman: University of Oklahoma Press, 1941.

Mardock, Robert W. *The Reformers and the American Indian.* Columbia: University of Missouri Press, 1971.

Mayhall, Mildred P. *The Indian Wars of Texas.* Waco, Tex.: The Texian Press, 1965.

———. *The Kiowas.* Norman: University of Oklahoma Press, 1962.

McConnell, Joseph Carroll. *The West Texas Frontier.* Palo Pinto, Tex.: Texas Legal Bank & Book Co., 1939.

Methvin, Rev. J. J. *In the Limelight: Or, History of Anadarko.* Anadarko, Okla.: n. p., n. d.

———. *Andele: Or, The Mexican Kiowa Captive.* Anadarko, Okla.: Plummer Printing Co., 1927.

Mishkin, Bernard. *Rank and Warfare Among the Plains Indians.* New York: J. J. Augustin, 1940.

Momaday, N. Scott. *The Way to Rainy Mountain.* Albuquerque: University of New Mexico Press, 1969.

Morrison, William B. *Military Posts and Camps in Oklahoma.* Oklahoma City, Okla.: Harlow Publishing Corp., 1936.

Nye, Col. Wilbur Sturtevant. *Bad Medicine & Good: Tales of the Kiowas.* Norman: University of Oklahoma Press, 1962.

———. *Carbine & Lance: The Story of Old Fort Sill.* Norman: University of Oklahoma Press, 1937.

——. *Plains Indian Raiders*. Norman: University of Oklahoma Press, 1968.

Priest, Loring B. *Uncle Sam's Stepchildren: The Reformation of United States Indian Policy, 1865–1887*. New Brunswick, N.J.: Rutgers University Press, 1942.

Prucha, Francis Paul. *Guide to the Military Posts of the United States*. Madison, Wis.: State Historical Society of Wisconsin, 1964.

Richardson, Rupert N. *The Comanche Barrier to South Plains Settlement*. Glendale, Calif.: Arthur H. Clark Co., 1933.

——. *The Frontier of Northwest Texas, 1846–1876*. Glendale, Calif.: Arthur H. Clark Co., 1963.

——, and Rister, Carl Coke. *Greater Southwest*. Glendale, Calif.: Arthur H. Clark Co., 1935.

Rickey, Don, Jr. *Forty Miles a Day on Beans and Hay: The Enlisted Soldier Fighting the Indian Wars*. Norman: University of Oklahoma Press, 1963.

Rister, Carl Coke. *Border Captives: The Traffic in Prisoners by Southern Plains Indians, 1835–1875*. Norman: University of Oklahoma Press, 1940.

——. *Fort Griffin on the Texas Frontier*. Norman: University of Oklahoma Press, 1956.

——. *The Southwestern Frontier, 1865–1881*. Glendale, Calif.: Arthur H. Clark Co., 1928.

——. *Southern Plainsmen*. Norman: University of Oklahoma Press, 1938.

Sandoz, Mari. *The Buffalo Hunters, The Story of the Hidemen*. New York: Hastings House, 1954.

——. *Cheyenne Autumn*. New York: McGraw-Hill, 1953.

——. *Hostiles and Friendlies*. Lincoln: University of Nebraska Press, 1959.

Schmeckebier, Laurence F. *The Office of Indian Affairs: Its History, Activities, and Organization*. Baltimore, Md.: John Hopkins Press, 1927.

Stroud, Harry A. *Conquest of the Prairies*. Waco, Tex.: The Texian Press, 1968.

Tatum, Lawrie. *Our Red Brothers and the Peace Policy of President Grant*. Philadelphia, Penn.: J. C. Winston & Co., 1899.

Toole, K. Ross. *Probing the American West: Papers from the Santa Fe Conference*. Santa Fe: Museum of New Mexico Press, 1962.

Toulouse, James R., and Toulouse, Joseph H. *Pioneer Posts of Texas*. San Antonio, Tex.: The Naylor Company, 1936.

Trenholm, Virginia Cole. *The Arapahoes: Our People*. Norman: University of Oklahoma Press. 1970.

Utley, Robert M. *Frontier Regulars: The United States Army and the Indians, 1866–1891*. New York: Macmillan, 1973.

Vestal, Stanley. *New Sources of Indian History 1850–1891*. Norman: University of Oklahoma Press, 1934.

———. *Queen of the Cowtowns: Dodge City.* New York: Harper and Brothers, 1952.

———. *Warpath and Council Fire: The Plains Indians' Struggle for Survival in War and in Diplomacy, 1851–1891.* New York: Random House, 1948.

Wallace, Ernest. *Texas in Turmoil, 1849–1875.* Austin, Tex.: Steck-Vaughan Co., 1965.

———, and Hoebel, E. Adamson. *The Comanches: Lords of the South Plains.* Norman: University of Oklahoma Press, 1952.

Webb, Walter Prescott. *The Story of the Texas Rangers.* New York: Grosset and Dunlap, 1957.

———. *The Texas Rangers: A Century of Frontier Defense.* Boston, Mass.: Houghton Mifflin, 1935.

Wellman, Paul I. *The Comancheros.* Garden City, N.Y.: Doubleday & Company, Inc., 1952.

———. *Death on the Prairie.* New York: Macmillan, 1934.

———. *Indian Wars of the West.* Garden City, N.Y.: Doubleday & Company, Inc., 1947.

Wilbarger, J. W. *Indian Depredations in Texas.* Austin, Tex.: Hutchings Printing House, 1890.

Wright, Muriel H. *A Guide to the Indian Tribes of Oklahoma.* Norman: University of Oklahoma Press, 1951.

(Articles)

Algood, Samuel Y. "Historic Spots and Actions in the Washita Valley up to 1870," *Chronicles of Oklahoma,* Vol. V, No. 2 (June 1927).

Archambeau, Ernest R. (ed.). "The Battle of Lyman's Wagon Train," *Panhandle-Plains Historical Review,* Vol. XXXVI (1963).

Baird, Maj. G. M. "General Miles's Indian Campaigns," *Century Magazine,* Vol. XLII (1891).

Barrett, Arrie. "Western Frontier Forts of Texas, 1845–61," *West Texas Historical Association Yearbook,* Vol. VII (1931).

Beach, James H. "Old Fort Hays," *Transactions of the Kansas State Historical Society,* Vol. XI (1910).

Becker, W. J. "The Comanche Indian and His Language," *Chronicles of Oklahoma,* Vol. XIV, No. 3 (Sept. 1936).

Bender, A. B. "The Texas Frontier, 1848–1861," *Southwestern Historical Quarterly,* Vol. XXXVIII, No. 2 (Oct. 1934).

Bieber, Ralph P. "Some Aspects of the Santa Fe Trail, 1848–1880," *Chronicles of Oklahoma,* Vol. II, No. 1 (Mar. 1924).

Bryan, Frank. "The Llano Estacado: The Geographical Background of the Coronado Expedition," *Panhandle-Plains Historical Review,* Vol. XIII (1940).

Buntin, Martha. "Difficulties Encountered in Issuing Cheyenne and Arapaho Subsistence, 1861–70," *Chronicles of Oklahoma,* Vol. XIII, No. 1 (Mar. 1935).

———. "The Removal of the Wichitas, Kiowas, Comanches, and Apaches to the Present Agency," *Panhandle-Plains Historical Review,* Vol. IV (1931).

Butler, Joseph. "Pioneer School Teaching at the Comanche-Kiowa Agency School, 1870–1873," *Chronicles of Oklahoma,* Vol. VI, No. 4 (Dec. 1928).

Cabannis, A. A. "Troop and Company Pack-Trains," *Journal of the U. S. Cavalry Association,* Vol. III (1890).

Campbell, Walter S. "The Cheyenne Dog Soldiers," *Chronicles of Oklahoma,* Vol. I, No. 1 (Jan. 1923).

Connelley, William E. "The Treaty Held at Medicine Lodge," *Collections of the Kansas State Historical Society,* Vol. XVII (1928).

Crane, R. C. "General Mackenzie and Fort Concho," *West Texas Historical Association Yearbook,* Vol. X (1934).

———. "Settlement of Indian Troubles in West Texas, 1874–75," *West Texas Historical Association Yearbook,* Vol. I (1925).

———. "Some Aspects of the History of West and Northwest Texas Since 1845," *Southwestern Historical Quarterly,* Vol. XXVI, No. 1 (July 1922).

———. "Some Early History of the Panhandle-Plains Region," *Panhandle-Plains Historical Review,* Vol. VIII (1935).

Crimmins, Col. M. L. "The First Line: Or, Army Posts Established in West Texas in 1849," *West Texas Historical Association Yearbook,* Vol. XIX (1943).

———. "Fort McKavett, Texas," *Southwestern Historical Quarterly,* Vol. XXXVIII, No. 1 (July 1934).

———. "Notes on the Establishment of Fort Elliott and the Buffalo Wallow Fight," *Panhandle-Plains Historical Review,* Vol. XXV (1952).

Debo, Angie. "History and Customs of the Kiowas," *Panhandle-Plains Historical Review,* Vol. VII (1934).

———. "Social and Economic Life of the Comanches," *Panhandle-Plains Historical Review,* Vol. III (1930).

D'Elia, Donald J. "The Argument Over Civilian Or Military Control, 1865–1880," *Historian,* Vol. XXIV, No. 2 (Feb. 1962).

Doran, Thomas F. "Kansas Sixty Years Ago," *Collections of the Kansas State Historical Society,* Vol. XV (1923).

Dunn, William Edward. "The Apache Mission on the San Saba River; Its Founding and Failure," *Southwestern Historical Quarterly,* Vol. XVII, No. 4 (Apr. 1914).

Essin, Emmett M., III. "Mules, Packs, and Packtrains," *Southwestern Historical Quarterly,* Vol. LXXIV, No. 1 (July 1970).

Foreman, Grant. "Historical Background of the Kiowa-Comanche Reservation," *Chronicles of Oklahoma,* Vol. XIX, No. 2 (June 1941).

———. "The Texas Comanche Treaty of 1846," *Southwestern Historical Quarterly,* Vol. LI, No. 4 (Apr. 1948).

Fritz, Henry E. "The Making of Grant's Peace Policy," *Chronicles of Oklahoma,* Vol. XXXVII, No. 4 (Winter 1959–60).

Garfield, James A. "The Army of the United States," *North American Review*, Vol. CXXVI (1878).

Garfield, Marvin. "The Military Post as a Factor in the Frontier Defense of Kansas," *Kansas Historical Quarterly*, Vol. I, No. 1 (Nov. 1931).

———. "Defense of the Kansas Frontier, 1864–1865," *Kansas Historical Quarterly*, Vol. I, No. 2 (Feb. 1932).

———. "Defense of the Kansas Frontier, 1866–1867," *Kansas Historical Quarterly*, Vol. I, No. 4 (Aug. 1932).

———. "Defense of the Kansas Frontier, 1868–1869," *Kansas Historical Quarterly* Vol. I, No. 5 (Nov. 1932).

Godfrey, Edward S. "Cavalry Fire Discipline," *Journal of the Military Service Institution of the United States*, Vol. XIX (1896).

Green, L. D. "The Army and the Indian," *Harper's*, Vol. XXXVIII (1894).

Grinnell, George Bird. "Bent's Old Fort and Its Builders," *Collections of the Kansas State Historical Society*, Vol. XV (1923).

Griswold, Gillette. "Old Fort Sill: The First Seven Years," *Chronicles of Oklahoma*, Vol. XXXVI, No. 1 (Spring 1958).

Hadley, James A. "The Kansas Cavalry and the Conquest of the Plains Indians," *Collections of the Kansas State Historical Society*, Vol. X (1908).

Haley, J. Evetts. "The Comanchero Trade," *Southwestern Historical Quarterly*, Vol. XXXVIII, No. 3 (Jan. 1935).

Hanks, Jane. "Law and Status Among the Kiowa Indians," *American Ethnological Society Monodgraph*, Vol. I (2nd printing, Seattle, 1966).

Harmon, George D. "The United States' Indian Policy in Texas, 1845–1860," *Mississippi Historical Review*, Vol. XVII (1930).

Hickok, H. R. "Our Cavalry Organization as Viewed in the Light of Its History and of Legislation," *Cavalry Journal*, Vol. XXII (1912).

Hill, Frank P. "Indian Raids on the South Plains," *Panhandle-Plains Historical Review*, Vol. VII (1934).

———. "The South Plains and Our Indian History," *West Texas Historical Association Yearbook*, Vol. XII (1936).

Holabird, S. B. "Army Wagon Transportation," *Ordnance Notes*, No. 189 (Washington, D.C.: Apr. 15, 1882).

Holden, William C. "The Buffalo of the Plains Area," *West Texas Historical Association Yearbook*, Vol. II (1926).

———. "Frontier Defense, 1846–1860," *West Texas Historical Association Yearbook*, Vol. VI (1930).

———. "Frontier Defense, 1865–1889," *Panhandle-Plains Historical Review*, Vol. II (1929).

———. "Frontier Defense in Texas During the Civil War," *West Texas Historical Association Yearbook*, Vol. IV (1928).

———. "Immigration and Settlement in West Texas," *West Texas Historical Association Yearbook*, Vol. VII (1931).

Hughes, Pollyanna B. "Adobe Walls May Rise Again," *Texas Parade,* Vol. XV, No. 5 (Oct. 1954).

Hunt, F. A. "Adobe Walls Argument: An Indian Attack on a Party of Buffalo Hunters," *Overland Monthly,* Vol. LIV (May 1909).

Hunter, J. Marvin, Sr. "The Battle of Palo Duro Canyon," *Frontier Times,* Vol. XXI, No. 4 (Jan. 1944).

Kenney, M. M. "Tribal Society Among Texas Indians," *Southwestern Historical Quarterly,* Vol. I, No. 1 (July 1897).

Koch, Lena Clara. "Federal Indian Policy in Texas," *Southwestern Historical Quarterly,* Vol. XXVIII, No. 4 (Jan. 1925), and Vol. XXIX, Nos. 1 and 2 (July and Oct. 1925).

Leckie, William H. "The Red River War of 1874–75," *Panhandle-Plains Historical Review,* Vol. XXIX (1956).

Leeper, Paul S. "Satanta and His Trial," *Frontier Times,* Vol. VII, No. 7 (Apr. 1930).

Linton, Ralph. "The Comanche Sun Dance," *American Anthropologist,* Vol. XXXVII, No. 3, Part 1 (July–Sept. 1935).

Little, Edward Campbell. "The Battle of Adobe Walls," *Pearson's Magazine,* Vol. XIX, No. 1 (Jan. 1908).

Lowie, Robert Harry. "Societies of the Kiowas," *American Museum of Natural History, Anthropological Papers,* Vol. XI, Part 11 (1916).

McNeal, T. A. "The Indians Agree to Abandon Kansas." *Transactions of the Kansas State Historical Society,* Vol. VI (1897–1900).

Mead, James R. "The Little Arkansas," *Transactions of the Kansas State Historical Society,* Vol. X (1908).

Mellor, William J. "Military Investigation of Colonel John M. Chivington Following the Sand Creek Massacre," *Chronicles of Oklahoma,* Vol. XVI, No. 4 (Dec. 1938).

Mitchell, Sara Brown. "The Early Days of Anadarko," *Chronicles of Oklahoma,* Vol. XXVIII, No. 4 (Winter 1950–51).

Montgomery, Mrs. Frank C. "Fort Wallace and Its Relation to the Frontier," *Collections of the Kansas State Historical Society,* Vol. XVII (1928).

————. "United States Surveyors Massacred by Indians (Lone Tree, Meade County, 1874)," *Kansas Historical Quarterly,* Vol. I, No. 3 (May 1932).

Mooney, James. "The Cheyennes," *Memoirs of the American Anthropological Association,* Vol. I, Part 6 (1907).

————. "The Kiowa Indians." *Seventeenth Annual Report of the Bureau of American Ethnology,* Part 1 (1897).

Muckleroy, Anna. "The Indian Policy of the Republic of Texas," *Southwestern Historical Quarterly,* Vol. XXV, No. 4 (Apr. 1922), and Vol. XXVI, Nos. 1, 2, and 3 (July and Oct. 1922 and Jan. 1923).

Nesbit, Paul. "Battle of the Washita," *Chronicles of Oklahoma,* Vol. III, No. 1 (Apr. 1925).

Nichols, Col. G. W. "The Indian: What We Should Do with Him," *Harper's,* Vol. XL (Apr. 1870).

Nye, Col. Wilbur Sturtevant. "Excitement on the Sweetwater," *Chronicles of Oklahoma,* Vol. XVI, No. 2 (June 1938).

———. "An Indian Raid into Texas," *Chronicles of Oklahoma,* Vol. XV, No. 1 (March 1937).

———. "Kiowa Sun Dance," *Chronicles of Oklahoma,* Vol. XII, No. 3 (Sept. 1934).

Oswald, James M. "History of Fort Elliott," *Panhandle-Plains Historical Review,* Vol. XXXII (1959).

Peery, Dan W. "The Kiowas' Defiance," *Chronicles of Oklahoma,* Vol. XIII, No. 1 (Mar. 1935).

———. "The White Kiowa Captive," *Chronicles of Oklahoma,* Vol. VIII, No. 3 (Sept. 1930).

Petter, Rodolph C. "Sketch of the Cheyenne Grammar," *Memoirs of the American Anthropological Association,* Vol. I, Part 6 (1907).

Porter, Kenneth Wiggins. "Negroes and Indians on the Texas Frontier," *Southwestern Historical Quarterly,* Vol. LIII, No. 2 (Oct. 1949).

———. "The Seminole Negro-Indian Scouts, 1870–1881," *Southwestern Historical Quarterly,* Vol. LV, No. 3 (Jan. 1952).

Prickett, Robert C. "The Malfeasance of William Worth Belknap," *North Dakota History,* Vol. XVII (1950).

Ramsdell, Charles W. "Presidential Reconstruction in Texas," *Southwestern Historical Quarterly,* Vol. XI, No. 4 (Apr. 1908).

Rathjen, Fred. "The Physiography of the Texas Panhandle," *Southwestern Historical Quarterly,* Vol. LXIV, No. 3 (Jan. 1961).

Richardson, Rupert N. "The Comanche Indians at the Adobe Walls Fight," *Panhandle-Plains Historical Review,* Vol. IV (1931).

———. "The Comanche Reservation in Texas," *West Texas Historical Association Yearbook,* Vol. V (1929).

Rister, Carl Coke. "Fort Griffin," *West Texas Historical Association Yearbook,* Vol. I (1925).

———. "Harmful Practices of Indian Traders of the Southwest, 1865–1876," *New Mexico Historical Review,* Vol. VI (1931).

———. "The Significance of the Destruction of the Buffalo in the Southwest," *Southwestern Historical Quarterly,* Vol. XXXIII, No. 1 (July 1929).

———. "The Significance of the Jacksboro Affair of 1871," *Southwestern Historical Quarterly,* Vol. XXIX, No. 3 (Jan. 1926).

Rossi, Paul A. "Run the Buffalo, A Story of the Hide Hunters," *The American Scene,* Vol. X, No. 3 (1969).

Russell, Don. "The Army of the Frontier, 1865–1891," *Westerners Brand Book,* Vol. VI (1949).

Schmitt, Karl. "Wichita-Kiowa Relations and the 1874 Outbreak," *Chronicles of Oklahoma,* Vol. XXVIII, No. 2 (Summer 1950).

Seton, Ernest Thompson. "The American Bison or Buffalo," *Scribner's Magazine,* Vol. XI, No. 9 (Oct. 1906).

Sheffy, L. F. "The Experimental Stage of Settlement in the Panhandle of Texas," *Panhandle-Plains Historical Review,* Vol. III (1930).

Shipp, W. E. "Mounted Infantry," *Journal of the U. S. Cavalry Association*, Vol. V (1892).

Smith, Col. C. C. "Old Military Posts in the Southwest," *Frontier Times*, Vol. VII, No. 9 (June 1930).

Spier, Leslie. "Notes on the Kiowa Sun Dance," *American Museum of Natural History, Anthropological Papers*, Vol. XVI, Part 6 (1921).

Steele, Aubrey L. "Lawrie Tatum's Indian Policy," *Chronicles of Oklahoma*, Vol. XXII, No. 1 (Spring 1944).

Street, William D. "Cheyenne Indian Massacre on the Middle Fork of the Sappa," *Transactions of the Kansas State Historical Society*, Vol. X (1907–8).

Tate, Michael L. "The Frontier of Northwest Texas During the Civil War," *Chronicles of Oklahoma*, Vol. L, No. 2 (Summer 1972).

Taylor, Alfred A. "Medicine Lodge Peace Council," *Chronicles of Oklahoma*, Vol. II, No. 2 (March 1924).

Wallace, Edward S., and Anderson, Adrian S. "R. S. Mackenzie and the Kickapoos: The Raid into Mexico in 1873," *Arizona and the West*, Vol. VII (1965).

Waltman, Henry G. "Circumstantial Reformer: President Grant and the Indian Problem," *Arizona and the West*, Vol. XIII (1971).

West, G. Derek. "The Battle of Sappa Creek, 1875," *Kansas Historical Quarterly*, Vol. XXXIV, No. 2 (Summer 1968).

————. "Baldwin's Ride and the Battle of Lyman's Wagon Train," *English Westerners' Special Publication*, No. 1 (London: 1964).

White, Lonnie J. "The First Battle of the Palo Duro Canyon," *Texas Military History*, Vol. VI (Fall 1967).

Wyman, Walker D. "The Military Phase of Santa Fe Freighting, 1846–1865," *Kansas Historical Quarterly*, Vol. I, No. 5 (Nov. 1932).

INDEX

Abolitionists, 140
Adaptability, 2, 7
Adobe Walls, 35–36, 46, 56, 59, 60, 61, 63, 132; attack, 60ff., 66; battle, *viii*, 67–78, 79, 80, 95, 101, 103, 109, 115, 130, 173; casualties, 78; fortifications, 130; war party, size, 65
Alcohol, *vii*, 59, 57
Algonquin, 7
Alvord Council (1872), 14–15
Americanophiles, 23
Americans, *viii*, 5; and Indians, relationship, 2–3, 4, 5ff., 17. *See also* United States *and under* tribe
Amon Carter Museum of Western Art, *xi*
Anadarko, 115, 116, 170, 186; Agency, 97–98; catalyst, 191; fight, 117ff., 123, 147, 214; renegades, 147ff., 152, 166, 190
Anderson, Charles G., *xii*
Apaches, 2, 3, 15, 38, 171
Arapahoes, *vii*, 1, 6, 7, 8, 13, 19, 38, 42–44, 49, 52, 200, 204, 205, 215; buffalo, 24; characteristics, 19, 200; peace: chiefs, 19, 31, 44, policy, 125; reservation, 11; United States, 7–8; war, 56
Arkansas River, 1, 11, 22, 23, 24; "dead line," 22, 24, 25
Armitage, Harry, 72
Arms (and ammunition), 28, 29–30, 60, 62, 68, 71, 72, 74, 90,

117, 127, 133, 144, 162, 181, 217; gun runners, *vii*, 49–50, 171
Asa-toyah-teh, Chief, 14, 53–54, 108, 117
Atah-lah-te (Loud Talker or Feather Head), 87
Atchison *Squatter Sovereign*, 140
Augur, Christopher C., 39, 100, 101, 146, 169ff., 182ff., 190, 206–7
Austin, Stephen F., 4

Bailey, David, 91, 92, 93
Baldwin, Frank D., 78, 128ff., 135, 149ff., 157, 158, 192–94; characteristics, 193; expedition, 78; honors, 193; strategy, 193
Bandidos, 85
Barrett, Ed, 119, 120
Battey, Thomas C., 3–4, 15, 18, 39, 48, 57, 115
Bear's Paw, Chief, 162, 163
Beaumont, Eugene B., 172, 173, 174, 180
Beede, Cyrus, 40, 41, 108
Belknap, William Worth, Secretary of War, 106, 212
Bellfield, George, 76
Bennett, Andrew S., 215
Bent, George, 14, 45, 134, 137, 165, 215
Bent, William, 33
Biddle, James, 127, 133
Big Bow, Chief, 18, 41–42, 57, 82, 113, 131, 148, 149, 154, 205, 213

Big Moccasin, 199
Big Red Meat, Chief, 16, 115ff.,
　123, 190, 191, 205; death, 214
Big Tree, Chief, 17, 19, 48, 80, 83,
　108, 213; parole, 148; policy, 148;
　surrender, 189, 190; trial, 170
Bird, Chief, 213
Bison, extermination, *viii. See*
　Buffalo
Black Beaver, Chief, 119
"Black Comanche," 95
Black Horse, Chief, 16, 114, 214,
　215–16, 219
Black Kettle, Chief, 12, 19;
　massacre, 8
Blackmore, William, 23, 24
Blaine, Martha, *xi*
"Blue Billy," 60
Blue Shield, 148–49
Boehm, Peter M., 173, 174
Born, "Dutch Henry," 32, 61
Botalye, 148–49, 154, 155, 158, 159,
　160
Box, James, 39
Bristol, H. B., 127
Brooke, General, 46
Buell, George P., 51, 105, 183, 187,
　190–91, 207
Buffalo: destruction, 20, 22ff., 37,
　43, 44, 109; Great Southern Herd,
　26; guns, 28, 29–30, 71, 74, 75;
　hides, trade, 21–23, 36; hunters
　(-ing), *vii,* 1, 2, 11, 21ff., 36,
　37–38, 59ff., 63, 76, 77, 96, 128,
　130, 218, atrocities, 130–31,
　characteristics, 31ff., policy, 33,
　"runners," 24, 25, 29, 36, scouts,
　150, supply post, 35–37 (*see*
　Adobe Walls), teams, 30, and
　traders, 64; and Indians, 2, 11, 24,
　26, 27, 37, 39–40, 59; legislation,
　25; migration, 26, 36; number, 21,
　26; poacher, 51, 52; runners, 71;
　soldiers, 191
Buffalo Good, Chief, 122
Buffalo Indians, 1–20

Buffalo Wallow, 160, 161; battle,
　147, 163–64, 178; defined, 160
Buffalo War, *ix,* 59–66
Bull Bear, Chief, 16, 54, 193, 201

Cache Creek, 110, 111, 114
Caddoan tribes, 115, 119–20
Cameron Creek, 91
Campbell, David, 129
Campbell, Henry, 218
Camp Supply, 13, 31, 41, 44, 46,
　60, 95, 98, 166; commandant,
　156; location, 131; interpreter
　(*see* Chapman, Amos)
Canada, Ojibway, 7
Canadian River, 26, 33, 104
Cannibalism, 55, 233
Cap Rock, 104, 105, 136
Carefoot, Carol, *xi*
Carnal, Ed, 87–88, 91, 208
Carpenter, Lewis H., 121, 191
Carson, Kit, 33
Castillo de San Marcos, 211;
　National Monument, *xii*
Cator, Bob, 76
Cator, Jim, 76
Chaffee, Adna R., 133–34, 191
Chapman, Amos, 31, 60–61, 64,
　131, 132, 158, 159, 160, 165
Charlton, John B., 171
Chee-na-bony, Chief, 121–22
Cheevers, Chief, 112, 205, 214
Cherokee, 4
Cheyenne(s), *vii,* 1, 7–8, 10, 13, 19,
　31, 38, 42–44, 52, 54, 59, 65, 75,
　78, 79, 110, 133ff., 139, 147, 149,
　166–67, 170, 192, 197, 198ff.;
　Agency (*see* Darlington); agent,
　11, 12; alcohol, 49; buffalo, 24;
　chiefs, 19, 42, 44, 136, 178, 193,
　215, peace, 31, 38, 45, 56, 59,
　72, 96, war, 96, 139, 201, 220;
　customs, 223; Dog Soldiers, 10,
　19, 38, 42–43, 56, 96, 191, 193,
　201, 203; massacre, 8; prisoners,
　215ff.; raids, 95ff., 102;
　reservation, 11; Southern, 1, 6–8,

14, 44; surrender, 191, 193, 199, 201ff.; war policy, 125; warriors, 41, 46. *See* Lone Tree Massacre
Cheyenne-Arapaho, 8, 9; Agency, 46, 95, 97; agent, 37; reservation, 27, 45, 101
Cheyenne-Pawnee, 82
Chickasaw country, 47
Chivington, John, 8, 12, 219
Churches, 12–13
Cimarron River, 25, 26, 33, 129
Civil War, 8, 13, 39, 84, 107, 125, 127, 140, 172, 211; "boy wonders," 125–26; debts, 99; post-, era, 2; POW camp, 143; Second Manassas, 101, 127
Clarke, Ben, 41, 131, 132, 148
Coke, Richard, 84, 85
Collier, John, 114
Collinson, Frank, 29
Colorado, 8, 9, 78, 95, 144
Comancheros, 4, 5, 49, 57, 149, 175
Comanche(s), *vii*, 1, 3, 7, 13, 26ff., 52–53, 69, 79, 83, 92, 96, 99, 107, 117ff., 153, 156ff., 174ff., 205, 206, 208; alcohol, 49; Americans, 5–6; bands, 15–16; characteristics, 14, 16, 19, 71, 79; chiefs, 14–15, 16, 114, 178, war, 31, 39, 190, 214; hideouts, 95; hostiles, 115; imprisonment, 213ff.; internment, 110ff.; and Kiowas, 8, 9; Kotsoteka, 14, 15, 85, 170, 190; language, 14; moon, 173; Nokonis, 14, 15–16, 109, 112, 114ff., 213; number, 14; peace faction, 109; Penatekas, 14, 53, 54, 60, 109, 112, 114ff.; Quahadi, 14, 15, 16, 50, 52, 53, 54, 85, 109, 114ff., 167, 170, 190, surrender, 208–9, 211, 214; reservation, 11; strategy, 155, 162; Sun Dance, 53, 54; surrender, 189, 191; Texans, 4–5, 6; United States, 85; war, 79; Yapparikas, 14, 39, 75, 112ff., 190, 191. *See* Adobe Walls, battle *and* Fort Sill

Commissioner of Indian Affairs. *See* Indian Commissioners
Compton, C. E., 47, 96, 127, 128, 129, 133, 139
Congressional Medal of Honor, 165, 193
Connell, Agent J., 115–16
Corn, Lee, 88, 92, 93
"Council House," 5, 6, 85
Covington, Agent, 219
Cowboys, 83–84, 114
Coyle, Mrs. John, 118
Crist, S. B., 141
Crow Indians, 17
Custer, George A., 9, 12, 25, 82, 126, 127, 169, 219
Cutler, Abram, 140, 142

Damron, Shad, 83
Dangerous Eagle, Chief, 80, 213
Darlington, Brinton, 13
Darlington Agency, 44, 45, 50, 59, 96, 97, 98, 99, 110, 125, 188, 207, 215
Davidson, John W. "Black Jack," 60, 97, 98, 105, 107ff., 118ff., 135, 147, 182–83, 194–95, 204–6, 211; Anadarko, 170; campaign, 186ff., 197ff.; characteristics, 107–8, 116, 185; expeditions, 191; Miles, 127; strategy, 120. *See* Haworth
Davis, E. J., 84, 85
Decker, Eugene, *xi*
Delano, Columbus, 38, 44, 106
Delawares, 115, 128ff., 133, 134; Chief, 119, 128
Department of the Missouri, 206
Department of the Platte, 101
Department of Texas, 183
Diplomacy, 3
Division of the Missouri, 100
Dixon, William "Billy," 23, 28ff., 36, 60, 64, 65ff., 78, 128, 131; "long shot," 77; scout, 158ff.
Dodge, Richard I., 22, 26–27
Dodge City, 22, 23, 28, 30, 32, 35, 76, 77, 101, 102

Do-ha-te, 80, 81, 82–83, 149, 214
Do-hauson, Chief, 5, 7, 9, 16, 17
Do-hauson the Younger, 9, 82, 83, 205
Donjon, 186
Dudley, Dave, 60

Eagle Heart, 201
Elk Chewing, Chief (Quirts Quip), 14, 39, 112
Esa-que, Chief, 75, 223
Expansionism, 7, 9, 143–44

Fairchild (hunter), 32, 33–34
Falling Leaf, Chief, 128, 133
Farming, 7
Farnsworth, H. J., 161, 192
Florida, 211, 213
"Foolish water." *See* Alcohol
Fort Bascom, 95, 105, 123, 161
Fort Clark, 169
Fort Cobb, 12
Fort Concho, 95, 105, 123
Fort Davis, 95
Fort Dodge, 22, 23, 26, 47, 95, 99, 105, 123, 125, 139, 169
Fort Griffin, 48, 95, 105, 123
Fort Hays, 21
Fort Larned, 10, 95
Fort Leavenworth, 101, 127
Fort McKavett, 95, 169
Fort Richardson, 92, 95
Fort Sill, 13, 14, 40, 53, 54, 70, 95, 97, 99, 100, 105, 107ff., 122, 123, 185, 189, 209, 211; characteristics, 110; commandant, 107 (*see* Davidson); Indians, 107ff., 114ff., 123, 148, 211ff.; Museum, *xii;* reputation, 186
Fort Stockton, 95
Fort Wallace, 95, 217
Fort Wise Treaty, 8
Fort Worth, *xi*
Fort Zarah, 95
Frazier, Steele, 26–27
Frontier, 28, 70, 84–85, 86, 98, 131, 139; politics, 140; press, 102,

126–27; protection, 95; recognition, 126
Fuller, Lieutenant, 162

Garfield, James A., 13–14
German, Adelaide, 144–47, 198; rescue, 193, 194
German, Catherine (Kate), 144–46, 197, 198–99, 200, 201, 202–3, 215, 219
German, Joanna, 144, 145–46, 147
German, John, 143
German, Julia, 144, 145–46, 147, 198; rescue, 193, 194
German, Lydia, 143, 144
German, Rebecca, 143–44, 147
German, Sophie, 144–46, 197, 198–99, 200, 201, 202, 215
German, Stephen, 143, 144
German kidnaping, 145–47, 193, 197ff., 203, 217
Gilmore, Quincy O. M., 187
Glass, William, 89–90, 92
Goodnight, Charlie, 175
Grant, Ulysses S., 44; Mackenzie, 169; "peace policy," 12–13, 99, 106–8
Gray Beard, Chief, 43, 96, 146, 192ff., 199, 200, 215; death, 220; surrender, 201
Great Dry Time, 78, 125
Great Plains, 21
Griswold, Gillett, *xii*
Guinn, Wallace, 120
Guitain, 50, 80, 81, 82, 92
Gunther, Captain, 180

Hambright, H. A., 217
Hancock, Winfield Scott, 9–10, 100; "war," 10
Hanrahan, James (Jim), 35, 36, 61, 64–65, 67–68, 69, 70, 73, 75
Hard, Henry E., 179
Hartwell, Charles A., 195
Hatfield, Lieutenant, 177, 178
Haworth, Agent James M., 16, 18,

19, 41ff., 50–53, 57ff., 80, 81, 96, 97, 108–9, 122, 181, 214, 223, 225; characteristics, 14, 107, 111, 112; Davidson, 107ff., 185–89, 207; reputation, 13–14; support, 207

Haworth, James Entricon (son), 42

Heap of Birds, Chief, 43, 96, 193, 201, 215

Henely, Austin, 129, 131, 217–20

Hennessey, Patrick, 97, 98

High Back, 201

Historians, 112; promilitary, 107

Hoag, Superintendent Enoch, 13, 40, 41, 43, 46, 47, 98, 103, 112, 189

Holmes, John "Antelope Jack," 60

Horseback, Chief, 15–16, 108, 109, 112, 213–14

Horse thieves, 31, 32, 44ff., 48, 61, 109, 203, 209; retaliation, 95

Houston, Sam, 4

Howard's Well wagon train massacre, 18

Ho-weah, Chief, 14, 113

Howling Wolf, Chief, 79

Hudson, Lieutenant, 80

Huggins, Jim, xii

Hunt, W. C., 83

Hunting Horse, 82–83, 88–89, 92

Huntsville Penitentiary, 81, 83

Indian Agents, viii, 8, 9, 10, 11, 12, 13–14, 31, 37–38, 108. See also under name

Indian Appropriation Act, 205

Indian Bureau (Agency), viii, 12, 41, 43, 52, 103, 203

Indian Commissioner(s), 41, 44, 98, 106, 108, 202; Board of, 13. See Smith, E. P.

"Indian exterminators," 85

Indians, vii, viii, 1, 3, 7, 30, 31, 37, 47, 158, 176, 178, 188ff.; alcohol, 49, 57; amnesty, 218; arms, 9, 11, 117; arrests, 199–200, 201; atrocities, 60, 92, 93, 97;

"auxiliaries," 33; bravery, 72, 155, 158, 162; Buffalo, 1–20; captives, 152–53; characteristics, 2, 4, 7, 37, 175; chiefs, 9, 11, 12, 19, 79, 80, most famous, 17, policies, 17–18, surrenders, 191 (see under name of Chief and tribe); commissary, 21–36 (see Buffalo); customs, 71, 72, 79, 81, 83, 92; enemies, 55–56, 85; families, 162, 163; guides, 174; hostiles, 190ff., 195, 200, 205; hunger, 40–44 (see Buffalo); hunting ground, 22; impersonating, 47, 48; income, 49; internment, 106, 110ff., 116, 123, 148; interpreters, 31, 165, 203 (see Bent, George); land surveys, 49; leader, 52 (see Isa-tai); life style, 37; magic, 149, 154; names, 232; nomads, 2; peace, 109, 189; policy making, 79, 80; POWs, 199; prophecy, vii, 149, 154; prowhite, 19; punishment, 212; raids, 7, 18 (see Lone Wolf and Medicine Water); religion, 37, 56; resistance, collapse, 197–209; status, 51; stereotype, 1–2; strategy, 155, 162ff., 174ff., 218; superstitions, 39, 49, 75, 83, 110, 112, 149, 179; surrender(s), 188–89, 191, 195, 199, 201ff., 207, 209, 211–21; tactics, 121, 122, 131, 132, 133, 149; unrest, causes, 40–41, 44, 48–49, 51–52; uprisings, 99ff., 101, 127ff.; warfare, 65–66, 68, 70–72, 77, rules, 146 (see also under Warfare); war parties, 85, 139, 141, 143, 145–46, 149ff., 154, 159, 200, 201; warrior societies, 69, 179 (see under tribe); white, 152, prisoners (see German kidnaping); women, 145–46, 154, 215, warrior, 139. See also under name of tribe, South Plains, and United States

Indian Territory, 11, 13, 23, 24, 25, 26, 27, 30, 31, 79, 95; law-enforcement officers, 44; reorganization, 206
Indian War (1874–75): beginning, 78
Inquisition, 3
Iron Mountain, Chief, 113
Iron Shirt, Chief, 178
Irving, Washington, 170
Isa-havey, Chief, 14, 53–54, 109
Isa-nanica, Chief, 114–15
Isa-Rosa, Chief, 14, 75, 114, 190, 191, 214
Isa-tai, Chief, 52–55, 57, 65ff., 70–71, 75, 78, 232
I-See-O, 82

Johnson, Andrew, 10, 100
Johnson, Andy, 70, 72
Jones, C. E., 130, 132
Jones, Harry C., 141
Jones, Horace, 108
Jones, John B., 84, 85–86, 87ff., 92, 208

Kansas, viii, 8, 9, 11, 13, 21, 22, 26, 44ff., 78, 146; buffalo, 22–24, 27, 30, 44, 46; Daily Commonwealth, 126–27, 136, 167; Indian frontier, 95; and Indian Territory, boundary, 24–25, 27; land survey, 140; Medicine Lodge Creek, 10; Military Division, 25; Pacific Railroad, 23; State Historical Society, xi; University, 140
Katakas, 1, 11, 56, 223; internment, 111, 113ff.
Keeler, "Old Man," 71, 73
Kellihan, Pat, 187
Kentucky, 84
Keuchler, John H., 141–42
Keyes, Alexander S. B., 195, 197, 199, 216
Kickapoos, 13
Kidnaping, 193, 197. See German kidnaping

Kiowa-Comanche Agency, 47, 48, 97, 100
Kiowas, vii, 1, 3, 4, 18, 19, 26ff., 39, 42, 52ff., 57, 59, 79ff., 87ff., 96, 97, 99, 107, 108, 117ff., 147ff., 153, 177ff., 187, 190ff., 205; Adobe Walls, 79; agents, 13, 14; alcohol, 49; Anadarko renegades, 147ff., 152; arms, 49–50; characteristics, 16, 17, 19, 79, 110, 149, 179; chiefs, 5, 7, 9, 16–17, 18, 50, 171, peace, 108, 111, 148, 160, 213, principal, 205, war, 18–19, 31, 39, 40, 41, 42, 80, 148, 162, 190; education, 39; god-founder, 80; internment, 110ff.; Kaitsenko, 17, 81; Katakas, 42; Kotsotekas, 206; leaders, 7; number, 16; on-de aristocracy, 16, 82; policy, 79, 80, 93, 148; "political deal," 17; Quakers, 15; refuge, 148; reservation, 11; strategy, 155; Sun Dance, 56–57; surrender, 188–89, 205ff., 213; Tsetanmas, 16, 17; warriors, 81, societies, 17 (see under name); Yapparikas, 205. See also Fort Sill; Lone Wolf; and Satanta
Kop'e-to-hau (Mountain Bluff), 160
Krumrein, Stephanie, xi
Kuehn, Claire, xi

Lamar, Mirabeau, 4–5
Land surveys, 49
Lawler, Ed, 120
Lawson, Charlie, 119, 120
Lawson, Gaines, 116–17, 118ff.
Lawton, Henry W., 171, 172, 173
Lean Bear, Chief, 193, 201
Lease, Henry, 76
Leavenworth, Henry, 5, 7, 9
Leavenworth, Kansas, 21
Lee Massacre, 18
Lefebvre, E. C., 44–45, 46, 96
Left Hand Bull, Chief, 193
Leonard, Fred, 71, 73

Lewis, Granville, 155, 166
Lewis, William H., 90, 156
Lincoln, Abraham, 100
Little Arkansas River, 9, 38
Little Arkansas Treaty, 8–9, 10
Little Crow, Chief, 191
Little Robe, Chief, 12, 19, 31, 38, 44, 45, 46, 56, 59, 95, 96
Little Rock, Chief, 12, 19
Llano Estacado, 95, 104, 132, 171, 190
Lone Tree massacre, 141–42
Lone Wolf, Chief, 16–17, 18, 40, 50–51, 56, 79, 80, 81ff., 91–92, 108ff., 117, 148, 160, 190, 205, 208, 212, 213; revenge raid, 79, 80–93; son, 50; tactics, 87, 91
Long Back, Chief, 201, 202
Looting, 181
Lost Valley, 84, 87, 88, 208; fight, 79, 80–93, 115
Loving, James C., 83, 87–88, 92
Lyman, Wyllys, 136, 151ff., 157, 165
Lyman's Wagon Train, 151, 153, 164; battle, 147, 154–59, 162, 166, 188

McDonald, Captain, 150
McFadden, Thompson, 128, 129, 133, 134, 136
Mackenzie, Ranald S., 105, 127, 135, 146, 167, 169ff., 191, 192, 195, 197, 206, 211ff.; characteristics, 169–70, 172, 182, 207, 209; "Column," 171ff.; command, 206; Indian nickname, 169; Miles, 206–7; orders, 171, 182; strategy, 171ff., 177, 180, 182. See Palo Duro Canyon, battle
McKibbon, Steve, 114
McLaughlin, N. B., 172, 173, 180
Maman-ti, Chief (owl prophet), 19, 80ff., 87, 93, 113, 148ff., 154, 160, 178, 190, 205, 208, 209, 213; death, 220; foster son, 152; prophecy, 92, 178, 214

Mamay-day-te, 82, 83, 91, 92
Man-yi-ten. See Woman's Heart, Chief
Marshall, J. T., 102, 126–27, 131, 193
Marshall, William, 167
Martin, A. J., 128–29
Martin, William "Hurricane Bill," 45, 46
Massacres, 8, 10, 13, 17, 18, 19, 123, 177, 199, 200; Lone Tree, 141–42; Sappa Creek, 218–20; Short, 199; Warren Wagon Train, 17, 83, 170; Washita, 13, 19
Masterson, William Barclay "Bat," 31, 34, 67ff., 73, 128, 131
Mayer, Frank H., 29
Medicine Arrows, Chief, 201
Medicine Lodge, 54, 99; Council, 7, 17, 25, 38, 71; Creek, 10; raid, 95, 96; Treaty, 18, 21ff., 27, 38, 44, 51, 223
Medicine Men (Do-ha-te), 19, 50, 52–53, 57, 65, 75, 80, 81, 96, 185, 213; apprentice, 82; and prophets, 149, 154
Medicine Water, Chief, 96, 139, 142ff., 147, 193, 199, 201, 215
Meloy, Harriet C., xi
Mexicans, 3, 149, 158, 160, 198; and Indians, 3–4, 18, 85; "traders," 171
Mexican War, 6
Mexico, 3, 4, 6, 8, 50; Old, 5, 6
Mihesuah (Comanche), 69
Miles, Agent John D., 13, 19, 37–38, 42ff., 50, 52, 59, 96ff., 112, 125, 185, 199, 200ff., 215; wife, 202
Miles, Nelson A., 40, 105, 125–37, 147ff., 158, 161, 164, 166, 169, 170, 183, 185, 193, 200ff., 216, 220; aide (see Baldwin, Frank D.); characteristics, 165, 167, 169, 194, 197, 206; command, 127; Davidson, 187; Expedition, 125, 127–37; guides, 174;

mistakes, 146; reports, 134–36; reputation, 127, 136–37, 207; scout, 131; strategy, 139, 166–67, 171, 188, 191–92, 197ff.; surrender ultimatum, 198; wife, 126, 128, 135, 167, 194, 197; writings, 170, 204. *See* German kidnaping *and* Mackenzie

Military Department of Texas, 98

Military Department of the Missouri, 9, 98, 100, 101

Minimic, Chief, 42, 96, 199, 215, 220

Missouri Division, 100

Mochi (Buffalo Calf Woman), 139, 145–46, 215

Modest, Ernest, 120

Modoc Indians, 212

Montana Historical Society, *xi*

Mooar, John Wesley, 22, 23, 28, 61–64, 70

Mooar, (Josiah) Wright, 21, 22, 23, 26–28, 29, 36, 61–64, 70, 136–37

Moore, George, 88–89

Morey, Marjorie, *xi*

Morris, Margaret F., *xii*

Morrison, William F., 203

Mosier, Ed, 98

Mow-way, Chief, 15, 114, 182, 190, 206, 214; village sacking, 170, 173

Mumsukawa, Chief, 178

Murphy, Johnny, 97, 98

Myers, A. C. "Charlie," 30–31, 34, 35, 61, 63, 64, 65, 71, 73, 76

Myles, John, 125

Nap-a-wat (medicine man), 19, 80

National Archives Federal Records Center, *xi*

Neill, Thomas H., 125, 188–90, 199, 200ff.; characteristics, 204–5; Davidson, 204; prisoners, 215ff., 219

Newcomb, J. G., 83

New Orleans, 100

New Spain, 4. *See* New Mexico

New Mexico, 4, 5, 19, 78, 95, 105

North Fork Red River, 56; War Council, 56, 57–58

North Plains, 1, 7, 10

Norvall, Stevens T., 216

Nueces River, 4, 86

Nye, Wilbur, 83, 107

Ogg, Billy, 68

O-ha-wa-tai, Chief, 178

Ojibway (Canada), 7

O'Keefe, Tom, 35

Oklahoma, 78; Historical Society, *xi*, 219

Olds, William, 35, 77

Old Whirlwind, Chief, 19, 38, 42, 46, 56, 65, 78, 96, 99, 136–37, 193

"Orator of the Plains," 17. *See* Satanta

Osages, 5; reservation, 143

Osborn, E. B., 19–20, 76, 214

Osborn, T. A., 46

"Outlawry" concept, 123

Owl prophets, 80, 81; emblem, 83. *See* Maman-ti

Pacer, Chief, 42

Palo Duro Canyon, 105, 149, 175–77; battle, 179–83, 187, 191, 192, 205, 206, 207

Panhandle-Plains Historical Museum, *xi*

Parker, Cynthia Ann, 53

Pawnees, 82, 115

Peace policy, 107; opposition to, 108. *See under* Grant, Ulysses S.

Petersen, Karen D., *xii*

Pike's Peak, 8

Plagues, 130, 151

Plains Indians, 4, 65ff., 72, 78, 212; culture, 69; horsemanship, 71

Plummer, Joseph H., 60, 128, 130, 132

Polk, James, 6

Poor Buffalo, Chief, 19, 121, 122, 154, 158, 179, 205

Pope, James W., 127, 133, 137
Pope, John, 46, 77, 98–99, 103–4, 127, 147, 183, 188, 217, 218; characteristics, 101–2, 166; command, 206; Miles, 127, 134, 166, 167; strategy, 125
Porter, Mel, 91, 92
Powder Face, Chief, 19, 31, 46, 56
Powell, Dr., 194
Prairie Fire, Chief, 113
Pratt, Richard H., 187, 194, 211ff., 220–21
Press, the, 126–27, 136, 140, 166, 167; frontier, 102, 126–27
Price, Mary Alice, xii
Price, William R., 105, 127, 161ff., 167, 178, 188, 191, 192, 194
Pruner, Pat, 120

Quakers, 18, 39, 46, 97, 114, 115, 189, 225; Executive Committee, 98; Indian Agents, 13–15, 123 (see under name)
Quanah Parker, Chief, 16, 53, 54–55, 56, 65–66, 70, 71, 72, 74–75, 77, 114, 175, 178, 208–9

Races, adaptability, 2
Rafferty, William A., 216ff.
Ransom, 146
Rath, Charlie, 22, 29, 35, 50, 60, 61, 64, 65, 70, 72, 73–74
Reconstruction, 84, 85
Red Cloud, Chief, 101
Red Moon (warrior), 41, 193, 201
Red Otter, Chief, 50, 51, 81, 83, 89, 205
Red River, 82, 86, 104, 114, 135, 149
Red River War (1874–75), viii, 21, 100, 125, 136, 161ff., 199; causes, viii; characteristics, vii–viii; end, 209, 211; Indian mistakes, 177; map, xxi. See Buffalo War
Red Warbonnet, Chief, 177, 179
Reservations, 8, 9, 10–11, 15, 27, 45, 51, 102, 128, 143

Richards, Agent Jonathan, 97, 112, 115
Richardson, Paula, xi
Rio Grande, 4
Robertson, Walter, 86, 90
Robinson, I. J., 132
Ross, Findlay, 116
Ryan, Dennis, 195

St. Augustine, Florida, xii
St. Louis, 183
St. Vrain, Ceran, 33
Salt Creek, 86, 87; Massacre, 177
"Salt Prairie," 83
San Antonio, Texas, 5, 100–1
Sand Creek, 8; Massacre, 10, 12, 13
Sanderson, George K., 111, 112–14
Sanderson, Lieutenant, 186, 187
Sand Hill, Chief, 193
San Saba Mission, 3
Santa Fe Trail, 6
Sappa Creek "Massacre," 218–20
Satank, Chief, 7, 17, 171
Satanta, Chief, 17, 40, 48, 79, 80–81, 82, 83, 87, 108, 113, 158, 177, 189; parole, 148, 190; policy, 148; prison, 190; surrender, 188–90; trial, 170; warriors, 114, 117
Scalawag law, 84
Schesventer, George F., xii
Schmalsle, William F., 150–53, 157
Schofield, George W., 186, 191
Scott, Hugh, 65
Scott ms., xii
Scouts, 31, 60, 62, 65, 78, 126ff., 134, 149ff., 158, 161, 171, 182, 187; Army, 41, 82. See Chapman, Amos, and under name
Seminoles: -Negroes, 177, 182, scouts, 171, 172
Shadler, Ike, 64, 69–70, 72, 76
Shadler, Shorty, 64, 69–70, 72, 76
Shaller, Rolla, xi
Shaw, James A., 140, 141–42
Sheridan, Philip H., viii, 13, 25, 99, 100, 102ff., 128, 136, 166, 182,

185; characteristics, 100; policy, 107, 212; reports, 136; strategy, 105–6, 127, 187–88; "winter campaign," 19, 25, 103, 195
Sherman, William T., 9, 11–12, 13, 39, 99ff., 105–6, 170; Miles, 126; policy, 107, 123
Shirley, William, 116, 118, 119, 120, 121
Short, Daniel Truman, 140, 141–42
Short, Frances (Mrs. Oliver F.), 140, 141
Short, Harry C., 140, 141
Short, Oliver F., 140–42, 146
Short massacre, 199
Shroder, Charles, 218
Sign language, xii, 14
"Singing wire," 122
Sioux, 2, 7, 10, 101
Sisk, Philip, 61, 62, 63
Slavery, 140
Smith, Edward P., 41, 44, 45, 106, 108, 112
Smithsonian Institution, xi
Society of Friends, 13. See Quakers
South, the, 100
South Plains, viii, 1, 2, 27, 96
South Plains Indians, vii, 1ff., 10, 12, 13, 39, 51; characteristics, 14, 19–20; chiefs, 17; Confederation, 1, 6, 7; life style, 19–20; unrest, causes, 44
Southwest, 2
Srack, Samuel B., 218
Staked Plains (El Llano Estacado), 16, 95, 104, 105, 115, 127, 149, 172
Stevens, G. W., 86, 88, 91
Stone Age coalition, 14
Stone Calf, Chief, 19, 31, 38, 56, 71, 72, 96–97, 198–99, 201–5; exoneration, 203
Striking Eagle, Chief, 17–18, 19, 49, 56, 59, 79, 80–81, 108, 110, 111, 113, 115, 123, 148, 160, 205, 213, 214, 220; death, 214
Strong, Henry W., 171, 173

Sturms, Dr. J. J., 206, 208–9
Summers, Mrs. Dale, xi
Sun Boy, Chief, 39, 80, 82, 111
Sun Dance, 53, 54, 56–57, 79, 81, 97, 109, 190
Supply trains, 161. See also Wagon trains
Surveyors, 139–41, 146

Tabananica, Chief, 14–15, 114, 191, 205, 214
Tafoya, José Piedad, 175–76, 178
Tah-bone-mah, 82, 83, 92
Talley, John H., 44–45, 46
Tatum, Laurie, 13, 108
Tau-ankia, 80, 82, 92, 110; revenge raid, 190
Teachers, 15, 115, 118
Tehan (Tehanna, or Texan), 152–54, 155–56
"Tehannas," 5, 6, 39
Téné-an-gopte (Eagle That Strikes with Talons, Striking Eagle), 17–18. See Striking Eagle, Chief
Tennessee, 84
Terry, Benjamin Franklin, 84; "Texas Rangers," 84, 85
Texas, vii, viii, 3, 6, 8, 14, 78, 84–85, 167; buffalo, 26, 27, 30; Department of, 146; frontier, 6; horse thieves, 44; Indians, 4–5, 6, 55–56, 85; panhandle, 9, 16, 27, 28, 36, 43 (see Staked Plains); Rangers, 83, 84ff., 115, Frontier Battalion, 84–86, 208, policy, 86; State Library (Austin), xi; university, xi–xii; war for independence, 4
Thompson, William A., 171, 174
Thrasher, Luther A., 140, 141–42
Tipis, 7, 37, 151, 191
Tonkawas, 55–56, 171, 174, 177, 179–80, 181, 182, 187; cannibalism, 233
Tosawi, Chief, 117, 118, 119
Trade (-ing), 1, 4, 5, 6, 14, 21–22, 33, 36. See Buffalo hunters

Treaties, *vii*, 6, 8–9, 10–11, 21, 51.
See also under name
Treaty of Guadalupe-Hidalgo, 6
Treaty of the Little Arkansas, 51
Tulé Canyon, 166–67
Tulé Creek, 135
Tyler, Billy, 73, 76

Union Pacific Railroad, 144
United States, 9; Indian Agents,
181; and Indians, *vii, viii*, 5, 6, 7,
12, 17, 31, 51, 59, policy, 12–13,
38–39, 40, 44, 106, 107–8 (*see*
peace policy *under* Grant, Ulysses
S.), surveys of lands, 49, treaties,
6, 8–11, obligations, 37, 39, 40,
war, 95–106; and Mexico, 6;
military administration, 100;
post-Civil War, 99–100
U. S. Army, *viii*, 17, 41, 44, 183,
186; blacks, 70, 97; buffalo
question, 24–27; central
command, 183; frontier forts, 95;
Indians, 45, 46, 77, 85, 99, 127ff.,
137, 139ff., 146ff., 154ff., 170,
174, 188ff., 195ff., 197ff., best
force, 169, 170, Bureau, *viii*,
policy, 123, 171, 199, strategy,
155, 180, 195, surrender, 204;
officers (*see* Miles, Nelson A. *and
under* name); strength, 99–100;
supply dispute, 166
U. S. Attorney General, 44–45
U. S. Congress, 10, 12–13, 51, 99
U. S. Interior Department, 12, 13,
38, 44
U. S. Library of Congress, *xii*
U. S. Senate, 9
U. S. War Department, 12, 99, 106,
136
University of Texas, *xi–xii*

Van Vliet, Stewart, 166
Van Zandt, Mary, *xii*
Viele, Charles D., 194

Wagon trains, 87, 97, 98; Lyman's,
151, 153, battle, 147, 154–59,
162, size, 154; wagonmaster, 63;
Warren Raid, 17, 83, 170
Wallace, Tommy, 60
War(fare): against whites, 38–39;
Buffalo, 59–66; causes, 40–41;
cultural significance, 2;
importance, 2–3; Indians, 3, 5,
54ff., 68ff., 71, 81, 91, 95–106,
mistakes, 87, paint, 183,
preparation, 54ff., tactics, 86–87.
See also under Indians; Red River
War; and U. S. Army
Warren Wagontrain Raid, 17, 83;
massacre, 170
Warrington, Lewis, 197
Warrior Woman, 139
Washington City, 44, 183; Indians,
39, 80, 148
Washita, massacre, 13, 19
Washita River, 82, 136
Water, scarcity, 135
Waterholes, "gyp water," 132
Watkins, William, 97
Webb, John, 26, 63
West, Dr. Elliott, *xii*
West Point, 125, 126
Wheeler (Texas Ranger), 88, 92
Wheelers (buffalo hunters), 28
Whirlwind, Chief. See Old
Whirlwind, Chief
White, James, 21
White Antelope, Chief, 201
White Horse, Chief, 10, 18, 42, 79,
206, 213
Whites, *vii*, 2–3, 38–40. See also
Americans
White Shield, Chief, 19, 31, 38, 42,
56, 79, 96
White Wolf, Chief. See Isa-Rosa,
Chief
Wichita Agency, 97, 115, 121, 122,
147, 189; location, 115–16. See
Anadarko
Wichita Mountains, 13
Wichitas, 115, 122
Wikoff, Captain, 187

Wild Horse, Chief, 16, 114, 178, 190, 208
Williams, George H., 44, 45, 46
Wilson, Lem, 62, 150–53
Wilson, Lieutenant, 86, 90
Wing, Ira G., 132, 150–53
"Winter Campaign," 12, 15
Wolf Robe (warrior), 199, 201, 202
Woman's Heart, Chief, 18, 113, 213
Woodward, Lieutenant, 117

Wright, Robert M., 60, 61–62, 72
Wrinkled-hand Chase, 185, 188–96, 200, 207
Wynkoop, Agent, 12

Yellow Fish, 69
Yellow Horse, Chief, 56, 139
Yellow Moon, Chief, 113
Younkin, C. George, *xi*